THE USABLE URBA

M avec
montonta

The Usable Urban Past:
Planning and Politics in the Modern Canadian City

EDITED, WITH INTRODUCTIONS BY
ALAN F. J. ARTIBISE
AND
GILBERT A. STELTER

THE CARLETON LIBRARY NO. 119
Published by Macmillan of Canada
in association with the Institute of
Canadian Studies, Carleton University

COPYRIGHT © Alan F. J. Artibise and
Gilbert A. Stelter, 1979

All rights reserved—no part of this book may
be reproduced in any form without
permission in writing from the publisher
except by a reviewer who wishes to quote
brief passages in connection with a review
written for inclusion in a magazine or
newspaper.

ISBN 0-7705-1793-5

Canadian Cataloguing in Publication Data

Main entry under title:

The Usable urban past

(The Carleton library; no. 119)

Bibliography: p.
ISBN 0-7705-1793-5 pa.

1. Cities and towns—Canada. 2. Municipal
government—Canada. 3. City planning—Canada.
I. Artibise, Alan F. J., date. II. Stelter,
Gilbert A., date. III. Carleton University.
Institute of Canadian Studies. IV. Series.

HT127.U82   307.7'6   C79-094911-3

Printed in Canada for
the Macmillan Company of Canada Limited
70 Bond Street, Toronto, Ontario,
M5B 1X3

The Carleton Library

A series of reprints, original works, and new collections of source material relating to Canada, issued under the editorial supervision of the Institute of Canadian Studies of Carleton University, Ottawa.

Director of the Institute and General Editor
S. F. Wise

Executive Editor
Virgil D. Duff *(Macmillan of Canada)*

Editorial Board
Marilyn J. Barber *(History)*
Dennis Forcese *(Sociology)*
David B. Knight *(Geography)*
Steven Langdon *(Economics)*
Maureen Molot *(Political Science)*
J. George Neuspiel *(Law)*
Derek G. Smith *(Anthropology)*

Publications Editor
James H. Marsh

For
J. M. S. CARELESS
Friend, Colleague, Scholar

CONTENTS

Preface

This collection of original essays represents some of the innovative historical research and writing being done on modern Canadian urban development. An interdisciplinary approach to the historical dimension of urban politics and planning is emphasized, with contributors representing the disciplines of history, geography, planning, and political science. Many of the essays are pioneering explorations into subjects which have received little attention; as a result the authors do not always share assumptions on fundamental questions. In our introductions to the sections, we take these differences into consideration and place the questions in the large perspective of the existing literature. We have also included a guide to sources of information on Canadian urban studies and a selected bibliography.

The publication of this book involved the co-operation and support of many people. We wish to thank the University of Guelph's College of Arts and Social Sciences for generous financial assistance. Our thanks are also due to Gerald Bloomfield for providing cartographic services and to Sue Bullock, Donna Pollard, and Puri Chadwick for assistance in typing (and retyping) the manuscript. It is also essential to thank Terry Crowley and W. W. Straka for their help in organizing the Canadian Urban History Conference held at the University of Guelph in May 1977. Several of the papers published here had their genesis at this conference.

We dedicate this volume to Professor J. M. S. Careless of the Department of History, University of Toronto. It is our personal tribute to a man who has made a rich and enduring contribution to the study of Canada's urban past. Through his own work on the concept of metropolitanism, and his enthusiastic encouragement of the work of many students and colleagues, Professor Careless has been a major force in the study of the Canadian city.

Alan F. J. Artibise, Victoria
Gilbert A. Stelter, Guelph

General Introduction

The Past in the Present: Exploring the Relevance of Canada's Urban Past

In a recent issue of *City Magazine*, the editors noted that "Canadians are characterized by their forgetting of the past, by their failure to retain and make use of their collective experiences".[1] Whatever the merits of this sweeping generalization in other fields, it certainly can be applied to Canadian urban studies. Canada's urban past has, until recently, been left by default to those exploiting the market for nostalgia. The numerous published studies of communities are usually characterized by antiquarianism and the distortion that comes of pages of meaningless or insignificant data and virtually no interpretation or analysis. Furthermore, in many volumes the past is naïvely seen as a continually unfolding success story in which all citizens, regardless of their economic standing or ethnic background, were united in meeting challenges and resolving problems. In short, much urban history has been more concerned with surface impressions and entertainment than with considered judgment.[2]

While the historical profession has thus been at fault for not writing scholarly urban history, social scientists studying Canadian urban development can also be indicted for being pre-eminently concerned with the present and having too little regard for the historical dimension. Within some social sciences, in fact, the historical approach seems to be regarded as little more than a hobby for those whose creative powers have failed. Those committed to serious history, on the other hand, have been reluctant to search for what might be called a "usable past", partly because they are wary of the abuse of history by non-historians. These abuses have included a tendency to use history to substantiate positions arrived at by other, non-historical means and to assert qualified historical opinion as fact.[3]

The lack of scholarly urban history and the disregard for the historical dimension by most students of the city have much to do with the contemporary failure to deal effectively with urban issues.[4] As Canadians tackle urban problems, they do so without the benefit of knowing the origin of cities, how or why they grow or decline, or even in what direction they are moving. Without a sense of history, politicians, planners, and the general public do not have the means to bring about the changes they desire. The result is frustration and confusion, whether in neighbourhood action groups, city hall, provincial departments of urban affairs, or the Ministry of State for Urban Affairs in Ottawa.[5] Moreover, most citizens lack any sense of continuity in their urban life and as a result cannot affirm their identity as members of communities that extend far back in time.

Fortunately, this unacceptable situation is changing. In recent years there has been an explosion of interest in the urban past among both professional scholars and the general public. Many of the problems outlined above have been overcome and an attempt is now being made to understand the complexities of urban development. The city in history is the focus of research for such specialists as planners, geographers, economists, demographers, and, of course, historians. All have begun to ask difficult and searching questions about the urban past, and the result is rarely either an antiquarian venture with genealogical overtones or historical boosterism. Instead, historical urban research, whether set in one city, in regions, or even in the country itself, is concerned with such broad questions as factors in urban growth, the origins and goals of planning, and the nature of municipal reform and politics.[6]

Scholars approach the question of the relevance of the past in understanding the present and planning the future in various ways: in some work it is explicit and part of the argument; in others it is less direct, only implied. But in virtually all recent scholarly work there is agreement on certain fundamental points. It is obvious, for example, that a city's site, its buildings, the early surveys and divisions of land, and the original location of residential, institutional, and commercial districts impose a measure of permanence on the form of a community. So, too, do the political structures and values rooted in the initial period of rapid urbanization. As two commentators have noted in another context, "Inertia is part of the dynamic of urban change: the structures outlast the people who put them there, and impose constraints on those who have to adapt them later to their own use. The fact is that the framework of growth, however hastily devised, tends to become the permanent structure."[7]

Despite this growing recognition of the role of the past in the present, the study of urban history is still in its infancy; many fundamental questions have yet to be asked, let alone satisfactorily answered. While studies of Ontario and western cities are proceeding briskly, the same cannot be said for those of the Maritimes or Quebec. Moreover, the very difficult problem of comparing the development of different cities in different regions has not even been begun. Nevertheless, several trends are evident that suggest that one can be optimistic about future developments in the field. Among these are the formulation of common questions about urban growth, planning and development, and urban government. Another related trend is an interdisciplinary approach which provides a breadth and scope to the study of the urban past that has not until recently been evident. The result, eventually, will be a common understanding of how the city is built; of how it came to be the way it is today.

The goal of this book, then, is not to give final answers to the many urgent urban problems of the country. There are no final answers, no ultimate master plans, but there are choices to be made. Together, the essays in this volume outline in certain key areas systematic ways of examining the urban past. The hope is that by outlining and analysing some of the issues, and by publishing what is now known about how the Canadian urban system worked in the past, scholars will be better able to select areas for future research. It is also to be hoped that an awareness of their urban history will help people decide for themselves intelligently what they can do to control and plan future urban development.

NOTES

1. *City Magazine*, vol. 3, no.1 (1977): 1.
2. See, for example, J. M. S. Careless, "Localism or Parochialism in Canadian History", *B. C. Perspectives*, no. 2 (1972): 4-14.
3. John Taylor, "Habitat 1976", Canadian Historical Association, *Newsletter*, no. 1 (1975): 5-8.
4. For an excellent discussion of this problem in the United States, see Sam Bass Warner, Jr., *The Urban Wilderness: A History of the American City* (New York, 1972), Chapter 1 and *passim*.
5. See, for example, James Lorimer and Evelyn Ross, eds., *The Second City Book: Studies of Urban and Suburban Canada* (Toronto, 1977), pp. 6-7 and *passim*.
6. Some of the best and most representative work to date has been collected in Gilbert A. Stelter and Alan F. J. Artibise, eds., *The Canadian City: Essays in Urban History* (Toronto, 1979). For a comprehensive bibliography see Alan F. J. Artibise, "Canadian Urban Studies: A Select Bibliography", *Communiqué: Canadian Studies*, vol. 3, no. 3 (1977): 51-123. For a description of current research, see Gilbert A. Stelter, "Urban History in North America: Canada", *Urban History Yearbook* (University of Leicester, England, 1977): 24-29.
7. H. J. Dyos and M. Wolff, "The Way We Live Now", in Dyos and Wolff, eds., *The Victorian City: Images and Realities*, vol. II (London and Boston, 1973), pp. 893-94.

I.

The Economic Framework

Introduction

Why do cities grow or not grow? What are the most relevant factors influencing or inhibiting growth? These questions are being examined by scholars from several different perspectives and it is useful to outline some of their underlying assumptions. One of the questions involves the role of cities in the development of the larger regional or national economy. Are cities the dynamic engine of growth, stimulating economic development, or are cities the end result, the product of such forces as the level of staples production and export? The argument for the positive role of cities—what might be called an "urban primary model"—has been presented by a number of urban economists. For example, Harvey Lithwick and Gilles Paquet point out that while the emergence of early Canadian cities depended on the growth of a region and the development of its resources, the process has been reversed in recent years. The larger cities aggressively generate growth; in fact, they argue, the "economic health of a region is now a function of the viability of the city within it."[1] On the other hand, an "urban dependency" model is presented in the following essay by James Simmons, an economic geographer. Simmons argues that the external demand for primary staples continues to be the key factor in urban growth. While large manufacturing centres are not as directly dependent on the health of the hinterland as are small regional centres, large cities nevertheless ultimately depend on the national production of staples for their well-being.

A second set of questions about urban growth involves the scale at which meaningful explanations can be made. Can a city's growth or decline be explained by internal factors, especially the role of individual leaders and groups, or must the larger national or international external forces be emphasized? Can an individual city's economy be explained without placing it into the context of a larger system of cities? Historians tend to emphasize the initiative of elites, either through private entrepreneurial action or through group efforts such as Boards of Trade or municipal councils, in accounting for urban growth.[2] Some of this initiative is referred to as "boosterism", which is usually confined to promotional activities to attract railways, industry, and immigrants, but may also include schemes to beautify cities or even to extend a city's boundaries. The emphasis at this scale is on people able to use their opportunity, or individuals and groups effectively responding or failing to respond to the possibilities emerging from external factors.[3]

At another scale, urban growth is explained by reference to trends in regional and national economic development and by an analysis of an urban system presumed to be national and international in scope. The idea that cities form a central component of a national heartland-hinterland relationship has become a well-established conceptual framework.[4] The story usually goes something like this: Cities and colonies which were once subservient to external metropolitan centres became dominant forces in their own right, especially with the introduction of the National Policy in 1879. Tariff barriers stimulated the growth of an urban-industrial complex along the Quebec – Windsor axis, while restricting the hinterland regions to staples production. The building of the transcontinental railroads greatly facilitated the flow of industrial goods to the hinterland and of staples to the cities of central Canada for processing or export.[5] In the following essay, Simmons argues this metropolis – hinterland arrangement in explaining Canadian urban development in terms of a highly interconnected network of urban nodes.[6]

The necessity of including not only impersonal and mechanistic forces, but of giving "faces" to growth forces is being increasingly recognized by social scientists. A good example is the conclusion to a section on "Growth Forces" in Leonard Gertler and Ronald Crowley, *Changing Canadian Cities*: "The forces described represent prevailing trends within which cities work out their destiny, but they are not ironclad. Growth is the result not only of these forces but also of the manifold actions of many people—migrant and stayer, entrepreneur and employee, elite and commonfolk. . . . All the ingredients for urban growth may be present but the skill and initiative of the entrepreneur is needed before development can take place."[7] In other words, an understanding of urban growth will come only from a synthetic view which focuses on the joint operation of several processes at various scales. Studies which emphasize different factors should not be seen as competing explanations, since they aid in the essential task of defining the nature of the problem and do not preclude the development of a comprehensive model of urban growth.

NOTES

1. "Urban Growth and Regional Contagion", in Lithwick and Paquet, eds., *Urban Studies: A Canadian Perspective* (Toronto, 1968), p. 37. See also Lithwick, *Urban Canada: Problems and Prospects* (Ottawa, 1970).

2. For examples, see Gilbert A. Stelter and Alan F. J. Artibise, eds., *The Canadian City: Essays in Urban History* (Toronto, 1979), especially Section III, "Metropolitan Growth and the Spread of the Urban Network".

3. Recent case studies include Alan F. J. Artibise, "Boosterism and the Rise of Prairie Cities, 1870-1913", and Leo Johnson, "The Ideology and Political Economy of Growth: Guelph, 1827 – 1927", both in Gilbert A. Stelter and Alan F. J. Artibise, eds., *Shaping the Canadian Urban Landscape: Essays in the City-Building Process, 1820 – 1920* (forthcoming).

4. For examples, see J. M. S. Careless, "Metropolitan Reflections on 'Great Britain's Woodyard'", *Acadiensis*, vol. 3 (1973): 103-09; Gilbert A. Stelter, "The Urban Frontier in Canadian History", in A. R. McCormack and Ian MacPherson, eds., *Cities in the West* (Ottawa,

1975), pp. 270-86; Peter Usher, "Hinterland Culture Shock", *Canadian Dimension*, vol. 8 (1972): 26-31.

5. The literature on this subject is immense and includes John Dales, "Canada's National Policies", in Dales, ed., *The Protective Tariff in Canada's Development* (Toronto, 1966); and D. V. Smiley, "Canada and the Quest for a National Policy", *Canadian Journal of Political Science*, vol. 8 (1975).

6. Other examples of this approach are Brian B. J. L. Berry, "Cities as Systems within Systems of Cities", *Economic Development and Cultural Change*, vol. 9 (1961): 573-87; and Gerald Hodge, "Regional and Structural Components of Urban Growth", in L. S. Bourne and R. D. MacKinnon, eds., *Urban Systems Development in Central Canada: Selected Papers* (Toronto, 1972), pp. 108-16.

7. *Changing Canadian Cities: The Next 25 Years* (Toronto, 1977), p. 152. For a similar view see Peter G. Goheen, "Industrialization and the Growth of Cities in Nineteenth-Century America", *American Studies*, vol. 14 (1971): 49-66.

1.

The Evolution of the Canadian Urban System

JAMES W. SIMMONS*

Over the last one hundred and fifty years the evolution of the Canadian urban system has been reasonably regular. The population has slowly been redistributed from rural to urban locations, the proportion of manufacturing jobs has grown, and more recently shifts towards service activities have occurred. Throughout there has been a continuing growth of per capita income.[1] But the steady progress of these curves across the graph, decade after decade, for the country as a whole, disguises the fact that these curves aggregate processes which vary widely over space. While one region is growing, another is declining. In different parts of the country urban growth may be based on such diverse processes as agricultural production, mining investment, or the expansion of the public sector.

The Canadian economy is, and has always been, strongly differentiated over space. Although people in the Windsor – Quebec corridor often forget it, the prosperity of the majority of cities in Canada is still based on the production of a single primary commodity. These primary commodities vary widely from region to region, and, of course, their production and its value varies widely over time. From year to year and from decade to decade the fluctuations in value of output of these regional staples is one of the major determinants of the pattern of urban growth rates. Complicating any analysis of growth is the inability to predict or control these fluctuations, which are largely the result of decisions made outside the country by markets, cartels, and corporations in London and New York. The regularities in urban growth which do occur result from the intricate network of economic relationships among cities. These fluctuations in the primary sector are diffused in a systematic fashion to other secondary and tertiary economic sectors in other cities, creating the composite pattern of economic change which can be observed in any one time period.

* I wish to acknowledge the assistance of John Britten and Jim Lemon who commented on an earlier draft of this article.

This essay focuses on the economic processes which initiate and transmit growth impulses in the Canadian urban system.[2] Where, and through which decisions, does growth occur? How does growth move from place to place in order to produce the patterns of urban growth which we observe consistently over time? The essay begins with a review of the main attributes of the Canadian urban system and its growth over time, drawing on present-day patterns and extrapolating back in time. The second part presents a simplified model of the interdependency of urban regions. The final section uses the model to interpret the historical evolution of the Canadian urban system.

THE CANADIAN URBAN SYSTEM

Some Definitions   The use of the term "urban system" as a framework for studying the space-economy over time implies at least two things. First, the economy of the country and its growth and change are considered to take place at a number of urban nodes. Thus, in Figure 1:1 Canada in 1971 is partitioned into 124 urban-centred regions. These urban-centred regions are groups of counties or census divisions aggregated around cities of over 10,000 population. By grouping a city with its immediate hinterland, the bothersome problems of definition involved in separating cities from rural areas can be avoided. In fact, the whole question of rural-urban differentiation is passed by and the focus turns instead towards the relative rates of growth, or decline, of urban-centred regions of different sizes and in different locations. The main advantage of this approach is that it identifies with each urban centre the real economic base of most Canadian cities: the agriculture or lumbering, mining or fishing in the nearby districts on which the town's merchants depend. It also implies that the very concept of disaggregating the national economy is important: cities grow in different fashions, and not precisely in parallel; hence growth in one location may be related to growth somewhere else.

The second characteristic of an urban system is a concern with the pattern of interdependency among cities—a central theme throughout this essay. How is the urban system organized? Which cities are linked to Winnipeg? And to which larger city does Winnipeg turn? The lines drawn in Figure 1:1 represent a hypothesis about present-day urban-system linkages, suggesting a simple hierarchical structure dominated by variations in population size and distance, and modified on occasion by a transportation system or a language barrier. This notion of urban-system organization will be elaborated in the second part of

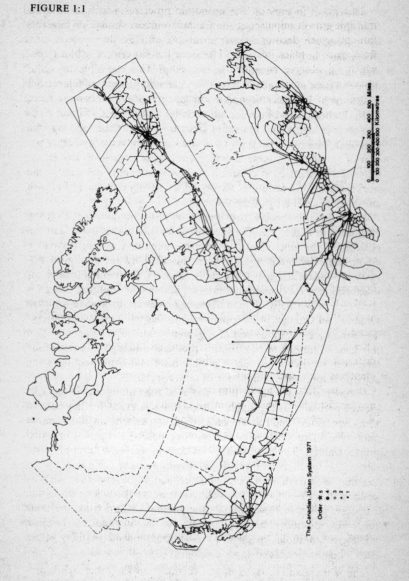

The Canadian Urban System 1971

Order
★ 5
● 4
○ 3
▲ 2
• 1

this essay, but in essence it assumes that no city operates in isolation from the rest of the space-economy. Information, money or migrants move from one place to another in regular patterns.

Describing the Urban System The most striking aspect of the Canadian urban system, examined in cross-section, is the high degree of differentiation of economic base from place to place. Canadian cities tend to be highly specialized in the production of one or two products, such as wheat, wood pulp, or automobiles. Although Canadian cities also share a highly uniform set of services (a post office, Holiday Inn, Canadian Tire store, etc.), which now account for sixty to seventy per cent of employment, these activities are largely derivative. Except for a handful of the largest centres it is the ten to twenty per cent of the workers in the mine, mill, or factory who determine the rate of growth and level of prosperity of the town.

The present-day spatial distribution of this economic specialization is mapped in Figure 1:2. The specialized activity makes up at least ten per cent of the labour force in an urban region. The census data on employment by industry have been modified by redefining all primary processing activities (pulp mills, smelters, fish plants) from manufacturing into the appropriate primary sector. The resulting pattern is stark indeed. Virtually all manufacturing cities are located in southern Ontario and Quebec, in the corridor identified by Yeates and others.[3] The urban regions in the rest of the country are largely dependent on the demand for one or two primary products, although in a few of the larger centres a combination of public-sector and light-manufacturing activities support the designation of service centre.

The map suggests that in 1971, just as in the nineteenth century, the growth processes of the staple economy are relevant for the bulk of Canadian cities. The income of a city is dependent on the quantity and value of production of the resource base, be it grain, or wood pulp, or nickel. These urban regions depend upon the level of world demand as much as on their own ability to produce. To a large extent the rate of growth in a particular location is beyond the reach of policy-makers in Ottawa, responding instead to the whims of nature, corporate policy in New York, or the gnomes of Zurich. At the same time, any governmental intervention into the national economy—a tax, a tariff, a quota—is bound to redistribute income spatially within such a highly specialized space-economy.

The manufacturing cities of the corridor, on the other hand, produce almost entirely for the Canadian market. Protected by a tariff wall soon after Confederation, they have grown in step with the

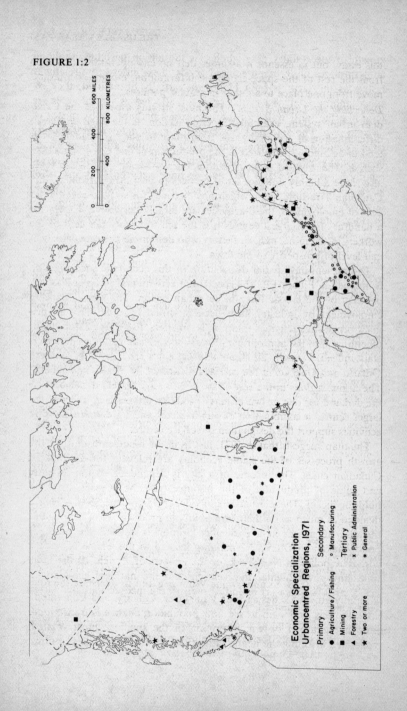

**Economic Specialization
Urbancentred Regions, 1971**

Primary	Secondary
● Agriculture/Fishing	○ Manufacturing
■ Mining	Tertiary
▲ Forestry	✕ Public Administration
★ Two or more	✱ General

600 MILES

800 KILOMETRES

400

200

400

0

growth of the country as a whole. As the nation becomes wealthier and consumes more manufactured goods, these cities grow relatively faster; as the tariff is built higher or partially dismantled, they respond appropriately. Particular cities are affected as special gates are built into the tariff wall—for foreign textiles perhaps, or by means of an auto pact. The auto pact, however, has made many manufacturing cities as sensitive to external demand (for Gremlins rather than Cadillacs) as any gold-mining town. Both Windsor and Sudbury grew rapidly between 1966 and 1971 and declined between 1971 and 1976, in step with the U.S. economy. Much of the discussion to follow, however, is concerned with the primary producing cities outside the corridor, and the very high-order centres, such as Toronto and Montreal, which serve them.

The Canadian urban system is highly integrated in the sense that changes in the economic base of one city are quickly communicated to other nearby cities and translated into relative rates of growth and decline. A good wheat crop means more money spent in the towns, more clerks in the stores, and more jobs. The jobs are filled by new residents from other cities or abroad. Money and jobs mean population growth; the lack of them leads to out-migration and population decline. It is as simple as that. Even the most inward-looking locations in Quebec or Newfoundland respond to the loss of jobs. Regional variations in wage levels and unemployment persist, but in the face of substantial migrations towards growth areas.

The map of internal migration flows in Figure 1:3 is the best evidence we have about the current pattern of urban-system organization.[4] Each arrow shows the direction of the most popular destination from each urban region. People from Yorkton go mainly to Regina; people from Regina go to Calgary, and so on. The pattern is basically hierarchical, linking each small centre to the nearest higher-order place. It indicates the regional structure of the country, suggesting the relative lack of contacts among cities in the Atlantic region, and the high level of integration among western cities. Because these arrows represent flows of migrants, rather than flows of commodities, the map shows clearly the language barrier in Quebec, eastern Ontario, and New Brunswick, across which very few people move. The use of migration also tends to undervalue Winnipeg and to overstate the role of rapidly growing cities such as Vancouver, Calgary, and Edmonton. None the less, we begin to see how population change is transmitted through the urban system, beginning in the smallest, most volatile economies, affecting the nearer cities first and the larger cities in turn, until gradually the network of linkages among cities is itself transformed. The migrants who transmit this change are primarily young people, age fifteen to thirty, and they respond to both economic and social opportunities.

FIGURE 1:3

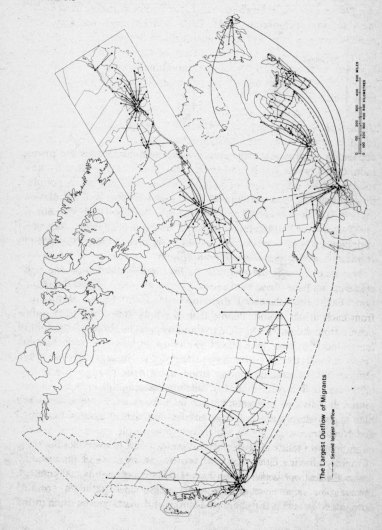

The Largest Outflow of Migrants

—————➤ Second largest outflow

FIGURE 1:4   Relationship among Components of the Urban System*

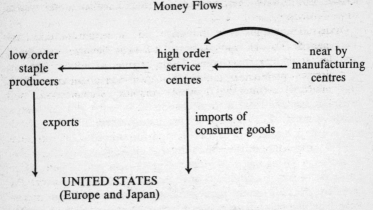

Money Flows

* Each movement of money results in a flow of commodities in the opposite
  direction.

The relationships among the main components of the Canadian
urban system are shown in Figure 1:4. Income from the sale of
primary products (largely in foreign markets) is allocated to the small
producing regions across the country, and the commercial system
moves it through the urban system to higher and higher order centres.
The main economic mechanism is the final demand linkage as defined in Watkins' discussion of the staple economy.[5] When the money
reaches the highest-order Canadian centres (Toronto and Montreal) it
creates both demand for manufactured goods from the nearby industrial cities, and demand for imported goods from abroad. The bulk of
imported consumer goods goes to these two cities for redistribution
elsewhere in the urban system. The external linkages of the urban
system play a critical role in urban growth or change in Canada,
although it is a role often difficult to measure. Not only trade relations, but flows of investment capital and migrants, as well as key
nodes in transportation and communication systems, are determined
externally.

A central feature of these economic relationships within Canada is
the dependence of larger service centres on the level of income and
rate of growth of their tributary areas. This is not an unusual concept,
but it requires some explicit hypotheses about the spatial structure of
the hinterlands if it is to be tested empirically. This will be done in the

section to follow. These relationships between urban growth and hinterland growth have been relevant for the Canadian urban system since fur-trading days.

Other relationships can be important, too, in certain locations and time periods. Forward and backward economic linkages are significant for certain primary activities. Transportation and military systems, or retirement preferences, impose their own inter-urban connections. The industrial corridor has a whole complex of connections, both internally and with parent firms outside the country. But the fundamental concept which explains the spatial expansion of urban growth in Canada is the level of world demand for various staple products and the articulation of their final demand linkages over space. From Brandon to Winnipeg to Toronto, a good crop and a good price generates urban growth along the commercial path. To predict the crop (i.e., climate) and the price on the world market is almost impossible. The limited understanding of urban growth which is attainable must focus on the commercial linkages among cities, and how they evolve through time.

Growth in the Urban System   A significant by-product of the growth processes of Canadian urban regions is a high level of uncertainty. A very large random (or at least unpredictable) component exists in the growth of any city or groups of cities. No one has been able to forecast rates of growth, and while one can always "explain" a given rate of growth in the past, the explanations are idiosyncratic, varying from city to city and decade to decade. The productivity of primary commodities changes rapidly over space and time. Weather, insects, plagues, and dry holes are not predictable. Commodity prices are imposed externally and change with the business cycle, with war and peace, and with the development of new technologies and new sources of production. Predicting urban growth rates in Canada is very much like playing the commodity market.

The uncertainty is observable in the history of most Canadian cities (Figure 1:5). The graphs display examples of annual rates of change in income level for a number of urban regions in Canada. The curves are already smoothed to eliminate the national growth rate and the national business cycle. None the less, rates of growth or decline of ten, fifteen, even twenty per cent per year can be observed. Over a decade these fluctuations may cancel out, but just as often may cumulate into sizable growth or decline.

The size of an urban region offers some protection. A larger place serves a wider territory, perhaps encompassing two or three different primary products, and the rates of growth aggregate into a regular pattern of growth, much like that of the nation as a whole. This explains the increase in regularity with city size shown in the graphs.

FIGURE 1:5

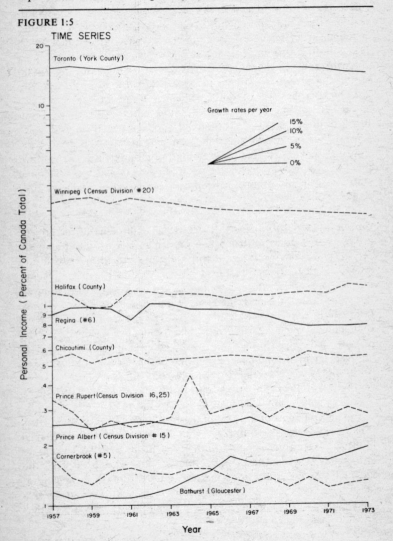

TIME SERIES

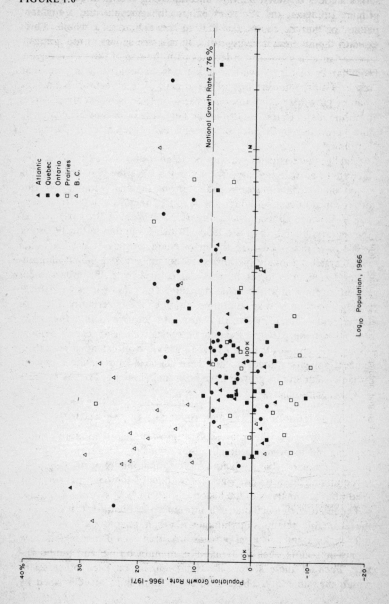

FIGURE 1:6

Another way of describing the uncertainty of growth is the graph in Figure 1:6, where the rate of growth is plotted against the size of city. Note first that there is no relationship between size of city and rate of growth. Small cities are just as likely to grow as large ones. Instead, the variance in growth rate declines with the size of the urban region, with larger places growing at about the national growth rate. The result of all this uncertainty in the growth of small centres is that the map of growth rates in any one year or decade is markedly different from the map of growth rates in the next year or decade. The correlation between growth rates of cities in two different time periods is very low.[6]

Finally, there is evidence that no relationship has existed between the rate of growth and city size in Canada since the regular collection of population data began in 1851.[7] Strong regional variations in rate of growth do occur, although the favoured regions change from decade to decade: almost always Ontario, the West in the early part of the century, the North in the 1950s, British Columbia in the 1960s.

We have described here the main characteristics of the Canadian urban system: a highly specialized economic base, dependent on natural and economic forces beyond our control, with the urban nodes linked together in a hierarchic structure. The rate of urban growth is highly uncertain in space and time, although the uncertainty is less for larger centres. Neither size of centre, nor location within the urban system, nor the pattern of economic specialization appear to be consistent predictors of the rate of urban growth over extended periods of time. It appears, moreover, that these characteristics of the Canadian urban system and its growth have been maintained at least as far back as Confederation.

THE STRUCTURE OF INTERDEPENDENCY OF URBAN REGIONS

In order to make the processes of growth described above more explicit, and to permit generalizations about the long-term evolution in the Canadian urban system, a more formal model of urban growth is required. The next few pages apply some of the concepts currently used in urban analysis to the historical pattern.[8]

The interdependency matrix is introduced in Figure 1:7. It describes the economic relationships among n urban regions as a matrix of inter-regional inter-sectoral purchases. Within each urban region are k economic sectors, such as agriculture, manufacturing, and public service. Each of these sectors has some impact on each other sector within the same city. These intra-city relationships are described by the submatrices along the diagonal, in the way that an input-output matrix for Toronto would describe the main properties of that city's economy. Each one hundred office jobs leads to five hundred cleaning jobs, store clerks, school teachers, and so forth. The off-diagonal submatrices (e.g., inter-city (2, 1)) describe the impact on sector j of city (1) due to a change in sector i of city (2). For instance one hundred office jobs in Toronto may require one ton of paper from Trois Rivières. Many of these inter-city relationships are zero: the pair of cities are simply not related in any direct fashion as, for example, Prince Rupert and Val D'Or.

The vector on the left side of the diagram identifies the initial growth impulses which drive the model. Suppose, for instance, that for a given time period it were possible to identify the change in production of a given primary product in a given urban region. Wheat production goes up by ten per cent, and the real price per bushel by five per cent, generating a total income increase of fifteen per cent in city (1). The increase stimulates growth in other sectors within the community as described by the diagonal submatrix (1), but also carries over to a nearby larger centre—city (2)—where it increases the activity in the retail and service sectors. The increase in income of both city (1) and city (2) is carried over to the even larger centre, city (7), and so on, up the urban hierarchy. The final impact of all the initial growth impulses is the result of the initial vector acting through the interdependency matrix (that is, growth impulses moving throughout the urban system), a vector of net growth at each location, by each sector. This resultant growth is described by the final growth vector on the right side of the diagram.

Beyond the scope of this discussion is a whole social science devoted to specifying the properties of such an interdependency matrix, the mathematics of its application, and to qualifying its potential for forecasting. Instead, the structure of the interdependency matrix itself is of interest here. What places in the urban system are related to each other and how do these relations evolve over time? This exposition demonstrates the potential complexity of urban economic growth. Any real world model, and in particular, any verbal discussion of the process, inevitably abstracts a small number of relationships from this complexity. The abstraction is necessary because an interdependency matrix, such as the one portrayed above, is impossible to develop.[9] One hundred cities and fifty economic sectors would require twenty-five million relationships to be evaluated, linking each economic sector in Yorkton, for instance, to each sector in Noranda. Fortunately, for the urban analyst the Canadian urban system is quite simple. The great majority of these relationships are effectively zero. Yorkton has virtually no manufacturing sector; Noranda, virtually no agriculture. Moreover the two regions are not in direct contact. They are linked only indirectly, by means of a series of service centres. This means

FIGURE 1:7

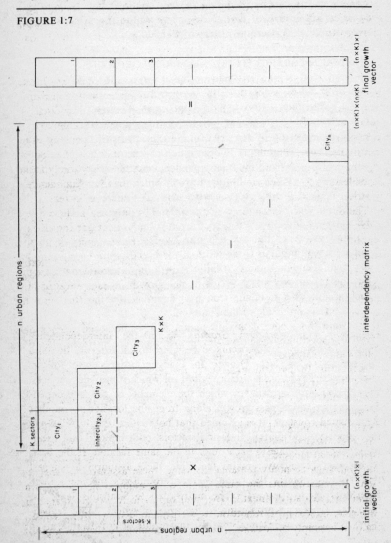

that it may someday be possible to measure the significant relationships in the Canadian urban system, at different time periods; and then to simulate the diffusion of growth throughout the urban system due to some initial disturbance such as a change in the price of oil.

This is not really the concern of this essay, however. The interdependency matrix can be used as a device for discussing the various ways in which growth or decline can occur within the urban system during various periods in the history of Canada.

THE INTERDEPENDENCY MATRIX AND URBAN GROWTH[10]

The point of using the elaborate conceptual framework of the interdependency matrix is to explore the various processes by which growth and change take place within the Canadian urban system. The discussion first differentiates between growth occurring within a stable interdependency matrix (the short term), and the effects of changing the matrix itself (the long term). A description of various kinds of urban-system organization and the interdependency matrices they imply follows, leading to a discussion of the ways in which the interdependency matrices determine the growth of particular cities or sets of cities.

The discussion concentrates on the primary producing and service cities outside the Ontario – Quebec corridor. The manufacturing cities have their own dynamics (described in most of the conventional literature on urban growth), in which the city size, location, and sectoral specialization are important. It should be noted, however, that the origins of many of these manufacturing cities in Canada are rooted in the local resource base.[11]

Long-term and Short-term Growth Within the interdependency framework urban growth occurs in response to an external demand for a primary product. Growth in a higher-order centre follows growth in the lower-order urban regions for which it provides services. This is *short-term* growth, in which the elements of the interdependency matrix which pass growth along from one location to another are assumed constant. It is assumed that both cities remain relatively the same size, and that all industrial sectors, both internal and external, continue to relate to each other in the same fashion. If the basis of Brandon's economy remains the same, these assumptions suggest that Toronto obtains the same share of Brandon's income growth from one year to the next.[12] The mail orders to Simpsons-Sears, for instance, increase in proportion to the price of wheat. More realistically, it is simply maintained that the magnitude of growth in a given city due to the initial growth vector is much greater than that induced by changes in the interdependency matrix.

Over five or ten years, however, the interdependency matrix may be altered significantly, generating *long-term* growth in the cities affected. Three kinds of long-term growth are possible. In the simplest, most dramatic kind of growth, a change in the urban-system organization might create a new linkage between a pair of cities or break one which existed before. A new highway might transfer the trade of Ottawa, for instance, from Montreal to Toronto. Spelt provides frequent examples of the impact of transportation networks and new transportation technology in the growth of small urban centres in Ontario.[13] More likely, the rapid growth of a tributary region might transform it into a competitor, as Toronto challenged Montreal around the turn of the century, and Kingston even earlier. Such a transfer accelerates the growth of the successful challenger, and slows down the growth of the loser. These rearrangements in the organization of the urban system result from the cumulation of differential growth rates in the competing regions over an extended period of time. In a truly random space-economy they represent the equivalent of a "lucky streak" for the winner. In reality, they may result from the development and exhaustion of a resource base, the shift in the terms of trade between different resource products, or between primary commodities and manufactured goods, or the extension of settlement in a frontier system. Winnipeg provides several examples through the years as its fortunes reflect changing relationships with an extensive hinterland. The settlement of the prairies from east to west gave Winnipeg an enormous initial advantage, which it maintained as long as the hinterland remained agricultural.[14] The discovery of a new resource base in Alberta, however, and the subsequent relative price shifts between oil and agriculture ultimately permit Calgary and Edmonton to compete on an equal footing.

The most widespread kind of long-term growth occurs when the proportion of income passed on from one level to the next higher level in the urban hierarchy changes. For instance, the presence of powerful scale economies in retailing has led to the relocation of certain kinds of stores from low-order to high-order centres. Highway improvements allow customers to shop directly in larger centres; the result is an increase in the proportion of income transferred upwards in the hierarchy and a modification of the final demand linkage. The effect on the urban system is widespread because it reduces the growth rate of low-order centres all across the country, even though this pattern of decline may be masked by the rapid short-term growth of small resource-based communities on the frontier. In various decades in the past such transfers of urban activities have occurred both up and down the hierarchy, favouring different size levels in different decades. Recently, for instance, a kind of decentralization of manufacturing, retailing, and population has occurred in Central Canada, which favours second-level cities (e.g., Barrie, St. Jean) at the expense of the very largest (Toronto and Montreal). In the rest of the country, in contrast, the very largest centres appear to grow most rapidly.

The third form of long-term growth is the incremental shift in the boundaries of trade areas that takes place over time. A shift in the relative size or range of services offered by competing cities, or an improvement in a transportation network transfers part of the trade area from one city to the other. Over the last twenty-five years Toronto has attracted an increasingly larger share of the trade of the Maritimes away from Montreal, until the latter now serves only the French-speaking areas. At the same time the intensity of Montreal's dominance of the latter has probably grown. In the West, Winnipeg is slowly losing much of Saskatchewan to Calgary and Edmonton, while the latter turn increasingly to Vancouver instead of Toronto.

Sorting out these various kinds of long-term growth is not easy. Data on inter-city contact is at present rudimentary. Historically one can only turn to transportation schedules, lists of customers, post-office records, and the like.[15] At the same time there is no alternative. These urban-system relationships of cities are critical components of urban growth for most of the country, although knowledge of the patterns and their stability is still speculative.

The Linkage Structure   How many of the twenty-five million possible linkages in the urban interdependency matrix can reasonably be discarded? Which linkages are essential to an understanding of urban growth? How is the urban system organized, and how does this organization change over time? Several different linkage arrangements are put forth, so that their relevance in different historical periods can be evaluated.

Consider first the city as an *autarchic* structure. Frequently cities are discussed in textbooks as if they had no external relationships, or as if each city deals independently with the world. All the significant linkages then occur in the submatrices along the diagonal of the interdependency matrix, and the inter-city linkages are effectively zero. There is no doubt that one hundred years ago cities were much more independent, in the sense that fewer goods passed from city to city. More food, clothing, and fuel was generated locally, and incomes were much smaller, reducing the overall level of personal consumption. At the same time, those linkages which did exist played an important role in the economic base of each community. Most urban regions in Canada at the time depended on the export of primary products, which took place through the same transportation network which delivered consumer goods. The result was, even then, a hierarchy of cities of increasing size, each providing more complex mixtures of goods and serving increasingly larger trade areas. The larger centres, like Montreal, gained income from their hinterlands by handling both exports of staples, and imports of consumer goods. In addition, massive inter-regional migrations adjusted the supply of labour to fluctuations in the local economic base. Although the overall level of economic interaction was much lower in the nineteenth century, the role of exports of local primary products, and the path of the growth impulse through the urban system, was comparable to the present.

It was suggested earlier that this interdependence could be represented by a *hierarchic* structure, in which growth moves upwards from the lowest centres to the highest. Such an organization has the advantage of simplicity: it requires only n linkages, one for each city to the nearest high-order centre. The validity of this model rests on the extreme distances between competing centres in much of Canada, as well as the great variations in city size. In reality, smaller centres often split their allegiance among two or even three locations. For instance, Chatham (Ontario) is served by both London and Windsor. The simplicity is also maintained by focusing on the final demand linkages, retailing and services, and eliminating the complexity of manufacturing production processes.

A controversial aspect of the hierarchical model is the assumption that growth impulses move up the hierarchy. Several writers working in more industrialized areas argue that the downward diffusion of industrial technology is an important source of urban growth.[16] Within Canada, in certain areas at certain times, growth impulses do appear to move from large cities to small. During the last decade, for instance, growth near large cities spreads outward to neighbouring smaller cities. In frontier regions settlers moved outward from the large centres, taking their capital goods with them. For many staples an increase in production may require a substantial investment from a corporate or financial headquarters in a larger centre. But in Canada, for the most part, the larger cities simply respond to the growth of the smaller centres. Ultimately their economic base is identical with that of their hinterlands. If one examines the growth of Canadian cities over time, the spatial pattern of growth is the single consistent observable regularity.

An alternative to the hierarchical model is the *fully interconnected* urban system in which the forward and backward linkages of an industrial complex determine the interdependency matrix. Size of city and distance would be important, but sources of raw materials and markets, and the complexities of corporate structures would create circuits of linkages, with many more links than nodes. Such a model may have relevance for the cities of the central Canada corridor during the most recent decades.[17] For the past it may be worthwhile to try to trace the flow of income for a staple such as wheat, backwards to the farm-implement industry and forward to the milling and storage complexes. These linkages are undoubtedly significant, but much less so than the final demand linkages described above. Beyond that, the operational difficulties of examining urban growth throughout the urban system on a sector-by-sector basis are overwhelming.

A final possible variation of the interdependency matrix modifies the fully interconnected matrix by incorporating intense regional linkages while ignoring inter-regional contacts which are either weak or are channelled through the larger centres. This interdependency matrix has blocks of intra-region inter-city linkages along the diagonal and zeroes elsewhere. It would represent pre-Confederation Canada very well, in that each colony dealt independently with the rest of the world (predominantly Great Britain or the United States). In terms of social or cultural contacts, as Figure 1:3 suggests, French-speaking Canada operates in this fashion today. The utility of knowledge of such patterns, for both economic and social phenomena, goes beyond urban-growth models since they permit the evaluation of such terms as "fragmented", "isolated", and "integrated" which are central to the interpretation of political events. The lack of contact among the Atlantic provinces, as compared to the western provinces, is still quite striking.

CHANGES IN THE INTERDEPENDENCY MATRIX OVER TIME

Over the last one hundred and fifty years the Canadian urban system has grown dramatically. The population is ten times larger, the number of urban nodes has increased in proportion, and the number of significant inter-city linkages has increased at least one hundred

times. The amount and content of each linkage has changed as well.
In addition the whole pattern of external relationships of the urban
system has been altered. None the less, the basic mechanisms of
growth remain the same.

The growth of the urban system has several implications for the
interdependency matrix. The magnitude of growth, and its concentration on the western periphery of the urban system, means that short-
term growth often cumulates into significant long-term changes. Important urban subsystems have been added in western Canada and
along the northern frontier, and their peripheral location leads to
growth in the limited number of centres in the pre-existing urban
system which are linked to them (the gateway effect). At the same
time, high levels of international migration and capital movement
permit rapid rates of growth and decline in low-order centres. An
urban system which grows rapidly has great capacity for sudden
change or redistribution.

Although the increased number of urban nodes in the system extends the number of possible linkages among cities (n cities permit n^2
linkages), this tendency is counteracted by the increasing size differentiation of cities. Whereas the largest cities in 1851 were Montreal
(57,000), Quebec (42,000), Toronto (31,000), and Saint John (23,000),
by 1971 the urban regions represented by Toronto and Montreal were
each over two million in population. Growing size differences in cities
extend the range of linkage magnitudes; they concentrate interdependencies into a hierarchical pattern by differentiating the range of
goods and services available at competing cities, so that Brandon and
Winnipeg are not competitive in any way. They also alter the relative
accessibility of locations. Even if one prefers to go directly to Regina
from Thompson, Manitoba, one still has to pass through Winnipeg to
get there. The very largest centres have polarized the linkage structure
so that Toronto, Montreal, and increasingly Vancouver, attract, generate, or process a very large proportion of business linkages.

The effect of the increased variation in city size on the interdependency matrix helps to compensate for the reduced effect of distance,
due to reduced transportation time and costs. It is now possible to
reach a major city from virtually any part of the country within four
hours. In the interdependency matrix, the blocks of regional linkages
are replaced by contacts with large centres in more distant locations.
Amherst, Nova Scotia, now deals with Halifax because it is bigger,
rather than because it is closer, but it may also increasingly deal
directly with Toronto. The role of medium-seized centres, such as

Sherbrooke and Kingston, in a hierarchical model may be declining as a result.

It is difficult to evaluate the changes in the magnitude and content of inter-city linkages themselves. It is possible that, on the production side, flows may not have changed all that much. The output of a farm may be greater and more specialized; it may require more fertilizer and more machinery; but by and large the linkages are similar. For some staples, of course, the production linkages now have almost no spatial ramifications. An oil pipeline, an iron-ore freighter, or a unit train carrying coal for export leaves little imprint on the parts of the urban system it passes through. The farmer as consumer, in contrast, has doubled and redoubled his real income, increasing his dependency on other locations, where, for example, he shops for a whole array of new products ranging from orange juice to television. The role of the final demand linkages in the interdependency matrix is greater than ever before.

The interdependency matrix in the Canadian urban system thus remains simple and direct despite the great technological changes in the economy. The initial growth impulses move in a very structured fashion to maintain regular growth in the largest centres. An essential source of stability in these linkages is the national boundary itself. Political institutions are the preconditions for the economic integration. The nature of Confederation, the barriers to external trade that it imposes, and the networks of communication and transportation that it initiates have helped to develop and maintain the interdependency matrix in its present form.

Some of the external linkages are beyond our control. It is possible to trace the regular transfer of external markets from the United Kingdom, to the United States, and now to the Orient (all of which accelerate the growth of the western cities); but the rise and fall of the demand for gold, aluminum, wheat, coal, or whatever cannot be predicted. Over a number of years the response of producing regions in Canada to this external demand cumulates into sizable differences in population and services in competing cities. This in turn alters trade areas. The discovery of oil at Leduc in Alberta ultimately reduced the role of Winnipeg in western Canada, as the development of hard rock mining in northern Ontario may have permanently altered the relationship between Toronto and Montreal. At some specific time the growth in a service hinterland, which initially feeds the growth of the higher-order centre, may begin to generate a competitor. This volatility in rate of growth and inter-city relationships within the Canadian urban system argues against any metropolitan-dominance model, in which a larger centre controls the destiny of smaller places.

Changes in Individual Linkages For the urban system as a whole the least important sources of long-term growth variations are those unique events which alter the relationships between a pair of cities. Such events affect only a few elements within the whole interdependency matrix, while the kinds of changes discussed above modify a large proportion of the relationships. None the less, changes in individual linkages are crucial to the historian interested in the growth path of a single city, and represent the most likely kind of research on interdependency in the immediate future.

The importance of a particular linkage is increased to the extent that the simple hierarchic structure holds. With each city linked to a single higher-order centre, and carrying with it the relationships of a number of smaller places, a transfer in allegiance of a higher-order centre can be of considerable significance to the system as a whole. The Atlantic provinces provide several examples of realignment and readjustment, plus some potential linkages that have never been consummated. The original colonies, continually conscious of their differences, were linked together only under protest. The Intercolonial Railway, following Confederation, placed Halifax within reach of central Canadian manufacturers and wholesalers, made Moncton an important city (at the expense of Saint John), but did not link together the region itself. No gateway city (like Winnipeg) emerged. Instead of processing the regional staples (like Vancouver), Halifax depends on the military and transportation roles assigned to it by the federal government and the province; and despite the efforts of federal planners to make it the pre-eminent "growth centre" of the Maritimes, other urban regions prefer to look to Toronto or Montreal. Perhaps the Intercolonial aborted the development of a regional subsystem in the Maritimes; or the lack of coal near Halifax dispersed the Nova Scotia industrial base too thinly.[18]

Changes in transportation networks or technology account for relatively few linkage changes in a hierarchic system. Except perhaps in the earliest stages of the Canadian urban system, new transportation systems tend to reinforce the patterns of the old, because of the political clout of established cities, the innate locational attributes, or increasingly, the scale advantages of larger places. Perhaps the changing pattern of external linkages deserves more explicit attention. Internal linkages for both the consumption and production respond to the shifts in predominant external linkages from east to west: from Great Britain to the eastern United States, to the West Coast and the Orient. The relative importance of the various ports of entry shift—both the ports themselves and the mode of transportation—but more important, these nodes anchor the internal distribution network of the country. The role of Toronto and Montreal in the Canadian urban system depends in part on their intense linkages with New York and the eastern United States. For example, these two cities generate seventy per cent of the entire passenger movement across the United States border. As the United States economy moves to the south and west the advantages for distributing their goods within Canada may also shift.

A notable set of new economic linkages are those of the public sector. Every provincial capital city, as well as Ottawa, has grown faster than the province it serves over the last two decades, reflecting the transfer activities from the private to the public sector. Ottawa then, defines a new set of interdependencies, linked to all parts of the urban system.

Conclusions A consideration of the growth paths of all Canadian cities over a long period suggests three major components of any growth model:
1. Uncertainty. A considerable proportion of urban growth is unpredictable, due to the openness of the Canadian economy, and its continued dependence on primary products.
2. The Resource Base. The distribution and properties of staple products largely determine the location and timing of urban growth in smaller centres. It is not industry or entrepreneurial skill but the ability of the hinterland to generate wealth which is essential.
3. The Network of Interdependencies. The linkages between cities redistribute income from one location to another. They are essentially conservative, in that they maintain size and dependency relationships among cities. The larger the city, the more it depends on situation rather than on a site resource base.

Of these three components the most useful in understanding the urban system is the last. The study of urban economic growth requires the explicit specification of spatial interdependencies, in such a way that their magnitudes can be evaluated and their stability measured. Until then it is difficult to make much sense of the complex patterns of urban growth.

NOTES

1. See, for example, Leroy O. Stone, *Urban Development in Canada* (Ottawa, 1967); R. Marvin McInnis, "Long-run Changes in the Industrial Structure of the Canadian Workforce", *Canadian Journal of Economics*, vol. 4 (1971): 21-36; R. Marvin McInnis, "Long-run Trends in the Industrial Structure of the Canadian Work Force: Regional Differentials, 1911-1961", mimeo (Kingston: Department of Economics, Queen's University); James W. Simmons, *The Growth of the Canadian Urban System*, Research Paper No. 65 (Toronto: University of Toronto, Centre for Urban and Community Studies, 1974).

2. The important references for this discussion are the studies of the United States urban system by John R. Borchert, "American Metropolitan Evolution", *Geographical Review*, vol. 57 (1967): 301-22; and Michael P. Conzen, "A Transport Interpretation of the Growth of Urban Regions: An American Example", *Journal of Historical Geography*, vol. 1 (1975): 361-82; Michael P. Conzen, "The Maturing Urban System in the United States, 1840-1910", *Annals of the Association of American Geographers*, vol. 67 (1977): 88-108; the analysis of urban growth in England and Wales by Brian T. Robson, *Urban Growth: An Approach* (London, 1973); and the work on Southern Ontario by Leslie Curry and Geoffrey Bannister, "Forecasting Township Population of Ontario from Time-Space Covariances", in L. S. Bourne, *et al.*, eds., *Urban Futures for Central Canada* (Toronto, 1974), pp. 34-59; and Geoffrey Bannister, "Population Change in Southern Ontario", *Annals of the Association of American Geographers*, vol. 65 (1975): 177-88; Geoffrey Bannister, "Space-time Components of Urban Population and Change", *Economic Geography*, vol. 52 (1976): 228-40.

3. Maurice Yeates, *Main Street: Windsor to Quebec City* (Toronto, 1975). See also D. Michael Ray, *et al.*, eds., *Canadian Urban Trends*, vol. 1, *National Perspective*, (Toronto, 1976).

4. A more extensive discussion of the 1966-71 migration pattern is found in James W. Simmons, *Migration and the Canadian Urban System*, Research Paper No. 85 (Toronto: University of Toronto, Centre for Urban and Community Studies, 1977).

5. Melville H. Watkins, "A Staple Theory of Economic Growth", *The Canadian Journal of Economics and Political Science*, vol. 24 (1963): 141-58.

6. James W. Simmons, "Short-term Income Growth in the Canadian Urban System", *The Canadian Geographer*, vol. 20 (1976). 419-31.

7. Simmons, *Growth of the Canadian Urban System*.

8. Examples of applications of the interdependency concept include a study of interregional migration in California by Andrei Rogers, *Matrix Analysis of Interregional Population Growth and Description* (Berkeley and Los Angeles, 1968); studies of leads and lags in unemployment in the United States by L. J. King, E. Casetti, and D. Jeffrey, "Economic Impulses in Regional System of Cities: A Study of Spatial Interaction", *Regional Studies*, vol. 3 (1969): 213-18; an analysis of Quebec cities by Claude Marchand, "Spatial-temporal Relationships in the Quebec Urban System", in Bourne, *et al.*, *Urban Futures . . .*, pp. 178-93; and the discussion of inter-regional multipliers in Canada by Yeates, *Main Street*, pp. 183-90.

9. Only in the last two years has a crude interregional, intersectoral model been developed for the provinces of Canada: Richard C. Zuker, "An Interprovincial Input-Output Model: Version III", Mimeo (Ottawa: Economic Development Analysis Division, Department of Regional Economic Expansion,

1976). Prior to this the only example was a two-region model for Canada and the United States: Ronald I. Wonnacott, *Canadian – American Interdependence* (Amsterdam, 1961).

10. This section draws upon an extraordinary dissertation which pulls together an extensive literature on urban growth, interaction, and interdependence. Eric S. Sheppard, "Interaction Feedback Modelling: Explorations into Configurations, Flows and the Dynamics of Spatial Systems", PHD diss., University of Toronto, Department of Geography.

11. James M. Gilmour, *The Spatial Evolution of Manufacturing: Southern Ontario, 1851-1951*, Research Publication No. 10 (Toronto: University of Toronto, Department of Geography, 1972).

12. In another paper the proportion of income passed along from one level of cities to the next is evaluated. Although the results are not wholly convincing, they do indicate that the basic relationships are stable from one year to the next: Simmons, "Short-term Income Growth . . . ".

13. Jacob Spelt, *Urban Development of South-Central Ontario* (Toronto, 1972).

14. The concept of the "gateway city" has been used to explain the rise and relative decline of Winnipeg in the West: Andrew F. Burghardt, "A Hypothesis About Gateway Cities",
Annals of the Association of American Geographers, vol. 61 (1971): 228-40.

15. The trade relationships of Winnipeg with the East and with other western centres during the 1880s have been traced in this manner: Donald Kerr, "Wholesale Trade on the Canadian Plains in the Late Nineteenth Century: Winnipeg and its Competition", in H. Palmer, ed., *The Settlement of the West* (Calgary, 1977), pp. 130-52.

16. For example, Allan R. Pred, *Urban Growth and the Circulation of Information* (Cambridge, Mass., 1973); and Brian J. L. Berry, "Hierarchical Diffusion: The Basis of Development Filtering and Spread in a System of Cities", in N. H. Hansen, ed., *Growth Centres in Regional Economic Development* (New York, 1972), pp. 108-38.

17. James W. Simmons, "Interaction Among the Cities of Ontario and Quebec", in L. S. Bourne and R. D. MacKinnon, eds., *Urban Systems Development in Central Canada*, Research Publication No. 9 (Toronto: University of Toronto, Department of Geography, 1972), pp. 198-219.

18. L. D. McCann, "Staples, Urban Growth and the Heartland-Hinterland Paradigm: Halifax as an Imperial Outpost, 1867-1914", paper presented to the Canadian Urban History Conference (Guelph, 1977).

II.

Politics and Municipal Government

Introduction

Although there is a relatively large body of literature devoted to Canadian municipal government and politics, there is still no book-length study that satisfactorily deals with the political history of urban Canada.[1] There are many reasons for this situation. Urban government and politics is a difficult subject and generalizations cannot easily be made as the patterns of development of individual cities and regions vary so much. The fact is that local government, by its very nature, tends to differ from city to city and from region to region. Problems faced in large metropolitan centres, such as Toronto or Montreal, usually differ significantly from those in smaller centres, such as Fredericton or Victoria. Similarly, the situation that exists in newer communities, such as resource towns in the north, is not at all like that found in older, established centres.

A second reason for a lack of general studies is that urban government and politics are far more complex than they at first appear. Far from being agencies that concern themselves only with such mundane tasks as ditch digging, garbage removal, and street repair, local governments also deal with such vital issues as planning, public health, economic growth, immigration, and public ownership of water, hydro, and transportation systems. Indeed, the actions of city governments across Canada have had much to do with the country's development.

The key role local government played in shaping urban Canada means that studies must be concerned with a wide variety of problems and areas. Studies of municipal government must, furthermore, concentrate on two different but interrelated topics. On the one hand, it is essential to understand the machinery and statutory powers of local governments and deal with the technical problems they face in providing municipal services. On the other hand, students of urban government must analyse the forces that influence the manner in which the formal institutions work, forces such as pressure groups, economic conditions, personnel, and ideologies.

Still another reason for the dearth of historic studies of urban

government and politics is that political scientists, caught up in the
study of other questions, have virtually ignored the urban area. Many
potential writers have been captives of the myth that the study of
municipal government is uninteresting because it is non-partisan.
When they do turn their talents toward the study of civic government,
it is usually to deal with some contemporary issue or problem; little, if
any, attention is paid to the influence of the past on the present.[2] As a
result, the study of the experience of urban government has been left
by and large to historians.[3]

While all these problems have so far prevented the publication of a
sound political history of urban Canada, the work that has been
completed has been impressive both in volume and scope and some
agreement is emerging about the nature and role of the political
structures and processes that exist in urban communities. The most
important consensus has been reached on the point of the continuing
influence of past decisions, particularly those made during the important "reform" era that lasted from the 1880s to the 1920s. The structural forms and the accompanying ideology of local government formulated during this period—involving city-wide rather than ward elections, boards of control, commission government, and city managers, and concepts such as non-partisanship and municipal politics as
"business"—are still with us in large part. In many cities, the form of
government instituted at the turn of the century remains intact or has
been only slightly modified. The ideology of the urban-government
reform movement appears to have congealed as an important component of the Canadian political culture. It has not only removed many
issues from the arena of political debate, but it often affects present-
day decision-making in crucial ways.[4] Elected and appointed civic
officials, for example, inherit a "system" that was established or
evolved in response to the needs and values of a society quite different from that of the present. It is thus difficult, if not impossible, for
these officials to redirect the structures and processes of local government to focus on issues now considered vital to urban residents.[5]

One of the most significant elements of this inherited system is the
relative powerlessness of municipal governments. Civic corporations
are today often denied the possibility of undertaking a vital role by
the fact that significant powers have been removed from their purview
by the statutory establishment of a bewildering array of autonomous
boards and commissions. Also, there has been since the early 1900s an
increasing trend toward provincial control over, and intervention in,
city activities. As urban problems grew more complex and severe, the

ability of local government to deal with them became diffused over a wide range of agencies and levels of government.

Several examples illustrate this loss of autonomy. In terms of general municipal supervision by provincial governments, every province had by the early 1950s fully operational departments of municipal affairs, most with extensive powers to supervise, influence, and control local governments. Furthermore, both prior to and after the establishment of such ministries there was an expansion of legislation providing for greater provincial control over many local government functions. Ontario provides perhaps the most advanced example of this phenomenon, although it was general throughout Canada. The Municipal Act entry in the index of the *Revised Statutes of Ontario* for 1950 contains cross-references to sixty-five other provincial acts affecting local government. Some of these date to the pre-1914 period, and are generally guiding or prohibitive in nature, but most date from after the First World War. Some of the latter are the Ontario Housing Act (1919), the Factory, Shop, and Office Building Act (1932), the Department of Municipal Affairs Act (1935), the Municipal Health Services Act (1944), and the Ontario Municipal Improvement Act (1950).[6]

While the loss of municipal autonomy was in large part a result of provincial intervention, it was also partially self-inflicted. One of the ideas that grew out of the urban reform movement of 1880-1920 was that municipal affairs was "business" and that it could best be dealt with by appointed "experts". In Winnipeg, for example, there was a multiplicity of civic boards and commissions in operation prior to the Second World War: the Board of Commissioners of Police (1884), the Public Parks Board (1893), the Playgrounds Commission (1909), the Hospital Commission (1911), the Civic Charities Endorsement Bureau (1913), the Social Welfare Commission (1917), the Winnipeg Housing Commission (1919), and the Auditorium Commission (1932). There were as well a number of inter-municipal agencies and organizations that fragmented further the power of the local government. These included the Winnipeg and St. Boniface Harbour Commissioners and River Control Board (1912), the Greater Winnipeg Water District (1913), the Greater Winnipeg Sanitary District (1935), and the St. James – Winnipeg Airport Commission (1937). Significantly, this diffusion of power among boards and agencies did not become a matter of concern until the 1950s when serious discussion of fundamental changes to local government structures finally took place.[7]

The history of this loss of autonomy and its impact on modern urban centres has only recently been undertaken and much research remains to be done on this and many other topics. Although a good start has been made on the study of some issues, cities (Toronto, Montreal, Winnipeg), and regions (western Canada), many have yet to be examined in any detail. In other words, the important general study must wait for more thematic and particular studies of urban government and politics throughout Canada, and especially in central Canada and the Maritimes. There is also a need in all areas for more studies that concentrate on separating out what was unique to a particular city or region and what was not. Only in this way will it be possible to arrive at the goal of studies that identify the seminal forces that determine the structures and processes of local government. Once this knowledge is available, the problems created by urbanization will be more easily tackled and solved.

Each of the five essays in this section deal with an important aspect of municipal government and politics. While these essays represent only a small portion of the work completed in recent years, they do provide a number of conclusions of importance not only to urban specialists but also to everyone interested in understanding the Canadian city. Moreover, through the examination of such fundamental topics as the nature of the reform movement, the class basis of municipal government, and the relationship of municipal and provincial government, these studies provide useful models for work in these areas by other students of urban government and politics.

NOTES

1. See the bibliography in Section IV, this volume. The most recent study— D. J. H. Higgins, *Urban Canada: Its Government and Politics* (Toronto, 1977)—devotes only thirty pages to the "evolution of municipal government".

2. See, for example, the essays in L. D. Feldman and M. D. Goldrick, eds., *Politics and Government of Urban Canada* (Toronto, 1976). See also N. H. Lithwick and Gilles Paquet, eds., *Urban Studies: A Canadian Perspective* (Toronto, 1968), pp. 202-74 and *passim*.

3. For a representative example of recent work see the section on "Urban Reform" in Gilbert A. Stelter and Alan F. J. Artibise, eds., *The Canadian City: Essays in Urban History* (Toronto, 1977).

4. See Gilbert A. Stelter and Alan F. J. Artibise, "Urban History Comes of Age: A Survey of Current Research", *City Magazine*, vol. 3, no. 1 (1977): 22-36.

5. T. J. Plunkett, "Perspective", *Urban Focus*, vol. 6 (1977): 1.

6. For an excellent general discussion of this development see John Taylor, "Urban-Industrial Society and the Decline of Local Autonomy in Twentieth-Century Canada". Mimeo. (Ottawa: Carleton University, 1977).

7. H. Carl Goldenberg, *et al.*, *Report of the Royal Commission on the Municipal Finances and Administration of the City of Winnipeg* (Winnipeg, 1939).

2.

The Modern City Realized:
Toronto Civic Affairs, 1880 – 1915

JOHN C. WEAVER

For upright Torontonians in the 1880s, civic reform had implied a reduction of saloons and the election of honest men.[1] The latter represented the prime barrier against corruption, since few equated the realization of good government with structural change. Thus in 1887, after having read evidence of an attempt to defraud the city, Mayor Howland resignedly addressed Council. Rather than presenting proposals to overhaul civic administration, he stated that "no amount of care and forethought can anticipate or provide against the ever varying forms and methods of fraud. An Army of Inspectors could not prevent dishonest intention from achieving some measure of success."[2] By 1915, however, a series of concurrent local and international events had inspired the raising of an "Army of Inspectors", complete with a general staff of commissioners, auditors, and advisory bodies—the entire force backed by pressure groups such as the Civic Guild and the Bureau of Municipal Research. If Howland gave expression to the old spirit, a *Globe* editorial of 1902 capsulized the new:

> We will be told that what is needed in municipal councils is better men, not new laws or constitutions, but the fact remains that you may have good men while your instrument of government is not favorable to giving them an opportunity of showing their worth.[3]

In sum, though the temperance and moral dimensions remained (personified by J. W. Bengough and F. S. Spence), the remedy of the patrician was yielding to the administrative arrangements of the expert with efficiency rather than moral purity the objective. Moral exemplars were still valued, but not as highly as efficient administrators with broad powers. The best government no longer seemed dependent upon a handful of honest men on low salaries; it meant a smoothly functioning and well-paid bureaucracy.[4] There had occurred a shift from reform with morality as focal point to that with an institutional thrust.[5]

To a degree, this change naturally accompanied the growing complexity of municipal affairs and the parallel emergence of specialists devoted to measuring the performance of an enterprise. Among these, chartered accountants, civil engineers, architects, and political economists were prominent. Against a backdrop of judicial inquiries disclosing corruption and carelessness, such professionals, joined by economy-conscious businessmen, pressed for the establishment of an orderly city. This clear explanation of municipal reform, however, is complicated by an additional consideration. Partisanship often edged into the ferment for change. Most active reformers claimed Liberal affiliation. With Conservatives and Orangemen holding sway in the city, Liberals readily embraced innovations that seemed capable of upsetting the Tory apple-cart. All of this, it must be emphasized, appeared in a North Atlantic context where ideas from the United States, England, and Germany mingled in public lectures, journals, and universities. Like most North American cities in this yeasty era, Toronto chose to exchange gross inefficiency for the foibles of executive or bureaucratic remedies. Moral and Christian impulses were supplemented by bureaucratic and scientific dimensions, influencing the decision-making process, the control of public services, alterations to the environment, and the tenor of social work.

I: THE "SHAME" OF THE CITY

At the turn of the century, expansion, the loose ends of administrative practices, and a form of machine politics in Toronto offered diverse temptations. Contracts for improvements, civic franchises, irregular bookkeeping methods, and a lax political morality beckoned to men with a keen appetite for shady opportunities. One need only consider the career of George Elliott—a man on the make, "too much given to alcohol", a promoter of stocks, and a part owner of a gravel company. Whenever "there was anything going through the Council that was interesting", Elliott could be found at City Hall or at his "desk" in the Red Room of Scholes' Hotel. Working from both sites he fixed contracts and licences. Elliott's known accomplishments included a licence for an abattoir, contracts for a paving brick company, a special water rate for the City Dairy, and the purchase of a cold storage plant for the St. Lawrence Market from a firm that had retained his services. Such results were attained by offering political support to an influential alderman, direct bribes, or more devious techniques. On one occasion the resourceful lobbyist arranged to have a truculent alderman called to the telephone just as a crucial vote was underway.[6]

Elections were anything but model exercises in democracy. The

Globe was not being entirely partisan when it attacked the notorious Ward Two Conservative Association. "Watering the ballot box and creating votes with a lead pencil", were practices well known to that group.[7] One of the leaders of the Association, an Orangeman, had struck a bargain with Mayor Shaw in 1899. In return for supporting the Mayor, by turning out the Orange vote, John Thompson and a cohort, John Noble, were appointed Chief and Deputy Chief of the Fire Department.[8] Even more flagrant abuses appeared in the 1903 election. A Deputy Returning Officer, Samuel Thompson, had stuffed ballot boxes. At first, when questioned he feigned misdirected goodness: "I just had an insane desire to do a kindness for people I took a fancy to." Later he confessed that an aldermanic candidate had employed him.[9] Of course, lesser evils, the generous distribution of beer or cigars, had a more accepted role in civic politics.

The firehalls, throughout the period, had "the reputation of schools of scandal". Eventually, in 1915, the duo of Thompson and Noble were caught with their hands in the civic cookie jar and resigned. They both had exploited department men and equipment for private gain, including the construction of houses.[10] Other employees of the city had availed themselves of similar practices. John Chambers, Commissioner of Parks, resigned in 1908; he had been selling Parks Department surplus material and retaining the proceeds. Among his peccadilloes, Chambers had directed park employees to raise mushrooms and vegetables which he sold to a St. Lawrence Market vendor. For many years Chambers had exhibited plants belonging to the city at the Annual Industrial Exhibition. In the years 1905, 1906, and 1907, he received and kept $1,004 in prizes. More bizzare were the infractions of E. H. Carter, zoo-keeper. He stocked his larder with bread and meat destined for the Riverdale Park animals. Carter also ran an exotic pet business and sold fat and bones to a rendering company.[11] The Works Department lacked colourful opportunities, but the pattern of graft held true to form. In 1902, an employee had used the carpenters working under him to build the frames for his house. Moreover, the storekeepers' books seldom balanced.[12] Juggling ledgers required no great ability; the system lacked inspection. A commotion resulting from missing tax funds in 1898, for example, showed that tax collectors operated with no surveillance. They retained tax rolls in their possession for three years at a time.[13]

To secure one of these rewarding posts or a more subordinate position, aspirants needed no special skill or training. Thompson and Noble applied political pressure, but nepotism proved convenient too.

The Deputy Returning Officer saw to it that his brother worked as his
assistant; Fred Carlton, Assistant Superintendent at Queen's Park, was
the son of the Superintendent. Clearly, the civil service lacked professional rigours. Indeed, as late as 1915, applications for positions or
promotions in the Fire Department came before the Chief alone, and
in some instances applicants made use of aldermen to obtain their
appointments.[14] The *Globe's* accusations, therefore, had an authentic
ring:

> To a very considerable extent the standing committees of Council are now
> employment bureaus, and the heads of departments, with exceptions, are
> tempted to give more heed to pleasing the Aldermen than to insuring the
> efficiency of their departments by the employment of only capable civic
> servants.[15]

The most colourful of the political manipulators was Dr. Beattie
Nesbitt. One would not have suspected his former eminence on April
14, 1912, as he stepped from an elevator in the Cook County Hall and
into the custody of J. E. Rogers of the Ontario Police Force, charged
with fraud. Draped in a threadbare suit, Nesbitt smiled and approached the cluster of Toronto newspaper men. "I see the Ward
Associations are keeping at work."[16] According to a *Globe* reporter,
Nesbitt's new beard and loss of weight had given him "the appearance of a Jewish rabbi".[17] Both Nesbitt's remark and the reporter's
description rekindled memories of the doctor's close political association with the Toronto ethnic community. Nesbitt, a former member of
the Ontario Legislature, a mayoralty candidate, and business promoter had earned his political spurs in the mid-1890s when he led the
Young Conservative Association in a revolt against the party establishment.[18] His hallmark then and throughout his career, a brash
populism, made party regulars blanch, though they did not hesitate to
use his machine. He was denied a provincial Cabinet post because of
the belief that "Dr. Beattie Nesbitt may have his own game to play
and may not be amenable to party discipline".[19]

Nesbitt's early support of a few progressive causes and his posture
as the "workingman's friend" illustrate the difficulty of maintaining a
black-and-white evaluation of bossism. Adam Beck's biographer admitted that Nesbitt "was one of the First Politicians of Ontario to
openly espouse the public ownership of electricity".[20] The boss also
must be granted some credit for familiarizing newcomers in "the
Ward" with a tolerant side of Protestant Toronto. Precisely because a
machine like that run by Nesbitt committed itself to preservation and

aggrandizement rather than to fulfilling a creed, it was an instrument in cracking the social exclusiveness of an otherwise very inflexible community. This should provide no basis for nostalgic praise of boss Nesbitt, but it does relate him sympathetically to social changes that other politicians deplored.

Many of these changes occurred in "the Ward". By "the Ward", Torontonians had in mind an imprecisely defined region of their city. "The Ward" served as a subjective shorthand designation for Toronto's foreign quarter. Confusion as to the exact blocks encompassed by "the Ward" resulted, in part, from an amalgamation of wards in 1891. Originally, "the Ward" conformed in its location to St. John Ward, running from Queen to Bloor Street and bordered by Yonge and College (present-day University Avenue). All of these were busy thoroughfares, yet the interior of "the Ward", a compressed network of streets and narrow lanes, was a little-travelled area. After 1891, St. John Ward became part of a much larger civic unit, Ward Three, but "the Ward" label stuck to the St. John area, which from the 1880s to the turn of the century housed the bulk of the city's Italian and Jewish population. Further confusion as to its location arose after 1900 from expansion as the foreign population spilled over into the streets to the west. A report in 1918 noted a district resembling "the Ward" developing west of University Avenue while a housing study conducted in 1934 actually placed "the Ward" almost entirely west of its position at the turn of the century. The best definition for an understanding of "the Ward" and particularly what it meant to the rest of Toronto appeared in a 1918 study of poverty. According to it, "the Ward" constituted "a condition, an attitude of mind toward life, a standard of living—not merely a geographic locality". Intrinsic to this notion and to popular use of the term was a tone of contempt. Civic reformers and "city beautiful" exponents hoped that it would be "wiped out by the complete substitution of stores, factories, and public buildings".[21] Instead, it grew, "boiling over into adjacent areas". This presented a dilemma, for if they were simply to tear down "the Ward" they might only "create slum conditions in other parts of the city, even in the suburbs".[22] "The Ward", therefore, was treated by good and proper Torontonians as a blemish whose foreign contagion was best kept from the sanctity of the suburbs.

In 1901 Ward Three contained 99 per cent of the city's Jewish population, 78 per cent of its black, 75 per cent of the Italian residents, and 62 per cent of the Chinese. By contrast, only 19 per cent of Toronto's British population resided there. But Ward Three included much more than the compressed knot of cottages that once had been St. John ward. North of "the Ward", around the attraction of Queen's Park, spacious residences contrasted with the immigrant dwellings; here could be found a community of well-to-do Anglo-Saxons. Hence the concentration of foreigners in a specific area was even greater than that suggested by the Census for all of Ward Three in 1901. When Dr. Charles Hastings compiled his report on the city's central district, in 1911, the area that he focused on was "the Ward" where he found 1,207 Jewish families and 180 Italian families along with over 60 non-Anglo-Saxon families.[23] But these bare indicators only touch a few of the many traits that set the area apart, for the immigrants clustered there were sheltered in quite distinctive housing and they brought new cultural dimensions to Toronto in a span of little more than two decades.

Like many waves of immigrants arriving in North American cities, the Eastern European Jews who came to Toronto moved into a district where land use was on the verge of transition. Investors waiting for the business district to move west of Yonge Street into St. John Ward rented out small brick or plaster cottages as unimproved single-family residences. Of 1,319 residences in 1909, 1,083 were occupied by tenants. In most instances, the rent obtainable for such places would have barely paid taxes; owners were content to accept low returns with the prospect of eventual profits on soaring real estate values. With no interest in erecting new houses or repairing dwellings, investors allowed conditions to deteriorate. Many of the characteristically small houses were heated only by kitchen stoves and they often lacked indoor plumbing. As late as 1916, the Health Department discovered thirty-five houses wholly lacking a water supply. Inhabitants of "the Ward" considered themselves fortunate if they lived near the Harrison Bath House in the Centre Avenue neighbourhood.[24] The *Globe*, alarmed by conditions in "the Ward", unsympathetically and foolishly editorialized that the situation would improve once foreigners were taught "the value of sanitation". That economic forces rather than culture contributed to the circumstance was not acknowledged. It was far easier to assume that "an educational campaign to make good Canadians" would resolve social problems.[25]

In these narrow houses, the occasional cigar maker or tailor set up trade to supplement wages earned from regular employment. A few such tradesmen, like Louis Issen and Isaac Sternberg who worked in the needle trades for Imperial Manufacturing, felt the injustices of official harassment as they paid fines and court costs for working at their own premises on Sunday. Though the dwellings were small, over-crowding was not excessive by standards of the day. On an average, in 1909, six individuals occupied each house. None the less, the New York Bureau of Municipal Research, conducting a Toronto survey in 1913, found fourteen men in three rooms at 88 Walton Street and twenty-seven in six rooms at 72 Terauley Street. Both were in the heart of "the Ward".[26]

Quite as apparent as the deteriorating housing was the district's ethnic culture and, like the untidy buildings with their broken plaster exteriors, the mix of languages, religions, and economic activities caused concern in the predominantly Protestant city. With Minto's Kosher Restaurant and the Lyric Theatre on Terauley Street as well as the seven synagogues that were scattered throughout "the Ward" by 1910, the area had the appearance of a separate and a distinct society. Representative of its growth and character, and also of its westward movement, was the acquisition of the New Richmond Methodist Church on McCaul Street for Congregation Beth Hamidrash Hagadol in 1907. Other institutional features also marked the area. To meet educational pressures and to make "good Canadians" out of newcomers, authorities had established a special school on Louisa Street and later replaced it with the Hester Howe School on Elizabeth.[27] At the former, nine-tenths of the pupils came from Russian Jewish families. School inspector Hughes, interviewed in 1902, noted the necessity of creating such an institution without a rigid grade system because "during the last four years a great number of Jews, principally from Russia, have settled in the school districts of Louisa, Elizabeth, and McCaul streets". Hard pressed, many of the families had their children take up part-time employment. A few youngsters sold bagels on the streetcars, but a more general practice was to peddle the *Telegram* and its rivals. Hughes considered the Jewish lads "by all means, the best and thrifty newsboys". But to secure a licence, newsboys had to attend a school. The special one on Louisa Street satisfied the requirement. Once dismissed from classes, they would rush down to the newspaper buildings and carry off bundles to Yonge Street.[28] The regulation of the newsboys was just one of several ways in which Toronto authorities sought to control activity; shops and peddlers also required licences and were the subject of police scrutiny.

Along Queen and Simcoe streets, the community's dealers in second-hand clothing had set up shop. To outsiders it was a disorderly region set quite apart from their norm. One "old-timer" recalled: "We will journey up York Street to Queen. On this East side all second-hand shops, clothing, jewellery, tools, etc., also the spot where detectives go looking for stolen goods". His memory was keen enough. For example, the *Toronto Star* reported on December 31, 1901, that "Leopold Kurtz was committed for trial on a charge of receiving a cloak and ruff belonging to Miss Aggie Kitchen, knowing them to be stolen. Kurtz, it came out, was carrying on a second-hand business with a licence". With every instance of infractions and appearances before Magistrates' Court it became easier to stereotype all residents of "the Ward" as real or potential criminals. On the other hand, "respectable" Torontonians arrested for infractions often were released without an appointment in court.[29] For various reasons, then, the teeming back-streets and lanes, an unknown territory to most middle-class citizens, were simply seen as breeding grounds for immoral activity. It should be observed that, though drinking and disturbances occurred, disorderly houses and houses of ill-repute were not part of "the Ward" culture but centred near the Cabbagetown region to the east.[30]

While the surge of immigration from the 1880s to the First World War injected novel cultural and social elements into Toronto, it likewise created a new political ingredient. What is interesting in this context is to consider how politicians responded to "the Ward". To be sure, Toronto Liberals and civic reformers did court the foreign vote, but the causes with which many of them were associated made efforts in this direction strained. Mayor Fleming, a reform mayor whose claim to innovation rested on mundane administrative changes, including the amalgamation of the street watering and scavenging departments, went to the voters in December 1893, claiming: "I am satisfied that your streets have never been kept as clean before." When a voice from the audience inquired about St. John ward, Fleming replied: "Now I am not as familiar with St. John Ward as you are."[31] His statement neatly summed up a Liberal and civic reform weakness. Civic reformers had little intention of understanding the people of "the Ward" on their own terms. Keeping the Sabbath holy, working for temperance, and acting as jealous guardians of the public purse, reformers frequently marched out of step with life in "the Ward". Although it did not occur in "the Ward", the arrest of Mrs. Meyer on Lake Shore Road for selling a five-cent cigar to Constable Twigg in violation of the Lord's Day Act was an incident that made righteous reformers appear meddlesome. On Sundays in "the Ward" policemen peddled around the blocks on their bicycles watching for the illicit movements from within the shops.[32] Causes and crusades, implying licences and regulations, had little meaning for individuals adjusting to a new setting.

It was a Liberal Ontario Legislature that passed "An Act to Prevent Profanation of the Lord's Day".[33] Conservatives, on the other hand, had proceeded with very pragmatic arrangements involving new residents. Louis Catone, vice-president of the Italian Benefit Society, frankly stated that he would support Conservative mayor Oliver Howland because "he was as friendly with the Italian man after the election as before".[34] Of course not all members of the party approved of rubbing shoulders with aliens but ward organizers like Harry Piper, and later Beattie Nesbitt, embraced the immigrant. Piper, an alderman who represented St. John Ward with only three years' interruption between 1877 and 1888, had established the first political contacts with the Toronto Jewish community, being "famous for his practice of taking a cartload of flowers through the Ward for distribution to the ragged children of poverty there".[35]

From the late nineties until his political demise in 1907, it was Nesbitt who held "the Ward", knocking Liberal opponents and Conservative rivals into a cocked hat. Like his sage American contemporary, Plunkitt of Tammany Hall, the doctor knew there was "only one way to hold a district. . . . you must study human nature and act accordin'. . . . to learn real human nature you have to go among the people, see them and be seen."[36] A *Star* editorial, written with tongue in cheek, suggested how well Nesbitt knew his ward:

> The Third Ward is our microcosm, and here the Doctor makes his strongest appeal. His qualities are, so to say, universal. He has views in regard to feeding the poor and starving which find him favour with the Hungarians. He has subtlety, finesse,—and that naturally attracts the Russians. His silk hat is dazzling. It has Polish enough to put the Poles under a spell. Moreover, he is serious enough for the Syrian. Outside the Ward, too, the Doctor is all things to all men. He has wit for the Irish; he has girth to catch the eyes of the German; he can have Scotch for the asking.[37]

In a new and often hostile environment, with reformers perpetually demanding regulations and licences and Protestant churches attempting to gain converts,[38] the residents of "the Ward" found a relaxed and reasonably tolerant atmosphere in Nesbitt's machine. It was far easier to associate with Nesbitt who once said he would "not assume to dictate to anyone on moral or sentimental questions" than it was to find a basis for accord with reformers backed by the self-righteous Rev. James Alexander Macdonald, editor of the *Globe*, or clergymen like Dr. Richard Wilson of Trinity Methodist Church who, in an address before the annual meeting of the City Mission wondered, "by what authority . . . was the picture of our Lord Jesus Christ turned to the wall in this city?|... We are not living in New York."[39] Anti-Semitic remarks, for example by the upright reformer Goldwin Smith, could only enhance Nesbitt's drawing power, for he astutely posed as the immigrants' friend. At a rally on Chestnut Street, a copy of the Toronto *News* with an editorial referring in uncomplimentary terms to "the Ward's" Jews was handed to him. After reading the first few lines, he refused to go further and denied that the *News* was truly a Conservative paper. When some three hundred destitute "Bulgarians" arrived in Toronto, Premier Whitney declined aid until conferring with Ottawa authorities. The boss, knowing how to grandstand for the constituents, demanded immediate support.[40] Still, like Piper, Nesbitt realized that kind words and gestures required an occasional support-ing action. When Conservatives formed the provincial government in 1905, Nesbitt loosened rewards for party faithfuls. Well-heeled Con-servatives registered opposition, but the doctor's faction triumphed. Interviewed about the many changes in the provincial offices in the city, he defended them without admitting they were purely patronage decisions.

> As regards the justices of the peace this has become largely an honorary office. Many of the old justices have been retained, the appointment changes being really due to increases in the list. As regards marriage licence issuers, much the same may be said, and as regards the Division Court Clerks and bailiffs, it was from their ranks that many of the most active canvassers for the Reform party were drawn. And with regard to the licence inspectors the Government laid it down as a matter of policy that it should have officials known to be in full sympathy with their party.[41]

Despite protestation that these activities did not necessarily mean patronage, Nesbitt's statement suggests the categories of appointment which were open to political consideration.

Through Nesbitt it is possible to reconstruct some impression of Toronto's social and cultural atmosphere, including barriers and paths to adjustment for Toronto immigrants at a particular time. What takes form is not a picture of a muted and secure city where men like Goldwin Smith and George Taylor Denison debated Canada's des-tiny. Untidy, narrow-minded, segregated into different societies, at times violent and often venal, Nesbitt's Toronto shared attributes with many North American cities at the turn of the century. The Anglo-Saxon community that characterized Toronto received the thin edge of social transformation between 1890 and 1910. Toronto also partook of another feature of North American urban evolution as its expanding business district furthered peripheral land speculation and made inexpensive housing temporarily available to the new arrivals from Eastern and Southern Europe. By land economics and immigration, a portion of the city consisting of sub-standard housing became identified with aliens.

Like many North American cities experiencing a transformation due to immigration, streetcars, and suburbs, Toronto had come to resemble a network of villages linked by services, but separated by culture and social status. Efforts of sorts were made to paper over the divisions by enforcing a particular model of conformity. The regulatory impulse, the enforcement of the Lord's Day, and the creation of a special school for the foreign population represent exertions of an established community to perpetuate its patterns of culture. Without the flexible practices of men like boss Nesbitt, Toronto might have been even more divided and cold than it was. On the other hand, politicians like Nesbitt did not use public office as an instrument for social change; they were not the pioneers in health and housing reform. Nesbitt and his kind—"the glad handers"—had little to do with the modern city desired by reformers.

II: REFORM BY ADMINISTRATIVE FIAT

Civic reformers in 1894–95 had hoped that their innovation, the Board of Control, would place Toronto on a sound administrative footing, curtailing ineptitude as well as the ability of special interests to penetrate civic government. They had expected too much, but the failure of this lone remedy only encouraged an enthusiasm for additional "refinements". Institutional revision definitely had come to stay. For fifteen years and beyond, Toronto politicians would discuss, reject, modify, or adopt a range of measures which, for the sake of simplicity, can be categorized. First, there were the demands for a fortified executive. In reform tracts and editorials this figured as a saintly body dedicated to the public interest, shunning partisan politics and capable of handling the many details of administration. Second, and related to the previous goal, were pleas for a well-paid and professional civil service. Reformers often blurred the distinctions between an executive and a civil service; in simple terms they wanted strong men on top. The blinking owls and vultures on Councils (a reform analogy too often close to the mark) were to be cut down to size by "big men".[42] Finally, there came steps to deter the falsification of books. A good deal of reform zeal went into assembling necessary, if mundane, instruments for internal inspection.

During the first years of the century, reform aspirations continued to centre on the Board of Control and revisions to the mode of selecting controllers. By the legislation of 1896, controllers were aldermen elected from among their fellow members of Council. The Cabinet concept, after a fashion, had had a bearing on this process. It was, however, through the selection procedure that the hand of ward politics was felt on what had been meant to be a pristine executive body. Well before the formal elections, candidates lined-up support and concluded backroom agreements. To the pious *Globe*, this represented an impediment to clean government and, incidently, an obstacle to Liberal involvement in civic management. The effective Conservative ward organizations and the Conservative majority in Council resulted in Tory domination on the Board of Control. The overall consequence: "There is not a single Liberal at the head of a civic department. . . . Most of these men [the heads] are not only conservatives, but active in the party organization."[43]

Whatever the mix of motives, the *Globe* conducted a campaign to have controllers elected at large.[44] The selection of the Board for 1903 particularly nettled. Council predictably picked members of the old gang. This moved the *Globe* to declare "that the people at large could have made a better choice".[45] Backing up this position in Council was Alderman Urquhart who already had proposed a series of revisions for Board of Control. In addition to at-large elections he advocated abolition of Council's committees and a concomitant strengthening of the Board of Control.[46] Here the hypothesis of Liberal partisanship and reform has considerable strength. Urquhart, one of the *Globe's* favourite sons, was elected second vice-president of the Ontario Liberal Association while Mayor in 1904.[47] It is also worth noting that he sought federal gifts for Toronto just before the municipal elections of 1906.[48] One of Urquhart's proposals, the at-large election, passed into law.[49] Citizens received four ballots any or all of which could be cast for a candidate. This new format ran counter to the traditions of parliamentary and representative government. The Board of Control was henceforth not responsible to Council; with the system of multiple ballots and at-large election, its members had no constituency. Toronto was acquiring a constitution that coincided with an American ideal—the separation of powers.

Reformers did not rest satisfied with the executive as represented by the reconstituted Board of Control. Council through its committees, they believed, still had far too much executive authority. Moreover, the commission idea had come into vogue, internationally, nationally, and locally. The federal government had appointed a Board of Railway Commissioners in 1903 and established a Civil Service Commission in 1908. In 1904 Edmonton adopted a charter, drafted by C. W. R. Biggar, a Toronto lawyer and former City Solicitor, which included an executive commission. In the United States the Galveston commission plan gained popularity.[50] Though details differed, commissions were basically meant to bar political meddling from government. Ideally, they were to accomplish this by having their members and powers placed beyond partisan political pressure; it was hoped they would attract capable administrators. Several variants touched Toronto.

Regular but unsuccessful pleas for the abolition of Council and rule by an appointed or elected commission had appeared since 1894 when introduced by Goldwin Smith.[51] The issue received a thorough airing in 1912 when one of Canada's foremost municipal reformers, Toronto businessman, academic, and Liberal, Samuel Morley Wickett, selected it as a topic for an address and pamphlet. Discussion concerning it had been vigorous and Wickett set out to contribute to the issue.[52] His position was curious and reflected Toronto's position at the junction of British and American culture. Reformers generally favoured the American concept of separation of powers and a strong municipal executive. But the British heritage still had some significance. Thus Wickett, a man who was as important as any in fostering American municipal ideas in Toronto, opposed government by commission because it ran contrary to British democratic practices.[53]

Though a Council appeared in Wickett's blueprint, his overall design betrayed a bias against such an organ being anything but a forum for discussion. He suggested that a remodelled Board of Control would hold office for a period longer than Council, sit in Council, and preside over the chief committees of Council. Writing to Sir John Willison, former editor of the *Globe* and then editor of the *News*, Wickett added more details. He proposed that an agitation might be initiated in Toronto "to have Council appoint a Board of Control who shall be the best available administrators and appointed for say six-year periods at a fair salary". He felt that the Board of Control, with modifications that would further reduce the status of Council, could become a forceful executive instead of suffering from the turmoil of annual elections and the pestering of Council's committees. Making the executive responsible to an elected body, a solid tradition on other levels of government, was not his ambition for the city; rather, "giving cohesion to what is now fragmentary and amateurish" cornered his

FIGURE 2:1   Morley Wickett

SOURCE: Kenneth Kilbourn.

attention. A Council was provided for in Wickett's blueprints, but his
overall design would have left it emasculated. The real work of city
government would be done by a revised Board of Control "who shall
be the best available administrators and appointed for say six years at
a fair salary".[54]

How Toronto's civic administration evolved owed much to the thoughts and actions of Wickett. As a graduate student in Political Economy at Vienna and Leipzig, Wickett developed great esteem for Austrian and German civil services and their statistical practices. As a manufacturer involved in his family's leather goods firm and a prominent figure in the Canadian Manufacturers' Association, he appreciated sound fiscal and bookkeeping practices. Returning from his studies abroad in 1897, Wickett was struck by how the activities of municipal authorities fell critically below the needs imposed by a modern industrial state. Frequent elections and routine administrative matters, in his evaluation, provided "two unnecessary obstacles [which] shut out many able men" from civic service.[55] In numerous speeches and articles between 1902 and 1915 there surfaced an intense distaste for the cut and thrust of politics. It was a lamentable fact, Wickett told the first conference of the Canadian Political Science Association, that so many political barriers prevented the proper citizens from entering civic life.

> A candidate has to face a great many things. He has to face a campaign. He has to face local opinion; the lodges; political influence; the possibility of criticism. And there is, in addition to all these things, the competition with the glad-hand artist who is abroad in the land and makes his presence known in every street—all of us who run for city council have to face him.[56]

To reduce the attraction of "the glad-hand artist", like the dethroned Nesbitt, he wanted to see popular power curbed. On the whole, Wickett expressed satisfaction with the municipal franchise in Canada, for unlike municipalities in the United States, those in Canada were "regarded more as a species of joint stock company, only those contributing the capital being allowed to share in the direction of its affairs".[57] However, he felt that future actions could upset the balance. Already campaigns had been mounted to extend the franchise; thus socially and ethnically undesirable groups soon might be drawn into politics and they had "little ground for interest in civic affairs".[58] Presumably, Wickett felt that the city was solely the domain of its native-born landholders.

Another of Wickett's goals was the reduction of the number of wards. A previous amalgamation in Toronto, he claimed, had "helped much toward weakening the influence of ward politicians".[59] But his most original and revealing suggestion appeared in 1907, as apart of a major study, *Present Conditions*.[60] Requesting "business before politics",[61] he proposed that corporations be granted the franchise. As-

sessed and taxed for the support of city services, companies were
deprived of the franchise. To Wickett, this did not seem consistent
with "the theory of representation". Ontario should alter its Corporation Act so that stockholders would qualify as freeholders and be able
to vote in the wards where the corporation held property.[62] To clear
away the tedium and clutter of administration that he saw as the
second impediment to attracting "the best men" for civic leadership,
Wickett hoped that the role and independence of city department
heads would be bolstered so that they could keep routine matters
away from policy-makers.[63] This might not only free the councillors
from excessive duties but also exclude them from sources of patronage. To ensure independence and non-partisan behaviour, he suggested that the tenure of department heads should be made secure
from "temporary local influence".[64] He also stressed making municipal service more rewarding.

> The customary standard of salaries paid to officials is low considering the
> interests at stake. It must be raised if a municipal civil service as the field for
> a career is to be made possible and if men are to be secured whose services
> will relieve councils of the infinite details of municipal administration.[65]

Compounding the detraction of low wages, municipal bureaucrats
received no prestigious attention. A few medals and some words of
praise from the Governor General or Lieutenant Governors, Wickett
believed, would do much to enhance the stature of functionaries and
reduce temptation.[66] In summary, "the Prussian Municipal machinery" served as a prototype since it provided municipal servants with
training, solid wages, security, pensions, independence, and suitable
pomp.[67]

Schemes to reduce the latitude for popular involvement in municipal government and to secure proficient civic servants were regularly
accompanied by a third consideration—more refined statistics. As
early as 1899, Wickett had pressed for the creation of a "statistical
Board at Ottawa" with the Imperial Board of Austria as a model.[68]
Writing in 1902, Wickett noted that there should be a complete system of reports from each city department. "The cost of well-edited
reports and civic yearbooks is trifling in comparison with the services
that such publications are capable of rendering to municipal government."[69] Throughout 1907 and 1908, in his pamphlet *Present Conditions* and in a series of articles, Wickett continued to press for sophisticated statistics and meaningful bookkeeping practices in government.
A passing reference to the need for "uniform bookkeeping, full statist-

ical returns from municipalities" in *Present Conditions* was expanded into a direct set of proposals presented to the Union of Canadian Municipalities. He began his argument to that body by noting the magnitude of municipal receipts and expenditures. "The grand total possibly foots up to several times that for the Provinces and perhaps exceeds the budget of the Federal Government itself."[70] The lack of fiscal order in Toronto contrasted with the Imperial supervisory councils in Austria and Germany; the confusion in city books also must have seemed markedly different from the records of a well-managed business. To remedy this condition, Wickett recommended standardized accounting practices for all Canadian municipalities.[71]

Elected as a Toronto alderman in 1913, with the blessings of the *Globe*, Morley Wickett worked assiduously for the implementation of his urban-reform objectives and met with some success. At Council meetings, he opposed attempts to institute city government by commission and instead worked for the hiring of expert administrators to direct, not replace, Council.[72] One important aspect of Toronto's administrative growth was to be directly affected by Wickett's exertions in this area. The city's finances had been allowed to fall into a state of appalling disorder. Back taxes went unpaid, large public works lacked co-ordination with the Finance department, the sinking fund was not used to best advantage, and debentures were being sold with limited bidding.[73] From his position within the Toronto establishment, Wickett set out to secure the services of a competent business leader to rectify the fiscal problems of the city. Specifically, he had in mind Thomas Bradshaw, a financier well versed in bonds and banking—"the well-known authority on securities and investments".[74]

Arrangements to press Bradshaw into service were conducted outside as well as inside City Hall; in 1915, Wickett drew newspaper executives and businessmen into a campaign to exert pressure on Council, the Board of Control, and the Mayor.[75] As part of his campaign, Wickett published a series of open letters, emphasizing the chaotic state of Toronto's finances.[76] After a year of such groundwork, Toronto Board of Control agreed to create a powerful office "to be known as the Commissioner of Finance" with virtual veto power over every city department. Finally, in March 1916, Bradshaw received his appointment "at an annual salary of $15,000".[77] This squared with Wickett's aim of appointing well-paid experts. The experiment justified his efforts, for Bradshaw's accomplishments did save the city great expense.[78]

As Chairman of the Transportation Committee, Wickett drafted his most prophetic document. Viewing the area around Toronto as part of an organic whole which shared its economy with the city, he began to consider planning for the region as a necessary concomitant to future prosperity. In part, Wickett detected savings for the city if a far-reaching plan were undertaken. During his campaign for fiscal reform, he observed that the city often paid for improvements, such as bridge construction and street widening, that raised property values in areas outside the Toronto boundary. Why, he questioned, should these locales not carry some of the burden?[79]

His report, however, rejected the common practice of annexing municipalities. This expedient stood condemned because it was cumbersome and only applied to immediately contiguous municipalities, not to those beyond. What Wickett wanted instead of annexation was the creation of an institution that would reach out further without implying the disappearance of existing municipal units. The desired goal was "simply the coming together of a group of municipalities for the purpose of carrying out certain services which they can do jointly more effectively than they could singly". The area to be taken in by the endeavour was pragmatically defined "as limited by the maximum time that a workman can afford to take going to his work day-by-day. . ." . For the Toronto district this would mean approximately a metropolitan boundary of Oakville, Brampton, Aurora or Richmond Hill, Markham, and Port Union.[80] Well aware of developments in Europe and the United States, he turned to the precedents of the Boston, London, and Berlin municipal areas and then prescribed a plan for Toronto. A Council composed of representatives from the participating municipalities was to appoint an executive of three Commissioners.

    a) An Electric Commissioner. His duty it would be to take charge of the development of inter-municipal electric lines, location of local industries and residential centres, lighting, telephones, etc.

    b) A Road and Parks Commissioner. His duty it would be to take care of road construction and make provision for parks, playgrounds, and other breathing spaces.

    c) A Health Commissioner. His duties would have to do with sewage, water and related services.[81]

Toronto would eventually have a metropolitan organization, but not until 1953.

The Commission concept attracted further interest and was recommended as a means of reforming the administration of the Fire Department. Being major ratepayers and consumers of city services, businessmen had a direct interest in the efficiency of all city operations, but the Fire Department had a special importance. When two investigations into its conduct turned up irregularities, the cry went forth for reform and a fire commission. Judge Denton, presiding at the investigations, recommended such a body and noted the American experience.

> In the principal [sic] cities of the northern States the fire brigades are governed by a commissioner or commissioners. They are appointed in different ways. In some cities there are three commissioners; in others four; in others five, and in some there are six. In some places they are appointed by the Mayor, the term of office being from three to six years, one or more commissioners retiring alternately. In other cities the nominations of the Mayor must be confirmed by the Council....
>
> A commission selected in this manner is considered to be semi-independent. [... The] members acquire during their tenure of office an expert and scientific knowledge ... and should produce a more efficient and useful fire brigade than one that is under the control and governed by a constantly changing body of municipal representatives with many and varied municipal problems on their hands.[82]

The Riverdale Business Men's Association supported the idea and Council drafted a measure. The commission designed by Council would have been appointed and composed "of a member of the Board of Trade, a member of the City Council, and a member of the Fire Underwriters' Association"; Board of Control rejected the idea.[83]

While efforts to establish a galaxy of commissions occasionally faltered, largely because of opposition to creating too many high-salaried positions prone to patronage use, the executive arm and bureaucracy were strengthened. Throughout the period, Council and the Board assented to appointing individual Commissioners to manage several departments. The appointment of Bradshaw as a Finance Commissioner represents one outstanding example. Considering the likelihood of increased expenditures in the Works Department and in the Water Works Department, the judge presiding at the Works Department investigation of 1911 concluded "that a general business manager or Commissioner of Works should be appointed with full supervision over all expenditures of both these departments".[84] Council and Board of Control approved and appointed a Commissioner of Works with the grand salary of $8,000 a year.[85] Earlier, in 1908, as part of the aftermath from the parks investigation, Council hired two

chartered accountants to investigate civic bookkeeping practices.
Among their conclusions was a suggestion to appoint a City Auditor;
Council approved and established the office.[86]

Piece by piece, ineptitude and leeway for corruption were being
chipped away and replaced with modern management techniques.
The chartered accountants, for example, also had proposed double-
entry accounting, balance sheets, and a system of grading civic servants.[87] One important non-profit agency, the Bureau of Municipal
Research, furthered this pursuit of meticulous efficiency and economy. The Bureaus in the United States received backing from the
business community and stressed the importance of attending to the
details of urban affairs rather than working for broad charter revision.[88] The impelling force behind the founding of the Toronto bureau came from an accountant, John I. Sutcliffe. His plan for a few
friends to meet in a luncheon discussion group grew into a more
ambitious plan after a visit to New York and Philadelphia in 1913
where he talked with the staff of the New York bureau, met with the
President of the City College, saw Clinton R. Woodruff of the National Municipal League, who had visited Toronto in 1907, and interviewed the head of the Russell Sage Foundation.[89] After reporting to
his friends, "it was decided to call a larger meeting to consider the
advisability of engaging the New York Bureau of Municipal Research
to make a Survey of the Civic Administration in Toronto."[90]

To provide potential supporters with some notion of what a survey
comprised, Sutcliffe had invited Henry Bruère, director of the New
York bureau, to address his group—tentatively called the Civic Survey
Committee. Bruère responded and appeared on July 10, 1913, to
present a speech that appealed to the business and professional audience. "We believe," he stated, "that if you recognize city government
for what it is—a great service corporation, you can get efficient service
by dealing with city government problems as you would any other
great corporation."[91]

It was decided then to raise a fund sufficient to hire the experts of
the New York bureau to conduct a comprehensive survey of the
administration of Toronto. Members felt that the New York experts'
experience in having "studied the methods of leading cities on the
Continent and in America" could be of use in sorting out the civic
problems of Toronto. To meet the five thousand dollar cost, a Committee of One Hundred Citizens was formed with each member
pledging to contribute or collect fifty dollars. Morley Wickett actively
participated in these meetings and when the New York experts came

to Toronto he co-ordinated the meeting between them and officials at City Hall.[92] The end result of the investigations, a thick, typescript document, detailed a variety of recommendations.[93] Portions of the report, accusing Toronto authorities of inefficient bookkeeping, incompetence in the Fire Department, personal influences in Public Works appointments, and many other inadequacies and abuses, appeared in the press.[94] These, in turn, prompted the Fire Department investigation.[95] Concurrently, the group organized a "citizens ticket" for municipal elections with the ubiquitous Wickett as their man in Ward Two.[96] Finally, in a petition for a provincial charter, the Toronto bureau provided the new reform movement with a quintessential statement. No spirit of moral crusade appeared as it dryly promised "to promote efficient and economic government; to promote the adoption of scientific methods of accounting and reporting the details of public business, with a view to facilitating the work of public officials; to secure constructive publicity in matters pertaining to public problems, and to these ends to collect, to classify, to analyse, to correlate, to interpret, and to publish facts as to the administration of government".[97] Specific campaigns held to these goals as the Bureau recommended an independent Civil Service Commission for Toronto, a Central Purchasing Department, a Transportation Commission, and the reorganization of charity efforts to eliminate duplication.[98]

III: UP-GRADING THE ENVIRONMENT

In his capacity as Chairman of the Transportation Committee, Wickett had touched another important dimension of Toronto's future. For years public ownership of the Toronto Street Railway Company had been debated; in 1910 the city initiated service on a small municipally owned streetcar line; by a plebiscite in 1909 Torontonians approved a subway in principle.[99] Transportation and commuting, to civic leaders, had come to assume high priority. Whereas city dwellers once had been concerned about the existence or absence of a service—never mind who owned it—they now took its presence for granted. Streetcars and electric power had arrived. Those who had brought these services into Toronto increasingly became portrayed, with cause, as villains. Citizens grumbled over inconvenience, fares, omissions, shoddy work, and reluctance to expand services. Franchise privileges granted out of need for something at once and smoothed into being by the oil of graft were becoming regarded as acts of theft.[100] Public ownership had had advocates in the initial stages of utility development. However, implementation came with the compelling force of "booster" arguments. Ironically, this same growth orientation had contributed to the hasty handling of franchises in the first place. Now advocates of boom found that private utilities were far too cautious with their expansion programs. The rising attack on slums was also drawn into the issue. Environmental reformers attributed overcrowding, in part, to the reluctance of the Toronto Street Railway to lay tracks into newly annexed suburbs.

> Toronto cannot hope to cope with the slum problem until it secures control of transportation. Every day's delay in extending the railway lines to outlying districts adds to the menace of the tenement districts. Again and again Dr. Hastings in reports and at meetings of the Board of Health has laid stress upon the necessity of securing access to suburban properties where land will be available.... The city must secure adequate transportation or pay the penalty in disease and crime and immorality.[101]

With important policies soon anticipated in this area, civic authorities began to consider the methods of administration. Looking into this, the Board of Control for 1913 suggested that Council apply to Queen's Park for legislation creating an appointed traffic commission with power to hold, construct, and operate civic cars. Two special reports by Wickett's committee supported the recommendation.[102] The forthcoming provincial legislation became the basis for the Toronto Transportation Commission. Pressure for other departmental or specialized commissions (a piecemeal approach to the project of city government by a single commission) already had been brought to bear and would continue.

A commission to administer and expand the city park system, an idea raised during the parks investigation of 1907–08, was one of several schemes that went unrealized.[103] The silk-stocking members of the Civic Guild, also known as the Toronto Guild of Civic Art, stood four-square behind endeavours to purge parks and planning of graft and inefficiency with a commission. Organized in May 1897, the Guild had initially limited itself to securing mural decorations for the city's public buildings. Dwindling interest brought it to the verge of collapse in 1900; that year only eleven paid membership dues. International activity in urban planning and the "City Beautiful" Movement in the United States prompted a revival. Reconstituted, it became dedicated to beautifying streets, public squares, and parks; to the stimulation of a pride in the improvement and care of civic and private property; to the goal of making Toronto an agreeable and pleasant city. In December 1907, the Guild sponsored a lecture-luncheon in conjunction with the Canadian Club and invited Clinton Rogers Woodruff to speak. Woodruff, Acting Secretary of the American Civic League, spoke on parks, planning, and the smoke nuisance.[104] The following year membership reached nearly four hundred and in 1909 the Guild published a glossy and ambitious description of its aims. Illustrated with views of the great plazas of Europe and the Americas, the report betrayed a bias in favour of symmetry and vistas; it showed little appreciation for the city as a complex social organism. The report maintained that Toronto should and could construct the broad avenues of a Washington or a Buenos Aires and that the city might well develop a central core like Cleveland's "Court of Honor".[105]

Originally dedicated "to promote and encourage civic art", the Guild's touchstone was "planning" with both beauty and efficiency in mind. Home Smith, a Harbour Commissioner and member of the Guild executive, likened city planning to the ambitious work of harbour development that Toronto had undertaken; both, he felt, related to the expeditious movement of men and material under the aegis of progress.[106] He, like Morley Wickett, was a businessman of the young progressive mould, unwilling to condone the status quo so long as new and promising thoughts streamed in from the United States and Europe. Smith and other Guild leaders were men of business, patrons of art and learning who, for reasons of civic pride and boosterism, were determined to make Toronto a world city. Specifically the Guild advocated street widening and a pair of avenues ripping diagonally across the city's grid from the northeast and northwest to converge near the business centre.[107] Although they alleged that traffic congestion prompted their concern, no data was adduced to justify diagonal avenues as a proper remedy. Moreover, they did not consider the related loss of housing. It is likely that the sheer aesthetics of a drafted plan, the pride of working to bring "beauty and dignity ... to the internal area of the city", served as motives.[108] As with a later plan, the clearing of a new avenue (Federal Avenue) sweeping up from Union Station to a point near City Hall, the purpose was essentially visual.[109] Beyond a tampering with street layouts and a weakness for an architecturally conceived and symmetrically drafted city, the Guild pushed for actions of unquestioned merit. It saw the eventual need for subways and as part of its park plans, it recommended the expropriation of the Scarborough Bluffs.[110]

If physical or visual order interested the Civic Guild, so did administrative order. Alarmed by vivid confirmation of malfeasance in the

Parks department, letters flowed into Council favouring a Parks Commission composed of appointees from the professions or business. In
this cause the Guild joined the Ontario Association of Architects, the
Engineers Club, the Riverdale Business Men's Association, the Board
of Trade, and the Island Association.[111] This interest of professional
and business associations further marks their relation to reform.
Though Board of Control continued to reject by-laws establishing a
Parks Commission, the idea had indirect or latent importance. The
Guild devoted continuing publicity to the idea and reinforced the
more general theme of an administration set safely beyond the whim
of voters. "Is it not time," questioned a Guild editorial, that "we in
Canada approached a little nearer the German idea and regarded
municipal administration wholly as business and very important business?"[112] Aside from proselytizing in this direction, the Guild succeeded in promoting and participating in a short-lived precursor to
the Toronto Planning Board. Responding to the Guild's requests for
planning, Council created and financed a Civic Improvement Committee that functioned from 1909 to 1912. The important aspect of this
body lies in its composition. It did not operate as a committee of
Council, rather it consisted of both members of Council and private
citizens—essentially the executive of the Guild.[113]

In each of the above steps, the Guild helped to identify urban
planning with an appointed commission, professional designs, and
hence remoteness from political or community pressure.[114] This assisted the fracturing of civic government into administrative bodies
with murky lines of responsibility and authority. The persistence of
these trends can be detected in subsequent efforts to place planning
on a permanent basis. All members of the 1928 Advisory City Planning Commission were appointed. The Toronto Planning Board, established in 1942, consisted of appointees and one member of Council to act as a liaison.[115] Thus what should have been developed as
an important area of public policy, with Council or even community
participation, emerged as the prerogative of professionals and businessmen.

Fiscal restraints after 1913 rendered the grandiose schemes of City
Beautiful unattainable, but the concept of an attractive and efficient
city had resilience. The gradual elimination of "the Ward" by hospital and government construction, the shaping of University Avenue
into a monumental thoroughfare, the burying of overhead cables,
and the introduction of land use controls were all derivatives. The
break away from a grid plan, the boulevards, vistas, and parks were

ideas that spilled over into the private sector, influencing ambitious new land developments. It is not surprising that Civic Guild executive member Home Smith absorbed these embellishments into his extensive suburban project, Humber Valley Surveys: Riverside, Bâby Point, Glebe, Bridge, and Old Mill. In addition to park land and a boulevard, Home Smith's scheme employed restrictive covenants. There could be no attached or semi-detached homes; dwellings were to have a minimum value; fence heights and building lines were designated; businesses, signs, and billboards were banned. The venture represented a considerable advance in real estate development. The bulk of nineteenth-century property development had been conducted by land auction with few developers' controls. Humber Valley came closer to the form of the "packaged" suburbs commonly associated with the post-1950 era.[116]

Home Smith's suburban plan was not typical, but the construction of new brick homes in lesser surveys with various covenant restrictions figured as significant elements in a major building boom between 1907 and 1913. New housing, however, had little direct effect on the quality of shelter for lower-income groups. Indeed, it pushed up housing costs. "The building of . . . larger houses than fall within the means of the workingman taxes to the full cities and in consequence little provision is made for the man with an income of $10 to $15 per week."[117] In terms of real wages rents had been racing upward for many years. A study by James Mavor, Morley Wickett's mentor, concluded that between 1897 and 1906 rents for a sample group of Toronto workingmen's dwellings had doubled.[118] The Dominion government's Board of Inquiry into the Cost of Living recorded a sixty to seventy per cent rent increase between 1900 and 1913.[119] Along with cost, the quality of cheap housing came under sharp review from Dr. Charles Hastings, the Medical Officer of Health.[120] One of the more tangible responses to the housing problem was the Toronto Housing Company, incorporated in 1912 to raise workingmen's dwellings. City Council, the Civic Guild, the Toronto District Labour Council, and civic reformers were all convinced of the need for action, particularly after the 1911 Hastings report. Thus formation of a limited dividend company occurred early in 1912 with the sanguine belief that it was possible to construct decent and inexpensive shelter.[121]

A speaking campaign to launch the company attracted the city's reform notables, including Jesse McCarthy, a dynamic and versatile reformer, who bridged the social gospel and the business efficiency elements of progressive reform. A former superintendent of agencies for the Temperance and General Insurance Company, McCarthy was manager of the Aetna Insurance Company when he sat as a member of City Council.[122] An ardent Methodist and temperance man, "but not a crank in the accepted use of the term", he stood for a business-like management of civic affairs and was remarkably active in promoting health measures.[123] Hospital expansion, pure milk, water filtration, inspection of slaughterhouses, improved voter registration, and public-owned utilities were issues that he advanced before Council. Along with Dr. Hastings, it was alleged that McCarthy's work contributed to the reduction of the death rate by communicable diseases from 130 per 100,000 in 1910 to 30 in 1914.[124] Like many reformers throughout North America, he maintained that significant improvements in health and housing would occur when workingmen could ride public transportation to new suburban communities. In this connection, the Toronto Housing Company established its first two housing projects close to streetcar lines.[125] Unfortunately, the attempt to secure inexpensive yet decent housing in the suburbs was not the simple panacea that McCarthy and the Toronto Housing Company had anticipated. Economic recessions and the sheer expense of building better housing diminished the Company's expectations and achievements. None the less, the housing problem had been established as a matter for public concern. It would be raised again in Toronto civic history with the 1934 "Bruce Report" and the construction of Regent Park in the early 1950s.[126] Interestingly, certain of the Toronto Housing Company's problems would recur. One of these was ratepayer opposition to multiple-family units and the related fear of depreciated property value.[127]

Innovations pertaining to slums proceeded in another of the era's emerging professions. By the early twentieth century social workers had begun to shed philanthropic and social gospel associations, establishing themselves as a distinct field within the social sciences, and gradually having to operate with government aid and review. The career of "child-saver" J. J. Kelso chronicles some features of the transformation. Kelso had been initiated into the world of the deprived urban child during his work as a police and court reporter, a position that likewise affected the social conscience of contemporary New York reformer, Jacob Riis.[128] Seeing the neglected, Kelso vowed to "give up ambition, turn aside from cherished hopes, and plead for these little ones who perished by the wayside".[129]

In 1886, at twenty-two years of age, he began work that occupied his next fifty years. An amateur and a Christian, Kelso was also sentimental, good-hearted, and vain. He received considerable acclaim, but did not let the public forget his trials: "I sorrowed, suffered, and sacrificed for others, because that was the burden that was laid upon me."[130] "I firmly believed and I do still," he wrote, "that God was working through me and that I was merely his instrument in demonstrating the possibility of reclamation work when undertaken in His name."[131] The revealing word "reclamation" infers his moralistic values. Children became delinquent owing to a social environment which taught unacceptable notions; the key to reclamation was the inculcation of socially approved values. Therefore, when Kelso spoke out against child labour, particularly the use of newsboys, he not only felt that newspapers were exploiting children, but that "such thrusting out on the streets, of mere infants, familiarized them with all vices and profanity of the worst society".[132] In 1889, Kelso led a deputation from the Humane Society to the office of the Police Commissioners to demand a by-law licensing and regulating the use of newsboys. That many such youths, from immigrant families in "the Ward", supplemented family incomes was not fully appreciated. The same concern with protecting the child from immoral influences took Kelso, into campaigns for Juvenile Courts, separation of youthful offenders from "criminals", playgrounds, and the placement of Children's Aid Society youths in the countryside.[133] The temptations and unnatural conditions of the urban environment were staple theories with Kelso thus he favoured foster homes in the country "where there is every incentive to right living and the development of thrifty and industrious habits".[134]

> A child in a poor family in a city is so cramped and hindered and restricted in his development, that artificial means have to be supplied for his legitimate play activities. In a country district, there are plenty of open spaces and children have live play fellows.[135]

Instead of "live play fellows", a number of youths found farmers eager for cheap labour. Kelso, a shrewd enough manipulator of publicity, also used urban and rural settings for photographs depicting striking "before and after" portraits of waifs.

The transition from the amateur volunteer guided by moral values and an agrarian ideal to a civil servant proved disappointing for someone with voluntary and romantic sentiments like Kelso. Social workers were becoming concerned with professional standards, advanced training, and managing agency budgets.[136] In his 1909 Re-

port for the Bureau of Neglected Children, Kelso seemed disturbed
by the modernization and bureaucratization of his organization.
"Much of the success of the Children's Aid movement in earlier
years", according to him, "was due to the willingness to be of service, and the greater success has often been met with dealing with
matters that did not come definitely within provisions of the Children's Protection Act. This special work is no longer possible as the
Audit Department had decided to require all work done to be strick-
ly within the terms of the Act, where expenditure is involved."[137]

Hints of the shifting from a sectarian and conversion-oriented social work into a secular and "scientific" pattern arose in other circumstances. Casebooks of early twentieth-century social workers indicate their attempts to comprehend poverty and delinquency in
pseudo-clinical terms rather than by measuring the moral environment. Included were evaluations of mental competence, literacy, and
medical histories.[138] In 1911, when Boss Nesbitt fled to Chicago to
avoid arrest for fraud, immigrant adjustment was on the verge of
receiving assistance from an essentially non-sectarian settlement
house movement. A multi-denominational association of social reformers and philanthropists founded the Central Neighbourhood
House. An important feature was that with Protestants, Catholics,
and Jews behind it, the House advanced no doctrine—unlike many
other mission and settlement house efforts which sought converts.
When the head worker, Miss Neufeld, resigned in 1915, she delivered a farewell message that indicated hope for a changing relationship between "the Ward" and "Toronto the Good":

> This Settlement was established in the Fall of 1911 to foster the spirit of
> neighbourliness, and to promote the highest type of social citizenship. The
> rapid rise of industrial centres, complicated by the large influx of immigrant
> groups, had made much more conscious and organized effort necessary.
> Mutual misunderstandings between the earlier settlers and the newcomers
> who cling to the language and traditions of their fatherlands, made for
> suspicion and distrust which must be broken down by a sympathetic inter-
> pretation of the needs of each group to the other.[139]

Symbolic of new directions toward understanding was the fact that,
while Nesbitt languished as a fugitive on Chicago's Drexel Avenue,
youths at the settlement house were formed into a model parliament
and were instructed in the "wholesome fun of playing at being adult
citizens".[140] With this exercise and, more important, through an ambitious program to teach conversational English, the House worked to

improve communication between "the Ward" and its surrounding environment in ways not provided for by the *quid pro quo* of "boss politics". The night courses, sports, and social clubs organized by the House represented a change from Piper's flowers, Nesbitt's cigars, and the patronage of both.

IV: CONCLUSION

Reform campaigns had peaked by 1915. New officials had been appointed to operate with proper management and budgetary practices. The Bureau of Municipal Research, launched with a full-time director, was publishing a regular series of bulletins and preparing an occasional research report. Thompson and Noble of the Fire Department, appointed under the mores of the backroom, resigned in 1915 after Courtroom exposure. The same year, the Department replaced horsedrawn fire engines with six trucks. Beattie Nesbitt had passed from the scene, dying a few hours after being acquitted of fraud in January 1913. Morley Wickett, only forty-three, died suddenly before Christmas, 1915. Generally, Torontonians could look forward to a better life, for sanitary and water supply improvements had reduced mortality rates. Social workers and a Juvenile Court, in very formative stages, represented a change from the neglect Kelso had found as a journalist. But to suggest that Toronto had secured many attributes of a modern city does not mean that all was perfection.[141] Achievements in health, public transportation, and civic economy were possible because they bolstered the city's reputation or were intrinsic to the expectations of the middle class and the business community. Reforms that implied an expense with negligible direct returns to ratepayers had a more difficult road. The Toronto Housing Company, for example, incurred ratepayer opposition. Indeed, the Company's situation in the private sector indicated where governments set the boundary between public and private concerns. Understandably, the most enduring of reform concepts was an ethos of economy and efficiency. The notion that urban decision-making required technical skills and the corollary that professional control reduced waste were concepts which encouraged bureaucratic expansion. The basically conservative nature of ratepayers eyeing tax bills, the emergence of a professional and managerial middle class and periods of fiscal stringency after 1913 made fertile ground for the ideals of Morley Wickett.

In its accomplishments, limitations, and excesses, the character of Toronto civic affairs for decades to come had been charted at the turn of the century.

NOTES

1. City of Toronto Archives, Scrapbook on City News, 1886–1887; Desmond Morton, *Mayor Howland, The Citizens' Candidate* (Toronto, 1973), *passim*. City of Toronto Archives henceforth cited as Toronto Archives.

2. Toronto Archives, 1.1–0.3, Folio No. 17, folder marked "Alderman Piper Bribery Charges, 1888". Mayor Howland to Council, December 5, 1887.

3. *Globe*, November 12, 1902, p. 6.

4. Stan Kutcher, "J. W. Bengough and the Millennium in Hogtown: A Study of Motivation in Urban Reform", *Urban History Review*, no. 2–76 (1976): 30-49; Ann Boyer, "F. S. Spence: His Social Ideas and His Reform Career", unpublished graduate paper, McMaster University (1977).

5. For a parallel thesis on an American city see Augustus Cerillo "The Reform of Municipal Government in New York City", *The New York Historical Society Quarterly*, vol. 57 (1973): 51-71.

6. Toronto Archives, 1.1–04, Folio No. 4, "Civic Investigation *Re* Puddy Brothers, 1905-1906", pp. 22-28, 580-92, 671.

7. *Globe*, November 5, 1902, p. 6.

8. Toronto Archives, 1.1–03, Folio No. 1, "Fire Brigade Investigation", *passim.*

9. Toronto Archives, 1.1–04, Folio No. 24, "Investigation into Civic Elections, 1904", pp. 766-70.

10. "Fire Brigade Investigation", p. 161 and *passim.*

11. Toronto Archives, 1.1–04, Folio No. 34, "Parks Investigation Report, April 11, 1908", *passim.*

12. Toronto Archives, 1.1–04, Folio No. 3, "Works Department Investigation, 1911", pp. 6-37. Also see "Investigation into Toronto Water Works at the Main Pumping Station, 1899", (1899), pp. 2-19.

13. Toronto Archives, Unlabelled Scrapbook, 1898–1901. See also *News*, June 2, 1898.

14. *Toronto Fire Department Investigation*, 1915, pp. 589-90.

15. *Globe*, November 2, 1903, p. 4

16. *Globe*, April 15, 1912, p. 1; *Evening Telegram*, April 15, 1912, p. 16.

17. *Globe*, April 12, 1912. p. 1

18. See Nesbitt's address as Chairman of the Organization Committee of the Young Conservative Association quoted in *Toronto World*, September 14, 1893, p. 1.

19. Public Archives of Ontario, Whitney Papers, J. A. Macdonell to Whitney, April 15, 1905. Also J. P. Whitney to E. C. Whitney, January 3, 1908.

20. W. R. Plewman, *Adam Beck and the Ontario Hydro* (Toronto, 1949), p. 30.

21. Toronto, Bureau of Municipal Research, "What is 'the Ward' Going to do with Toronto" (1918). Ken Tilling in Hugh Garner's *Cabbagetown* knew "the Ward" in 1929 when it still was identified with Italians and Jews. See *Cabbagetown* (Richmond Hill, 1973), p. 71; and Albert Rose, *Regent Park, A Study in Slum Clearance* (Toronto, 1958), p. 39. The dynamic growth and shifting area of immigrant colonies as well as the persistent labelling of such communities as if they were static has been observed for cities in the United States. See Humbert S. Nelli, "Italians in Urban America: A Study in Ethnic Adjustment", in James F. Richardson, ed. *The American City: Historical Studies* (Toronto, 1972), p. 161.

22. "What is 'the Ward' Going to do with Toronto", p. 5.

23. Dominion of Canada, *Dominion Census, 1901*, pp. 344-45. See also *Special Report on the Foreign Born from the Records of the Fifth Census*, pp. 32-34, 42-43; Toronto Archives, 1.1–04, Folio No. 5, "Report of the Medical Health Officer Dealing with the Recent Investigation of Slum Conditions in Toronto" (1911), pp. 5-7.

24. Toronto Archives, 12–05, Folio No. 2, clipping, Rae Corelli, "The Ward", *Star*, February 22, 1964.

25. *Globe*, December 13, 1904, p. 7; December 1, 1906, p. 6.

26. New York Bureau of Municipal

Research, "The City of Toronto, Canada: Report on Physical Survey" (1913), p. 4.

27. Interview with Jacob Charendoff, February 20, 1975. Mr. Charendoff was raised in "The Ward". See also Robert Harney and Harold Troper, *Immigrants: A Portrait of the Urban Experience, 1890 – 1930* (Toronto, 1975), pp. 109-42.

28. Corelli, "The Ward"; Stuart E. Rosenberg, *The Jewish Community in Canada*, 2 vols (Toronto, 1970), I, p. 153; *Star*, November 6, 1900, p. 7; December 20, 1902, p. 4.

29. John Fierheller, a McMaster University graduate student researching crime in Toronto in the late nineteenth century, has found this distinction by comparing precinct records of arrests with court records. I am indebted to Mr. Fierheller for this information.

30. C. S. Clark, *Of Toronto the Good: The Queen City of Canada as it is* (Montreal, 1898), *passim*; Queen's University Archives, Flavelle Papers, Flavelle to W. K. McNaught, January 4, 1906. In this long letter, Flavelle, a former member of the Board of License Commissions, describes and names some of the city's more notorious pubs and hotels.

31. *Telegram*, December 23, 1893, p. 4.

32. *Star*, November 22, 1902, p. 20; interview with Jacob Charendoff.

33. Rosenberg, *The Jewish Community in Canada*, I, p. 178.

34. *Star*, December 27, 1902, p. 18.

35. Clark, *Of Toronto the Good*, p. 85.

36. W. L. Riordon, *Plunkitt of Tammany Hall* (New York, 1963), p. 25.

37. *Star*, December 13, 1907, p. 8.

38. Rosenberg, *The Jewish Community in Canada*, I, pp. 158-160.

39. *Globe*, December 21, 1905, p. 14.

40. B. G. Sack, *History of the Jews in Canada* (Montreal, 1965), p. 235; *Star*, November 3, 1900, p. 3; *Toronto World*, December 4, 1907, p. 3.

41. *Star*, November 28, 1905, p. 1.

42. *Globe*, December 2, 1902, p. 6.

43. Ibid., December 22, 1905, p. 4.

44. Ibid., January 3, 1903, p. 6.

45. Ibid., January 13, 1903, p. 4.

46. *Minutes . . . of the Council of . . . the City of Toronto . . . 1902* (Toronto, 1903), pp. 270-71; "Report No. 1 of the Committee on Legislation and Reception", Appendix A., ibid., p. 64.

47. *Globe*, November 24, 1904, p. 8.

48. Ibid., December 28, 1905, p. 3.

49. "Report No. 4 of the Committee on Legislation and Reception", Appendix A, *Minutes . . . 1904*, p. 204.

50. Harold A. Innis, *A History of the Canadian Pacific Railway*, 2nd ed. (Toronto, 1971), p. 186; J. E. Hodgetts, William McCloskey, Reginald Whitaker, V. Seymour Wilson, *The Biography of an Institution, The Civil Service Commission of Canada, 1908-1967* (Montreal, 1972), pp. 25-26; *Daily Edmonton Bulletin*, November 23, 1903, p. 3.

51. Smith was still supporting the idea in 1902. *Globe*, November 17, 1902, p. 6.

52. The Literary and Scientific Society at the University of Toronto sponsored a debate on the substitution of government by commission for the system of government by Council. Supporters of the commission lost. *Minutes . . . 1912* (Toronto, 1913), p. 471; *Globe*, November 16, 1912, p. 8.

53. Morley Wickett, "City Government by Commission", an address before the Canadian Club of Hamilton, delivered in November 1912 (Toronto, n.d.).

54. Public Archives of Canada, Sir John Willison Papers. Wickett to Willison (January 17, 1912; May 27, 1913).

55. S. M. Wickett, *City Government in Canada*, University of Toronto: Studies. History and Economics, vol. II (Toronto, 1902), pp. 21-22.

56. S. M. Wickett, "A Toronto Viewpoint", Canadian Political Science Association, *Papers and Proceedings of the First Annual Meeting, Ottawa, September 4-6, 1913* (Kingston, 1913), pp. 131-32.

57. Wickett, *City Government in Canada*, p. 10.

58. Ibid., p. 55.

59. *The Municipal Government of Toronto*, University of Toronto:

Studies. History and Economics, vol. II (Toronto, 1902), p. 35.

60. Writing to John Willison, Wickett stated that he hoped "Present Conditions" would be used as a program for change by "our municipal reformers". Willison Papers. Wickett to Willison (December 28, 1907).

61. S. M. Wickett, *Present Conditions*, University of Toronto: Studies. History and Economics, vol. IV (Toronto, 1907), p. 170.

62. Ibid., pp. 166-67.

63. *City Government in Canada*, pp. 21-22.

64. *The Municipal Government of Toronto*, p. 42.

65. *Present Conditions*, p. 154.

66. *Globe*, January 16, 1914, p. 6; December 21, 1915.

67. "City Government by Commission", p. 9.

68. Mavor Papers. Wickett to Mavor (May 17, 1899).

69. *City Government in Canada*, p. 22.

70. S. M. Wickett, "Municipal Publicity through Uniformity in Municipal Statistics", *Canadian Municipal Journal*, vol. 4 (1908): 453.

71. Ibid., 454.

72. Toronto, *Minutes . . . of the Council of . . . the City of Toronto . . . 1914* (Toronto, 1915), p. 515.

73. *Globe*, January 14, 1914, p. 91.

74. Ibid., January 31, 1914, p. 5.

75. Willison Papers. Wickett to Willison (February 16, 1915).

76. S. M. Wickett, *Toronto's Need of Reform* (Toronto, November, 1915).

77. *Minutes . . . 1916*, p. 65; Appendix B, Ibid., p. 49; Board of Control, "Minute Book of Board of Control, January – June, 1916", item 1350.

78. Toronto Archives, "Financial Letterbook, September 29, 1915 to February 18, 1918"; Thomas Bradshaw to T. L. Church (April 8, 1920), quoted in *Minutes . . . 1920*, p. 559. Bradshaw served as an advisor to many municipalities in subsequent decades. See Thomas Bradshaw, "A Discussion of Municipal Finance and Administration", *Dalhousie University Bulletins on Public Affairs*, no. 3 (Halifax, 1937).

79. S. M. Wickett, "Open Letter No. 1", *Toronto's Need of Reform*, pp. 6-7.

80. S. M. Wickett, Memorandum *re* Metropolitan Area (Toronto, 1913), p. 1; *Canadian Annual Review* (1913): 350.

81. Memorandum, p. 4.

82. Toronto Archives, 1.1 – 04, Folio No. 2, "Toronto Fire Department Investigation, Report of His Honour Judge Denton", pp. 70-73.

83. *Minutes . . . 1915*, p. 55, Board of Control Report No. 14 and No. 34, Appendix A, ibid., pp. 549, 1264.

84. Works Department Investigation, 1911, p. 38.

85. By-law No. 6094, Appendix B, *Minutes . . . 1912*, p. 437.

86. Henry Barber and Harry Vigeon, Special Auditors under Reference of Council, "Report", dated 13th April, 1908 (Toronto, 1908), pp. 31-32, 41; *Minutes . . . 1909*, pp. 126-27.

87. Ibid., *passim*.

88. Norman Gill, *Municipal Research Bureau, A Study of the Nation's Leading Citizen-Supported Agencies* (Washington, D.C., 1944); Jane S. Dahlberg, *The New York Bureau of Municipal Research, Pioneer in Government Administration* (New York, 1966).

89. Toronto Bureau of Municipal Research, *Minute Book, April 1913 – September 1914*, John I. Sutcliffe to John Macdonald and John Firstbrook (April 15, 1913) (Copy). Toronto Bureau of Municipal Research, Minutes of Meeting (May 19, 1913) and Minutes of Meeting (May 28, 1913). I am grateful to the Bureau for the courtesy extended when using its records.

90. Ibid., Minutes of Meeting (May 19, 1913).

91. Ibid., Address of Henry Bruère, Minutes of Meeting (July 10, 1913).

92. Ibid., Minutes of Meeting (October 13, 1913).

93. The City of Toronto, Canada, Report on a Survey of the City Treasury, Assessment, Works, Fire and Property Departments, Prepared for the Civic Survey Committee by the New York Bureau of Municipal Research (1913).

94. *Globe*, January 21, 1914, p. 7; January 23, 1914, p. 7; January 26, 1914, p. 7; February 3, 1914, p. 8; February 4, 1914, p. 7.
95. "Toronto Fire Department Investigation, Report of His Honour Judge Denton", p. 51.
96. *Globe*, December 27, 1913, p. 2.
97. Toronto Bureau of Municipal Research, *Minute Book, February 9, 1914 to May 29, 1914*, p. 24. Copy of Petition to Government of Ontario.
98. Toronto Archives, Bureau of Municipal Research Collection, *Bulletins*, Number 2 to 90 (March 18, 1914 to September 23, 1921).
99. *Globe*, December 25, 1909, p. 6; *Globe, Saturday Magazine*, December 28, 1912, p. 2.
100. Toronto Archives, 1.1 – 03 Folio No. 3, "In the Matter of the Investigation before His Honour Judge McDougall ... Evidence", 5 vols. (1894).
101. *Daily News*, November 5, 1913, p. 1.
102. *Minutes ... 1913*, p. 19; Report no. 2 and Report no. 3, Appendix A, *Minutes ... 1914*, pp. 1902-03, 2154-55. *Statutes of the Province of Ontario 1914*, Chapter 98, p. 51.
103. *Globe*, December 6, 1907, p. 4; *Minutes ... 1908*, p. 73. Council approved the measure but it was rejected by the Board of Control. Appendix A, ibid., pp. 333-38. Also See, *Minutes ... 1914*, p. 318.
104. Rosalyn Berger, "History of Planning Organization in Toronto", City of Toronto Planning Board (1958), pp. 1 – 2; *Globe*, December 10, 1907, p. 7.
105. *Globe*, December 24, 1906, p. 6; Guild of Civic Art, *Report on a Comprehensive Plan for Systematic Civic Improvements in Toronto* (Toronto, 1909), p. 5.
106. *Globe*, November 28, 1912, p. 6; R. C. Home Smith "Our Present Duty Towards Toronto's Future", addresses delivered before the Canadian Club of Toronto (1912 – 1913), pp. 81-88. The changing focus for the Guild and its rise and decline are best traced in the "Minutes of the Toronto Civic Guild", 1897-1914; "Minutes of the Executive Committee of the Toronto Civic

Guild", 1911-1914, 1916-1919; Baldwin Room, Toronto Municipal Library.
107. W. A. Langton, "A Plan For Toronto", *Report on a Comprehensive Plan*, p. 9; Toronto Archives, Guild of Civic Art, "Plan, College Street Widening", (October 5, 1911).
108. *Report on a Comprehensive Plan*, p. 14.
109. Civic Improvement Committee, *Report of Civic Improvement Committee for the City of Toronto, 1911* (Toronto, n.d.), plate number 1.
110. Guild of Civic Art, *Monthly Bulletin*, vol. 1 (1911): 1.
111. *Minutes ... 1908*, pp. 174-75, 194. The Guild noted that several American cities had created Parks Commissions, *Report of Civic Improvement Committee* (1911), p. 10.
112. *Monthly Bulletin*, vol. 1 (1911): 6-7.
113. *Report of Civic Improvement Committee*, (1911), p. 5.
114. *Monthly Bulletin*, vol. 2 (1913): 3.
115. Berger, "History of Planning Organization in Toronto", pp. 3-5.
116. For the Home Smith project see Toronto Archives, uncatalogued brochures, *Humber Valley Surveys* (Toronto, 1912), pp. 1-24. The changing character of urban land development is discussed in Michael Doucet, "Building the Victorian City: The Process of Land Development in Hamilton, Ontario, 1847-1881", PHD diss., University of Toronto (1977). Packaged suburbs are discussed in George A. Nader, *Cities of Canada: Theoretical Historical and Planning Perspectives*, 2 vols. (Toronto, 1975), I, p. 333.
117. *Canada Labour Gazette*, August, 1912, p. 143.
118. *Financial Post*, February 15, 1908, p. 3.
119. Canada, *Board of Inquiry into the Cost of Living*, vol. II, p. 519.
120. *Report of the Medical Health Officer Dealing with the Recent Investigation of Slum Conditions in Toronto* (Toronto, 1911).
121. For the background on housing reform and the operation of Toronto Housing Company, see Shirley

Spragge, "A Confluence of Interests: Housing Reform in Toronto, 1900-1920", this volume, Chapter 10.

122. *Toronto News*, December 30, 1914, p. 2.

123. *Toronto News*, December 20, 1913, p. 1; *Minutes . . . of the Council of the City of Toronto, 1910* (Toronto, 1910), p. 344; *Minutes . . . of the Council of the City of Toronto, 1911* (Toronto, 1911), pp. 340, 367, 486.

124. *Star*, December 30, 1914, p. 6.

125. Spragge, "A Confluence of Interests".

126. *Report of the Lieutenant-Governor's Committee on Housing Conditions in Toronto* (Toronto, 1934); Rose, *Regent Park, A Study in Slum Clearance, passim.*

127. Spragge, "A Confluence of Interests".

128. J. J. Kelso, *Early History of the Humane and Children's Aid Movement in Ontario, 1886-1893* (Toronto, 1911), pp. 1-13; Jacob A. Riis, *The Making of an American*, Roy Lubove, ed. (New York), pp. 200-33. For the emergence of a reform-minded press see Paul Rutherford, "The People's Press: The Emergence of the New Journalism in Canada, 1869-99", *Canadian Historical Review*, vol. 56, no. 2 (1975): 169-91.

129. Ibid., p. 13.

130. Ibid., p. 5.

131. Walter Baker, "J. J. Kelso", *Canadian Welfare* (November-December, 1966), p. 252.

132. Kelso, *History of the Humane and Children's Aid Movement*, p. 37.

133. Neil Sutherland, *Children in English-Canadian Society: Framing the Twentieth-Century Consensus* (Toronto, 1976), pp. 115-23.

134. J. J. Kelso, "Farm Life the Most Wholesome", *Tenth Annual Report of the Superintendent, Neglected and Dependent Children of Ontario, 1902*, Ontario Sessional Papers, Number 43 (1903), p. 32.

135. *Thirty-sixth Annual Report, 1929*, Ontario Sessional Papers, Part II, pp. 6-7.

136. Roy Lubove, *The Professional Altruist: The Emergence of Social Work as a Career, 1880-1930* (Cambridge, Mass., 1965), *passim.*

137. *Sixteenth Annual Report, 1909*, Ontario Sessional Papers, Number 26 (1910), p. 9.

138. See the excerpts from casebooks quoted in "What is 'The Ward' Going to Do with Toronto", pp. 38-54.

139. The Central Neighbourhood House, *Year Book* (1915), n. p.

140. The Central Neighbourhood House, *Year Book* (1912), n. p.

141. For evaluations of the reform movements from the perspective of labour and socialists see Wayne Roberts, "Progressivism and the New Civic Spirit in Toronto", forthcoming PHD diss., University of Toronto.

3.

The Municipal Government Reform Movement in Western Canada, 1880-1920

JAMES D. ANDERSON

During the period of rapid urban growth and industrialization around the turn of the century, the public functions of the city became increasingly important to various urban groups in Canada. Local governmental institutions were called upon to provide essential services to a rapidly expanding population and to burgeoning industry. Regulation of business and labour, provision of subsidies to industry, supply of water, gas and electricity, health and sanitation services, and taxation were a few of the activities of local governments which had an increasing material effect on groups within the city.

The early importance of urban government in the Canadian political economy can be indicated in various ways. One such measure is the rate and extent of urbanization. By 1912, an estimated 45 per cent of Canadians were concentrated in urban centres of 4,000 or more.[1] Even in western Canada, often depicted as an agricultural frontier, the urban growth was phenomenal: as early as 1901, the population of the prairies was 25 per cent urban; by 1911, the prairies were 35 per cent urban. The rate of increase was most remarkable in the five largest prairie cities. During the period 1901–16, Winnipeg's population (including adjoining St. Boniface) grew from 45,000 to 187,000 and became Canada's third largest city. In the same fifteen-year period, Edmonton's population multiplied from 4,100 to 53,800; Calgary grew from 4,400 to 56,000; Regina rose in size from 2,200 to 26,100; and Saskatoon developed from a tiny hamlet of 113 to a city of 21,000 people.[2]

The public expenditures of large urban centres also reflects the role of the city as a significant unit of the Canadian state. At the turn of the century, for example, the budgets of Winnipeg, Toronto, and Montreal exceeded those of the respective provinces in which they were situated.[3] Large cities also have had a considerable degree of local autonomy with respect to taxation and expenditure. But even to the degree that local jurisdictions act as agencies of senior governments, the way in which they carry out these duties has a differential impact on socio-economic groups in the city. There has always been a strong element of "politics" in the "administration" of programs at the local level.

The era of the rise of the modern city in Canada between 1880 and 1920 was characterized by a heightened struggle over the role and function of local government. A logical connection was often made between the importance of local government to a particular class and the need to take steps to insure that it serve that class interest. This argument was perceived and acted upon by both business and labour groups. For example, a member of the Chamber of Commerce of London, Ontario, made this point in his address to the Ontario Municipal Association in 1919:

> If the mercantile and other business interests of a community are to progress there must be a close relationship between the Chamber of Commerce and the city government. Legislation to protect the community merchant and the money he invests annually in taxes from the transient cannot be effected without co-operation between the two forces. Fire, police, health, and the necessary protection for every business cannot be secured without close relationship between the two.[4]

Labour groups slowly began to contest business hegemony in local government. In the second decade of the century, organized labour sought a measure of power at City Hall. They did so in Winnipeg, for example, "because local bodies controlled housing, sanitation, public health, charity, and other departments of public effort".[5]

In this context, it is possible to analyse the movement for municipal reform which swept across the nation around the turn of the century. The urban reform movement originated in the latter decades of the nineteenth century and culminated in the aftershock of the First World War. It coincided, not accidentally, with the initial period of rapid urbanization and industrialization in Canada. The movement, which included a variety of causes, can be viewed as a campaign by which identifiable interests sought to ensure that their respective interests and values would dominate in the local political economy, and that the benefits and sanctions emanating from local institutions would conform to their various conceptions of the public interest.

A principle objective of the reform movement was the alteration of the structure and function of civic government itself. Reformers did not stop at campaigns to change the personnel of local government. The local "constitutions" or civic charters, they found, were not enshrined in the British North America Act but were, in fact, relatively easy to change by the dominant forces within the community. And when new cities arose, particularly in western Canada, it was possible to model the form of government on the latest reform schemes because the inertia of an older organizational framework was relatively insignificant compared to that of eastern cities.

The reform era around the turn of the century was also the time of the "great barbecue"—a time of burgeoning capitalism in which often the successful businessman was the folk hero. It was also a period in which "there was general agreement that the chief duty of government was to produce material prosperity by supporting business enterprise".[6] It was a period in which organized labour was weak and its legitimacy dubious as the reaction to the Winnipeg General Strike of 1919 (and earlier actions by labour) suggests.[7]

It was necessary for business to use the instrument of local government to promote growth, to help in establishing economic dominance over the rural hinterland, to compete with rival urban centres, to control wages and working conditions, and to confer public legitimacy on corporate objectives. A related and important factor in local government reform was the desire by business to keep input costs low through municipal ownership of utilities such as gas, electricity, and waterworks.

The incentive to bring municipal utilities under sound public management was compelling. A University of Toronto political economist calculated that municipally owned waterworks systems in Canada charged 50 per cent less than private waterworks for the same service.[8] Similar results were claimed for other utilities which were taken under municipal ownership. For example, the *Canadian Municipal Journal* reported in 1911 that over the five years the city of Calgary had been operating its electric lighting plant, the rates had been reduced by 45 per cent relative to those charged previously by a private concern.[9] When Winnipeg ended its reliance on a private electrical franchise in 1911, the new public hydro-electric facility reduced the cost of power in Winnipeg from nine cents to three cents per kilowatt hour. The *Manitoba Free Press* credited the availability of inexpensive power for an influx of new manufacturing concerns to the city and, not incidentally, a real estate boom: "[Public] power is the force which has carried real estate upwards in phenomenal bounds, and which has created many fortunes for the holders of property."[10]

In Winnipeg and other cities, plans for restructuring local government were linked expressly to the need for efficient operation of municipal utilities. It was essential that these vital services be operated on principles of businesslike efficiency and economy. Therefore, it was of crucial importance to "reform" the inefficient council-committee form of local government by introducing features characteristic of the private business corporation. For example, the city charter of Edmonton, which incorporated the latest reform principles, "was designed with special regard to the question of municipal ownership".[11]

The conception of "local government as business" relegated the notion of representation of non-business interests to a position of little or no importance. As a prominent Toronto reformer, academic, and businessman, Samuel Morley Wickett, wrote in 1902, "Throughout Canada the Municipality is regarded more as a species of joint stock company, only those contributing to the capital being allowed to share in the direction of its affairs."[12] According to the prevailing ideology, the only segment of the community which contributed to the civic coffers were those who paid business or property taxes. Tenants and other urban residents with little income or property were denied the right to vote in civic elections and plebiscites long after universal manhood suffrage had been won at federal and provincial levels.[13]

Other urban groups sought an expansion of the public role of the municipality and control over its operation because of its importance to them. Organized labour concentrated its attack, however, on the restrictive franchise provisions in local elections and the high property qualification necessary to run for civic office. Often, labour's preoccupation was with the immediate concerns of wages, working conditions, public transportation costs, housing, and social services.[14] Much, if not most of the political thrust of labour was directed at the provincial level because the provincial legislation could effect any of these policy areas, including the laws governing local elections.

The structural forms and the accompanying ideology of local government formulated during the municipal reform era are still largely intact. In many cities, the form of government (for example, the board of control or commission board plan) instituted at the turn of the century remains intact or has been only slightly modified. The city-wide, or at-large, local electoral system has persisted until very recently in many cities, and the "non-partisan" sentiment is still a potent force in urban politics. The ideology of the urban reform movement appears to have congealed as an important component of the Canadian political culture. It clearly defines present-day civic decision-making in crucial ways and also relegates many policy concerns to the realm of non-decision; that is, it removes many issues from the arena of legitimate debate.

In recent years there has been a noticeable reaction against the ideology and institutions implanted by turn-of-the-century municipal government reformers. Ironically, municipal government "reform" has come full circle. In the early years of the century, for example, a typical municipal reformer was opposed to ward elections, against open party politics in municipal matters, and in favour of strengthening the civic executive or bureaucracy. The present-day urban reformer, however, is in favour of ward elections, often advocates a form of local partisanship, and supports measures designed to shift power away from the civic bureaucracy or executive to the elected council. Yet, the recent reaction to the earlier conception of municipal reform cannot be understood adequately without some knowledge of the character of reforms popularized by an earlier generation. Just as buildings, land titles, and the location of residential and commercial districts impose a measure of permanence on the physical form of the city, so too do the political structures and values rooted in the initial period of rapid urbanization and industrialization. As two noted historians suggest, "Inertia is part of the dynamic of urban change: the structures outlast the people who put them there, and impose constraints on those who have to adopt them to their own use."[15]

The purpose of this chapter is to examine the bias inherent in many of the features of Canadian municipal government reform. The focus here is on the prairie region of western Canada with particular attention to Alberta. The West, as historian Paul Rutherford has pointed out, "was a veritable laboratory for reform",[16] and municipal reform was perhaps most fully worked out in Alberta cities. Yet, little has been written on urban government reform in the region.

In order to determine the nature and extent of the class, ethnic, or partisan bias of local government reform in western Canada, it is necessary to make some analytical distinctions concerning urban reform in general and urban government reform in particular. Distinctions must be made among groups advocating various reforms as well as among the reform proposals themselves. The rhetoric of reform very often masked the reality. Indeed, the very term "reform" is far from value-free. In the following section, a brief analysis of the core features of Canadian municipal government reform is developed.

MUNICIPAL GOVERNMENT REFORM DEFINED AND DELIMITED
In this study, the municipal reform "package" is examined as it relates to the attempt to change the structure and function of urban political institutions. At the outset, it is useful to distinguish between the social

reform element of the movement and the campaign for structural reform. Paul Rutherford's statement points out the need to make such analytical distinctions:

> Clearly there were different concerns sheltered under the umbrella of urban reform—the elimination of vice and crime, social justice, the creation of a healthy environment, the regulation of utility corporations, the beautification of the industrial city, town planning, and the remodelling of the municipal government.[17]

While there was some overlap of personnel between groups advocating moral, humanitarian, and social reform on the one hand, and good government advocates on the other, the emphasis of the social reformers like J. S. Woodsworth was not primarily directed to revamping the structure of civic government. Woodsworth, for example, was perhaps the greatest crusader of his time for measures such as the improvement of the conditions of the slum, civic charity, and health and sanitation. He was not, however, a central figure in any campaigns for civic charter reform. It appears that urban reform groups pressing for humanitarian reforms usually were made up of clergymen, women's groups, temperance advocates, and academics. However, the typical leaders of campaigns for local government reform, particularly in the West, were leading businessmen, usually members of the boards of trade.[18] An analytical distinction, therefore, must be made between the structural and humanitarian elements of the movement.

The interrelated group of reform measures which are examined below include measures designed to reform civic elections and revamp the structure of the city council and civic bureaucracy. These proposals constituted the core of municipal government reform and were motivated by an underlying political ideology. They were often linked to each other in reform campaigns in particular cities and were frequently bound together in specific city charter reforms. Usually, they were instituted by a distinct socio-economic segment of the community. Specifically, the core features of municipal government reform consisted of the following:

1) *Abolition of ward elections*: At-large elections or elections based on large, socially heterogeneous wards were to replace the prevailing practice of electing councillors from relatively small wards.

2) *Civic executive and bureaucratic reform*: In order to separate policy-making from administration and to strengthen the bureauc-

racy and/or executive relative to the city council, a number of civic charter reforms were recommended. The most common forms adopted in Canada included variations of the following: (a) the Board of Control; (b) the Commission Plan; (c) the Board of Commissioners; and (d) the City Manager Plan.[19]

3) *Non-Partisanship*: In Canada, non-partisanship was held to be a consequence of civic executive reform and at-large elections Nevertheless, it can be considered an institutional reform in that it implied the absence of political parties from municipal elections. It did not involve legal changes as it did in the United States, where the removal of the political-party designation from the ballot and measures such as primary elections were designed to insulate local elections from political-party activity.[20]

4) *The Municipal Reform Ideology*: This political ideology provided the rationale for municipal institutional reform. As such, the ideology embodied the attitudinal counterpart of structural reform. Some of the key tenets of the reform ideology can be stated as follows:

   a) City government is primarily business, not politics.[21] It should therefore be run by administrative experts, particularly successful businessmen,[22] on business-like principles of efficiency and economy.

   b) A clear distinction between policy and administration in civic government is necessary.[23] City Council should function in the same fashion as a board of directors of a private corporation, giving broad policy direction only. The administration (implementation) of policy should be left entirely to the civic administration or a small executive elected at large, the duties of which are to correspond to that of the manager of a private business firm.

   c) The public power of the civic corporation must be centralized by (i) shifting power from the council, and (ii) abolishing ward elections so that councillors elected from the city at large can safely ignore the parochial interests based on class, ethnicity, or geographic location within the city.[24]

   d) Party politics must be kept out of municipal "business" since local government is largely technical and administrative in nature. In the absence of political parties in local elections, however, it is appropriate for the most prominent ratepayers (that is, those who have the greatest interest in the municipal corporation) to guide the voters in order to elect the right kind of candidates to civic office.[25]

While at-large elections, commission or manager-style forms of administration, along with non-partisanship constituted the institutional core of the municipal reform movement, the attitudinal counterpart of these structural measures was the municipal-reform ideology. There was a great measure of unanimity among Canadian municipal reformers on these features. Together, they would take city government out of the hands of parochial politicians whose loyalties were to individual wards and would instill the principles of efficiency and economy in a business-like local government. Moreover, the scuttling of wards and the removal of important policy matters from the council to either a small executive elected at large or a professional civic administration would both decrease the potential for patronage available to councillors and eliminate the electoral base of the "logroller" or ward-heeler at the same time. Thus, these measures would eliminate the chief incentive for political-party activity at the local level. Most importantly, by changing the basis of representation, municipal reform would "prevent the candidature of inconspicuous men".[26]

There were a number of other important proposals for change in municipal government current during the reform era which cannot be considered part of the core of the municipal-reform movement. The extension of the franchise is one such example. Reformers, as well as the schemes they devised, often reflected a general reluctance to broaden the franchise. A related factor, the property qualification for holding municipal office, was similarly regarded. Reform schemes often provided for a higher rather than a lower property or income qualification. A host of examples could be given. The Montreal reformer's campaign for a board of control retained provisions for a restrictive franchise and a very high property qualification for civic office.[27] Edmonton's "reform" charter of 1904 contained a provision which in plebiscites on referred money by-laws allowed as many as four votes to burgesses according to the amount of property each owned.[28] The effect of this provision was significant. For example, the City of Edmonton's voters' lists for 1914 contained a high proportion of names of persons and corporations with two, three, or four votes each. Of the fifty-two names on the first page of the list (which appears to be representative of the entire list), twenty-eight burgesses were allowed more than one vote for a total of fifty-five votes. The remaining thirty names on the list were allowed only one vote each.[29] Thus, not only were non-property owners excluded entirely from plebiscites on money by-laws, but large property owners wielded at least twice as much voting power as those who held little property.

In Regina, where the Edmonton charter was adopted virtually intact, a cumulative voting clause was incorporated into the draft charter which would have permitted large property owners as many as sixteen votes (four votes in each of four wards). This provision, however, was modified by the Saskatchewan legislature such that a property holder could vote only four times—once in each ward in which he owned property.[30] Yet, reformers heralded the Edmonton city charter of 1904 and its imitations adopted in other western cities as the latest innovations in progressive civic reform.[31]

The restrictions with respect to voting for municipal candidates during the reform era were little better than the provisions for plebiscites on money by-laws. In Calgary, for example, the *Herald* estimated that 50 per cent of property owners did not have a sufficiently high assessment to qualify for the vote.[32] At the peak of municipal reform activity in Winnipeg in 1906, that city's population was 101,057, but only 7,784 were qualified to vote in the civic election.[33] In Montreal, at the turn of the century, an estimated 30 per cent of otherwise qualified electors were disfranchised for failure to pay the municipal water tax and other municipal rates.[34] The franchise was further weighted in favour of the substantial owners of property in almost all cities by the provision that electors could vote in each ward in which they held property. Alan Artibise notes that this provision enabled wealthy electors in Winnipeg to cast up to seven ballots each. In the 1910 election in Winnipeg, for example, there were an estimated six thousand repeaters on the voters' list.[35]

The failure of reformers to press for an extension of the franchise to the non-property-owning segment of the population was not a mere oversight. A noted Canadian reformer, Samuel Morley Wickett, for example, proclaimed in an article published in 1907 that Canada's municipal franchise was a positive feature of the Canadian municipal system in that it gave tax-paying corporations the vote and that it excluded from the voters' lists those with little or no income or property, thereby operating "chiefly against newcomers of various classes and nationalities who have little ground for interest in civic affairs".[36] The property or income qualifications for municipal office were usually left intact in the reformers' campaigns to restructure city government in the prairie region. In some cases, reformers actually succeeded in raising such qualifications so that leading businessmen could be persuaded to seek election to these newly created municipal positions. Thus, when the board of control scheme was adopted in Winnipeg in 1906, an accompanying "reform" raised the property qualification for the mayoralty candidate from five hundred to two thousand dollars—a fourfold increase. The candidates for the board of control were also required to own property worth at least two thousand dollars in order to qualify.[37] When Calgary civic leaders devised a city charter in 1893, they included a provision by which councillors were required to meet a property qualification of one thousand dollars. This factor prevented over 65 per cent of Calgary ratepayers from qualifying for municipal office in 1889.[38] In 1906, the City of Medicine Hat set a property qualification of one thousand dollars for the offices of both mayor and alderman.[39]

Not surprisingly, city councils and in particular mayoralty offices, were usually beyond the reach of even skilled workers during the reform period. Max Foran's study of Calgary during the period 1884 – 95 reveals that "on no occasion did artisans or labourers run for [civic] office".[40] And in Winnipeg Henry Huber's research demonstrates that all of the successful mayoralty candidates were members of the Board of Trade and of the Liberal or Conservative parties.[41]

Even direct legislation provisions (initiative, referendum, and recall) cannot be considered core features of the Canadian movement for municipal government reform. Only a minority of reform campaigns resulted in the adoption of these measures. The direct legislation features were more noticeable in southern Alberta cities where American immigration was pronounced. Even here, however, the percentage of voters required to initiate policies or recall errant legislators was high. For example, when Lethbridge adopted the American style commission form of civic government in 1913, it incorporated the direct legislation provisions of initiative, referendum, and recall which formed part of the populist crusade of the progressive era. These three key features of direct democracy provided the means by which a stated number of qualified voters, by signing a petition, could (a) initiate legislative proposals which the Commission would be required to consider; (b) force the Commission to submit matters to a referendum; or, (c) "recall" one or more Commissioners by petitioning that the offending local legislator(s) again submit to a special election in order to be confirmed in, or removed from, office. However, the proportion of electors required to petition in order to exercise these democratic provisions was high. In order to force the Commissioners to submit a by-law to a referendum, twenty per cent of the number of voters polled in the preceding election were required to sign a petition to this effect. An identical number of voters were required to initiate proposed local legislation, which the Commission could either ratify or submit to a referendum. The recall petition required the signatures of fifteen per cent of the number of voters in the preceding election.[42]

To ensure that these democratic mechanisms would be used sparingly, if at all, the Lethbridge Commission petitioned the Alberta legislature in 1914 to raise the number of signatures required to bring into play the referendum and recall provisions.[43] By 1916, the Commissioners were successful in securing a charter amendment which increased the number of voters required to set in motion the initiative, referendum, and recall procedures to the virtually prohibitive level of 35 per cent, 25 per cent, and 25 per cent respectively.[44] The Lethbridge charter contained other provisions which also fell short of the populist ideals supposedly embodied in direct legislation. In order to exercise the franchise for example, a resident required a property or income qualification of two hundred dollars and in addition representatives of private companies were allowed to vote.[45]

These examples illustrate the point that it is important to discover what democratic measures reformers usually *excluded* from schemes for restructuring civic government. While extension of the franchise, reduction in property qualifications for office, and direct legislation were well-known devices designed to give the average citizen a greater voice in civic affairs, most successful reform campaigns in Canadian cities seem to have excluded them or included them only reluctantly and then in a somewhat emasculated form. Yet, the newspapers, minutes of labour councils, and similar sources prove that these features were often advocated by labour and other non-elite segments of the community at the time.[46]

THE ROOTS OF REFORM

A study of the historical roots of reform in the Canadian context should lead to the discovery of some of the most significant indigenous factors which gave rise to the movement. Social scientists have assumed too often that the Canadian municipal reform movement was simply an imitation of the great American crusade against the corrupt urban political party machine. In a recent study, for example, the authors declare that Canada was "a country lacking in the social conditions that gave rise to the movement".[47] This statement could not be more misleading. While the influence of the American movement must be acknowledged, the fact that local government reform in Canada was unique in some respects and that it differed in degree if not in kind from its American counterpart in other respects makes it dangerous simply to assume that Canadian local government was an offshoot of the American movement.[48] Nor can western Canadian local government reform be considered entirely derivative of Ontario adaptations of American reform models. While the West was indeed a "laboratory" in which the reform formulae of central Canadians were applied, it is not at all clear that the application of these experiments conformed to the prescriptions of the self-proclaimed spokesmen of the new "civic science" living in Toronto or Westmount. More importantly, it is possible to conclude from the evidence now available that the *results* of these experiments in revamping civic government and politics in the West were not nearly as benign as leading central Canadian reform advocates had proclaimed.

During the reform period, the form and style for civic political institutions in the rapidly growing cities of the prairies were closely patterned after the Ontario model. The Baldwin Act passed in 1849, often called the "Magna Carta" of Canadian local government, was virtually replicated in the municipal legislation of the Northwest Territories, and later, the prairie provinces.[49] The Ontario municipal system was copied in the West in part because it was the "nearest established system", and because many western settlers came from Ontario.[50] Bob Edwards (later the editor of the *Calgary Eye Opener*) described the residents of Edmonton, for example, as persons whose homes contained "nothing but the pictures of deceased Ontario relatives".[51] Moreover, Ontario-born men in large part formed the elite in western centres. As Samuel Morley Wickett observed at the turn of the century with respect to the West:

> Owing largely to the fact that so many Ontario men have accepted municipal appointments or entered into the practice of law in its leading cities, the municipal system of Ontario has in many respects served as a model.[52]

An Ontario boyhood was also a distinguishing characteristic of many members of western boards of trade and city councils. These organizations co-operated in spearheading most campaigns for local government reform in the West. Four of the six mayors of Winnipeg who held office between 1901 and 1914 were from Ontario, and all six were members of the Board of Trade.[53] Both the original act of incorporation of Winnipeg and the subsequent adoption of the Board of Control in 1906 were based closely on the form of government prevailing in Toronto at each time.[54] When Edmonton obtained its charter in 1904, the former solicitor of the City of Toronto and editor of the *Municipal Manual* of Ontario, W. H. Biggar, was called in to assist in the formulation of the local constitution which subsequently served as the basis for similar legislation in Calgary, Regina, Saskatoon, and other western cities as well as the first general act governing cities in Alberta. Indeed, because of the innovative provision for administration by a board of commissioners, and other reform features, the Edmonton charter was widely imitated in the West. Edmonton became the quintessential "reform" city in western Canada. In fact, the Edmonton charter constituted a virtually perfect institutional realization of the ideology of the leading central Canadian reform advocates who were prevented from imposing their ideal model so completely upon the cities of their own region because of the inertia of tradition in these older urban centres. The Edmonton charter included provisions for a small council; an explicit allocation of significant powers to an appointed board of commissioners; a distinct separation of legislative and administrative functions; virtually complete municipal ownership of utilities; a cumulative voting clause which allowed holders of property to cast up to four votes on referred money by-laws; and a property qualification for municipal voters.[55]

Both the pre-reform and the reform models of local government in the West were based on Ontario precedent. The Ontario reform schemes themselves, however, had been influenced by American models. Ontario cities during the reform era often modified their traditional form of government, characterized by political decentralization and legislative dominance, by grafting on to the civic body politic the latest American reform structures. American "good government" influence also penetrated the West through the medium of periodicals, newspaper reports, and books as well as more directly by virtue of the trips by leading western reformers to American municipal conventions. Some civic leaders in the West had even spent some part of their lives in the United States and were likely influenced by American ideas concerning local government. Mayor W. D. L. Hardie of Lethbridge, for example, emigrated to the United States when he was twenty years of age and later returned to Canada to become the "mayor" of the American-style commission government instituted in that city in 1914.[56] Sanford Evans, Mayor of Winnipeg, had also spent some time south of the border, obtaining his MA degree at Columbia University.[57]

Municipal government reform in the West, however, was also influenced by social and economic forces which differed from central Canadian patterns in crucial respects. A massive influx of "unassimilable" non-English-speaking immigrants was an important western Canadian phenomenon during the reform era, and the fear of immigrant voting strength was a factor in the way in which western municipal reform developed. Labour militance, based on the industrial union tradition of working-class British immigrants, was most prevalent in the West before 1919. The desire to harness the instrument of the local unit of the state to attract railways became a virtual obsession with western business leaders who, unlike their central Canadian counterparts, could not rely on water transportation and nearby markets. The municipal borrowing power was also particularly important to business in the West, where capital was scarce and the need for an economic infrastructure (roads, bridges, utilities) was pronounced. Municipal non-partisanship was also doubtless reinforced by the strong antipathy of westerners to the established parties controlled in central Canada.

THE CLASS CHARACTER OF MUNICIPAL GOVERNMENT REFORM IN THE WEST

The most direct way to discover which groups benefited or suffered from reform measures adopted in urban centres in the West is to examine the circumstances surrounding the introduction of key features of reform in specific cities and the changes these reforms brought about. Because existing research on individual prairie cities is not very extensive, conclusions about the manner in which core features of civic reform affected different socio-economic groups in these jurisdictions must be based on incomplete evidence. Enough is known, though, to provide considerable support to the contention that the thrust of local government reform tended to reduce or make more difficult the *representation* of the working class, lower-status ethnic groups, and the electoral organizations they supported in the civic political arena. A related bias apparently introduced by reform structures and ideas was a reduction in the degree of *responsiveness* of local government to the needs and demands of workers and non-English-speaking immigrants, particularly Slavs and Jews. These immigrant groups were, however, almost entirely working class during the reform period. Similarly, the electoral organizations attempting to represent labour drew their support from working-class and immigrant districts. Local government reform had the effect of reducing the power of immigrant groups and labour-based slates in civic politics. It is, therefore, possible to treat such ethnic and partisan bias as another form of class bias.

The central contention of this study, then, is that the general effect of civic government reform in western centres was detrimental to working-class interests. This does not imply that reform was in all respects or in every instance disadvantageous to the interests of lower-class or lower-status ethnic groups.[58] It can be argued, for example, that civic non-partisanship (supported by labour as a rule) was a device which served to lure workers away from the bosoms of traditional parties and to enlist them in the ranks of the "independent" parties of labour. However, the cry of non-partisanship was also a signal for the coalition of anti-labour and anti-socialist Liberals and Conservatives in the local political arena.[59] The political affiliations of local councillors during the reform period suggests that the "non-partisan" features of reform was, on balance, perhaps not in the objective interest of labour.

The analytical distinctions set out earlier in this paper can now be employed to determine, in a tentative way at least, the class interest that reform measures appear to have served. Each of the following core features of local government reform will be considered: (a) the abolition of wards or the adoption of large wards; (b) civic administrative reforms designed to shift power from the council to a civic executive and/or bureaucracy; (c) non-partisanship; and (d) the ideology of municipal government reform. The reform ideology will be discussed in the context of each of the structural reforms for which it provided the philosophical basis.

a) *The Attack on the Ward System*

A major feature of the municipal government reform movement in western cities was the campaign to abolish wards. Edmonton's at-large system dates back to its origin as a city in 1904, for example. Calgary changed to an at-large electoral system in 1913 as a result of a narrow victory by an anti-ward lobby in a plebiscite. Wards were abolished in Victoria in 1912, and eight years later the number of wards in Winnipeg were reduced from seven to three.

In addition to the strong attack on the ward system emanating from central Canada and the United States, the system of apportionment of municipal expenditures by wards and the control of expenditures by individual councillors were widely criticized by civic leaders as being a parochial, corrupt, and inefficient practice. The alleged extravagance and favouritism practised by the city councillors of Winnipeg was one of the key factors which prompted the Board of Trade to mount a reform campaign in that city in 1885. With the victory of the reform group, power over divisional expenditures were withdrawn from individual aldermen and vested in council.[60] With respect to the prairie region in general, the official journal of most municipal associations on the prairie provinces, the *Western Municipal News*, campaigned against the ward apportionment tradition ceaselessly in part because "work is very often placed with the friends of the councillor of the division".[61] The main motivation behind the campaign to abolish the ward system, however, was the desire to change the basis of representation. J. M. S. Careless has pointed out that urban centres on the prairies developed segregated districts based on sharp differences in income levels, quality of housing, and ethnic make-up at a very early stage in their growth.[62] Working-class and Eastern European groups, concentrated in particular wards, were occasionally able to elect "one of their own" to urban councils.

During the first two decades of the century, Jewish and Ukrainian groups, concentrated in Ward Five in Winnipeg's distinctive North End, elected several representatives to city Council. The first successful Jewish candidate, Moses Finkelstein, elected to Council in 1904, wrote later that an organized effort by the Jewish community to obtain representation on Council began in the first few years of the century. By 1912, the Ukrainian community of Ward Five was able to celebrate the success of T. Stefanik in the Winnipeg civic election with an enthusiastic parade down Main Street.[63] Organized labour was also able to mount a challenge of sorts to the dominance of business interests on civic councils with the aid of ward elections. Of the 515 councillors elected in Winnipeg between 1874 and 1914, a total of 21 have been identified as "artisans and workingmen". At least several of these had strong links with organized labour which actively supported their election.[64] Winnipeg's ward system was evidently still an important factor later in the reform period when economic conditions associated with the First World War and its aftermath increased both union strength and militancy. By the end of the second decade of the twentieth century, labour had almost gained control of Winnipeg city council but then lost ground rapidly when the basis of representation was changed through the reduction in the number of wards. The abolition of wards or the change to a few large wards were both perceived by reformers as measures designed to prevent the representatives of non-elite groups in city councils. At-large or large-ward elections would have the added effect of inducing prominent businessmen to run for office by reducing the necessity for candidates to engage in personal canvassing and otherwise to mend political fences.[65]

Urban electoral reforms also greatly increased the costs of campaigning. Very little has been discovered to date on financing of early municipal elections in the West but it is possible to get an indication of the effect of the at-large system on election expenses by examining evidence from eastern cities with populations similar to that of growing western centres. In 1913, for example, the mayor of Halifax noted that it cost candidates for the board of control from five thousand to ten thousand dollars to run in a city-wide contest. Therefore, he declared, "if you abolished the ward system they [the incumbent ward representatives] would not be liable to run." However, the mayor of London responded to this concern by describing the procedure in his city where a "Citizen's Committee" dominated by representatives of business organizations recruited and nominated a group of candidates and provided the campaign expenses of this approved slate.[66] In the West, at-large contests for civic office also increased the power of those groups able to finance a city-wide campaign[67] and consequently made it more difficult for low-income segments of the community to win local office. As a noted authority on Canadian local politics observed, "Experience shows that many of those who can retain office under the ward system fail to return to council when a change is made to the general vote basis."[68] A comparison between cities with ward and at-large elections seems to support this view. For example, in the absence of a ward system in Edmonton, labour and Eastern European immigrant groups concentrated in the eastern section of the city were largely unsuccessful in obtaining representation on city council despite organized attempts to do so.[69] In Winnipeg, however, labour groups and Jewish and Slavic immigrant communities elected several spokesmen to Council early in the century.[70] In the twin cities of Port Arthur and Fort William, a similar effect of the two different forms of local electoral system is suggested, although other factors cannot be discounted. During the reform period, local candidates affiliated with labour often won election in Ward One in Port Arthur but suffered defeat in Fort William which had city-wide elections. The ward system of the former city was seen as a threat by the civic establishment, as the remarks of Port Arthur's Mayor Oliver at a municipal convention suggest:

In Port Arthur, we have one ward in which there are about 7,000 people of whom about 5,500 are foreigners, who have not been long enough in Canada to any more than know how they are to vote. They do not know anything about government, nor do they try to study it, and by voting at-large we try to get the aldermen elected who have the best interests at heart.[71]

Since an at-large system was part of the reform inspired "business government", it was more credible to businessmen. The mayor of Red Deer, for example, quoted approvingly the words of President Elliot of Harvard University: "to the performance of business functions in an honest and intelligent manner, the notion of representation by districts of population has no sensible application."[72] When wards were abolished, businessmen could run for office with reasonable confidence that they would be insulated from popular pressures.[73] "The would-be Cincinnatus in the business community would only put down his tools to govern, not to engage in politics."[74] Electoral reform in Calgary is a case in point. When an at-large system was adopted there in 1913, it appears to have had an effect on the recruitment of candidates for local office as well as on the results of the election itself. The Conservative *Calgary Herald*, pleased with the first election campaign under the at-large system, commented in an editorial on December 2, 1913: "We cannot say that the abolition of the ward system is responsible but it is a fact that some first class businessmen have permitted their names to go before the people." The *Herald* was equally pleased with the results of the election, expressing mock surprise that no labour-supported candidates had won. It suggested that labour's fate may have been owing to the candidacy of unusually prestigious candidates that had run for the business faction.[75]

b) *Civic Executive and Bureaucratic Reform*

The board of control, the commission form, the board of commissioners, and city manager forms were all adopted in Canadian cities. As with local electoral reform, revamping the civic executive and bureaucracy was designed to reduce the representation of lesser men and to enshrine the principles of business efficiency in the municipal corporation. Four schemes were adopted, with some variations, by western cities. The board of control scheme, first adopted in Toronto, spread to Winnipeg, Montreal, Hamilton, Ottawa, and other cities. It removed considerable power from the common council and transferred it to a group of controllers elected at-large who formed an executive body superior to the council. This "super-group" usually assumed particular responsibility for finance and the awarding of civic contracts. In Ottawa, for example, the finance committee of Council was abolished when the board of control was adopted. A similar centralization of power in fewer and more expert hands was accomplished by the elected-commission form of local government adopted in Saint John in 1912 and in Lethbridge in 1913. Three to five commissioners were to be elected at-large, each of whom would have responsibility for a particular department of civic administration.

The elected-commission form, an American scheme, is not to be confused with the appointive board of commissioners form which flourished in western Canada. The board of commissioners plan implied not only the concentration of authority but an explicit removal of administration from the inexpert hands of elected councillors. Edmonton's council-board of commissioners charter adopted in 1904 expressly placed administration in the domain of several appointed civic bureaucrats. While the mayor was ex-officio member of the board, his role was largely that of liaison between council and the board. The scheme soon spread to Regina, Saskatoon, Red Deer, and other cities. In Saskatoon, there was for some time a single commissioner—in effect, a city manager. Finally, the well-known city-manager plan, first adopted by Westmount in 1913, placed much of the power of policy initiation and implementation in the hands of a single appointed official.

While it has been pointed out that Canadian civic executive/bureaucratic reform schemes often retained the council committee system and ward elections, it is nevertheless the case that these structural changes weakened the elective component of city government. In Red Deer the board of commissioners replaced council committees, the former administrative units of City Hall.[76] Commissioners in Edmonton and other cities could be fired only by a vote of two-thirds of council. Hence, the civic public power shifted towards the appointed arm of government or toward an elite executive body elected from the city at-large. As John Weaver points out, "Reformers often blurred the distinctions between an executive and a civil service; in simple terms they wanted strong men on top. The blinking owls and vultures on councils (a reform analogy too often close to the mark) were to be cut down to size by 'big men'."[77]

Not only were reformed civic structures adopted as a rule as the result of campaigns by local boards of trade and the press, but the recruitment of candidates and campaigning for the newly restructured government was often more assiduously pursued by elites. Lethbridge provides a striking example. When the first election for the three-member commission government took place in 1913, "the citizens' slate, composed of three candidates selected by a body of seventeen prominent businessmen and representatives of the two political parties, triumphed".[78] Again, Alberta cities were in the vanguard in revamping the structure of local administration. The commission-board form was pioneered in Edmonton and set the pattern for the most common bureaucratic structure in prairie cities. Calgary initiated a system of elected commissioners along with mayor and council that was very similar to the board-of-control form. Red Deer followed Edmonton's lead in erecting a powerful commission board during the reform period and Lethbridge abolished city council entirely in 1913 in favour of a three-member elected commission closely modelled after the American city commission plan.

c) Non-Partisanship

The proposition that there has been an inherent class bias to local non-partisanship has been given very little attention by Canadian scholars.[79] It is nevertheless possible to formulate some of the main questions or hypotheses concerning this important plank in the reform platform.

One of the untested assumptions of Canadian social science re-search on municipal non-partisanship is that the anti-party sentiment in Canadian local politics was largely imported from the United States. According to the conventional academic view, the importation by Canadian reformers of the American municipal non-partisan senti-ment and institutional devices designed to eliminate local party poli-tics was both inappropriate and ironic; after all, Canadian cities at the turn of the century were not bastions of machine politics and urban party bosses.[80] This argument is wrong on two counts. First, the impetus for the movement for non-partisanship in municipal politics was often a product of indigenous conditions. Second, there was a distinctly partisan dimension to Canadian municipal politics of the reform era. In fact, party politics have long been present in local elections and the council deliberations in Canadian cities. Though partisan groupings have not been as organized and powerful as Amer-ican civic machines, led by the local party boss, in at least one of the senses in which "machine politics" is used (that is, corrupt politics) Canadian cities during (and since) the reform era have had spectacu-lar cases of local graft and patronage. The Cannon Commission, established by the Province of Quebec, reported in 1909 that Montreal politics had been "saturated with corruption" since 1892. Eight alder-men were found guilty by the inquiry.[81] In Toronto and Winnipeg, provincial inquiries discovered similar, if less sensational, examples of local corruption.[82] In all three cases these revelations were used by "non-partisan" reformers as a springboard to power at City Hall.

Calgary, too, was the scene of civic scandals involving land deals by aldermen in 1904. Two aldermen were thrown out of office by the Chief Justice and three city officials resigned in disgrace.[83] Frequent scandals such as these led J. S. Woodsworth to declare in 1909, "Already we have had revelations of municipal corruption, of the party machine in our civic elections and the 'handling' of the foreign vote."[84]

Another indigenous factor in the development of local non-partisan sentiment in Canada was the widespread practice of political-party competition for local office. Rival political-party activists in municipal contests often denounced their opponents for bringing "irrelevant" party considerations into the local political arena. Partisan and factional rivalry even characterized early township politics in Upper Canada and the first election in the City of Toronto was an open contest between Reformers and Tories.[85] In the West, local coalitions of Conservatives and Liberals co-operated on civic councils to "save the city from socialism". Organized labour also developed parties such as the Independent Labour Party and the Dominion Labour Party to challenge Liberal-Conservative hegemony in city councils.

The strong non-partisan tradition of western Canada with respect to the domination of political parties based in central Canada was apparently a reinforcing factor in local non-partisanship. While this anti-party feeling was strongest among rural groups, it easily penetrated the cities in the West. One linkage was apparently through rural migration to the urban centres; a second was through farmer-labour political exchange within organizations such as the Alberta Non-Partisan League in which William Irvine played a leading role.

A brief examination of the activities of the Alberta Non-Partisan League reveals the interaction of farmer and labour elements in the West in a common crusade against the established party system. The non-Partisan League, born of agrarian discontent in North Dakota, penetrated Saskatchewan and Alberta, where it made some impact during the period between 1916 and 1922. The Alberta Non-Partisan League, of which Irvine was secretary, originated in Calgary in 1916 and adopted a platform attacking the established party system and calling for extensive public ownership. The first objective of the League was "to overcome partisanship by the election of a truly people's government and the establishment of a business administration instead of a party administration".[86] By "business administration" Irvine and his associates clearly meant honest and efficient administration in the interest of the masses, rather than government by and in the interests of business. In fact, the League's activities were directed at reducing, not increasing, the degree to which business interests dominated all levels of government. In addition to the League's strong ties to the United Farmers of Alberta, Irvine and other League members were involved in setting up the Labour Representation League in Calgary in 1917 in co-operation with the Calgary Trades and Labour Council. By 1919 the Labour Representation League had evolved into the Independent Labour Party and later in the same year, it became the Calgary branch of the Dominion Labour Party. These parties of labour succeeded in electing a few candidates to municipal, provincial, and finally, federal legislatures with the victory of William Irvine in East Calgary in 1921.[87]

The philosophical and electoral challenge to the established traditions at the local level was not confined to Calgary. At the urging of the Labour Representation League of Calgary,[88] an organization with the same name was set up in Edmonton by leading members of the Trades and Labour Council of the capital city. It, too, was transformed into the Independent Labour Party and then the Dominion Labour Party by 1919. It also achieved a measure of success in Edmonton civic elections in the post-war years. In the 1919 Edmonton local election, for example, three aldermanic candidates nominated by the Dominion Labour Party were successful. In addition, the winning mayoralty candidate, Joe Clarke, had the endorsation of the DLP.[89] It is important to note that urban labour groups, influenced by the persuasive anti-party tradition of prairie farmers as well as by the experiences of workers themselves with the established parties, evolved from a position outside the party system to active participation in third parties. This process was particularly noticeable at the municipal level toward the end of the reform era when almost every western city developed a local organization centred on organized labour which supported candidates for civic office. Because local government was generally perceived as a matter of administration, local labour groups could contest municipal elections and still claim to be unsullied by party politics. The edict of Samuel Gompers forbidding union involvement in party politics, enshrined in some union constitutions, was not interpreted as applying to municipal elections. And since urban trades and labour councils were set up explicitly to deal with the common concerns of various unions within the city, it was natural that such organizations would attempt to secure workers' representation on urban councils.[90]

If non-partisanship served as a rationale for labour and socialist forces to act as a party in civic affairs without suffering the full force of hostility to the established party system, it also served as a convenient cover for local wings of established parties to coalesce in civic politics, disguised as citizens' committees or good government groups of various designations. Covert partisan coalitions of Liberals and Conservatives in such organizations as the Winnipeg Citizens' League could generally be counted on to prevent "socialists" and labour representatives from capturing city hall.[91] The anti-party rhetoric of such local party coalitions was a highly effective, if dishonest, way of discrediting electoral organizations of labour, which were often accused of representing narrow class interests rather than the general good of the city population. Mayor William Short of Edmonton, for example, warned delegates to a 1907 municipal convention in Alberta that "the trade union's political party may place a man in the council irrespective of his fitness".[92]

Local coalitions of Liberals and Conservatives were motivated by more than the threat of political activity by labour, however. The need for leading business figures to co-operate politically at the local level was usually stronger than the partisan differences which might exist among them. This was so particularly in the precarious economic climate of the prairies where such co-operation was so obviously in their joint pecuniary interest. As long as their "economic tutelage"[93] existed, open competition between Liberals and Conservatives in civic politics was a luxury neither group could afford.

On balance, the non-partisan camouflage appeared to have benefited Liberal and Conservative business-oriented interests in prairie cities during the reform era. Labour was apparently disadvantaged in several related ways by non-partisanship. First, pervasive anti-party sentiments of the voters in general apparently prejudiced them against any civic group that made a point of calling itself a party—as did the Independent Labour Party and the Dominion Labour Party. Second, to counter the charge of radicalism and narrow class motivations in civic contests, labour usually nominated the most respectable, hence most moderate, members of its leadership. Winnipeg Alderman and Mayor S. J. Farmer, for example, was a "gas and water" socialist[94] who later in his political career as CCF leader in the Manitoba legislature, accepted a cabinet post in the "non-partisan" government of John Bracken. Bracken became national leader of the Conservative party in 1942.[95] Similarly, J. A. Kinney, a labour alderman in Edmonton during the period of the First World War, drew the fire of some of his labour colleagues for his moderate position on civic issues.[96]

Third, because party lines in civic elections were not as clearly drawn as in contests at the senior levels, voters were forced to cast about for other ways of choosing candidates. They were influenced to some degree by the partisan biases of influential community institutions. Chief among these agencies offering political advice was the local newspaper. The success rate of candidates endorsed by newspapers has not been systematically studied in western cities, but fragmentary evidence suggests that it was significant. For example, in the Calgary civic election of 1913, seven of the eight candidates endorsed by the Conservative *Calgary Herald* were successful.[97]

The examples listed above are some of the more obvious ways the non-partisan ideology operating in local politics may have manifested a class bias. On balance, it was apparently easier for labour to elect representatives to the provincial level than to civic office.[98] The effect of the franchise provisions, which was more liberal in provincial elections than in local contests, must also be considered a contributing factor. There is little doubt, however, that by openly engaging in party-like activity rather than making a vague claim to represent all interests in the city, labour suffered a backlash from many voters who believed that such obvious partisanship was inappropriate for the management of the civic business.

d) *The Ideology of the Local Government Reform Movement*

The specific tenets of the reform ideology have been discussed in relation to the structural reforms to which they were linked. It is important to bear in mind the close relationship between structure and ideology, for the legacy of reform is an attitude of mind as much as it is a particular set of institutional arrangements. While the ideas and institutions of reform cannot be divorced in an analysis of the movement, it is possible to expand upon two general themes in reform thought, both of which were decidedly anti-democratic in their implications. First, reformers had a restrictive notion of what municipal matters were political in nature and therefore subject to a measure of popular participation if not control. Second, their views were dominated by a profound sense of *noblesse oblige*: a belief that those who were best suited to the task of governing the city had a civic duty to accept local office and would, because of their superior virtue, rule in the best interest of all urban residents.

Reformers sought to expand the domain of administration in local government and narrow the realm of legislation or "politics". For example, reformers persistently argued that,

> City government is mostly, almost entirely, administrative. What laws are enacted in the city hall have mostly the nature of bylaws which any board of directors of a large company would pass for the expedition of ordinary business.[99]

Since municipal matters were held to be essentially administrative, almost any challenge to the status quo could be dismissed as political meddling. Thus, at a 1917 convention of the Union of Alberta Municipalities, a resolution asking for conscription of wealth was ruled out on the basis that it was political.[100] Yet, there was nothing political about the invitation by the Calgary City Commissioners to a committee of the Board of Trade to sit in and offer advice when the 1915 civic estimates were being considered. The *Calgary Herald* editors described the commissioners' invitation as "an exhibition of good sense", since the Board of Trade was made up of a "body of recognized representative citizens".[101] Structural reformers also consistently claimed that municipal government was primarily a technical task, to be operated to the maximum feasible extent by experts on the basis of "scientific" principles.[102] By their invocation of a civic science and by raising the expert to the pinnacle of the municipal corporation, reformers forged a weapon with which they could effectively beat down competing claims regarding structural reform based on value premises they did not share.

The fact that the reform model of local government was anti-democratic in the extreme was rarely mentioned by leading reform spokesmen. Even the well-known view of municipal government as the school of democracy was not held to be inconsistent with municipal reform philosophy. Democratic traditions and practices could be learned in local councils, to be applied when councillors graduated to senior levels of government. For example, to a leading thinker in the municipal reform movement, municipal councils were "schools of democracy" because "they train the crowd for public life in wider fields".[103] The anti-democratic strain in reform did not go completely unnoticed. The director of the Toronto Bureau of Municipal Research, H. L. Brittain, warned in 1917 that because local government was perceived as a technical matter, "impatient people have been able to accept frankly some form of benevolent despotism".[104]

THE POLICY IMPACT OF MUNICIPAL GOVERNMENT REFORM

The self-proclaimed "benevolence" of reforms must be qualified in light of the policies they pursued or chose to ignore in practical situations. If they were able to admit on occasion that the schemes

they proposed involved government by an elite, they were nevertheless adamant in their view that reform regimes would govern only in
the interests of all the people of the city. Modern writers on municipal
history have kept alive this rosy interpretation of reform, claiming that
while the movement was elitist and anti-democratic, in that it reduced
the power of lower-status groups to influence urban public decision-
making, it none the less contributed to rationalizing and modernizing
urban life. It was, in this view, an exercise in "saving the Canadian
city". Significantly, the chief proponent of this interpretation of reform examined almost exclusively the ideas, not the actions, of municipal reformers and focused heavily on central Canada.[105]

The class character of reform can be seen clearly in the responsiveness of reform councils to various groups in the community. Often,
what reform councils failed to deal with is as significant in this regard
as the issues they chose to consider. Many important concerns were
relegated to the realm of "non-decision-making". Copp's study of the
conditions of the working class in Montreal is a case in point. In a
wave of protest over the 1909 revelations of civic corruption, a board
of control was adopted in Montreal and a reform regime was swept
into office. Yet, "throughout the four years of the 'regime of honest
men' nothing significant was accomplished. The Committee of Citizens and its candidates were fascinated with new boulevards and city
beautification."[106]

Similarly, the first reform regime elected in Winnipeg in 1884 with
the solid backing of the Board of Trade quickly ended the extravagance and graft of the previous council by instituting tighter accounting procedures. But it also reduced substantially the wages of civic
employees and cut relief expenditures by 58 per cent over the preceding year, despite the fact that unemployment was high and the need
for relief was great.[107] In Edmonton, the city council eagerly financed
the expansion of street railway lines and other municipal services to
land situated far beyond the populated area of the city, thereby
increasing the value of the property held by real estate interests.
When the economic boom collapsed after 1913, the council tried to
solve the problem of a heavy debt and a dwindling tax base by
dismissing some civic employees and reducing the salaries of others.[108]
In Canada, as in the United States, the reduction of civic expenditures
by reform councils "was often made at labour's expense".[109]

Reform regimes were also less responsive to the needs of the districts of the city inhabited by working-class families and lower-status
ethnic groups. It was this type of inequality that the Edmonton Trades

and Labour Council sought to correct when, in 1907, it decided to endorse those candidates who would fight for "the equal expenditure of the city in its different sections".[110] The policy bias of reform councils with respect to the poorer segments of the urban population took yet another form. The hiring practices of "honest" reform regimes were decidedly discriminatory. For example, in 1921, when Winnipeg's population was 33 per cent non-Anglo-Saxon, only 6 per cent of civic employees were drawn from this minority group.[111]

Civic reformers did little to stop another practice which involved the expenditure of municipal funds for private gain. During the reform era, western cities followed the example of their eastern counterparts in offering manufacturing firms, agribusiness, railways, and other industries bonuses in the form of cash grants, free land, tax exemptions, bond guarantees, and low utility rates. In this way, revenue raised from the less well-off urban residents by means of a regressive municipal tax system was spent in an attempt to attract and retain industries or railways. Despite the official rhetoric of reform spokesmen, which was strongly against bonusing, western civic elites were driven by their booster ambitions to continue to compete with rival centres by offering bonuses.

In the early phase of the reform era, spectacular concessions offered to industry and railways encountered little opposition from reform leaders. An example often cited is the $200,000 cash bonus granted the CPR by the City of Winnipeg in 1882, to which was added a parcel of land and an exemption from civic taxation in perpetuity. By 1909, Winnipeg had foregone more than $900,000 in tax revenue because of these bonuses.[112] Similarly, in 1906, Edmonton granted the Grand Trunk Pacific Railway a cash bonus of $100,000 and free land estimated at $60,000 to encourage the company to locate its line in the city.[113] In addition, Edmonton followed a policy of granting free light and water to firms for a period of five years after their establishment in the city.[114] In 1905, Calgary exempted the Alberta Portland Cement Company from payment of property taxes for a period of twenty years.[115] By 1911, Calgary was offering entrepreneurs industrial sites at cost, a low assessment rate and a seven-year tax holiday on buildings and stock.[116] In 1905, a by-law was passed by the Lethbridge council granting tax exemptions and rebates on water rates to the CPR.[117] A year later the Lethbridge city fathers guaranteed forty thousand dollars in debenture bonds of the Medicine Hat Woolen Mills Company.[118]

The reform elements themselves recognized some of the harmful

effects of the system of competitive bonusing and a great outcry
began against the practice, led by boards of trade and civic officials.
Yet, their opposition was usually based on the unfair advantage bonusing provided to firms seeking to compete with those already established in the community. For example, the Winnipeg City Solicitor
explained in 1910,

> Very often a person who has been a citizen in town or city for a number of
> years and has established a moderately sized plant of an industrial charac-
> ter, never asks for any concessions, and never gets any; but five men,
> perhaps four of them straw, will form themselves into a joint stock com-
> pany, come along and establish a rival concern, get concessions by way of a
> bonus or exemption or free sites, and set up in opposition to the other man
> who has been paying taxes for a large number of years to the municipality
> and [has] helped in this way to build up the municipality. If you grant
> concessions to industrial concerns, it should apply generally.[119]

If the bonusing craze did not slacken during the reform era, it
became more subtle and refined in form. A great deal was spent on
promotion schemes, including advertising, employing professional
civic boosters, and sending civic representatives on missions to other
cities to attract industries. For example, in 1905, the Edmonton City
Council granted the Board of Trade $3,500 for publicity purposes; in
1911 it gave the board fifteen thousand dollars to promote the city as
a haven for private investment. In 1910, Edmonton's industrial committee sent a former member of the Board of Trade to central Canadian and American cities to lure manufacturing firms to the Alberta
capital. Upon his return, he recommended that rather than bonusing
specific industries, the city should provide "at minimum cost suitable
sites and adequate power, light and water at low rates".[120]

Restrictions on bonusing placed in city charters did not stop the
practice. Despite these limitations, Alberta cities, for example, regularly sought and obtained amendments which permitted them to offer
substantial concessions to individual firms. Significantly, it was the
rural-dominated Alberta legislature which legislated against municipal
bonusing in 1913. Even this stipulation, however, did not put an end
to municipal concessions to private industry. Calgary, for example,
obtained an amendment to the legislation in 1914 which permitted the
expenditure of up to fifteen thousand dollars on civic promotion and
incentives to enterprises to establish in the city.[121] For a number of
years after the provincial legislation designed to end bonusing, Edmonton continued to tax land only, thereby exempting industrial or
other establishments from rates on improvements.

There was a close relationship between the policy of municipal ownership and the practice of bonusing industries. In fact, the former was often perceived by reformers simply as a more sophisticated form of the latter. The Mayor of Medicine Hat explained the connection lucidly: "The town with something to offer which is equivalent to a bonus, frequently escapes being required to put up a cash bonus. Municipal ownership and industrial progress go hand in hand."[122] Time and again, members of reform councils stressed the point that municipally owned utilities would serve to entice industry. In 1910, it was argued in the Edmonton Council debates that "cheap power is essential in order to induce manufacturing establishments to locate in the City of Edmonton".[123]

Yet, municipal ownership was not an article of faith among reformers. As John Weaver has pointed out, municipal ownership often came about by default; frequently after a private franchise had been granted to a firm that could not fulfil the terms of the agreement with the city, or in cases where a private concern could not be found to provide the service. Public power came to Edmonton in 1902, for example, when a frustrated town council bought out the private power company because it refused to up-grade its plant.[124] Similarly, when Edmonton's growth created a need for an improved water system, city officials found they could not interest private capital in providing the service because "we were a mere village, with comparatively little but high expectations to justify our ambitions".[125]

Municipal ownership, or as it was sometimes called, "municipal socialism", was not justified as a rule in terms of the benefits it would bring to the urban residents as such. Alan Artibise, for example, demonstrates that in the campaign for a municipally owned power system in Winnipeg, "public good was simply a dividend; it was not the operating principle".[126] The gas and water socialists were not opposed to a society dominated by private ownership; rather, they sought to make it more viable. One of the founders of the Union of Canadian Municipalities and a leading reform spokesman for example, made this point in 1909:

> It seems to be necessary to constantly rebut a notion...that we are the enemies of private enterprise, of lighting and power companies and street railway companies and of all capital. On the contrary, we are the true friends of capital and all private enterprises.[127]

The above discussion indicates that reformers sought to ensure that civic policy-making favoured their class interests. In the current writing on municipal reform in Canada, this point is usually conceded.

However, two historians have recently made the very valid point that the reformers' victories were seldom complete. They point out that other forces in the community were able to assert themselves either through modifying the reform structures to make them more democratic or by electing representatives to council.[128] It is true that men of modest means, including workers, did get elected to city councils during the reform era, despite the reformers preference for leading businessmen. At best, however, this argument provides a useful qualification to the interpretation of the reform movement as a victory for an entrenched urban elite. Even though structural reforms were not always implemented in the "pure" form (for instance, the ward system was never abolished in Winnipeg), the ideological crusade which invariably accompanied institutional reform was itself a potent factor in directing policy-making along certain lines. In the West reformers were able to exercise a virtual ideological hegemony with respect to the ends local government should serve.

Moreover, many leading businessmen, especially in western cities, did accept elective civic office.[129] Equally important, in many cases where business leaders themselves did not run for office, they were often instrumental in recruiting and supporting lesser business figures in local elections. A striking example of this phenomenon was the 1884 civic election in Winnipeg, in which leaders of the Board of Trade were accused by a Winnipeg newspaper of nominating their "clerks" for local office. This criticism was something of an overstatement (the board's mayoralty nominee was a law partner of the CPR's legal counsel in the West); yet, it was also appropriate since the council of "clerks" proceeded to implement to the letter the anti-labour policy of economic retrenchment that their more prestigious backers had advocated.[130] A study of the Winnipeg elections at the end of the reform period revealed a similar pattern. The fifty-six member executive of the Citizens' League which sponsored a majority of successful candidates in the 1919 election was made up almost entirely of leading business and professional men who resided in the more exclusive sections of the city.[131] As the noted critic of liberalism, Ralph Milibrand, states,

> members of the upper classes do not necessarily or even very often take a direct part in local and state government. But this does not mean that they do not form a crucial reference point for those who do run these units of government. In the light of the real economic power which business enjoys, and of the prevailing culture which legitimizes this power, the question

whether top executives or middle ones actually run for election and serve in state and local government appears grotesquely irrelevant.[132]

The impact of reform on the lives of urban residents cannot, however, be assessed adequately unless the role of non-elites in the movement is examined. Current research concentrates almost exclusively on the prominent business elements that led campaigns for local government reform in the West. Yet workers and the non-English-speaking immigrants were lukewarm or actively opposed to reform. Future research might well focus on the role of organized labour and Eastern European immigrants in reform campaigns. Labour was more militant in western than in central Canada, at least until 1920, and local trades councils were active participants in civic politics. In the West, too, labour was led by British immigrants who brought with them a tradition of civic involvement associated with the British Labour Party and the Fabian socialists. Moreover, the reform movement coincided with the great influx of European immigrants into the region. Since there is reason to believe that reform in the West was in part a response to the perceived threat posed by these newcomers, the role of immigrants in reform should be of more than passing interest.

CONCLUSION

The movement for municipal government reform between 1880 and 1920 coincided with the rise of important urban centres on the prairies. Western cities eagerly adopted the most up-to-date reform structures. The ideology of municipal reform was readily accepted by the disciples of the philosophy of rapid urban growth who formed the business and governmental elite of these centres. The central question for students of the reform movement (the class of reform) is, therefore, most fruitfully examined in the context of urban development in the prairie region. The research which has been published to date on municipal reform in the West had tended to confirm the view that the core features of reform had the effect of making it much more difficult for working-class elements of the population to elect representatives to civic government. It also indicates that reform measures made city government less responsive to the needs of the lower-status urban groups who were segregated into distinct areas of prairie cities.

Similar to other social movements, the crusade for municipal government reform was directed *against* something. Chiefly, it was motivated by a desire to remove the amateur from civic government. The petty politician, the saloon keeper, the self-conscious representative of an ethnic bloc, or the nominee of organized labour was seen by the urban elite that spearheaded the drive for structural reform as the chief obstacle to civic progress. Progress, in turn, was defined by reformers almost exclusively in terms of the role of municipal corporation in supporting the aims of business. This class bias is most clearly evident in the campaign for local governmental or structural reform. Too often, researchers have confused the goals of the structural reformers with those of reformers like J. S. Woodsworth whose primary goals were the social and humanitarian reform of the city. Local government reform is perhaps of greater significance because it structured the role of the municipal corporation in the local political economy.

Finally, the reform legacy is still clearly evident in the West today. The recent history of Alberta cities, for example, proves that both the structures and the ideology of the movement for municipal government reform have had an important influence on civic decision-making ever since. The reform structures have persisted with little or no alteration. Both Calgary and Edmonton, for instance, retain the council board of appointed commissioners, a system which was pioneered in Edmonton in 1904. In Edmonton, the four members of the appointed commission board are full-time employees, earning approximately forty thousand dollars per year while the twelve members of council spend only part of their time on civic matters and earn twelve thousand dollars each. The relative power of the elected and appointed arm of this "reform" administration can be inferred from this comparison. Similarly, the ward system, which was abolished in Calgary and Edmonton in the early years of the century, was not reinstated until the 1960s, and even then the large wards that were adopted did little to improve representation of lower-income groups. For example, in the 1971 Edmonton election based on four large strip wards, two-thirds of the aldermen who were elected came from the higher-income south side of the city which contained only one-third of the city's population.[133]

The ideology of reform is still a potent force in present-day civic politics as well. A recent sample of Edmonton voters revealed, for example, that only 13 per cent favoured party politics in civic elections. A province-wide opinion survey taken in 1971 also indicated that only 25 per cent favoured the involvement of "party-type organizations" in local elections.[134] The class character of the reform ideology can also be clearly detected in municipal election campaigns. An observer of a recent Edmonton election noted that business experience was the most advertised virtue of successful candidates.[135] The reform belief that "local government is business" was more provocatively stated by the present mayor of Edmonton who denounced his potential rival for the chief magistrates position in these words:

But he has had no business experience. He's been a school teacher, I've worked in business all my life, and we're running a business.[136]

NOTES

1. S. Morley Wickett, "City Government by Commission", Canadian Club of Hamilton, *Addresses* (Toronto, 1912), p. 3.

2. Paul Voisey, "The Urbanization of the Canadian Prairies, 1871-1916", *Histoire sociale /Social History*, vol. 8 (1975): 84, 91.

3. S. Morley Wickett, "Present Conditions", in S. M. Wickett, ed., *Municipal Government in Canada*, University of Toronto: Studies. History and Economics, vol. II (Toronto, 1907), p. 149.

4. J. H. Laughton, "Chambers of Commerce and City Government", *Municipal World*, vol. 29, no. 12, (1919): 176.

5. Lionel G. Orlikow, "A Survey of the Reform Movement in Manitoba, 1910-1920", MA thesis, University of Manitoba (1955), pp. 85-86. See also A. Ross McCormack, "The Origin and Extent of Western Labour Radicalism: 1896-1919", PHD thesis, University of Western Ontario (1973), p. 256.

6. Frank Underhill, *In Search of Canadian Liberalism* (Toronto, 1960), p. 197.

7. For example, troops were used against strikers in Winnipeg in 1906. The state was not prepared to tolerate militant action by unions. See W. L. Morton, *Manitoba: A History* (Toronto, 1955), pp. 304-05.

8. A. H. Sinclair, "Municipal Monopolies and their Management", in Paul Rutherford, ed., *Saving the Canadian City: The First Phase, 1880-1920* (Toronto, 1974), pp. 35-36.

9. "Municipal Ownership in Calgary, Alberta", *Canadian Municipal Journal*, vol. 7 (1911): 95.

10. Quoted in Alan F. J. Artibise, *Winnipeg: A Social History of Urban Growth, 1874-1914* (Montreal, 1975), pp. 99-100.

11. Alderman Wilfrid Gariepy, "A Daring Experiment in City Government", *Municipal World*, vol. 20, no. 11 (1910): 289. See also William Short, "Municipal Government by Commission", *Canadian Municipal Journal*, vol. 3 (1907): 143-46.

12. S. Morley Wickett, "City Government in Canada", in Wickett, ed., *Municipal Government in Canada*, p. 10.

13. By 1889, manhood suffrage applied to all federal and provincial elections in the provinces and territories in the West and Ontario. See W. L. Morton, "The Extension of the Franchise in Canada: A Study of Democratic Nationalism", Canadian Historical Association, *Annual Report* (1943), p. 78.

14. These concerns are clearly highlighted in the deliberations of the Edmonton Trades and Labour Council between 1905 and 1920. See the *Minutes of the Edmonton Trades and Labour Council*, Alberta Provincial Archives, Edmonton, for this period.

15. H. J. Dyos and Michael Wolff, "The Way We Live Now", in H. J. Dyos and Michael Wolff, eds., *The Victorian City*, 2 vols. (London, 1973), II, pp. 893-94.

16. Paul Rutherford, "Introduction", in Rutherford, ed., *Saving the Canadian City*, p. xiii.

17. Ibid. A number of students of municipal reform distinguish governmental reform as a separate

aspect of the movement. See, for example, John C. Weaver, "Elitism and the Corporate Ideal: Businessmen and Boosters in Canadian Civic Reform, 1880-1920", in A. R. McCormack and Ian MacPherson, eds., *Cities in the West: Papers of the Western Canada Urban History Conference held at the University of Winnipeg, October 1974* (Ottawa, 1975), pp. 48-73.

18. John C. Weaver, "Framing an Executive: The Western Cities, 1904-1912" (Kingston, Ont.: Institute of Local Government, Queen's University, n.d.). Some prominent advocates of moral and humanitarian reform of the city were also involved in civic government reform, as in the case of businessman H. B. Ames of Montreal. His proposals with respect to local government reform, however, included a high property qualification for local office and a restricted franchise. See Michael Gauvin, "The Municipal Reform Movement in Montreal, 1886-1914", MA thesis, University of Ottawa (1972).

19. Each of these forms of civic administration can be described as follows: (a) the board of control consisted of an executive body of several controllers, usually elected at-large, with executive and administrative powers superior to those of the council; (b) the commission plan implied the elimination of the city council, which would be replaced by three to five commissioners elected at-large, each of whom would be responsible for a particular aspect of civic administration; (c) the board of commissioners scheme included a strengthened bureaucracy consisting of several appointed officials (with the mayor an *ex-officio* member) designed to take over all of the "administrative" duties, leaving council the power of legislation only; and (d) the manager plan was very similar to the board of commissioners, except that all administrative matters were to be handled by a single appointed

manager whose role was held to be analogous to that of a manager of a business corporation. The city council was to continue to perform the legislative function.

20. An American exception to this general pattern was the charter which set up an American-style commission form of local government in Lethbridge in 1913. The Lethbridge charter contained a clause expressly forbidding the printing of a political party label on the local ballot. See *Statutes of Alberta*, 1913, Chap. 22, Sec. 24. The wording of this clause was identical to the ballot restrictions in the charters of Spokane, Washington, and Grand Junction, Colorado. See Carl D. Thompson, "The Vital Points in Charter Making from a Socialist Point of View", *National Municipal Review*, vol. 2 (1913): 421.

21. For example, a leading municipal reformer, Samuel Morley Wickett, stated in 1902 that "Municipal administration is, after all mainly a technical task". See Wickett, "City Government in Canada", p. 22.

22. Businessman and civic reformer, Herbert Ames of the Volunteer Electoral League of Montreal, proudly announced the victory of one of the League's candidates over a corrupt ward politician in 1892. The reform candidate was chosen because he was "a businessman of recognized ability and sterling integrity". Herbert B. Ames, "The 'Machine' in Honest Hands", in Rutherford, ed., *Saving the Canadian City*, p. 308.

23. See, for example, C. J. Yorath, "Municipal Finance and Administration", Commission of Conservation, *Report of the Conference on Urban and Rural Development in Canada*, Winnipeg, (May 28-30, 1917), p. 32.

24. H. H. Gaetz, "Municipal Legislation", *Western Municipal News*, vol. 4 (1909): 1078-81; Ontario, Commission on Municipal Institutions, *First Report*, 1888, p. 31; James Bryce, *The American Commonwealth*, 2 vols. (new ed., London, 1928), I, p. 651.

25. In Canada many cities had blue ribbon "citizens' committees" which functioned as quasi-parties in recruiting, endorsing, and financing civic candidates who were then expected to represent the "citizens'" class interests.

26. S. M. Wickett, "Municipal Government of Toronto," in Wickett, ed., *Municipal Government in Canada*, p. 38.

27. In 1893 the Montreal Volunteer Electoral League, of which reformer Herbert Ames was president, obtained an amendment to Quebec's civic electoral laws which "provided for the disfranchisement of mere boarders and lodgers". Ames, "The Machine in Honest Hands", p. 309.

28. Gariepy, "Daring Experiment in City Government", p. 291.

29. City of Edmonton, *Voters' List*, 1914.

30. Earl G. Drake, *Regina: The Queen City* (Toronto, 1955), p. 122.

31. Wickett, "Present Conditions", pp. 166-67.

32. *Calgary Herald*, August 5, 1887, cited by Max Foran, "The Calgary Town Council, 1884 – 1895: A Study of Local Government in a Frontier Environment", MA thesis, University of Calgary (1970), p. 45.

33. Henry Huber, "Winnipeg's Age of Plutocracy, 1901-1914", research paper, History Department, University of Manitoba (1971), p. 30.

34. R. Stanley Weir, "Some Notes on the Charters of Montreal and Related Statutes", in Wickett, ed., *Municipal Government in Canada*, p. 295.

35. Artibise, *Winnipeg*, p. 40.

36. Wickett, "City Government in Canada", p. 22.

37. J. S. Woodsworth, *My Neighbor* (new ed., Toronto, 1972), p. 116.

38. Foran, "The Calgary Town Council", p. 44.

39. *Statutes of Alberta*, 1906, Chap. 63.

40. Foran, "The Calgary Town Council", p. 46.

41. Huber, "Winnipeg's Age of Plutocracy", p. 32.

42. See *Statutes of Alberta*, 1913, Chap. 22; Mayor W. D. L. Hardie, "Straight Commission Government", *Canadian Municipal Journal*, vol. 12 (1916): 545-47.

43. "Municipal Affairs in Alberta", *Canadian Municipal Journal*, vol. 10 (1914): 475.

44. *Statutes of Alberta*, 1916, Chap. 33.

45. Ibid., 1913, Chap. 22.

46. See, for example, *Minutes of the Edmonton Trades and Labour Council, 1905-1920.*.

47. J. G. Joyce and H. A. Hosse, *Civic Parties in Canada* (Toronto: Canadian Federation of Mayors and Municipalities, 1970), p. 15.

48. The class bias of municipal government reform in Canada and the United States appears to have been similar, however. On this point, see Samuel P. Hayes, "The Politics of Reform in Municipal Government in the Progressive Era", *Pacific Northwest Quarterly*, vol. 55 (1964): 157-69.

49. C. W. Biggar, "Some Notes on the Growth of Municipal Institutions of Ontario", *Canadian Law Journal*, vol. 33 (1897): 18.

50. Kenneth Grant Crawford, *Canadian Municipal Government* (Toronto, 1954), pp. 19-20.

51. Quoted by J. G. MacGregor, *Edmonton: A History* (Edmonton, 1967), p. 130. For an example of the pressure from prairie settlers for the Ontario Municipal form, see Jane McCracken, "Yorkton during the Territorial Period, 1882-1905", *Saskatchewan History*, vol. 28 (1975): 105-06. J. E. Rea has adapted a useful theoretical perspective to the early development of the west as a "fragment" of Ontario political culture. See his article, "The Roots of Prairie Society", in David P. Gagan, ed., *Prairie Perspectives* (Toronto, 1970), pp. 46-55.

52. Wickett, "City Government in Canada", p. 7.

53. Huber, "Winnipeg's Age of Plutocracy", p. 39.

54. Artibise, *Winnipeg*, pp. 18, 56.

55. The features of the Edmonton city charter outlined in this paragraph are enthusiastically explained by Gariepy in "A Daring Experiment in City Government". Edmonton continued to set the pace in urban reforms in such areas as the adoption of the single tax: i.e., taxation based

on land values with no tax on
improvements (buildings). The fame
of its charter extended far beyond
Canada, as an article in an American
journal attests. See Fred Bates
Johnson, "A City that Taxes Things
as they are", *World's Work* (August
1910): 13292 – 13294. The editor of
the *Canadian Municipal Journal*,
Harry Bragg, noted in 1913 that
Edmonton had for some time been
well known for its "up-to-date"
legislation because it had adopted at-
large elections, the single tax, and
the (appointed) commission board
form of administration. See "City
Government League of Edmonton,
Alta.", *Canadian Municipal Journal*,
vol. 9 (1913): 443.

56. Ajax, "Some Big Municipal Men:
Mayor Hardie of Lethbridge",
Canadian Municipal Journal, vol. 12
(1916): 54.

57. *Western Municipal News*, vol. 4
(1909): 1105. For a more detailed
account of the American influence
on municipal reform in Canada, see
James D. Anderson, "Nonpartisan
Urban Politics in Canadian Cities",
in Jack K. Masson and James D.
Anderson, eds., *Emerging Party
Politics in Urban Canada* (Toronto,
1972), pp. 5-21.

58. See Gregory S. Kealey and Peter
Warrian, "Introduction", in Gregory
S. Kealey and Peter Warrian, eds.,
Essays in Working Class History
(Toronto, 1976), pp. 9-10.

59. For example, the Citizens' League of
Winnipeg and the Non-partisan
Association of Vancouver are local
coalitions of political party activists.
The former originated at the end of
the reform era.

60. David Spector, "The 1884 Financial
Scandals and the Establishment of
Business Government in Winnipeg",
Prairie Forum, vol. 2, no. 2
(November 1977): 167-78.

61. *Western Municipal News*, vol. 11
(1916): 35.

62. J. M. S. Careless, "Aspects of Urban
Life in the West, 1870-1914", in G.
A. Stelter and A. F. J. Artibise, eds.,
*The Canadian City: Essays in Urban
History* (Toronto, 1977), pp. 125 – 41.

63. Murray S. Donnelly, "Ethnic
Participation in Municipal
Government: Winnipeg, St. Boniface
and the Metropolitan Corporation of
Greater Winnipeg", *Report of the
Royal Commission on Bilingualism
and Biculturalism* (Ottawa, 1965), pp.
21-22.

64. Artibise, *Winnipeg*, pp. 26-27.

65. The latter sentiment was expressed
by Thomas Sharpe, the mayor of
Winnipeg, as one of the arguments
for adopting the board of control
form of government. See Weaver,
"Framing an Executive", p. 4.

66. Mayor Bligh of Halifax and Mayor
Graham of London Ont. quoted in
Canadian Municipal Journal, vol. 9
(1913): 404.

67. The substantial financing provided
by the anti-labour Citizens'
Committee of Winnipeg is a case in
point. See Paul Barber, "Class
Conflict in Winnipeg Civic Politics:
The Role of the Citizens' and Civic
Election Organizations", research
paper, History Department,
University of Manitoba (March,
1970).

68. Crawford, *Canadian Municipal
Government*, pp. 84-85.

69. See, for example, *Minutes of the
Edmonton Trades and Labour
Council*, October 21, 1907,
November 6, 1916.

70. In Winnipeg, however, lower-status
populations were more concentrated
in distinct districts than in
Edmonton. Organized labour was
also a stronger force in Winnipeg
than in Edmonton.

71. Jean Morrison, "Community in
Conflict: A Study of the Working
Class and its Relationships at the
Canadian Lakehead, 1903-1913", MA
thesis, Lakehead University (1974).

72. Gaetz, "Municipal Legislation", p.
1080.

73. Ontario Commission on Municipal
Institutions, *First Report* (1888), p.
31.

74. Michael Bliss, *A Living Profit:
Studies in the Social History of
Canadian Business, 1883-1911*
(Toronto, 1974), p. 127.

75. *Calgary Herald*, December 15, 1914.

76. Commissioner A. T. Stephanson, "Red Deer's System of Government by Commission", *Western Municipal News*, vol. 6 (1911): 15-16.

77. See John C. Weaver, "The Modern City Realized", Chapter 2.

78. *Calgary Herald*, December 9, 1913.

79. Most studies of the implications of local non-partisanship focus on Canadian cities during the last decade. See, for example, Masson and Anderson, eds., *Emerging Party Politics*.

80. Crawford, *Canadian Municipal Government*, pp. 55, 57; Harold Kaplan, *The Regional City* (Toronto, 1965), p. 30.

81. Gauvin, "The Municipal Reform Movement in Montreal".

82. Dennis Carter-Edwards, "Toronto in the 1890s: A Decade of Challenge and Response", MA thesis, University of British Columbia (1973). See also, Spector, "The 1884 Financial Scandals".

83. Grant MacEwan, *Calgary Cavalcade: From Fort to Fortune* (Edmonton: The Institute of Applied Arts, 1958), pp. 123-27.

84. Woodsworth, *My Neighbor*, p. 127.

85. See John McEvoy, *The Ontario Township*, University of Toronto Studies in Political Science, No. 1 (1899), p. 30; and F. H. Armstrong, "William Lyon Mackenzie, First Mayor of Toronto: A Study of a Critic in Power", *Canadian Historical Review*, vol. 48 (1967): 309-31.

86. *Alberta Non-Partisan*, vol. 3, no. 12, p. 9. Cited by A. M. Mardiros, *Biography of William Irvine* (forthcoming). I am grateful to Tony Mardiros of the Philosophy Department, University of Alberta, for allowing me to read his manuscript.

87. Mardiros, *Biography of William Irvine*.

88. In a letter, the Calgary Labour Representation League urged the Edmonton Trades and Labour Council to form a labour party in Edmonton. The Edmonton Labour Representation League was founded after the TLC in Edmonton had discussed "the platform and

principles" of the Calgary League. *Minutes of the Edmonton Trades and Labour Council*, January 3, April 16, May 7, and June 4, 1917.

89. William Askin, "Labour Unrest in Edmonton and District and its Coverage by the Edmonton Press, 1918-1919", MA thesis, University of Alberta (1973), p. 39.

90. W. J. C. Cherwinski, "Organized Labour in Saskatchewan: The TLC Years, 1905 – 1945", PHD thesis, University of Alberta, Edmonton (1971), pp. 225-56.

91. Paul Barber, "Class Conflict in Winnipeg Civic Politics: The Role of the Citizens' and Civic Election Organizations", honours essay, University of Manitoba, Winnipeg (1970).

92. William Short, "Municipal Government by Commission", *The Canadian Municipal Journal*, vol. 3 (1907): 144.

93. The phrase is used by Evelyn Eager, "The Conservatism of the Saskatchewan Electorate", in Norman Ward and Duff Spafford, eds., *Politics in Saskatchewan* (Don Mills, Ont., 1968), p. 4.

94. Paul Phillips, "'Power Politics': Municipal Affairs and Seymour James Farmer, 1909-1924", in McCormack and MacPherson, eds., *Cities in the West*, pp. 159-80.

95. Bracken gave as one of his chief qualifications for the post of Conservative leader his ability to check the growth of the CCF. See Lloyd Stinson, *Political Warriors: Recollections of a Social Democrat* (Winnipeg, 1975), p. 100.

96. Askin, "Labour Unrest in Edmonton", p. 58.

97. *Calgary Herald*, December 6 and December 9, 1913.

98. Artibise, *Winnipeg*, p. 38.

99. Frank Underhill, "Commission Government in Cities", in Rutherford, ed., *Saving the Canadian City*, p. 132.

100. *Western Municipal News*, vol. 12 (1917): 285.

101. *Calgary Herald*, October 15, 1914.

102. See, for example, J. O. Miller, "The Better Government of our Cities", in

Rutherford, ed., *Saving the Canadian City*, p. 352.

103. S. Morley Wickett, "A Toronto Viewpoint", *Papers and Proceedings of the First Annual Meeting of the Canadian Political Science Association* (Ottawa, September 4-6, 1913), p. 136.

104. H. L. Brittain, "Municipal Finance and Administration", in Commission of Conservation, *Conference on Urban and Rural Development*, p. 20.

105. Paul Rutherford, "Tomorrow's Metropolis: The Urban Reform Movement in Canada, 1880 – 1920", Canadian Historical Association, *Historical Papers* (1971), pp. 203-24. See also Rutherford, ed., *Saving the Canadian City*.

106. Terry Copp, *Anatomy of Poverty: The Condition of the Working Class in Montreal, 1897 – 1929* (Toronto, 1974), p. 147.

107. Spector, "The 1884 Financial Scandal".

108. The remarkable success of real estate interests in obtaining the extension of street railway and other municipal services to their far-flung property holdings is analysed by several writers. See John C. Weaver, "'Tomorrow's Metropolis' Revisited: A Critical Assessment of Urban Reform in Canada, 1890-1920", in Stelter and Artibise, *The Canadian City: Essays in Urban History*, pp. 393-418; Alan F. J. Artibise, "Boosterism and the Development of Prairie Cities: 1871-1913", Paper delivered at the Canadian Urban History Conference, University of Guelph (May 1977); and Edmund H. Dale, "The Role of Successive Town and City Councils in the Evolution of Edmonton Alberta", PHD thesis, University of Alberta (1969).

109. James Weinstein, "Organized Business and the City Commission and Manager Movements," *Journal of Southern History*, vol. 28 (1962): 178.

110. *Minutes of the Edmonton Trades and Labour Council*, November 4, 1907.

111. Donnelly, "Ethnic Participation in Municipal Government", pp. 50-51.

112. Theodore A. Hunt, "How Municipalities should Deal with Corporations", *Western Municipal News*, vol. 5 (1910): 12.

113. *Western Municipal News*, vol. 1 (1906): 198.

114. *Canadian Municipal Journal*, vol. 8 (1912): 315.

115. Statutes of Alberta, 1906, Chap. 55. For a number of other bonuses granted by Calgary city council, see Max Foran, "Early Calgary 1875 – 1895: The Controversy Surrounding the Townsite Location and the Direction of Towns in the Expansion", in McCormack and MacPherson, eds., *Cities in the West*, pp. 38-39.

116. "Calgary, Alberta", *Canadian Municipal Journal*, vol. 8 (1911): 341.

117. *Statutes of Alberta*, 1906, Chap. 24.

118. Ibid., 1908, Chap. 23.

119. Hunt, "How Municipalities Should Deal with Corporations", p. 11.

120. Dale, "The Role of Successive Town and City Councils", pp. 32-33.

121. *Statutes of Alberta*, 1914, Chap. 14.

122. Mayor F. G. Forster, "Development of Natural Resources under Municipal Ownership", *Canadian Municipal Journal*, vol. 2 (1906): 134. Forster noted that the yearly benefit to a single firm using his city's cheap gas was equivalent to a bonus of $2,500. Ibid., p. 135.

123. Cited in Weaver, "'Tomorrow's Metropolis' Revisited".

124. Ibid., pp. 14-15.

125. William Short, "Municipal Ownership in Edmonton", *The Western Municipal News*, vol. 9 (1914): 192.

126. Artibise, *Winnipeg*, p. 101.

127. W. D. Lighthall, "Annual Report to the Union of Canadian Municipalities", *Western Municipal News*, vol. 4 (1909): 1267.

128. H. V. Nelles and Christopher Armstrong, "The Great Fight for Clean Government", *Urban History Review*, no. 2 – 76 (1976): 50-66.

129. See, for example, Artibise, *Winnipeg*; and J. M. S. Careless, "The Development of the Winnipeg Business Community, 1870-1890",

Politics and Municipal Government 111

Transactions of the Royal Society of Canada, series 4 vol. 8 (1970): 239-54.

130. Spector, "The 1884 Financial Scandals".

131. This information first appears in Barber, "Class Conflict in Winnipeg Civic Politics", pp. 2-3. It then appears in J. E. Rea, "The Politics of Conscience: Winnipeg after the Strike", Canadian Historical Association, *Historical Papers* (1971), p. 278.

132. Ralph Miliband, *The State in Capitalist Society* (London, 1973), pp. 154-55.

133. *Edmonton Journal*, January 3, 1972.

134. Robert Gilsdorf, "The Popular Basis of Urban Political Institutions: 'Reformed' Institutions and Centralization in Edmonton", paper delivered at the Annual Meeting of the Canadian Political Science Association, Toronto (June 4, 1974), pp. 9-10; and Robert Gilsdorf, "Cognitive and Motivational Sources of Voter Susceptibility to Influence", *Canadian Journal of Political Science*, vol. 6 (1973): 626n. In the Edmonton survey, voters were asked if they favoured involvement of the three major parties in local politics. In the provincial survey, the question referred to "party-type organizations".

135. James Lightbody, "Edmonton Politics: Business as Usual", *Canadian Forum*, vol. 52 (1972): 8-9.

136. *Edmonton Journal*, November 22, 1976.

4.

Montreal's Municipal Government and the Crisis of the 1930s

TERRY COPP

The spring of 1940 is not likely to be remembered for the financial crisis that overcame the government in the city of Montreal. The invasion of France and the fall of the Chamberlain government occurred less than a week before the city was forced to default on the first of two bond issues which came due in May and June 1940. As the French army collapsed under the shock of the German offensive, Montreal passed under the control of the Quebec government's Municipal Commission. Camillien Houde and his City Council were relegated to an empty advisory role. The flamboyant mayor still had some months of freedom left before his internment for opposition to national registration, but his twelve-year struggle to dominate and shape the politics of his native city was over. Houde would return to the mayor's office with renewed popularity, but his role would henceforth be that of a figurehead, a rotund, comical "Mr. Montreal" symbolizing the élan of the city, but also symbolizing the end of the populist politics which Houde had stood for.

The humiliation of Camillien Houde and the takeover of his city were no doubt partly owing to political considerations. The volatile Houde had made enemies in all sectors of the highly partisan world of Quebec politics. But the new, deliberately undemocratic, form of government imposed on Montreal was a clear indication that Houde was correct when he charged that the Depression had ruined Montreal, and that now those who had tried to help the unemployed were to be replaced, "par les gens du Board of Trade, qui n'ont jamais aid qui n'ont offert que des critiques".[1]

In a strong speech to the Quebec legislature, Houde reviewed his efforts to stave off bankruptcy. He defended the quality of municipal administration, pointed to the new tax measures he had introduced, recalled the representations he had made to senior levels of government, and told his silent audience: "If we had followed the advice of the bankers and economists, we would have had to leave the unemployed to die of starvation."[2]

Houde's speech won him renewed respect but no concessions. City Council would henceforth consist of ninety-nine members, one-third elected by property owners (only one in ten Montrealers owned their own home), one-third by all electors, with a final one-third appointed by various organizations. Council would appoint an executive committee, but the popularly elected mayor would not be eligible to sit on this all-powerful body.[3] The city was to be made safe for the bond holders.

The story behind the events of May 1940 is bound up in both the history of the city and in the particular circumstances of the Great Depression. The collapse of municipal credit, the dramatic career of Camillien Houde, and the "corporatist" city charter of 1940 are incidents which serve as illustrations of structural problems in the evolution of Canada's metropolis, problems which reached crisis proportions during the 1930s. It would be foolish to suggest that all of these problems were unique to Montreal. Even a casual reading of the briefs presented to the Royal Commission on Dominion-Provincial Relations by various Canadian municipalities is enough to demonstrate that Montreal's agonizing struggle to maintain a minimal relief system during the 1930s was but a variation of the problems of other Canadian cities. A number of western cities had been forced to default well before Montreal was pushed to the wall. A detailed account of Montreal's story gives a valuable specificity and detail to an important problem in Canadian urban history and Quebec political history.

Montreal, similar to all Canadian cities, was a creature of its provincial government. The city's charter granted the popularly elected municipal council the power to raise revenue from a property tax, a business establishments tax, municipal licences, and from an occupant's levy known locally as a "water tax". The levels of such taxation were controlled by the provincial legislature and were subject to occasional re-adjustment when the "Montreal Bill" received its annual review by the Quebec Legislative Assembly and Council. Montreal also possessed the authority to borrow up to 15 per cent of its assessed valuation, a privilege denied to many other Quebec municipalities.[4]

During the 1920s Montreal's ordinary revenues increased by 20 per cent on a per-capita basis, but this increase was grossly inadequate in view of the need for long-overdue improvements in many municipal services. In 1926 Montreal's ordinary expenditure amounted to $39.60 per person in comparison to Toronto's outlay of $54.50. The vital field of public health received one-seventh of the allotment available in

Toronto. Much attention was focused on the public health question after 1926, and expenditures in this area gradually rose to levels comparable to Toronto.[5]

Increasing revenues were quickly swallowed up by these and other improvements, but no additional money was made available to deal with the massive municipal debt which the city had accumulated during its hectic three decades of growth. By 1929 the city's net funded debt amounted to 185.2 million dollars, or $238 per capita.[6] Montreal had become accustomed to solving its revenue shortages by extensive borrowing.

The provincial government, by contrast, pursued an extremely conservative fiscal policy, maintaining the lowest per-capita expenditures of any province and the second lowest per-capita debt. Representation in the provincial legislature was of course heavily weighted towards rural areas and Montreal's needs were usually accorded a very low priority.

The quality of Montreal's municipal administration had long been under attack from business organizations and self-styled reform groups. Local politicians were equally enthusiastic in levying charges of maladministration at their opponents. There was no doubt a good deal of corruption in municipal politics; the normal lubrication of big city government, patronage, kickbacks, bribes, were generally believed to be commonplace and some of the charges may have been true. However, the fundamental difficulty confronting civic administration in Montreal was an inadequate tax base, not corruption at City Hall.

This problem was compounded by the existence of a number of autonomous municipalities within and around the city, each of which used the urban area without liability for costs incurred by Montreal. All of these suburban cities, including the predominantly working-class towns such as Verdun, Lachine, and Montreal East, were in relatively sound financial shape in the 1920s, and were far better able to cope with the financial pressures encountered during the 1930s.[7] The desirability of a genuine system of metropolitan area government seems obvious, but there was in fact strong resistance from virtually all quarters to any expansion of the Montreal Metropolitan Commission's authority. Not only the suburban proponents of local autonomy but the Montreal politicians were opposed to metropolitan government which they associated with business and professional "good government" forces.

The relative prosperity of the late 1920s masked structural problems both in municipal finances and in the basic economy of the Montreal region. The city had tripled in size during the first thirty years of the century but its economy had experienced growth rather than modernization. The traditional mercantile functions of the city were as always dependent on servicing the growth centres of the Ontario and western Canadian economy. If such growth faltered, the harbour, the banks, the railways, and the other components of Montreal's metropolitanism would be highly vulnerable. The secondary manufacturing sector, which accounted for one job in four, was in many ways less diversified than it had been in the late nineteenth century. Almost all the new highly technical industries of the early twentieth century had bypassed the city. Instead of automobiles, agricultural implements, machine tools, steel, and electrical apparatus, the city continued to depend on food processing, textiles, the needle trades, and other low-wage, labour-intensive activities. Montreal had long been a magnet, selectively attracting a large pool of unskilled labour, the group most vulnerable in periods of economic contraction.[8] The impact of the Great Depression was felt immediately in Montreal. By June 1, 1931, 20 per cent of the male labour force and 10 per cent of the female labour force were without work. During the winter of 1931-32 more than one hundred thousand Montrealers were on relief.[9]

Montreal's civic administration was in the hands of the remarkable Camillien Houde in 1930. Houde had been elected mayor in 1928, but during his first term City Council was firmly controlled by Alderman A. A. Desroches, representing Hochelaga, who was also Chairman of the city's Executive Council. Houde organized a slate of candidates for the 1930 election and conducted a vigorous campaign against the "Desroches Clique" levying the standard charges of maladministration and scandalous conduct. Houde's own program consisted of routine promises to improve public health, lower transit fares, and reduce utility rates. No particular attention was paid to the high unemployment levels of the winter season, which were not responding to the normal corrective, the arrival of spring. Houde and his slate swept all before them, capturing control of City Council. Houde received a majority of 40,847 votes, the largest in the city's history.[10]

The main thrust of federal, provincial, and municipal unemployment relief during 1930 and 1931 was towards public works projects, though provision was made for minor amounts of direct assistance. Montreal borrowed over twenty million dollars at the very high rate of 6 per cent, to pay its share of expenditure on relief projects during the two years.[11] Houde and his associates spent public works money with a fine disregard for administrative niceties such as adequate accounting practices.[12] Work projects were oriented towards maximizing employment, and by 1932 Houde claimed that eighteen thousand additional workers, "the majority taken from the ranks of the unemployed",[13] were at work on public works initiated by the city.

The federal Unemployment Relief Acts had made provisions for small amounts of direct relief in 1930 and 1931. In Montreal such assistance was channelled through the traditional private denominational organizations which distributed funds according to their own procedures. The St. Vincent de Paul Society maintained its responsibility for the French Catholic community, 60 per cent of the population, and by the end of 1932 it was providing support for an average of 34,000 families a month, mainly the same families in each month. The Society was dispensing close to one million dollars each month, and more than three thousand volunteers were spending their evenings trying to maintain the policies outlined in the *Manuel du visiteurs du pauvre*.[14] The *visiteurs* were supposed to try and tailor their assistance to family needs and apparently did so. *Bons* or vouchers, redeemable at local stores, were issued. Other *bons* for rent, fuel, clothing, and even school books were provided. The Society continued to visit the sick, provide counselling, help families find new accommodation, and run interference between the needy and their creditors.

Within the Protestant community, direct relief to the able-bodied unemployed was provided by the Emergency Unemployment Relief Committee, an organization established in the winter of 1924 to cope with seasonal unemployment. This Committee worked in conjunction with the Protestant Employment Bureau and relief was available so long as the head of the family reported to the Bureau every second day and had his card signed weekly by his local church minister. By 1933 between four and five thousand families were receiving rent assistance, a fuel allotment and a weekly ration as follows:

9 lbs. stewing beef	2 lbs. sugar
¾ lb. salt pork	½ lb. cheese
20 lbs. potatoes	2½ lbs. beans
4 lbs. carrots and onions	2 lbs. prunes
4 lbs. rolled oats	1 lb. peanut butter
2 lbs. rice	2 lbs. Lassie's syrup
3 bars Lennox soap	

This ration was supplemented by bread and milk to a maximum of two loaves and two quarts a day.[15]

English-speaking Catholics without work were the responsibility of agencies operated by the Federation of Catholic Charities, and more than two thousand families were registered with the Federation. A further one thousand families received assistance through the Baron de Hirsch Institute during a normal week in 1933, bringing the total number of families on relief to around forty-two thousand. This estimate does not include single men and women living outside family units, but it does include an unknown number of families for whom unemployment and dependency were old problems which predated the Depression. It would be reasonable to suggest that the number of Montrealers living on relief of one form or another reached the two hundred thousand mark during the winter of 1932-33. When the civic authorities took over relief administration in August 1933, there were some sixty thousand names on the various relief rolls and an estimated 205,000 persons dependent on direct assistance.[16] These figures apply to the city of Montreal proper and not the metropolitan area, and, therefore, represent just less than one-quarter of the 874,000 residents of Montreal. The winter of 1933-34 was the worst period of the Depression, with the total of municipal relief dependents reaching 250,000, 28 per cent of the population.

A survey of the occupational background of relief recipients prepared in the winter of 1932-33 indicates that the hourly wage earners bore a disproportionate burden of unemployment. Professionals accounted for just 2.6 per cent of the total, and other white-collar workers 10.1 per cent. The remaining 87.3 per cent was made up of wage earners.[17] (Blue-collar workers accounted for approximately two-thirds of the 224,000 males in the Montreal labour force.) In late 1933, then, one in every four males in the labour force was on relief, but the number of male *wage earners* on the dole was one in three. These figures also suggest that French-speaking Montrealers, heavily over-represented in the unskilled and semi-skilled occupations, bore a disproportionate share of unemployment and were much more dependent on relief than the English-speaking population.[18]

Between 1933 and 1939 the number of heads of families on relief never fell below thirty-three thousand. The "best" year, 1936, saw a monthly average of 114,988 heads of families, dependents, and single individuals on the dole. When the Department of Municipal Assistance discontinued the relief in 1940, there were still ten thousand families receiving aid.[19]

The distribution of government funds by private agencies came under vigorous attack in 1932. Local merchants frequently found that *bons* or other vouchers could not be quickly cashed and joined the chorus of criticism. The private agencies lacked the administrative facilities to "control" expenditure and were lumped together with the Houde administration as having engaged in "maladministration and ruinous extravagance".[20]

The municipal election of 1932 was fought essentially on this issue. Fernand Rinfret, a former minister in Mackenzie King's government, ran for mayor on a platform of financial reform. The goal, Rinfret said, was "the establishment of a new financial stability at City Hall". One of the first duties of a new administration would be "to restore the confidence of the bankers and financiers in the financial solidarity of the metropolis".[21] Taxes could not be raised, so strict economy must be enforced.

Rinfret's success in the 1932 election seems surprising in view of the efforts of Houde to combat unemployment. Perhaps the vote reflects the too-often ignored reality that the large majority of the population held on to their jobs during the 1930s and thus retained their notions of unemployment as a personal failing, an individual responsibility. Certainly Houde's vote dropped dramatically in most parts of the city. Even his home ward, Ste. Marie, was won by Rinfret.[22] Other explanations are equally possible, however, and only a very detailed study of the election would produce a more informed estimate.

Rinfret's election coincided with a general decline in government support for public works expenditures as the major form of depression relief. Direct assistance, the dole, became the favoured mechanism for dealing with unemployment. By 1933 more systematic methods of administering direct assistance were developing in most Canadian cities as officials attempted to bring expenditures under control.

Nowhere did the need for better administrative control of relief seem more serious than in Montreal. Dominion government officials were appalled by the casual accounting methods of the city's private agencies. One inspector dispatched by Ottawa to find out how the St. Vincent de Paul Society was operating reported that "although they handle a half a million dollars a month and maybe more, they have no office and no bookkeeping system".[23] The Society flatly refused to co-operate with the enquiry, to the point of rejecting a request to supply the government with the names of the presidents of the various parish councils. The inspector noted that the Society's director "could not describe the system in detail, but added some were receiving *bons*, others cash, and others goods".[24] The charitable practices of the Society were simply no business of the government.

The other Montreal agencies were more co-operative with Dominion government inspectors, but their information simply reinforced the picture of administrative chaos. No one seriously suggested that the private agencies were corrupt, but they did appear to be "extravagant" and, even worse, unsystematic. In February 1933, the St. Vincent de Paul Society forestalled further government interference by announcing that it would no longer handle unemployment relief. City Council moved to appoint a Civic Unemployment Commission (the Terrault Commission), which took over all direct assistance to able-bodied unemployed in the spring of 1933. Private charity was left with the responsibility for the sick, the aged, infirm, crippled, and widows.

The Commission quickly lost credibility when it resorted to a system of using the secretaries of city aldermen as agents for job hiring on city projects. A scandal developed in July 1934 when it was alleged that Commission employees had accepted bribes to redeem the *bons* of certain large companies while smaller merchants were being told that funds were not available.[25] Terrault was forced to resign and a new Unemployment Relief Commission under Brigadier-General E. B. de Panet was appointed. Panet, a "dollar-a-year" man borrowed from the CPR, moved to introduce "modern business practices" into relief administration.[26]

Camillien Houde had swept back into power in April 1934 in the aftermath of the worst winter in the city's history, and Panet's appointment was the first concrete fulfillment of his campaign promise to bring the best available men to the aid of the beleaguered city.

With a quarter of the population on relief, Montreal was barely maintaining basic services. Relief cheques were not sent out in April because the federal government refused to forward further funds until errors and irregularities in Montreal's accounts were corrected. Many landlords had not been paid in months and hundreds of evictions were reported.[27] The city's streets had deteriorated and no money was available for repairs or street cleaning. Houde ran a low-key campaign, making few promises but reminding his audiences that when he was in office he was accused of "having spent too much money. But you ate. . . . You had your boots, your clothes and your landlords got their rent."[28]

The new Unemployment Relief Commission moved quickly to set up a highly organized relief system. By mid-1935 there were more than eight hundred full-time employees working at the central office and in twenty district bureaus. A force of one hundred inspectors ran constant checks to ensure that no one was violating the rules, and much stress was placed on the penalties that would be incurred for giving a false oath or defrauding the city. In the first year of the Commission's existence, 866 cases were pursued by the investigators and 691 of these were cut off from relief or had their allocations reduced. Since more than forty thousand cheques were being issued each week, the number of cases of "fraud" uncovered by the vast investigating force seems quite small.[29] However, as the Depression continued it became harder and harder to get onto the relief rolls in the first place, and the investigators were strongly criticized for their inflexible interpretation of the rules.

Two categories of "employable unemployeds" were recognized by the Commission. Unattached men and women could obtain an allowance of $1.80 per week plus $1.38 as a rent allowance. The allotment for a family of five consisted of the following:

	FOOD	FUEL (Summer)	FUEL (Winter)	CLOTHING	RENT	ELECTRICITY (Summer)	ELECTRICITY (Winter)
Weekly	$ 5.05	$0.75	$1.35	$0.75	–	–	–
Monthly	$21.88	$3.25	$5.85	$3.25	$10.50	$0.70	$0.90

Summer total $38.58
Winter total $41.38

Relief was paid by cheque with direct payments to landlords and the Montreal Light, Heat, and Power Company. A medical fund based on a city contribution of $0.25 per relief recipient was created and a panel of doctors recruited. The head of the household was allowed to earn up to three dollars per week without penalty and the wife and children could seek employment, providing 50 per cent of their earnings was contributed to the family.[31]

Unattached men who were eligible for municipal relief found themselves under enormous pressure to enroll in the Dominion government's relief camps. When General Panet took over from the Terrault Commission, there were 8,614 bachelors, widowers, and separated husbands on the city lists. In less than a year that number had been cut in half. As Panet explained it, conditions of life in the camps might not be ideal but they were "at any rate a great deal better than life in the city at $1.80 a week".[32] Perhaps Panet was right, but when the King government cancelled the program in 1936, life-long residents of Montreal found that they had lost their residency status and could not get back on to the municipal rolls.

The Commission also enforced strict residency requirements, insisting that only persons resident in Montreal on May 1, 1933, were eligible for relief. During the winter of 1935 – 36, *The Montreal Star* carried this account of the plight of "transient families":

Denied the dole because they arrived here after May 1st, 1933, at the mercy of charity which has not the funds to maintain them, between six and seven thousand families embracing twenty thousand souls are in a desperate plight and the city administration is baffled because at least five hundred thousand ($500,000) would be required for winter food, fuel and shelter and the aldermen hesitate to tax real estate owners further for the benefit of people who drift during the crisis. Most of the families are from rural Quebec and in their home towns or villages there is no dole because their local communities cannot support it, so they filtered to the Metropolis in the hope of finding work or getting on the dole rolls.[33]

At first City Council accepted the Commission's ruling, but in January 1936 the residence requirement was moved forward to May 1, 1934, thus adding additional thousands to the city's relief rolls.[34]

The system of public relief developed by the Panet Commission was roughly comparable to the schemes in existence in other large Canadian cities. Toronto had established a municipal Department of Public Welfare in 1931 when it became apparent that the need for public assistance was likely to be prolonged. Relief assistance rates were generally higher in Toronto than in other Canadian cities, but then the amount of unemployment in the city was much lower and its financial resources were enormously greater than any other large Canadian urban centre. Hamilton operated its relief through a Public Welfare Board composed of private citizens and city council members. Winnipeg's Unemployment Relief Committee was appointed by city council, but operated as a separate organization. Vancouver, like Toronto, organized a civic relief department. Rates for these three cities were comparable to rates in Montreal.[35]

During his 1934 campaign Houde had made a specific commitment to conciliate the financial community by appointing an advisory committee composed of prominent businessmen. Dubbed the "Brains Trust", this Committee found that its immediate task was to persuade the Banque Canadien Nationale and the Bank of Montreal to refinance six million dollars due from the city on June 15. This crisis was overcome but it was clear that unless something drastic was done the city would go into bankruptcy. A wide variety of schemes to raise revenue were under discussion in the fall of 1934, but in the end Premier Taschereau rejected new provincial tax measures, though he did promise to accept a new tax proposal for Montrealers if city council could agree on what was required.

The Montreal Bill considered by the Quebec legislature in February of 1935 was a very controversial document. There was some basic agreement that the city's projected current deficit of 8.2 million dollars could only be dealt with by tax increases, but there was no agreement on the nature of the new taxes. Houde floated a number of trial balloons, including a tax on bank clearances, which brought outraged protests and threats to move bank offices to Toronto.[36] Eleven more or less distinct drafts of the tax proposals were required before the bill was actually presented. The final version was a much more regressive tax package than earlier versions.[37] The income tax component was reduced in importance, the 2 per cent sales tax and the increases in "water taxes" (paid by occupants, not owners) were especially regressive. The business tax surcharge was quite moderate. Nevertheless, projected revenue figures indicated that Montreal would be able to balance its budget in 1935.

The strength of establishment opposition to the measures is somewhat surprising. Most of the press (French and English), the Board of Trade, the Retail Merchants' Association, the Chamber of Commerce, and, of course, Houde's political opponents, joined in a chorus of denunciation. In 1935 groups, such as the Board of Trade, argued that extravagance, high administrative costs, and outright corruption were responsible for the city's financial embarrassment. The Board of Trade, the Chamber of Commerce, and other business groups went so far as to declare, in a paid advertisement, that only 5 per cent of the municipal debt was due to relief expenditures.[38] The large newspapers echoed this charge.[39] The statements of the official spokesmen of the business community are severe. No fair attempt at evaluating the origins of municipal debt could possibly lend support to their view, and their opposition to Houde's tax proposals requires further examination.

When the Board of Trade presented a brief to the Rowell–Sirois Commission, its analysis of the city's financial plight was little different than Houde's; it was generally a constructive and thoughtful study of the problems of municipal finance.[40] Why then did business groups behave in a narrowly partisan fashion in the arena of civic politics? The cause was most probably the exclusion of the business elite, particularly the anglophone elite, from power in civic politics. Ever since Médéric Martin had broken the gentleman's agreement to alternate English- and French-speaking mayors in 1914, City Hall had become a potentially hostile, always foreign territory in the eyes of the anglophone-dominated business community. Houde, like Martin, described himself as a man of the people, a defender of the poor against the "interests", the east end against the western wards, the French against the English. Houde's populist rhetoric, his flamboyance, and his French-Canadian nationalism created further suspicion and fear. Houde's fascination with Italian fascism and his earlier links with anti-Semites such as Adrien Arcand raised additional barriers to a *rapprochement* between the Mayor and much of the anglophone community.

In 1934 – 35 Houde seems to have been determined to try to end the bitterness and polarization along ethnic lines which had characterized the city since the First World War. He was equally ready to develop friendly relations with Taschereau and his ministers in Quebec City. No doubt political opportunism played a large role in these manoeuvres, but Houde was also motivated by the plight of the unemployed and the need to broaden support for the unemployment relief program. Unfortunately, no real *rapprochement* developed.

The election of Maurice Duplessis as Premier of Quebec created new difficulties for the city of Montreal. Houde had deeply offended the man who succeeded him as leader of the Quebec Conservative party, and Duplessis would not rest easy until Houde's power base was broken.[41] Duplessis had declared his intention to abolish Montreal's sales tax during his provincial election campaign, and shortly after "Le Chef" was installed in office Houde announced his resignation as Mayor of Montreal, declaring that the hostility of the new government made his task impossible.[42]

In the municipal elections of December 1936 Houde ran a poorly organized and badly financed campaign. He was narrowly defeated by Adhémar Raynault, a prominent *nationaliste* and Duplessis supporter. Raynault had vowed to abolish the sales tax but his commitment, like Duplessis', was quickly forgotten. Duplessis and Raynault did take action designed to curb relief expenditures in Montreal, however. Relief eligiblity regulations were sharply tightened and one entire category of recipients were struck off the relief rolls: female heads of families with young children. The rationale for this decision was that such women were not employable. In addition, it was suggested that the needy would be taken care of under the provisions of the new Mother's Allowance Act passed by the legislature in March 1937. In fact, the first payments under the Act were not made until December 1938, and then only to mothers having two or more children.[43] The average monthly payment under the act was thirty dollars, a bitter joke indeed.[44]

Approximately three thousand women were declared ineligible for relief in the spring, including "females incapable of procuring work, those living in a state of concubinage, unmarried mothers, widows with young children, and women with husbands in jail".[45] A demonstration of seventy-five women at City Hall led to a temporary restoration of relief funds entirely at city expense, but after suggestions of Communist influence behind the demonstration and a commitment from Quebec to make such women eligible for assistance under the Quebec Public Charities Act, they were permanently removed from the rolls.[46]

Duplessis and Raynault were also determined to bring the Panet Commission under their control. A committee composed of four aldermen and three outsiders began an investigation of the Unemployment Relief Commission on the grounds that its administrative costs had risen to 5 per cent of the budget. Before his committee reported Duplessis ordered the provincial police to seize the records of the Commission. Panet, his fellow commissioners, and ten department heads were suspended because of "ruinous and intolerable abuses".[47] The Premier declared that Panet might be a friend of the autonomy of Montreal but that, as Attorney-General, he would not permit Panet to violate the autonomy of the province. The angry public response to this action caused Duplessis to retreat and the Commissioners were reinstated. However, three months later Mayor Raynault and his Executive Committee announced the abolition of the Commission and the transfer of its work to the Municipal Health Department. The Mayor claimed that this was done to cut administrative costs.[48] Direct relief costs did decline in 1937 and 1938, but as a result of the new regulations not lower administrative costs.

Houde was able to win back the mayor's office in the 1938 municipal elections, but he did not devote his major energies to combatting Duplessis' depression relief policies. Shortly after his defeat in 1936, Houde had contested a federal by-election in Montreal – St. Henri, a working-class area which had long been one of his strongholds. Houde's campaign was based on opposition to the increase in military expenditures announced in the 1937 federal budget.[49] The official Liberal candidate, bolstered by the anti-participation statements of Cardin and Lapointe, won handily but the by-election marked Houde's return to the *nationaliste* mainstream. During 1938 and 1939, Houde became one of the leading figures in the anti-war crusade which was taking hold in French Canada. At one point he declared that in the event of war between Britain and Italy, French Canada would favour Italy. He was forced to retract this statement, but the whole affair is indicative of Houde's new preoccupation.[50]

Montreal's financial situation had been temporarily improved by the 1935 tax measures, but the city's share of relief costs still had to be paid for by borrowing. Since the legal limit for municipal debt stipulated in the charter had long since been reached, the city had resorted to short-term loans authorized by the provincial legislature. This "Additional Debt" had gradually assumed quite impressive proportions and by early 1940 Montreal was in an even worse financial position than it had been in 1934. The projected deficit for 1940 was eleven million dollars and there was no money available to redeem two bank loans, amounting to 6.6 million dollars, due on May 15 and June 1.[51]

The new provincial administration of Adelard Godbout had given responsibility for municipal affairs to Telesphore-Damien Bouchard, a long-time mayor of Ste. Hyacinthe, and an activist in the Canadian Union of Municipalities. Bouchard thought of himself as an expert on municipal administration. He was also an old enemy of Camillien Houde's. As rumours about Bouchard's plans for the city began to circulate, Houde launched a vigorous campaign to prevent a takeover by Quebec. He urged the government to wait for the publication of the Rowell – Sirois Report, which would include an analysis of municipal financial problems. During April and May 1940, Houde took his case into the enemy camp, speaking to a variety of business and professional groups. He proposed a number of alternate schemes, but the common threat was the gap between municipal responsibilities and municipal tax sources.

The recommendations of the Rowell – Sirois Report were finally made public on May 16. Houde must have felt thoroughly vindicated as local newspapers headlined the Commission's critique of Quebec provincial finances. The revelation that Quebec municipalities had paid 26 per cent of direct relief cost as against a national average of only 15 per cent was followed by a flat statement that Montreal's financial crisis was a direct result of relief expenditures. But it was too late. Montreal had passed under the control of the Quebec Municipal Commission the day before the Report was published. A civil servant, Honoré Parent, had been made sole administrator of Montreal's financial affairs until a new system of government was installed. Even more ironic was the announcement that Quebec would move to introduce a province-wide sales tax, an income tax, and substantial increases in corporate tax[52]—all measures which Houde had advocated for years.

CONCLUSION

During the 1930s the city of Montreal's share of direct relief costs amounted to some forty-four million dollars. Additional Depression-related expenditures on public works added at least another ten million dollars to the city's expenses. At the same time the level of spending on the reformed public health system rose by more than 100 per cent (1929 – 34). Overall, the city's ordinary expenditures rose by 25 per cent over 1929 levels in a situation where traditional revenue sources were static or declining. Montreal had borrowed the entire cost of direct assistance, and had consequently increased its net funded debt from 185.2 million dollars to 273.2 million (1938). In comparison, Toronto was able to survive the Depression without significant additional borrowing. At the end of April 1939, Montreal's net funded debt per capita (together with short-term bank loans) worked out to $338, in contrast to a figure of $145 in Toronto.[53]

The crisis in civic finances was, of course, only part of a broader problem. In 1926, manufacturing production per capita in Montreal had been equal to that of Toronto; by 1936 it had fallen to 71 per cent of the Toronto level. Despite the severity of the economic decline experienced by Montreal, the population of the city had risen steadily during the 1930s.[54] There were 120,000 more residents of Montreal in 1939 than there had been ten years before.[55] Bad as conditions were in the city, they were better than in the rural areas of Quebec.

The 1930s was a disastrous decade for Montreal and its citizens. Considering the financial constraints under which the city operated, the response of the municipal authorities was comparatively constructive. The three Houde administrations (1930 – 32, 1934 – 36, 1938 – 40), in particular, deserve at least sympathy for the defending of the city's relief system against constant attack.

Not even this much can be said for the provincial and federal governments. Unlike the cities of Canada, the senior levels of government possessed relatively great financial flexibility. The Taschereau government in Quebec met the crisis of the thirties by reducing expenditures, and in 1936 its per capita outlay was lower even than New Brunswick's. The provincial debt did rise slowly in the 1930s, but in 1937 the province had the second lowest per capita debt of the nine provinces.[56] Even after the relatively heavy expenditures of the Duplessis years, the province was, in comparison to Montreal, in sound financial shape, reporting budgetary surpluses. Moody's *Manual of Investments* continued to rate Quebec government bonds at Aa, the highest category.[57] Stewart Bates, in his *Financial History of Canadian Governments* prepared for the Rowell – Sirois Commission, noted that, "Considering the debt levels and tax systems of other Canadian provinces, Quebec appears still to have some latent reserves of credit and taxation with which to pursue new policies."[58] The same could not be said for Montreal, though Moody's, with its Ba rating for Montreal (a high rating compared to western Canadian towns), seems to have had more confidence in the city than the Canadian banks, which refused to extend further loans.

Professor John Taylor's stimulating article on "The Urban West: Public Welfare and a Theory of Urban Development", suggests that "in their unwillingness to face certain social responsibilities in the thirties and earlier, the cities established a pattern of provincial, federal, and private control that has made them today virtually impotent".[59] It can be argued that in Montreal at least there was more willingness to face social responsibilities among urban politicians and officials than among any other political elite. Montreal was powerless because it lacked any reasonable measure of financial autonomy, because it lacked political clout in the rural-dominated legislative assembly, and because the Depression in central Canada had remarkably little impact on the well-being of middle and upper classes who remained preoccupied with "sound" financial management.

Camilien Houde's role in defending the interests of the unemployed requires further comment. Houde was not a radical except in temperament; he sought no structural changes in society or government. He offered no solutions to the Depression but rather concerned himself with trying to prevent further suffering. Houde came out of Montreal's slum-ridden east end; he knew his constituency at first hand and tried to act on their behalf. But if Houde had achieved everything he wanted, the unemployed would have been only marginally better off. Slightly higher relief allowances, more public works, and less stringent relief regulations were all Houde really stood for. His emergence as a folk hero among working-class Montrealers stands more as a comment on Canadian political leadership in the thirties than as a tribute to Houde.

NOTES

1. R. Rumilly, *Histoire de Montréal* (Montreal, 1974), Tome 5, p. 20. An account of Houde's speech is in *Le Devoir*, May 17, 1940.

2. Ibid., p. 17.

3. See Honoré Parent, "L'Administration Municipale", in *Montréal Economique* (Montreal, 1943), p. 325, for details.

4. City of Montreal, *Report of the Director of Finance 1932*, p. 3.

5. Figures from Huet Massue, "Financial and Economic Situation of Montreal Compared with that of Toronto", mimeo, McLennan Library, McGill University (1940), n.p.

6. Ibid., "Introduction".

7. Montreal Metropolitan Commission, *Financial Statements and Assessments, 1930 – 1940*.

8. See Terry Copp, *The Anatomy of Poverty: The Condition of the Working Class in Montreal, 1897 – 1929* (Toronto, 1974), pp. 140-47.

9. *Census of Canada, 1931*.

10. Sabina Burt, "The Montreal Municipal Elections of 1930, 1932, and 1934", mimeo, Sir George Williams University (1974).

11. City of Montreal, *Report of the Director of Finance, 1932*, p. 4.

12. The files of the Dominion Government's "National Unemployment Assistance Commission", PAC, R. G. 27, 70/303 are crammed with correspondence on Montreal's failure to provide adequate accounting of its disbursements.

13. *Montreal Star*, March 25, 1932, p. 3. All the major Montreal newspapers carry similar news reports of municipal affairs. Usually the *Star*, *La Presse* and the *Gazette* carry the most complete accounts of City Council meetings and civic election campaigns.

14. Peter Kralik, "The Saint Vincent de Paul Society in Montreal During the Depression", mimeo, Sir George Williams University (1974).

15. *Montreal Star*, May 16, 1931. Cited in Sally Jones, "Unemployment and Relief in Montreal 1930-33", mimeo, Sir George Williams University (1974).

16. E. B. de Panet, *The Work of the Unemployment Relief Commission 1934 – 35* (Montreal, 1935), p. 4.

17. Leonard Marsh, *Canadians In and Out of Work* (Montreal, 1936), p. 356.

18. This inference is borne out by the statistics on the percentage of families on relief by ward. Papineau, Ste. Marie, and Cremazie wards all had more than 40 per cent on relief in 1934 while less than 1 per cent were on the rolls in English-speaking Notre Dame de Grace and just over 7 per cent in the predominantly English-language ward of St. Andrew. *Montreal Star*, March 3, 1934.

19. Montreal Department of Health, *Annual Report, 1933-1940*.

20. *Montreal Star*, March 30, 1932.

21. Ibid., March 30, 1932.

22. Burt, "Montreal Municipal Elections", p. 23.

23. Report of Inspector E. Trottier, Nov. 16, 1932, PAC, R. G. 27, 70/303, Box 155, File "Correspondence-Quebec-Relief City of Montreal", n.p.

24. Ibid.

25. *Montreal Star*, August 28, 1932, cited in June Macpherson, "The Administration of Unemployment Relief in the City of Montreal 1931-1941", graduate research essay, Concordia University (1975).

26. Panet, *Work of the Unemployment Relief Commission*, p. 2.

27. *Montreal Star*, February 24, 1934.

28. Ibid., April 6, 1934.

29. Panet, *Work of the Unemployment Relief Commission*, p. 4.

30. "The Realities of Relief: A Report Submitted by the Unemployment Study Group of the Montreal Branch of the Canadian Association of Social Workers", mimeo, Montreal (1938), p. 12.

31. Ibid., p. 13.

32. Panet, *Work of the Unemployment Relief Commission*, p. 5.

33. *Montreal Star*, December 2, 1935.

34. Macpherson, "Administration of Unemployment Relief in Montreal", p. 25.
35. "The Realities of Relief", pp. 6-9.
36. *Montreal Star*, February 9, 1935.
37. The most advanced tax proposal, which included a sharply progressive income tax to be levied on all citizens of the Montreal Metropolitan area, is described in the January 24, 1935, issue of the *Montreal Star.*
38. The advertisement appeared February 20, 1935.
39. *The Star, La Patrie, La Presse, Le Canada, Le Devoir,* and the *Gazette.*
40. *Brief of the Montreal Board of Trade to the Royal Commission on Dominion-Provincial Relations* (1938).
41. For an account of Houde's relations with Duplessis, see Conrad Black, *Duplessis* (Toronto, 1977).
42. Houde's letter of resignation was dated August 27, 1936, which was three and one-half months before the municipal election.
43. Macpherson, "Administration of Unemployment Relief in Montreal", p. 53.
44. *Quebec Statistical Yearbook, 1942*, p. 229.
45. City of Montreal, *Report of Investigating Committee re: Unemployment* (Montreal, 1937).
46. Macpherson, "Administration of Unemployment Relief in Montreal", pp. 54-55.
47. Ibid., p. 21.
48. *Montreal Star*, July 16, 1937.
49. Rumilly, *Histoire de Montréal*, p. 225.
50. *Montreal Star*, February 17, 1939.
51. Ibid., April 6, 1940.
52. Ibid., May 16, 1940.
53. Ibid., May 21, 1940.
54. Massue, "Financial and Economic Situation of Montreal Compared with that of Toronto".
55. Ibid.
56. Huet Massue, "Graphic Review of the Public Debt, Revenues and Expenses of the Dominion of Canada and of the Provinces of Ontario and Quebec, 1914-1937", McLennan Library, McGill University (1938), n.p.
57. *Moody's Manual of Investments—Government Securities* (New York, 1942).
58. Stewart Bates, *Financial History of Canadian Governments* (Ottawa, 1939), p. 173.
59. John Taylor, "The Urban West: Public Welfare and a Theory of Urban Development", in A. R. McCormack and Ian MacPherson, eds. *Cities in the West: Papers of the Western Canada Urban History Conference* (Ottawa, 1975), pp. 286-313.

5.

Continuity and Change: Elites and Prairie Urban Development, 1914-1950

ALAN F. J. ARTIBISE

Urban growth on the prairies in the period 1914 – 50 generally followed patterns established in the pre-war era. Between 1871 and 1913, numerous urban communities had been established and many had enjoyed a decade or more of rapid growth and prosperity. During these crucial years the urban network of the region was set and by the outbreak of the First World War, five cities had emerged as dominant urban centres.[1] These cities—Winnipeg, Regina, Calgary, Edmonton, and Saskatoon—have since remained the primary urban concentrations of the region (see Tables 5:1 and 5:2, Appendix). Indeed, continuity between urban development in the pre-1914 and post-1914 eras is more noteworthy than change. The continuing efforts of urban elites to promote the growth of their communities met with only limited success. Economic realities and the pull of the past (in the form of a rigid framework for growth established prior to 1914) proved too great to overcome until at least the 1950s. This is not to say that there was no change, only that in most aspects the years between 1914 and 1950 witnessed the playing out of old themes in new circumstances.

Aside from general economic conditions, over which prairie cities had little control, two themes remained especially important in influencing prairie urban development after 1914. First, as in the previous era, prairie cities continued to be controlled by small, closely knit elites who made and implemented critical decisions.[2] The decision-making process in prairie cities was relatively simple. From formulation to implementation, a small group, or commercial elite, controlled the process. Although several different organizations or institutions became involved along the way, membership in each was sufficiently redundant to ensure continuity from start to finish. Therefore, even though a desire for a particular policy may have originated during lunch at an exclusive club or during a game of golf, it quickly moved up the hierarchy to discussion in the press, at the Board of Trade, and finally, to implementation by City Council. Virtually the same individuals were involved in all these stages. In short, the phenomenon of redundant leadership was a major characteristic of prairie urban leadership. From club to church, bank to City Council, the urban elites of prairie cities formed an interlocking directorate.

The decision-making process, in addition to being dominated at all stages by a small elite, was a closed process as well. Citizen participation is a post-1950 phenomenon; prior to that date the elites neither bothered about nor were seriously bothered by significant opposition.[3] A variety of factors, including a restricted franchise, plural voting, effective propaganda, and a centralized form of government assured the elites that their conceptions of desirable public policy would prevail.

The second theme is that the elites clung to a particular and well-defined set of ideas about urban growth. They shared what can be called "the booster spirit", and from this mental set they drew different ways of dealing with particular possibilities and problems. The booster mentality was made up of a web of beliefs and attitudes, but a few stand out above the others. It included, as has been discussed in some detail elsewhere,[4] a belief in the desirability of growth and material success; a desire to encourage growth at the expense of virtually all other considerations; a high degree of community spirit within the local elite coupled with a high degree of distrust for competing elites in other centres; a scornful attitude toward organized labour, farmers, the poor, and anyone who did not support the growth ethic; a loose attachment to Social Darwinism; and a belief in the special role of local government in fostering urban growth.

These ideas had been put into practice freely in the years before the First World War. By 1914 the five major prairie cities had a firmly established framework for future development. This framework included a variety of elements ranging from particular patterns of physical development to special tax policies and government structures. The key element, however, was the attitude of the decision-makers. The pre-1914 experience confirmed in the minds of the elites in all five cities that a booster mentality was essential to continued growth. More than ever before, the elites subscribed to the belief that "cities are made by the initiative and enterprise of its citizens".[5] Not one of the tenets of the booster philosophy had been dislodged by past experience. In terms of attitudes toward railways, immigration, and industrial encouragement, labour, inter-city rivalries, and the role of government, the commercial elites of the cities entered the post-1914 era intent on following past practices.

The year 1914 was pivotal in the history of prairie urban development. Before lay prosperity and rapid growth, after came three decades of relative stagnation and almost continual crisis. This second era
in prairie urban development was one in which both the major cities
and the region itself suffered substantial declines in their growth rates.
This decline was apparent in two general areas. First, the four cities of
Winnipeg, Calgary, Regina, and Saskatoon dropped in the ranking of
Canadian cities by size between 1921 and 1941 (Table 5:3, Appendix).
Second, in regional terms, the prairies switched from being the fastest
to the slowest growing region in the country. The urban percentage of
the prairies' population increased by only 4.9 per cent between 1911
and 1941, while the increase was 16.9 per cent in British Columbia,
16.4 per cent in Ontario, 15.8 per cent in Quebec, and 10.2 per cent in
the Maritimes (Tables 5:4 and 5:5, Appendix).

This sharp decline in the growth rate of prairie cities took place
within the context of general economic difficulties. A severe recession
in 1913 was followed by the dislocation of war and a slow recovery, a
dismal decade of depression in the 1930s, and a second war. All these
events adversely affected prairie urban development. However, the
more rapid decline and slower recovery of the prairie cities compared
to cities in other regions suggests that internal problems played a
significant role.

The difficulties faced by the five major prairie cities fall into two
general categories: short term and long term. The immediate problems of the city were financial and most had their roots in the pre-war
boom era. The debt problem was the most serious. In the years
preceding 1914 the debts of all five cities had skyrocketed as capital
commitments were made quite out of proportion to the true economic
value of the cities' assessments and to actual need. In other words,
prairie cities spent millions of dollars on excessive expansion, including such things as the provision of streets and sewers for large areas
which remained vacant for years (Table 5:6, Appendix).[6] This pattern
of uneven development greatly increased both the initial and operating costs of providing utilities, streets, transportation, and school facilities. Besides throwing a heavy burden of annual debt charges upon
the cities, the uncontrolled expansion of the pre-war years also greatly
increased the current annual expenses so that for the whole decade of
the 1920s the cities were barely able to maintain their plants.[7] In
terms of debenture debt alone, for example, prairie cities had committed themselves to the following sums by mid-1913: Winnipeg,
$28,000,000; Edmonton, $22,313,968; Calgary, $20,633,605; Regina,

$4,036,151; Saskatoon, $7,620,088.[8] Some idea of the excessive nature of the debts of prairie cities is gained by comparing their per-capita debt to that of other Canadian cities. In 1917, the general debenture debt per capita was $129 in Winnipeg, $313 in Regina, $290 in Saskatoon, $242 in Calgary, $359 in Edmonton, $265 in Vancouver, $108 in Halifax, $71 in Saint John, $160 in Montreal, $150 in Toronto, and $96 in Ottawa.[9]

In the years following 1913, these huge debts were repaid with a great deal of difficulty. In every prairie city expenditures were reduced as city councils attempted to pay heavy service charges. In Saskatoon, for example, many "non-essential" services were cut and controllable expenditures were reduced by 52 per cent between 1914 and 1916. These reductions were accomplished by such measures as sharp cuts in city staff and decreases in appropriations for garbage removal, cleaning, and the maintenance of streets. The total annual expenditures of Saskatoon continued at a low level until 1920; only in that year did they again reach the 1913 figure.[10] In Regina, financial difficulties in 1914 resulted in substantially curtailed public works programs, aggravating an already serious unemployment program. Regina's financial difficulties continued throughout the 1920s; in 1922, for example, the city's curtailed relief policies caused severe hardship.[11] Winnipeg's overall budget was also cut in the years after 1913; the city's 1926 budget was almost $300,000 less than it had been in 1921, despite the fact that the demand for services increased considerably during this period. Expenditures on public improvements were also reduced; during the four years from 1921 to 1924, expenditures totalled only two million dollars, representing about one-quarter of the physical volume of such work carried out in a similar pre-war period.[12]

The burden of heavy debt charges was such that by 1925 the city of Winnipeg was spending 29 per cent of its total annual budget on this single item. In Saskatchewan, the same figure for cities was 43 per cent, while in Alberta it was 32 per cent. A similar figure for Ontario at the time was only 22 per cent.[13] A study of Calgary finances, published in 1956, made the following statement concerning the debt problem:

In 1921 debt charges reached 18 mills out of a total mill rate of 46.6 mills, and for several years was nearly one-third of the budget. The city never quite recovered until recently, despite the somewhat better times of the late 1920s, and with the depression of the thirties the city debt was made bearable only by the introduction of the Fortin Refunding Plan in 1937. The essentials of the Fortin Plan were that it lightened the load of annual charges by extending the term of debt to 25 years.[14]

The burden of the huge debts piled up during the boom was intensified in the years after 1913 when assessments and revenues fell rapidly (Table 5:7, Appendix). Furthermore, dropping revenues and assessments were coupled with an alarming increase in tax arrears (Table 5:8, Appendix). Many owners of urban land, which was assessed at highly inflated values, forfeited their land to local governments instead of paying taxes. The forfeited properties ceased to be tax sources and the taxation of remaining properties had to be increased if the same total revenue was to be obtained. If the property tax had been wider, that is, if it had included buildings and improvements as well as land, or if it had assessed buildings and improvements at a higher rate, taxes on land as such would have been lower and land owners would have had some further incentive to keep their land. As it was, urban lots assessed at inflated 1913 values were taxed prohibitively in many cases in terms of both incentive and ability of the owner to pay.

Municipal financial stability suffered a particularly fatal blow because of the high degree of land owned by non-residents. The attitude of this group, most of whom held land only for speculation, was that defaulting on their tax liabilities was the best way out of a difficult situation. Since the annual taxes on their property represented a high proportion of what they might salvage, most allowed the municipalities to take over their lands.

The general conditions experienced by the five prairie cities in respect to assessments, revenues, and tax arrears can best be understood by specific examples. In Saskatoon, the city's total revenue for 1913 was $856,714. In 1914, the figure was only $805,528, and it continued to drop until 1920. Only in 1921 did revenue exceed the 1913 figure. Accompanying the drop in revenue were several years in which Saskatoon suffered a deficit, including 1917, 1919, 1920, 1925, and 1930. Indeed, beginning in the latter year, Saskatoon, like most prairie cities, began to run a deficit for several years in a row.[15] During the period after 1913, Saskatoon also saw a great deal of property pass into the hands of the civic corporation through the failure of owners to continue tax payments.[16] In Winnipeg, Calgary, and Regina the total revenue of the cities also dropped for a time and then remained relatively stable throughout the 1920s, and all cities received thousands of lots for non-payment of taxes.[17]

It was in Edmonton, however, that the financial situation was most severe. During 1918, for example, no less than 52,155 lots were in tax arrears. Following the tax sale held that year, 30,189 were forfeited to the city. These were valued at $6,230,000 and carried tax arrears of $1,800,000. By 1918, the cumulative total of tax arrears in Edmonton was $8,000,000. During the decade of the 1920s the financial situation did not substantially improve. Between 1920 and 1930, no less than 43 per cent of the total area of the city (excluding the area occupied by streets) was forfeited in lieu of taxes.[18] The facile assumption is often made that Edmonton, and other prairie cities, were fortunate to have become the owners of so much land. But since Edmonton was carrying a debt during the 1920s that averaged well over ten million dollars per year, the city acquired the lands only at the expense of foregoing large sums of tax revenues.

Faced with mounting financial difficulties, Edmonton City Council cut back on services. Budgets of several city departments were reduced, relief expenditures were curtailed, and, during 1914, contracts already signed for sewer construction were broken. By 1921, the decline in appropriations for street maintenance resulted in a need "for urgent repair", while garbage-removal services fell below a level necessary "if the City is to be kept in a clean and tidy condition".[19] In short, while the situation never reached crisis proportions, there were serious problems.[20] Moreover, since little maintenance was carried out during the 1920s, or during the depression and war which followed, Edmonton was by 1945 "run down" and it faced a "backlog of deferred public works . . . which had to be cleared out of the way". In the post Second World War period, Edmonton's per-capita debt surged upward to become, by 1953, the highest in Canada.[21]

In all five cities attempts were made to shore up the crumbling financial structures of the civic corporations. Most notably, in a move away from the single-tax philosophy, a tax on buildings and improvements was either re-introduced or increased as an attempt was made to increase tax revenues. In Edmonton, beginning in 1918, buildings which formally had been exempt were to be taxed at 60 per cent of their value. Calgary increased its rate of assessment from 25 per cent in 1913 to 50 per cent by 1919, while Saskatoon increased the rate from 25 per cent to 35 per cent in 1920, and then to 45 per cent in 1922. Other taxes were also increased or introduced during the period following 1913. Calgary began a business tax in 1916; Edmonton in 1918. The latter city also obtained authority to impose an income tax on a progressive rate, rising from 1 per cent on the first one thousand dollars to 8 per cent on all income over ten thousand dollars. Despite liberal exemptions this tax produced a fairly good revenue for the three years 1918 to 1920. It was repealed in 1921 when the provincial government refused to authorize its continuance. Saskatoon introduced a civic income tax and an amusement tax. In all cities, however, taxation of real property continued to be the principal source of revenue, providing well over 80 per cent of municipal revenues.[22]

Together with sharply curtailed expenditures, the broadened tax bases of prairie cities did enable all of them to struggle through the First World War and the decade of the 1920s. But they did so only at great hardship to the residents of the cities. The burden of taxation rose sharply (Table 5:9, Appendix), particularly for property owners. This development was, perhaps, fair considering that many property owners in the cities were speculators; a group that had made huge profits in the pre-1913 period and could in the following years afford to pay higher taxes. But this still left in all centres a large group upon whom the real property tax was a heavy burden. The vast majority of the cities' residents had the bulk of their wealth in real estate, and they were forced to carry a greater part of the burden of government expenditures than others with different forms of property. In other words, the increased taxation of the 1920s had a differential effect on different groups of property owners. While many did manage to meet their tax bills, a large number did not.[23]

In the face of these severe difficulties, it is important to note that the city's boosters continued to implement policies designed to promote growth. Even while essential services were being cut or reduced and relief expenditures curtailed, public funds were expended or committed in the continuing search for renewed prosperity. Boards of trade continued to receive substantial civic funds to finance their activities, promotional literature continued to be printed and distributed, and tax concessions and other forms of bonusing were still held out to various businesses.[24] In no city was the entire strategy of planning for growth reviewed and found wanting. There was, to be sure, some tinkering with the mechanisms, but no major overhaul was contemplated or begun.

It was against this backdrop that prairie cities entered the dismal decade of the 1930s. During these years the majority of residents in the cities suffered severe hardship, but the onset of the Depression was not so much an abrupt beginning of problems for prairie urban centres as it was a deepening of problems already present. In the ten years following 1929, the five major cities came close to financial collapse. To the already massive burden of debt they carried was added the problem of major relief expenditures. Moreover, the Depression brought with it further decreases in assessment values and increased tax arrears and tax rates (Tables 5:7, 5:8, and 5:9, Appendix). In an attempt to cope, the cities turned to the mechanism of taking out bank loans with tax arrears as collateral. When arrears continued to mount and the banks shut off this source of revenue, payments to sinking funds were waived and money was "borrowed" from city-controlled trust accounts and sinking funds. These inexpedient practices, in turn, did much to damage the cities' credit ratings and by the early 1930s few were able to sell any of their bonds on the open market.[25]

The cities, of course, all survived the Depression but they did so only at tremendous cost to future generations. The mechanisms used to deal with the financial crisis varied in detail from city to city, but all had characteristics in common. First, the governments of all five cities clung to the taxation of real property as their main source of revenue, refusing to adopt new taxation policies that would have spread the burden more evenly across the population on an ability to pay basis. While it is true that the municipalities were prevented from entering some lucrative fields of taxation by the provinces, there were no legal reasons why they could not have made significant adjustments in terms of removing exemptions, reviewing assessment policies, or increasing the rate of taxation on improvements. All of these measures would have increased revenues and generally lowered the tax rate for all but a few in the city. Lower tax rates, in turn, might have enabled more property owners to hang on to their land rather than turning it over to the city for non-payment of taxes.[26]

A second characteristic of the prairie cities' response to the problems of the 1930s was that they all approached the question of relief of the unemployed in a parsimonious manner. Although the municipalities continued to provide some form of assistance to the poor and unemployed, they did so in a very niggardly fashion and hardship among these groups was widespread. The fact was that the governing urban elites believed that prosperity would soon return and end their difficulties. With this in mind, prairie municipalities wrote off the unemployed as a temporary problem.[27] It was this attitude that was also behind the third characteristic of urban policy in this period. All the cities adopted a policy of economic contractions and retrenchment: budgets were slashed, borrowing for public works was stopped, employees were let go, and salaries were cut. The effect, of course, was to slow down an already sluggish economy and to leave for the post-Depression period a backlog of deferred public works.[28] A fourth characteristic was that the cities attempted to refund their massive debts, spreading the mistakes of the past well into the future. In Edmonton and Calgary, for example, a refunding scheme was adopted in 1937 that provided for the consolidation of all funded debts and extended the maturity date for thirty years. Only in this way were these cities saved from financial collapse.[29]

A fifth characteristic of the prairie cities' approach to their problems in the Depression was that they turned to both provincial and federal governments for assistance. There is no doubt that help was needed, but the type of aid sought and received was not in the best interests of the cities. Instead of insisting on a re-allocation of responsibilities and financial resources, the cities accepted funds raised by the senior levels of government. Thus, while the cities were expected to administer relief funds, actual control and regulation passed out of local hands. In other words, the grants received from senior governments were conditional grants that seriously impaired local autonomy. Local autonomy was lost in two ways:

> [Municipalities] were told what to do and given the money (or some of the money) to do it. Or they were given the option of taking money on certain conditions or not at all. In the former case the compulsion was explicit; in the latter implicit. In either case, local autonomy was compromised. Identification of problems and the establishment of priorities could not be determined in the locality. Responsibility for problems and the power to solve them (especially fiscal power) was separated.[30]

Moreover, this pattern, once established, was in later years extended far beyond grants for unemployment relief.

All of these methods of coping with the financial crisis of the 1930s were to have long-range consequences for prairie urban development. In 1939, however, when war brought an end to the Depression, the most significant fact about prairie cities was that in each the governing elites clung stubbornly to the outmoded booster policies of the past; policies that by then exacerbated rather than helped to solve problems. Several elements of the booster mentality, born and nurtured in the pre-war boom era, were especially harmful. First, the elites in each city continued to see each other as competitors. This attitude had made some sense in the fluid pre-1914 period but it later became a serious impediment as the cities faced problems which required new attitudes. The civic elites recognized that substantial growth on the prairies could come only in the form of the development of a diversified economic base, but they attempted to achieve diversification on an individual rather than a co-operative basis. They failed to see that their problem lay not in the relative advantage of one city over another, but rather in the disadvantageous position of the prairies vis-à-vis central Canada. In a situation in which the National Policy and discriminatory freight rates had long before condemned the prairies as an economic colonial hinterland, subject to the mercantile aspirations of the politically dominant central Canada, solutions lay in provincial and regional (or even inter-regional)[31] co-operation rather than in inter-city rivalry.

Instead of co-operation, however, rivalry was rampant in the inter-war years. In Saskatchewan, for example, inter-city rivalry prevented the early development of a publicly owned and efficiently run power corporation, thus retarding rather than expediting the chances of industrial development in the urban centres of the province.[32] In transportation, inter-city rivalry over the question of freight rates continued throughout the period to divide the prairie region into competing camps.[33] And all cities continued to compete for new industry by following a ruinous policy of bonusing.[34] The individualist attitudes of prairie urban elites also worked to their disadvantage in another area. In their search for renewed growth in the 1920s and 1930s, prairie cities encouraged the influx of eastern Canadian and multinational firms. Viewed in the short-run, this was an understandable approach since it did bring immediate gains. But over time, it meant a reduction in local control over the cities' economies. The individuals who managed the branches of national or international firms rarely sank roots in the cities, since they were almost certain to be transferred in due course to eastern Canada or the United States. The consequence was that capital as well as entrepreneurial ability was not as available to prairie firms as it was to their counterparts in central Canadian cities. Prairie banks came to exist exclusively of branches staffed by temporary residents, who were authorized by their respective head offices to extend loans only to certain prescribed limits. Loss of local control of the economics of the prairie cities tended to become cumulative as eastern Canadian or American corporations purchased large local firms from their retiring founders.[35]

Even more significant than the lack of co-operation in these areas was the fact that the elites of prairie cities did not begin or support any political movement designed to significantly alter national policy. The regional protest movements that did spring up—the United Farmers, the Progressives, Social Credit—provided ample scope to bring about significant change in the relationship of the prairies and central Canada, yet all failed to achieve their major goals. One of the chief reasons for this failure was a lack of support from the conservative elites of the cities.[36] Indeed, the problems of the 1920s and 1930s widened rather than bridged the gulf that had opened between city and farm.[37] And while urban elites cannot alone be held responsible for the ultimate failure of prairie protest in the inter-war period, their lack of support contributed to the eventual disintegration of the movements. Without urban support, the agrarian protesters failed to develop cohesive party platforms; organized parties remained weak because they represented only the interests of farmers rather than the interests of all groups within the region.

This failure to rationalize relationships within either the provinces or the region was coupled with an equally serious failure to come to terms with other groups in the cities, particularly labour and non-Anglo-Saxons. Just as boosterism acted as a screen shielding urban elites from the realities or regional economic problems, so too did it screen them from the realities of social and economic inequality within the cities. Advocates and supporters of boosterism were intent on creating a community spirit based on voluntarism, without any basic revision to the system of economic inequity and social injustice that existed in all prairie cities. They did this by promoting the notion that all classes and groups shared the same basic interests and goals; that the various groups—management and labour, Anglo-Saxon and non-Anglo-Saxon, rich and poor—could be united solely on the basis of faith in the city, belief in its destiny, and commitment to its growth. The community image promoted by prairie urban boosters was one that was fashioned more out of will than out of reality, more out of wishful thinking than out of experience. The civic and business elites talked about understanding and common ties, about creating a store of wealth to benefit all citizens, but in fact were generally unconcerned about the vast majority of residents. The attitude of civic elites towards groups within the city had serious shortcomings. The belief that everyone in the cities shared the same interests and goals—and could be united solely on the basis of greater civic loyalty, that everyone could be content with the leadership of a select group of businessmen, was simply false. Class and ethnic differences in prairie cities were real and could not be confronted or denied by the "unifying" ideas of civic boosterism. The belief that growth would somehow solve all problems was undoubtedly a comforting thought for some, but it precluded any genuine understanding of the realities of both growth and community. In terms of labour, for example, the attitudes and policies of the elites resulted in a weak labour movement and a steady slippage of wages within the Canadian spectrum.[38] And, contrary to popular belief, weak unions and low wages did not promote investment and growth. Instead, these conditions "[sapped] the strength and drawing power of local consumer market[s], and [dissuaded] employers from making the effort to improve efficiency and to innovate".[39]

The image the elites attempted to foster was thus one that tended to retard rather than stimulate growth.[40] It did not provide an outlet for all groups in the city to have a choice in the orientation of their community in specific directions; rather, the bulk of citizens were frustrated and discontented. This lack of a realistic, widely held set of values meant that positive community behaviour could not be mobilized to promote the cities' potential. Instead, continuing tensions within the city diverted attention from the prairie cities' main problem —their rigid relationship to the Canadian economy. The almost exclusive orientation of the elites to immediate growth blinded them to the potential of long-term development. The cities in the inter-war years reacted to external events that seemed beyond their control; they induced or attempted to induce new industries to locate without deciding whether the net effect was good or bad; and they permitted private and public bodies to make decisions that would not be reversible for generations.

A new era of prairie urban development began with the outbreak of the Second World War. Stimulated by a war economy prairie cities were, by the early 1940s, showing signs of coming out of their long slump. In national terms, the prairies experienced a rate of urban growth (11.1 per cent, Table 5:5, Appendix) greater than that of any other region, but the prairies still remained the least urbanized section of the country. Within the region, the growth achieved by the five major cities was uneven (Table 5:2, Appendix). Winnipeg, Regina, and Saskatoon witnessed only moderate growth. While Winnipeg and Saskatoon retained their respective positions in the hierarchy of Canadian cities, Regina declined in rank from seventeenth to eighteenth place (Table 5:3, Appendix). Moreover, each of these cities' rate of growth for the decade 1941-51 fell below the national average of 29 per cent.[41] In contrast to these three centres, Calgary and Edmonton grew rapidly as they benefited from the rapid expansion of the oil and gas industry in Alberta. Both grew much faster than the national average and both moved up in the hierarchy of Canadian cities.

The most significant observation that can be made about the decade of the 1940s, however, is that there were no fundamental structural changes in the economies of the cities; all five centres remained heavily dependent upon the processing of regional primary products and the collection and distribution of goods for their regional hinterlands (Table 5:10, Appendix). In other words, while there was some modest change in the economies of the five major cities, none was able to significantly supplement its basic central-place function with manufacturing and other national market activities. And although cities such as Edmonton and Calgary would continue for some time to grow rapidly as a result of the exploitation of non-renewable natural resources, the prospect of long-term growth for the prairie region's cities was poor without substantial economic diversification.[42]

This overview of prairie urban development suggests a number of tentative conclusions. In the first period of development, from 1870 to 1913, urban growth proceeded from a multiplicity of causes. Among them, the structures put in place by growth-conscious civic elites played a significant role in determining the rate and pattern of urbanization. But the framework for growth established in the early stages of urban development contained an implicit contradiction since the policies which fuelled growth in one era did not work in another. The free-wheeling boosterism of the fluid pre-1914 period was well suited to the time. When conditions changed, however, the very success of the framework made changes to it difficult; the old formula was viewed as a successful one and new, "radical" approaches were not easily or often adopted.

Moreover, it is doubtful that new structures would have had much impact, for two reasons. First, as prairie cities developed, their citizens lost more and more control over their own destinies. The introduction of provincial controls, through such agencies as departments of municipal affairs and special purpose boards, precluded certain actions being taken by city councils.[43] Similarly, the federal government increased its financial and jurisdictional control over urban centres. Together with the growth of branch plants and branch banking, these developments stripped the cities of most of their autonomy; by 1950, they had little power to initiate their own solutions to their own problems. Second, urban patterns, once firmly established, tend to become fairly stable, especially in terms of the relative relationships of cities within the system (Table 5:3, Appendix). In this situation, individual and group decisions do not have much impact on urban growth. Thus, in the absence of major changes which significantly alter economic relationships, the urban pattern on the prairies is unlikely to change dramatically.[44]

Two examples illustrate this point. Substantial new growth in prairie cities would most likely occur through their acquisition of some of the national market activities, now performed by central Canadian cities,[45] which possess numerous advantages over their prairie rivals. The addition of diversified, growth-oriented sectors, such as manufacturing, would require technological and financial assistance from the established central Canadian cities that is unlikely to be forthcoming. Moreover, such central Canadian cities as Montreal and Toronto have a great initial advantage in that they are already much larger than prairie cities and size itself enhances the ability to grow still more.[46] Also, since prairie cities already are hinterlands of central Canada, growth in them supports the dominant metropolitan centres by emphasizing the importance of the specialized services and products concentrated there.

Economic progress, characterized by the adoption of newly developed products and services, tends to confirm the ascendancy of the already established metropolitan centre[s]: innovations are customarily introduced first in such centres, and from here their subsequent general distribution tends to be controlled. The size achieved and resources acquired by the metropolitan centre[s] on the basis of undisputed ascendancy during the initial development of the hinterland, prove to be secular advantages which powerfully support [their] continuing ascendancy.[47]

Within the prairie region, the same process is at work. Winnipeg's initial advantage over other prairie cities has slowed their growth. In recent years, Edmonton and Calgary by-passed Winnipeg only because of their "luck" in discovering rich natural resources.

All this does not mean that prairie cities are necessarily doomed to remain colonies of central Canada, or that the human element has no further role to play in influencing urban growth. It does mean, however, that regardless of local growth policies, prairie cities are circumscribed by their region's dependent position within the national economy.[48] Established urban patterns, therefore, can be consciously altered only if the national economy is changed by political action.[49] However, a political solution is unlikely, if past experience is taken as a guide. Prairie cities have not been willing to co-operate either with each other or with their rural hinterlands to solve their many common problems. The key to success in the future lies in the recognition by prairie cities of their dependence on the resources of the entire region, for only when regional equality within Canada is achieved will prairie cities be able to look forward to substantial growth.[50]

TABLE 5:1 Population Growth in Selected Prairie Cities, 1871–1961

CITY	1871	1881	1891	1901	1911	1921	1931	1941	1951	1961
Winnipeg	241	7,985	25,639	42,340	136,035	179,087	218,785	221,960	235,710	265,429
Calgary	—	—	3,867	4,392	43,704	63,305	83,761	88,904	129,060	249,641
Edmonton	—	—	300(a)	4,176	24,900	58,821	79,187	93,817	159,631	281,027
Regina	—	800(b)	1,681(c)	2,249	30,213	34,432	53,209	58,245	71,319	112,141
Saskatoon	—	—	—	113	12,004	25,739	43,291	43,027	53,268	95,526
Moose Jaw	—	—	—	1,558	13,823	19,285	21,299	20,753	24,355	33,206
Brandon	—	—	3,778	5,620	13,839	15,397	17,082	17,383	20,598	28,166
St. Boniface	817	1,283	1,553	2,019	7,483	12,821	16,305	18,157	26,342	37,600
Lethbridge	—	—	—	2,072	8,050	11,907	13,489	14,612	22,947	35,454
Medicine Hat	—	—	1,570	3,020	5,608	9,634	10,300	10,571	16,364	24,484
Prince Albert	—	—	—	1,785	6,245	7,352	9,905	12,508	17,149	24,168
Portage la Prairie	—	—	3,363	3,901	5,892	6,766	6,597	7,187	8,511	12,388
Red Deer	—	—	—	—	2,118	2,328	2,344	2,924	7,575	19,612

NOTES: a) This is an approximation taken from City of Edmonton Records.
b) The population of Regina in 1882-1883 was between "800 and 900 souls". E. G. Drake, *Regina: The Queen City* (Toronto, 1955), p. 22.
c) Ibid., p. 71.

SOURCE: Institute of Local Government, *Urban Population Growth and Municipal Organization* (Kingston, 1973), Table II-1.

TABLE 5:2 Population Growth and Change in Major Prairie Cities, 1901-1961

YEAR	WINNIPEG		REGINA		SASKATOON		EDMONTON		CALGARY	
	Number	Per Cent Change	Number	Per Cent Change	Number	Per Cent Change	Number	Per Cent Change	Number	Per Cent Change
1901	42,340	—	2,249	—	113	—	4,176	—	4,392	—
1906	90,153	112.9	6,169	174.3	3,011	2564.6	11,126	116.4	11,967	172.5
1911	136,035	33.7	30,213	389.7	12,004	298.7	24,900	123.8	43,704	265.2
1916	163,000	19.8	26,127	-13.5	21,048	75.3	53,846	116.2	56,514	29.3
1921	179,087	9.9	34,432	21.8	25,739	22.3	58,821	9.2	63,305	12.0
1926	189,708	5.9	37,329	8.4	31,234	21.3	65,163	10.8	65,291	3.1
1931	218,785	15.3	53,209	42.5	43,291	38.6	79,187	21.5	83,761	28.3
1936	215,814	-1.4	53,354	.3	41,734	-3.6	85,774	8.3	83,407	-.4
1941	221,960	2.8	58,245	9.2	43,027	3.1	93,817	9.4	88,904	6.6
1946	229,045	3.2	60,246	3.4	46,028	7.0	113,116	20.6	100,044	12.5
1951	235,710	2.9	71,319	18.4	53,268	15.7	159,631	41.1	129,060	29.0
1956	255,093	8.2	89,755	25.9	72,858	36.8	226,002	70.7	181,780	40.8
1961	265,429	4.1	112,141	24.9	95,526	31.1	281,027	24.3	249,641	37.3

SOURCES: *Census of Canada, 1901-1961: Census of the Prairie Provinces, 1926, 1936, 1946.*

TABLE 5:3 Rank of Selected Canadian Cities by Size, 1901-1951

RANK	1901	1911	1921	1931	1941	1951
1	Montreal	Montreal	Montreal	Montreal	Montreal	Montreal
2	Toronto	Toronto	Toronto	Toronto	Toronto	Toronto
3	Québec	WINNIPEG	WINNIPEG	Vancouver	Vancouver	Vancouver
4	Ottawa	Vancouver	Vancouver	WINNIPEG	WINNIPEG	WINNIPEG
5	Hamilton	Ottawa	Hamilton	Hamilton	Ottawa	Ottawa
6	WINNIPEG	Hamilton	Ottawa	Québec	Québec	Québec
7	Halifax	Québec	Québec	Ottawa	Hamilton	Hamilton
8	Saint John	Halifax	CALGARY	CALGARY	EDMONTON	EDMONTON
9	London	London	London	EDMONTON	Windsor	Windsor
10	Vancouver	CALGARY	EDMONTON	London	Halifax	London
11	Victoria	Saint John	Halifax	Windsor	London	CALGARY
12	Kingston	Victoria	Saint John	Verdun	CALGARY	Halifax
13	Brantford	REGINA	Victoria	Halifax	Kitchener	Victoria
14	Hull	EDMONTON	Windsor	REGINA	Victoria	Kitchener
15	Windsor	Brantford	REGINA	Saint John	Saint John	Saint John
16	Sherbrooke	Kingston	Brantford	SASKATOON	Thunder Bay	Sudbury
17	Guelph	Peterborough	SASKATOON	Victoria	REGINA	Thunder Bay
18	Charlottetown	Hull	Verdun	Trois-Rivières	Sudbury	REGINA
19	Trois-Rivières	Windsor	Hull	Kitchener	SASKATOON	SASKATOON
36	—	SASKATOON	—	—	—	—
73	CALGARY	—	—	—	—	—
77	EDMONTON	—	—	—	—	—
97	REGINA	—	—	—	—	—
110	SASKATOON	—	—	—	—	—

SOURCES: *Census of Canada, 1931-1951.*

TABLE 5:4   Rural and Urban[a] Population Growth in the Prairie Provinces,
1901-1951 (in thousands)

	MANITOBA		SASKATCHEWAN		ALBERTA		TOTAL PRAIRIES		
	Rural	Urban	Rural	Urban	Rural	Urban	Rural	Urban	% Urban
1901	192	64	86	6	61	12	339	81	19.3
1911	269	193	413	80	264	110	946	383	28.8
1921	341	269	630	128	411	177	1,382	574	29.3
1931	357	343	735	187	504	228	1,596	758	32.2
1941	370	360	704	192	531	266	1,605	818	33.7
1951	337	440	579	252	489	450	1,405	1,142	44.8

NOTE: a) Urban population for the years from 1901 to 1931 represents the
population residing in incorporated cities, towns, and villages of
one thousand and over and incorporated municipalities of this size
range surrounding the larger cities which were later defined as
parts of the census metropolitan areas. For 1941 and 1951 the
urban figure also includes population residing in unincorporated
suburban parts of major urban areas.

SOURCE: "Analytical Report: Rural and Urban Population", *Census of Canada, 1956*, p. 26.

TABLE 5:5   Per Cent of Population Urban[a] in Canada's Regions, 1901-1951

REGION	1901	1911	1921	1931	1941	1951
British Columbia	46.4	50.9 (4.5)[c]	56.1 (5.2)	67.3 (11.2)	67.8 (0.5)	70.8 (3.0)
Prairies	19.3	28.8 (9.5)	29.3 (0.5)	32.2 (2.9)	33.7 (1.5)	44.8 (11.1)
Ontario	43.6	52.8 (9.2)	60.7 (7.9)	65.3 (4.6)	69.2 (3.9)	73.4 (4.2)
Quebec	38.2	45.9 (7.7)	52.0 (4.1)	59.7 (7.7)	61.7 (2.0)	67.0 (5.3)
Maritimes[b]	26.2	32.7 (6.5)	37.9 (5.2)	38.9 (1.0)	42.9 (4.0)	47.7 (4.8)

NOTES: a) See definition in Table IV, note (a).
b) Does not include Newfoundland in 1951.
c) Bracketed figures represent per cent increase for decade.

SOURCE: "Analytical Report—Rural and Urban Population", *Census of Canada, 1956*, p. 26.

TABLE 5:6 Area and Density of Population of Canada's Twenty Largest Cities, 1931

CITY	RANK By Pop'n	RANK By Density	POPULATION	Land Area in Sq. Miles	Pop'n Per Sq. Mile	Land Area in Acres	Pop'n Per Acre
Montreal	1	3	818,577	46.75	17,510	29,920	27
Toronto	2	2	631,207	34.00	18,565	21,760	29
Vancouver	3	14	246,593	43.96	5,610	28,434	9
WINNIPEG[a]	4	8	218,785	23.93	9,143	15,315	14
Hamilton	5	7	155,547	15.15	10,267	9,696	16
Québec	6	5	130,594	8.99	14,527	5,753	23
Ottawa	7	4	126,812	8.27	15,341	5,293	24
CALGARY	8	19	83,761	40.50	2,068	25,920	3
EDMONTON	9	20	79,197	42.50	1,864	27,200	3
London	10	11	71,148	11.30	6,296	7,232	10
Windsor	11	6	63,108	5.01	12,596	3,206	20
Verdun	12	1	60,745	2.23	27,240	1,427	43
Halifax	13	10	59,275	6.88	8,616	4,403	14
REGINA	14	16	53,209	13.14	4,049	8,410	6
Saint John	15	18	47,415	21.00	2,263	13,440	4
SASKATOON	16	17	43,291	13.25	3,267	8,480	5
Victoria	17	15	39,082	7.25	5,391	4,640	8
Trois-Rivières	18	9	35,450	4.00	8,863	2,560	14
Kitchener	19	13	30,793	5.43	5,671	3,475	9
Brantford	20	12	30,107	4.94	6,094	3,162	10

NOTE: a) If Winnipeg is combined with the adjacent City of St. Boniface, the density per square mile drops to 5581; per acre to 9.

SOURCE: Census of Canada, 1931.

TABLE 5:7 Net Assessment Values in Major Prairie Cities, 1901-1951 (in millions of dollars)

YEAR	WINNIPEG	REGINA	SASKATOON	CALGARY	EDMONTON
1901	21.3	—	—	2.3	1.3
1906	53.7	5.8	2.5	7.7	17.0
1911	157.6	26.9	23.3	52.7	46.4
1913	259.4	69.5	56.3	133.0	188.5
1916	278.7	51.2	37.6	84.1	132.4
1921	238.6	43.9	27.8	75.0	80.2
1926	232.6	39.5	28.3	59.0	58.8
1931	237.4	47.4	34.6	70.6	66.4
1936	198.3	42.1	33.6	61.2	54.0
1941	170.1	40.7	31.0	59.1	56.2
1946	183.8	41.3	31.9	66.3	77.2
1951	254.4	51.6	41.0	95.3	134.4

SOURCES: *Winnipeg Municipal Manuals, 1919, 1934, 1960; Regina Financial Statements, 1928, 1933, 1962; Saskatoon Municipal Manual, 1975; Calgary Municipal Manual, 1960; and Edmonton Financial Statements, 1935, 1952.*

TABLE 5:8 Value of Tax Arrears and Acquired Land (Vacant and Improved) in Major Prairie Cities, 1901-1951 (in thousands)

YEAR	WINNIPEG	REGINA[a]	SASKATOON	CALGARY	EDMONTON
1901	273	—	—	—	2
1906	442	—	—	—	2[b]
1911	798	62[c]	322[c]	—	208
1913	984	194	692	534	1,082
1916	3,168	612	1,002	3,497	5,250
1921	4,645	518	1,425	5,852	8,423
1926	4,931	411	1,860	5,482	6,592
1931	5,320	684	1,456	4,471	5,445
1936	12,000	1,389	3,094	6,406	6,154
1941	9,123	786	3,176	5,059	2,998
1946	621	972	1,559	3,152	1,069
1951	3,042	570	1,095	2,128	1,676

NOTES: a) Acquired land in Regina is recorded at a nominal value of one dollar. The figures shown for Regina, therefore, are for arrears only.
  b) Figures are for 1905.
  c) Figures are for 1912.

SOURCES: City of Calgary, *Financial Statements, 1913-1951*; City of Saskatoon, *Municipal Manual, 1975*; R. M. Haig, *The Exemption of Improvements in Canada and the United States* (New York, 1915); City of Edmonton, *Financial Statements, 1901-1951*; City of Winnipeg, *Financial Statements, 1901-1951*; City of Regina, *Financial Statements, 1901-1951*.

TABLE 5:9   General Tax Rates in Major Prairie Cities 1901-1951 (in mills)

YEAR	WINNIPEG	REGINA	SASKATOON	CALGARY	EDMONTON
1901	20.5	22.0	–	20.0	21.5
1906	17.9	15.0	18.0	22.0	10.5
1911	13.2	18.1	18.0	14.5	13.7
1913	13.0	14.0	18.0	18.7	16.0
1916	15.7	23.3	46.5	21.5	21.0
1921	30.0	43.0	45.0	46.6	39.9
1926	28.0	41.0	45.0	41.7	44.3
1931	34.5	48.0	45.4	47.0	49.5
1936	34.5	50.0	45.0	56.0	55.0
1941	36.5	49.5	44.3	44.5	51.5
1946	40.0	50.0	44.5	46.0	49.5
1951	44.5	61.0	55.0	60.0	56.0

SOURCES: *Winnipeg Municipal Manuals, 1927, 1945, 1961*; *Regina Financial Statements, 1928, 1933, 1962*; *Saskatoon Municipal Manual, 1975*; *Calgary Municipal Manual, 1974*; *Edmonton Financial Statement, 1926, 1959*; and "City of Edmonton Statistics", City of Edmonton Archives.

TABLE 5:10   Industrial Distribution by Percentage of the Labour Force of Major Prairie Cities, 1931-1951[a]

CITY	SECTOR[b]		
	Primary	Secondary	Tertiary
WINNIPEG:			
1931	2.2	25.6	65.2
1941	1.4	31.3	66.4
1951	0.7	33.1	65.5
REGINA:			
1931	2.2	22.8	69.8
1941	2.2	21.1	74.1
1951	1.4	20.2	76.4
SASKATOON:			
1931	2.6	20.2	70.1
1941	3.1	19.6	76.3
1951	2.1	22.6	74.7
CALGARY:			
1931	3.7	26.4	64.7
1941	2.9	28.0	68.0
1951	1.2	32.0	66.0
EDMONTON:			
1931	4.6	22.2	68.3
1941	2.9	27.3	68.8
1951	1.0	31.0	67.1

TABLE 5:10, Cont'd

NOTES: a) Comparable figures are not available for earlier years.
   b) The primary sector includes agriculture, fishing, hunting, and trapping. The secondary sector includes mining, manufacturing, utilities, and construction. The tertiary sector includes transportation and communications, trade, finance, insurance, and service.

SOURCE: Adapted from tables in P. A. Phillips, "Structural Change and Population Distribution in the Prairie Region: 1911-1961", MA thesis, University of Saskatchewan (1963).

NOTES

1. For a detailed discussion see Alan F. J. Artibise, "Boosterism and the Development of Prairie Cities, 1871-1913", in G. A. Stelter and Alan F. J. Artibise, *Shaping the Canadian Urban Landscape: Essays on the City-Building Process* (forthcoming).

2. See the articles by James D. Anderson and J. E. Rea in this volume, as well as the following: Alan F. J. Artibise, *Winnipeg: A Social History of Urban Growth, 1874–1914* (Montreal and London, 1975); Alan F. J. Artibise, *Winnipeg: An Illustrated History* (Toronto, 1977); E. G. Drake, *Regina: The Queen City* (Toronto, 1955); E. H. Dale, "The Role of the City Council in the Economic and Social Development of Edmonton, 1892-1966", PHD thesis, University of Alberta (1966); L. H. Thomas, "Saskatoon, 1883–1914", paper read before the Morton Historical Society, 1944; and J. H. Archer, "The History of Saskatoon", MA thesis, University of Saskatchewan (1948).

3. The exception to this generalization is Winnipeg where, from 1919, the commercial elite faced significant opposition from labour forces. The important point, however, is that the businessmen "never once lost control of council". See J. E. Rea, this volume, Chapter 6.

4. Artibise, "Boosterism and Prairie Urban Development".

5. *Regina Leader*, January 16, 1930.

6. See the maps in Artibise, "Boosterism and the Development of Prairie Cities".

7. See, for example, I. M. Nicoll, "Urban Municipal Finance in a Period of Expansion: A Study of the City of Edmonton", MA thesis, University of Alberta (1950), p. 112 and *passim*; and John Weaver, "Edmonton's Perilous Course, 1904-1929", *Urban History Review*, no. 2 – 77 (1977): 10-19.

8. Henry Howard, *The Western Cities: Their Borrowing and Assets* (London, 1914).

9. Commission of Conservation, *Urban and Rural Development in Canada* (Ottawa, 1917), p. 26. The figures cited are based on general debenture debt after deducting sinking fund and property owners' share of local improvements, but including debt of public utilities. The per-capita debt excluding public utilities debt was as follows: $40 in Winnipeg; $130 in Regina; $150 in Saskatoon; $100 in Calgary; $170 in Edmonton; $218 in Vancouver; $71 in Halifax; $11 in Saint John; $84 in Toronto; and $57 in Ottawa. Figures were not given for Montreal.

10. P. R. Creighton, "Taxation in Saskatoon: A Study in Municipal Finance", MA thesis, University of Saskatchewan (1925), Chapter IV.

11. See R. M. Haig, *The Exemption of Improvements From Taxation in Canada and the United States: A Report Prepared for the Committee on Taxation of the City of New York* (New York, 1915), p. 42; and Drake, *Regina*, pp. 179-80.

12. See City of Winnipeg, *Submission to Royal Commission on Dominion –*

Provincial Relations (Winnipeg, 1937), p. 25; and R. C. Bellan, "The Development of Winnipeg as a Metropolitan Centre", PHD thesis, Columbia University (1958), p. 313.

13. H. Carl Goldenberg, *Municipal Finance in Canada* (Ottawa, 1939), pp. 111-17. The figures for Saskatchewan and Alberta include all cities, not just Edmonton, Calgary, Regina, and Saskatoon.

14. *Report of the Royal Commission on the Metropolitan Development of Calgary and Edmonton* (Edmonton, 1956), Chapter VI, p. 5.

15. City of Saskatoon, *Municipal Manual*, 1975.

16. Saskatoon Board of Trade, *Annual Report for 1927*, p.11; Don Ravis, *Advanced Land Acquisition by Local Government; The Saskatoon Experience* (Ottawa, 1973), *passim.*

17. See E. J. Hanson, "A Financial History of Alberta", PHD thesis, Clark University (1952); Goldenberg, *Municipal Finance in Canada*; and H. C. Goldenberg, *Report on the Royal Commission on the Municipal Finances and Administration of the City of Winnipeg* (Winnipeg, 1939).

18. Dale, "Development of Edmonton", pp. 158-60; and *Royal Commission on Calgary and Edmonton*, Chapter VI, p. 25.

19. City of Edmonton, *Special Report on Assessment and Taxation* (Edmonton, 1921); and Weaver, "Edmonton".

20. For a general discussion of some of the problems of the 1920s see James Struthers, "Prelude to Depression: The Federal Government and Unemployment, 1918-1929", *Canadian Historical Review*, vol. 58, no. 3 (1977): 277-93.

21. *Royal Commission on Calgary and Edmonton*, Chapter VI, p. 41.

22. *Calgary Municipal Manual*, 1974, p. 38; Creighton, "Taxation in Saskatoon", p. 34; City of Edmonton, *Report on Assessment and Taxation*. I was unable to locate pertinent data for Winnipeg and Regina. It is possible, however, that few changes in taxation were made since of the five cities these two were in the best financial shape during this period. It can be noted that the

City of Winnipeg did attempt in the post-war period to secure authority from the provincial government to impose an income tax. It was unsuccessful, and in 1923 the province itself entered the field. See J. Harvey Perry, *Taxes, Tariffs and Subsidies: A History of Canadian Fiscal Development*, 2 vols. (Toronto, 1955), p. 245; and A. B. Clark, "Recent Developments in Western Canada", *Proceedings of the 13th Annual Conference of the National Tax Association* (New York, 1920), pp. 48-69.

23. For a general discussion of this problem see Goldenberg, *Municipal Finance in Canada*, pp. 96-100. The problem associated with the tax systems of prairie cities were magnified in Calgary when that city adopted a program of granting "relief of taxation" to certain areas of the city in 1915. The areas in question were parcels of land where, in the judgment of the city assessor, land was suitable only for agricultural purposes. Such relief, amounting to 25 per cent, was given in Calgary during the years 1915 and 1916. By 1917, owners of no less than 20,000 acres of land had applied for relief. Variations of this relief measure continued into the 1920s. See *Royal Commission on Calgary and Edmonton*, Chapter IX, p. 26; and Thomas Adams, *Rural Planning and Development* (Ottawa: Commission of Conservation, 1917), pp. 116-17.

These measures were obviously designed to relieve the tax burden on owners of certain properties in Calgary and could be defended on the grounds that any tax revenue from such property was better than none; a situation that might have occurred had the lands passed into the city's hands for non-payment of taxes. On the other hand, these parcels of lands, many of which were already sub-divided, had in virtually all cases been developed by speculators and the grant of tax relief to these groups only increased the burden on the rest of the community.

24. See, for example, Saskatoon Board

of Trade, *Annual Report for 1927*, *passim*; Artibise, *Winnipeg: An Illustrated History*, p. 116; and Dale, "Development of Edmonton", Chapter VIII.

25. In May 1933, for example, W. R. Taprell of James Richardson and Sons wrote J. B. Cross of the Calgary Brewing and Malting Company regarding the latter's investments in City of Calgary Bonds. The letter ended with this advice: "While, no doubt, you feel that in some way you may like to hold bonds of the City in which your Head Office is situated, we would like to point out that the City, by extreme mismanagement of their civic affairs, have not extended to corporations any attraction or assistance in making Calgary an attractive manufacturing centre through reasonable taxes and sensible government." City of Calgary Papers, Glenbow Archives. For other examples of problems in marketing bonds see Nicoll, "Edmonton", p. 97 and *passim*; *Submission of the Saskatchewan Urban Municipalities Association Presented to the Royal Commission on Dominion-Provincial Relations* (Regina, 1937); and *City of Winnipeg: Submission to Royal Commission on Dominion-Provincial Relations* (Winnipeg, 1937).

26. For a general discussion of tax problems, see W. J. Waines, "Problems of Public Finance in the Prairie Provinces", *Canadian Journal of Economics and Political Science*, vol. 3 (1937): 355-69.

27. John Taylor, "'Relief from Relief'- The Cities Answer to Depression Dependency", *Journal of Canadian Studies*, vol. 14, no. 1 (Spring 1979): 16-23.

28. Ibid. See also *Royal Commission on Calgary and Edmonton*, Chapter VI, p. 41; Goldenberg, *Report on Finances of Winnipeg*, p. 532; and *Commission of Inquiry Into Provincial and Municipal Taxation*, Papers, Provincial Archives of Saskatchewan, Regina—Box No. 1, File No. 2—"Report to Mayor and Council, Saskatoon, September 1936".

29. *Royal Commission on Calgary and Edmonton, passim*; Nicoll, "Edmonton".

30. John Taylor, "Urban – Industrial Society and the Decline of Local Autonomy in Twentieth-Century Canada" (unpublished paper 1977).

31. For an excellent discussion of the "narrowness of vision" on the part of prairie and maritime leadership see E. R. Forbes, "Never the Twain Did Meet: Prairie-Maritime Relations, 1910–1927," paper presented to CHA Annual Meeting, Fredericton, June 1977.

32. For a full discussion of power development and its impact on provincial and urban development see C.O. White, *Power for a Province: A History of Saskatchewan Power* (Regina, 1976).

33. See W. T. Jackman, *Economic Principles of Transportation* (Toronto, 1935).

34. Bonusing usually took the form of granting tax exemptions and/or low rates for power and water. See, for example, *Calgary Herald*, November 16, 1926; and "Report of the Railways, New Industries, Power and Development Committee", November 15, 1926, City of Calgary Papers.

35. See, for example, A. F. J. Artibise, "An Urban Economy: Patterns of Economic Change in Winnipeg, 1873 – 1971", *Prairie Forum*, vol 1, no. 2 (1977): 163-88; and Bellan, "The Development of Winnipeg as a Metropolitan Centre", pp. 486-89.

36. See Ian MacPherson, "Agrarianism and the Weakness of Prairie Regional Protest" (unpublished paper 1976).

37. See, for example, Artibise, *Winnipeg: An Illustrated History*, p. 152; and T. Flanagan, "Political Geography and the United Farmers of Alberta", in S. M. Trofimenkoff, ed. *The Twenties in Western Canada* (Ottawa, 1972), pp. 138-69.

38. See H. C. Pentland, "The Winnipeg General Strike: Fifty Years After", *Canadian Dimension*, vol. 6, no. 2 (1969): 17; Paul Phillips, "The National Policy and the Development of the Western

Canadian Labour Movement", in A. W. Rasporich and H. C. Klassen, eds. *Prairie Perspectives, 2* (Toronto, 1973), pp. 41-62; and Warren Caragata, "A Short History of the Labour Movement in Alberta", unpublished paper (1977).

39. Pentland, "Fifty Years After", p. 17.

40. For three discussions of the role of an urban image see N. H. Lithwick, *Urban Canada: Problems and Prospects* (Ottawa, 1970), pp. 52-53; B. A. Brownell, *The Urban Ethos in the South* (Baton Rouge, 1975); and Kevin Lynch, *The Image of the City* (Cambridge, Mass., 1960).

41. "Analytical Report—Rural and Urban Population", *Census of Canada, 1956*, Bulletin 3 – 2, p. 32. The average is of forty cities of 30,000 and over. The rate for prairie cities was as follows: Winnipeg, 6.2 per cent; Regina, 22.4 per cent; Saskatoon, 23.8 per cent; Calgary, 45.2 per cent; and Edmonton, 70.2 per cent.

42. Lithwick, *Urban Canada*, pp. 125-43.

43. The extent to which provincial controls have advanced in the prairie provinces is discussed in K. G. Crawford, *Canadian Municipal Government* (Toronto, 1954), pp. 344-55. Besides provincial departments of municipal affairs, agencies created by the provinces to supervise and control municipalities included a Local Government Board in Saskatchewan (1915), and the Municipal and Public Utility Board of Manitoba (1926).

44. One major change that could significantly alter relationships is a rapid advance in transportation technology which would reduce the "friction of distance". For a discussion of the importance of this factor see D. Michael Ray, "Urban Growth and the Concept of Functional Region", in N. H. Lithwick and Gilles Paquet, eds. *Urban Studies: A Canadian Perspective* (Toronto, 1968), p. 60 and *passim*.

45. Lithwick, *Urban Canada*, p. 134; Ray, "Urban Growth", p. 42.

46. Lithwick, *Urban Canada*, pp. 50-51.

47. Bellan, "Winnipeg as a Metropolitan Centre", p. 492.

48. See, for example, J. Howard Richards, *Saskatchewan Geography: Physical Environment and Its Relationship With Population and the Economic Base* (Saskatoon, 1975), pp. 47-53 and *passim*. One result of this continuing dependency is the prairie's poor showing in regard to manufacturing. Although the prairies contained 16.4 per cent of the country's population in 1977, their share of the country's manufacturing sales was only 9.3 per cent. And while manufacturing accounted for 25 per cent of Ontario's work force, 24 per cent of Quebec's, 16 per cent of B.C.'s, and 13 per cent of the Atlantic region's, it accounted for less than 10 per cent of the Prairie's. *Financial Post*, vol. 17 (1977).

49. Lithwick, *Urban Canada*, p. 73 and *passim*.

50. See the articles on the prairies in D. J. Bercuson, ed. *Canada and the Burden of Unity* (Toronto, 1977).

6.

Political Parties and Civic Power: Winnipeg, 1919 – 1975

J. E. REA

Much of the current interest in urban studies is saturated, quite understandably, with presentism. Contemporary analysis of modern urban problems seems, indeed, to be anti-historical; when, for example, activist investigators, righteous in their moral indignation, raise the hue and cry against land-development companies. The land developers, after all, are simply one of a number of pressure groups—albeit visibly successful—trying to persuade city councils across the country to favour their objectives or respond to their special pleading. It is certainly important, however, to seek to understand why one pressure group, such as the retail merchants' association, to cite an obvious case, may or may not be relatively more successful than, say, the neighbourhood community clubs or various cultural organizations. To put the question conversely, why does a city council appear to be susceptible to the blandishments of some special interest groups rather more than others?

While the vigour, tenacity, and avarice of the development lobby may be something to contend with, it seems equally, if not more, appropriate to direct historical research toward understanding how special interest groups in cities have operated, and with what success. While it is possible to deplore the current power and effectiveness of certain groups, it is also possible to ask if the fault may lie in the structure and ethos of civic politics in Canada. It seems imperative, in other words, that detailed historical analysis provide the necessary perspective in order to understand how both special interest groups and the community at large have been served by civic politicians over the long term. Comparative analysis, again over time, will provide an historical context in which to judge the efficacy, or lack of it, of civic administrations. It is therefore implied, in this line of argument, that cities must not be considered unique. The case-study approach, which is employed in this instance, must be followed by general, comparative examinations.

To determine whether or not the best interests of an urban community, in this case, Winnipeg, have been well or badly served, it is necessary to identify those who have made the important decisions in the city's development. If an identifiable group has been in a position to control events over a long period of time, it is possible, by examining its record, to conclude whether or not its primary concern was the public good or group interest. This chapter proposes to demonstrate the existence of a successful, long-lived, urban political party in Winnipeg and its less successful opposition. It will describe who those people were; how they sought and wielded power; and how they exploited an inadequate political structure. The intent, precisely, is to attack the presumption, for Winnipeg at least, that civic politics have been conducted on a non-partisan basis.

There are two general assumptions which underlie this study of Winnipeg over the fifty-five years ending in 1975. One of the legacies of the great Winnipeg General Strike of 1919 was the formation of two opposed groups shaped by the emotion and trauma of that confrontation; groups that perceived each other—almost apocalyptically— as battlers for the universal rights of labouring man, on the one hand, and on the other, as the defenders of a free, stable, and progressive society.[1] The labour movement, having failed to achieve its aspirations through mass economic action, turned then to the ballot box as an alternate means of gaining its objectives. Just as enthusiastically, the leaders of that segment of Winnipeg society which had broken the strike jammed their way, three thousand strong, into the Board of Trade building in August 1919 to reconstitute themselves as the Citizens' League of Winnipeg to ensure that political confirmation could be given to their recent victory. Although both groups have changed their names over the years, they have been consistent in their attempts to gain and exercise control of Winnipeg's civic government. The labour group, of course, now campaigns as the New Democratic Party. The Citizens' League, for its part, used several appellations over the years and is now known as the Independent Citizens' Election Committee. For convenience, the generic names of Labour and Citizens' League (despite the presumption of the latter) will be utilized.

The second assumption is the conviction that, in a free society, there is no such thing as a non-partisan election. Voters make their electoral choices for a variety of reasons including whim, prejudice, self-interest, ideology, religion, ethnicity, and so on. Any or all of these motivations can be harnessed by a skilful political organization to its own purpose. To suggest or assert that non-partisan politics is more objective or more altruistic, or indeed even possible in such circumstances, is either naïve or disingenuous.

This leads directly to the conclusion that the tradition of non-partisanship in city politics in Canada is neither natural nor theoretically justifiable. Indeed, non-partisanship, itself, has been used as a weapon in the struggle for political dominance in the modern history of Winnipeg, as it very likely has been in other urban centres. City voters have been far too gullible for too long. The claim that party government at the local level is inherently incompatible with civic virtue or efficiency is myth. Tales of wicked bosses and corrupt machines in the nineteenth century United States are hardly justification for abandoning the more legitimate British tradition of political responsibility. It is the abuse of party that should be condemned, not the party itself. If Winnipeg is any example—and there is no reason to consider it is unique—the alternative to a responsible party system is power without collective responsibility, which is even more readily susceptible to abuse and much more difficult to hold accountable.

At every civic election in Winnipeg since 1919, the Citizens' League campaigned on the slogan that party politics must be kept out of the city's affairs. It steadfastly denied that it was a party and its rhetoric attempted to capitalize on this theme; thus, in 1943, it offered candidates "with no sectional ties, no party ties, no ties of class, race, politics or religion". In 1948, the Citizens' League attempted to trade on the current tensions of the Cold War with the slogan, "use your ballot, guard your liberty, don't let Communists and party politicians run our city". The Citizens' League has never been accused of subtlety. As a final example, in 1951, the Independent Citizens claimed, "It's the PARTY politicians who are always advocating 'free services' ... which YOU PAY FOR through taxes included in your rent, in taxes on your homes, in licences and fees and many other hidden taxes. Vote INDEPENDENT this year.... Keep party politics out of city affairs."[2] The relevance, as usual, was obscure; the pejorative was the message.

The general contention is, therefore, that Winnipeg has had a functioning party system since 1919 and that the rhetoric of independent non-partisanship, employed consistently by one of the contending groups, has been a sham. Before testing this assertion, however, it should be pointed out that this study concentrates on the effective decision-makers, the aldermen. While the mayor receives much of the publicity and attention, it is votes in council, and its major committees, and how they are manipulated and deployed, which ultimately

determine policy. Management of the political machinery and major-
ity-group control of such key committees as Finance, Legislation, and
Public Works are the sinews of power. The average voter would never
notice, for instance, that a welfare program had been effectively killed
by the approval of an enigmatic "Motion to Refer".

The method employed has been twofold. A socio-economic profile
of all Citizens' League and Labour members of Winnipeg City Council was undertaken. With group identity established, party cohesion of
Citizens' League and Labour was tested by an analysis of roll-call
voting on important recurring issues throughout the period. The data
were then analysed to determine the credibility of the claim that the
"non-partisan" group did indeed serve the interests of all the residents
of Winnipeg.

During the first twenty-five years after the General Strike, from 1920
to 1945, Citizens' League and Labour, as social groups, have been
remarkably consistent. In drawing their collective portraits seven standard variables were employed: ethnicity, religion, place of birth, occu-
pation, quality of housing, education, and political affiliation.[3] Both
groups were heavily British and Protestant, but on all other tests
applied were almost completely dissimilar and drew their political
support from sharply distinct economic strata. It is worth remarking,
at this point, that the Citizens' League exhibited considerably more
electoral shrewdness than their opposition. Despite the polyglot nature
of Winnipeg's working class, Labour made little attempt to create an
ethnic constituency during these years, relying, presumably, on class
identification. Toward the end of the period, however, the League
began to give their support to candidates from non-British backgrounds.

Winnipeg City Council, from 1920 to 1971, was composed of a
mayor, elected on a city-wide franchise, and eighteen aldermen, based
on three six-member wards. Of the sixty-nine aldermen elected during
the period 1920-1945, sixty were members of the Citizens' League.
Labour succeeded in electing only 12 per cent of the Council membership. The electoral activity of the two parties was most intense
during periods of high emotion such as the immediate years after the
strike and during the Depression of the 1930s. Put another way, the
more threatening the challenge of Labour, the more cohesive and
effective the response of the Citizens' League. On only two occasions
during the period 1919 to 1945, and never again after that, did Labour hold as many Council seats as their opponents. In both those

instances, 1920 and 1934, the mayor had been endorsed by the Citizens' League, so that control by the latter was not seriously jeopardized.[4] Labour was never able to secure a majority, even during the most distracted times. The typical Council was controlled by the Citizens' League with a comfortable majority of two to one.

From the end of the Second World War until 1971, the pattern and personnel of Winnipeg politics remained essentially the same. At the latter date, the old boundaries of the former City of Winnipeg were extended to include all the surrounding suburban municipalities, creating a new political entity known locally as "Unicity".[5] However, throughout the preceding twenty-six years, from 1945 to 1971, the Citizens' League continued its dominance of City Council. They elected forty-four, or 61 per cent, of the aldermen while Labour's complement increased to only 26 per cent. There were, as well, three Labour Election Committee members (Communists) on Council during these years.

The socio-economic bias of the two groups remained generally consistent, although there were some significant changes. Unlike Labour, the Citizens' League continued to recruit and endorse candidates outside the British charter group to facilitate their electoral penetration of the working-class Ward III, an area of substantial ethnic complexity. They were willing, as well, to support women candidates in order to broaden their appeal. Even so, the class orientation of the League remained constant. Of their forty-four councillors from 1945 to 1971, thirty-two were businessmen or professionals, one was the retired Winnipeg Police Chief, and two women councillors were married to professionals.

The Labour party in Council showed even less inclination to change during these years despite their relative lack of electoral success. They continued to be overwhelmingly British and Protestant, but an interesting development in occupational categories did occur. Only one Labour alderman in this twenty-five-year period was a skilled tradesman. A rather startling percentage of their group were trade union officials or political party (that is, Co-operative Commonwealth Federation) employees. In other words, the civic Labour party became very much the political arm of organized labour, as opposed to the working class generally, despite its pretensions.

Thus, the basic polarization of Winnipeg politics, a presage of the General Strike, had almost become institutionalized during the years after the Second World War. The Citizens' League advertised itself as independent, responsible, businesslike, and committed to saving the city from the evils of partyism. They were tremendously successful electorally. The effect of their control on the evolution of Winnipeg, however, is another matter.

There is only one precise method of analysing legislative behaviour over an extended period of time. Recorded votes, or roll calls as they are usually known, are a permanent record of political activity, unlike the majority of City Council decisions, which are taken by voice vote or simply a show of hands. Roll calls are not customarily employed unless a member of Council considers a matter to be of unusual significance, or, more likely, wishes to have all his colleagues on the public record for political reasons.

To illustrate more sharply any changes or developments which have taken place over the fifty-five years from 1920 to 1975, the period was again divided into three units and each reviewed separately. The politics of the first twenty-five years were conditioned by the emotional legacy of the strike and the economic distress of the Great Depression. From 1945 to 1970, there was an almost ritualistic confrontation in which well-defined, recurring issues provoked complete polarization of the two groups. The third period, 1971-75, was examined to assess to what degree the traditional political alignments of Winnipeg were a continuing influence in the expanded Unicity.

The technique used to measure intra-group solidarity was the Rice Index, derived by converting the yeas and nays into percentages of the total number of the group who vote. These average cohesion percentages were then contrasted by group, employing the method known as inter-party likeness scales. The result was a ranking by degree of intensity of those issues which provoked the most rigid party divisions. The sample was purposely made large enough to ensure a reliable outcome. Every roll call vote in every odd-numbered year from 1921 to 1945 was included, a total of 321 recorded votes. These votes were then organized according to group affiliation to determine the relative cohesion of Citizens' League and Labour aldermen, and thus intra-group solidarity, in all those issues deemed important enough to demand a recorded vote. This exercise, using all the votes in the sample, produced an average cohesion rate for the Citizens' League of 71.38 and for Labour, 84.25. The results were tested to ensure that group numbers and personnel changes were not distorting factors in determining party cohesion. Rather, patterns of high-level cohesive voting have been related to the type of issues which customarily divided the two groups.

This type of voting comparison assumes that a party vote is one in which over half the Citizens opposed over half the Labour aldermen, a definition which would result in almost every one of the 321 votes falling within the category of party vote. It is clear, however, that some issues more sharply polarized the two groups. To isolate these more contentious issues would reveal much about party attitude toward matters coming before Council and thus the ideological and class orientation of Citizens' League and Labour. If, therefore, a party vote is defined as one in which 80 per cent of one group opposes 80 per cent of the other group, those issues which prompted the greatest conflict can be determined more precisely. Of the 321 roll-call votes examined, 134 fall within this more rigorous classification.

In the twenty-five years following the strike, these 134 party votes (80 per cent *vs.* 80 per cent) involved six policy issues which came up for debate and decision year after year. Four of these were economic issues—working conditions and wages of civic employees, public services, welfare costs, and rates of taxation (especially the business tax). The other two issues, electoral reform to broaden the municipal franchise to allow all voters to cast ballots on money by-laws, and City Council appointments to public boards and committees, were ideological in nature, or at least in the response they occasioned. Whenever these issues were raised, Citizens' League and Labour voted cohesively as opposing groups. A tabular arrangement of the results makes this obvious:[6]

ISSUES	NUMBER	CITIZENS AVERAGE COHESION	LABOUR AVERAGE COHESION
Social Welfare	48	96	98.4
Working Conditions and Wage Rates	23	100	100
Taxation Levels	5	100	100
Public Services	19	98	100
Council Appointments	25	100	100
Electoral Reform	14	98.6	100
TOTAL	134	98.7	99.7

On these recurring issues of substantial importance, Citizens' League and Labour were aligned against each other with almost perfect party discipline. So much for the claim of the Citizens' League that they were not a party.

The next twenty-five-year period, 1946-71, is marked by the same pattern of party consistency. The same sample, all roll-call votes in each odd-numbered year, 320 in total, was employed. The average cohesion of the Citizens' League was 79.72 and of their opponents, 88.47. Quite traditional issues such as rates of business taxation, electoral reform, Council appointments, and public services provoked disciplined party voting (80 per cent vs. 80 per cent). A new issue, involving questions of land use and zoning, began to spark heated debate. Class interest ideology and future development, therefore, were continuing, polarizing factors.

The final step in the analysis was to assess the political effect of the amalgamation of the metropolitan area of Winnipeg which resulted from provincial legislation in 1971. The spatial limits of Winnipeg were greatly extended to include all the surrounding suburban communities and its population more than doubled to greater than 550,000. The mayor was still elected on a city-wide franchise;[7] but the new Unicity Council was based on fifty single-member wards in which all councillors were elected for a three-year term. A novel, and very important, change was the introduction of an eleven-member Executive Policy Committee (EPC) which effectively controlled the major business of the Council. The Citizens group, through its voting majority on Council, have completely dominated the EPC since its inception. Not one non-Citizen member has ever been included. It acted as a quasi-Cabinet without, of course, the collective responsibility which would render it liable to an electoral accounting. The obvious question was whether or not the traditional class division would be carried over and extended to the political structure of the newly expanded city; or, rather, if some other factor, such as geographic polarization of the central city and the former suburbs, would disrupt the pattern of the preceding half-century.

Although only the four-year period from 1971 to 1975 has been examined, it is clear that the implementation of a unified city has had only a marginal impact on traditional party structures. If anything, party cohesion within the Citizens' group has increased on vital issues; that is, those issues now introduced and supported by the Executive Policy Committee which decided on policy and framed the crucial motions. Furthermore, while traditional polarizing issues have provoked party hostility as reflected in voting patterns, a new and divisive factor has been added. A commitment to the growth of Winnipeg was generally shared by most members of Council over the years. But, in recent years, a rising chorus of dissent has begun to challenge the assumptions which sustained this growth ethic, including, of course, one of the more apparent manifestations: the influence of the land development interests on City Council decisions. During the past five or six years, development matters have been the occasions for some of the sharpest exchanges in Council.[8] Problems of land use have assumed an increasing importance in the deliberations of City Council. These issues have invariably sparked a very high level of party regularity when brought to a vote.

The years 1973 and 1975 were selected for analysis in this section of the study to examine both the first Unicity Council and the second, elected in 1974. The immediate impression one gains from analysing the results is that party cohesion is very strong. There were 102 roll-call votes in 1973. The Citizens voted as a party (not simply a majority of them, but with a cohesion rate of 80 per cent or better) on fifty-six occasions, or 54.9 per cent of the time. The average cohesion of the Citizens on all votes was 78.44; they were slightly more cohesive on those issues sponsored by the EPC and responded with a rate of 82.8. If, however, the selection is further refined to isolate development issues, then party regularity almost approaches unanimity.

Labour, or the New Democratic Party (NDP), as one would expect, clearly demonstrates its public posture as a party. On 79 of the 102 roll-call votes, it voted as a party, that is with over 80 per cent cohesion. On all votes, Labour had an average cohesion rate of 88.87, and on those issues brought to Council by the EPC this rate rose to 90.68.

Two years later, in 1975, after the intervening election in 1974 had reduced the Citizens' majority, there were 149 roll-call votes. This was a substantial increase and can be partly accounted for by the frequency with which development-oriented issues increasingly divided City Council. The regularity of the Citizens' group remained consistent, 77.08 per cent of all roll-call votes and 80.16 per cent on those sponsored by the EPC. The party strength of the NDP suffered in 1975; its overall cohesion rate was 80.17, and on EPC issues it declined from 90.68 in 1973 to 80.84 in 1975. There was, however, a consistent defection of one member through the year, which, in a small group of nine, affected the NDP score greatly.

One further issue deserves comment at this point. The election of 1974 resulted in the appearance in Council of a group of ten independents.[9] In terms of socio-economic characteristics, they are indistinguishable, with one or two exceptions, from the Citizens. They hold what they have called "informal meetings" to consider issues coming before Council. It is probably too early to make any firm judgment of their political leanings or whether they are likely to develop into a cohesive group. It may be fairly pointed out, however, that on 62.7 per cent of all roll-call votes in 1975, a majority of the independents voted with a majority of the Citizens.

Several conclusions may be drawn from the Winnipeg experience. In the first instance, and most obviously, the claim of the Citizens' League and its successors that they are not a political party should be given little credence. On matters of substantial economic substance or ideological import, a disciplined party situation has existed and functioned in Winnipeg since 1920. The Citizens have exploited the appeal to non-partisanship with phenomenal success, never losing political control of City Council over the past fifty-seven years. The result has been that leadership has, to a large extent, been sacrificed to interest protection, as the roll-call votes make evident. The most serious effect, however, has been the evasion of responsibility. The facade of non-partisanship has thus led to the inability of the electorate to assign group responsibility and judge accordingly.

Two corollaries follow directly. Voter response to civic elections has been dismal. Despite the fact that civic government is closest to the people of all levels of political authority and directly affects the quality of their daily lives in terms of cost and services, the average turnout in Winnipeg from 1945 to 1969 has been 37.63 per cent. The major reason, it is contended here, is the incapacity of the electorate to make meaningful choices or, indeed, even to register an effective protest vote. Second, the non-partisan theme has led to an extraordinary number of carry-overs from one Council to the next. Without any choice between or among alternative policies or programs the average voter tends to seek familiar names. In Winnipeg, an incumbent alderman seldom loses; he either retires or dies. Again, from 1946 to 1969 and in 1974, of all councillors who offered themselves for re-election, 87.8 per cent were successful.

From the analysis of the data, therefore, it seems fair to conclude that the clearest charge against the Citizens' group and their anti-party tactics has been their consistent denial of collective responsibility which their control and exercise of power has surely entailed.

NOTES

1. J. E. Rea, "The Politics of Conscience: Winnipeg After the Strike", Canadian Historical Association, *Historical Papers* (1971), pp. 276-88. Prior to 1919, Winnipeg civic politics was dominated by a commercial elite devoted to virtually unrestricted growth. For an account see Alan F. J. Artibise, *Winnipeg: A Social History of Urban Growth, 1874-1914* (Montreal, 1975).

2. *Winnipeg Free Press*, November 11, 1943; October 23, 1948; October 20, 1951.

3. The data upon which this section is based may be found in J. E. Rea, *Parties and Power: An Analysis of Winnipeg City Council, 1919-1925*, Appendix IV, *Report and Recommendations*, Committee of Review, City of Winnipeg Act (Winnipeg: Manitoba Department of Urban Affairs, 1976). A detailed version of the early years of this study was published under the title, "The Politics of Class: Winnipeg City Council, 1919-1945", in Carl Berger and Ramsay Cook, eds. *The The West and the Nation: Essays in Honour of W. L. Morton* (Toronto, 1976), pp. 232-49.

4. See Paul Phillips, "'Power Politics': Municipal Affairs and Seymour James Farmer, 1909-1924", in A. R. McCormack and Ian MacPherson,

eds. *Cities in the West: Papers of the Western Canada Urban History Conference* (Ottawa, 1975), pp. 159-80; and A. B. McKillop, "The Communist as Conscience: Jacob Penner and Winnipeg Civic Politics, 1934-1935", in ibid., pp. 181-209. See also A. B. McKillop, "Citizen and Socialist: The Ethos of Political Winnipeg, 1919-1935", MA thesis, University of Manitoba (1970).

5. For a series of maps illustrating ward boundaries from 1920 to 1971, and the boundaries of Unicity, see Alan F. J. Artibise, *Winnipeg: An Illustrated History* (Toronto, 1977).

6. Rea, *Parties and Power*, p. 9.

7. There was considerable debate over this issue, since there was strong pressure to have the mayor elected by and from among the new Council of fifty. Such a procedure, in my view, would have been very salutary, since leadership and control (and thus responsibility) could be readily identified.

8. See, for example, R. Clark, *et al.*, "Reform Politics in Winnipeg: Opening Things Up", *City Magazine*, vol. 1, no. 3 (1975): 29-36.

9. They won largely at the expense of the citizens' group, but a close examination of this event is tangential to the main point of this chapter.

III.

Planning and the Realities of Development

Introduction

The history of Canadian planning and development is still in its infancy, but some of the outlines of the general picture have emerged. The basis for much of modern city planning stems from the urban reform era of 1890 – 1920. During these years many Canadians developed a heightened consciousness of the city, planning became professionalized, and the provinces introduced the legislative base for planning.[1] Canadian urban planning was not suddenly born in this period, of course, but was at least partially the product of two earlier phases of urban planning and development. In an initial phase, imperial officials determined the form of colonial towns. Central direction was evident in the planning of early Louisbourg, Halifax, Toronto, and others. Even some commercial enterprises were planned communities, as in the case of the Canada Company towns of Guelph and Goderich.[2] A second phase was represented by the Victorian era, when laissez-faire thinking dominated the question of who should make the decisions which would shape the community. It would be a mistake, however, to assume that planning did not take place during this period. Rather, planning was done at a private level, without regulation by municipal or provincial government. Many new towns founded by corporations in the late nineteenth century were built on the basis of plans drawn up by company officials, including Sudbury (Ontario), by the Canadian Pacific Railway Company, and Nanaimo (British Columbia), by coal barons in London.[3] In the larger cities, however, the results of the private decisions of thousands of individuals and corporations usually led to fragmented patterns of development.[4]

The modern phase of planning, ushered in around the turn of the century, was a response to the innumerable problems that accompanied the unregulated development of the Victorian period. These problems became more acute and apparent because of rapid urban growth. Between 1881 and 1921, the proportion of Canadians living in urban places doubled from about 25 per cent to almost 50 per cent. The largest cities were the main recipients of this growth. In the forty years after 1881, Montreal grew by four and one-half times to a total of 618,506, Toronto by six times to 521,893. Even more dramatic was the sudden emergence of Winnipeg and Vancouver in the first decade of the twentieth century, during which Winnipeg's size increased by more than three times and Vancouver's by almost four. Several factors contributed to this rapid population growth. One was the enlargement of boundaries. In Toronto in the 1880s, a series of annexations added Yorkville, Rosedale, the Annex, and several other outlying areas to the city. Montreal also annexed several suburbs, including Hochelaga in the 1880s, and incorporated nine more municipalities before 1919. An orgy of suburban subdivision in every major city placed enormous financial and physical strain on the central city's ability to supply services. A second factor was migration to the cities from other Canadian cities, from rural areas, and particularly from abroad. Foreign immigration significantly altered the racial composition of every major city, but especially of places such as Winnipeg where the foreign-born constituted 55.9 per cent of the population by 1911. In the eyes of many contemporary observers, rapid urban growth was creating problems of the kind usually found in European cities, for big cities seemed to breed disease, poverty, and crime. Slums had become more visible, and much of the working class was not properly housed.[5]

By the beginning of the twentieth century, Paul Rutherford has noted, "it was widely accepted that urban growth posed a serious menace to the future of the nation".[6] A host of reformers, including newspapermen, politicians, businessmen, and academics, cast about for solution to the city's ills.[7] Several concepts of city planning were developed, based on American and British experience. The most sweeping approach was the City Beautiful Movement, which was exemplified in the Chicago Exposition in 1893, but whose roots went back at least to the era of baroque planning. Supporters of this approach visualized a civic landscape of monumental public buildings, great diagonal boulevards, squares, and parks, and, especially, a magnificently designed Civic Centre.[8] Another approach to urban planning was the Garden City or New Town Movement, which originated about the same time. It was led by a British planner, Ebenezer Howard, who advocated a retreat from big city life to self-sufficient small towns surrounded by a green belt, with planned preserves for residential, cultural, commercial, and industrial uses.[9] The movement is described in more detail in several of the following chapters. The Garden City approach differed from the City Beautiful approach on the important question of the purpose of planning. While the City Beautiful advocates tended to emphasize urban aesthetics, Garden City planners stressed the health and housing of the residents. In several important respects, however, these two approaches had much in common. In both, planners would have a great deal of power (presumably with the support of government officials) in changing the existing urban structure or planning completely new towns. They both also stressed the segregation and sorting out of various urban functions—residential, commercial, industrial, and institutional. These common features merged, as Jane Jacobs has pointed out, and became the planning orthodoxy in North America.[10]

During the first thirty years of the twentieth century, Canadians experimented with a variety of these planning approaches. The emphasis shifted successively from aesthetics and the large-scale plan to the regulation of suburban expansion, to providing housing for workingmen, to zoning in order to segregate functions and protect property values. Some of these approaches were advocated or practised at the same time as others, but a rough periodization based on the dominating theme in a particular time period is possible. From the 1890s to the beginning of the First World War, the vision of the City Beautiful was in force. The professionals in town planning—architects, engineers, and surveyors—dreamed of coherent, unified streetscapes, of variations in street patterns, and of the grandeur of a city centre. Grandiose plans were drawn up for several cities, including Toronto in 1905 and 1909, Montreal in 1906, Winnipeg in 1913, Calgary in 1914, and Ottawa and Hull in 1915. Little came of these plans, usually because the public was horrified by the enormous costs involved in putting these plans into practice. By 1914, planners generally were denouncing the entire approach, arguing that beauty and aesthetics were not the top priority in solving urban problems.[11]

The City Beautiful idea was far from dead, however. The 1929 Bartholemew plan for Vancouver incorporated some of its basic principles and several other examples are cited in the following chapters. Perhaps the most spectacular adoption of the concept in a Canadian city took place late in the 1930s in Prime Minister Mackenzie King's supervision of the redevelopment of Ottawa as federal capital. King personally hired a French planner, Jacques Gréber, whose views coincided with his own on introducing a sense of grandeur into Ottawa. Whether the Gréber plan succeeded in this respect is debatable, but it certainly met Mackenzie King's needs. For example, after getting general agreement on the location of the War Memorial monument, King recorded in his diary: "I at once saw that I had my Champs Elysées, Arc de Triomphe and Place de la Concorde all at a single stroke."[12]

While the City Beautiful approach remained in existence, Garden City planning dominated the thinking of the professional planners and the public from 1914 to the mid-1920s.[13] The main channel for the Garden City approach was the federal government's Commission of Conservation organized in 1909. In response to advice from planners and reformers, the Commission brought in Thomas Adams, one of the leading British advocates of the movement, as their Town Planning Advisor in 1914. As a symbol of the Garden City idea, Adams was influential in promoting the development of urban planning in several respects. The first was provincial legislation regulating suburban expansion. Although planning was a local matter, Adams tactfully and persistently pressed for provincial legislation. Most of the provinces eventually adopted acts closely modelled on the British Act of 1909, or that part of it that dealt with municipal control over land-use planning. The necessity of controlling land likely to be developed was apparent to many observers, for the era was one of incredible suburban sub-division, far in excess of actual population increase. The second area of influence concerned the "New Town" aspect of the British movement. Adams was directly or indirectly involved in planning satellite towns, like Ojibway, an industrial suburb of Windsor, Ontario, and resource town like Témiscaming, Quebec, described in this section in the chapter by Oiva Saarinen. A number of other small resource towns planned during this period also reflected these general principles, including Kapaskasing, Iroquois Falls, and Arvida.[14] Suburban regulation and new towns, however, proved ineffective in coming to grips with the central concern of Garden City planning—the provision of housing for the working man and the poor. In fact, the suburban movement accentuated rather than alleviated the problem; it led to further fragmentation of the city into rich and poor because only the more prosperous could take part in the move away from the congested urban cores.

The question of whether government at any level would get involved in providing housing was one of the key issues of the period. Garden City advocates like Adams constantly pushed for intervention on the British model, but provincial governments made clear their reluctance to enter this field—all provincial planning legislation excluded the provisions of the 1909 British Act which concerned "The Housing of the Working Classes". The earliest housing schemes were thus of necessity privately initiated, combining philanthropy and investment, a practice popular in the United States. For example, Herbert Ames, a Montreal businessman, built a small group of model apartments, but his initiative was not imitated to any great extent by his business compatriots.[15]

In spite of a lack of action by private enterprise, city authorities generally remained aloof, and when civic government did get involved, it proved to be extremely minimal. Experiments in Toronto in 1913 and 1920 are examples. In one case the city guaranteed the bonds of a limited-dividend scheme of a joint stock company. In the other, a housing commission was appointed with clear instructions not to lose any city money. As described by Shirley Spragge in a chapter in this section, these ventures built over five hundred housing units, but this housing generally proved too expensive for low-income families. More popular with city officials was the strategy of improving housing through codes and strict code enforcement. Regulations were designed to ensure proper sanitary conditions, control the quality of tenement housing, and check the spread of slums. Codes, unfortunately, did not provide more or better low-income housing; if anything, they increased the cost of housing and reduced the available supply.[16]

The major government intervention in housing came, surprisingly, from the federal government, even though housing was under provincial jurisdiction. Between 1918 and 1924 the federal government operated a scheme to lend money to the provinces to encourage new housing construction. Most of the provinces participated; in Ontario, more than one hundred municipalities took advantage of the measures. Thomas Adams and other reformers hoped that this move signalled a new direction in government policy, but federal officials soon made it clear that it was a temporary measure to relieve the severe post-war housing shortages, especially for returning servicemen, and to reduce the threat of social unrest. The accession of Arthur Meighen to the office of Prime Minister cast the dye for a retreat from federal involvement. Symbolic of the federal move away from responsibility in the area was the abolition of the Commission of Conservation in 1921. The loan scheme was finally abandoned in 1923 – 24 and the federal government was not to return to the housing field until the crisis of the Depression in the 1930s.[17]

As housing reform declined as a positive force in the early 1920s, the pendulum swung back to a business-oriented approach to planning. Efficiency became the practical goal of reform, with planning seen as a rational, scientific activity. Technical experts were brought in to provide technical solutions. The trend was away from large-scale comprehensive plans to zoning as a means of achieving efficiency. The segregation of land uses was established on a legal-administrative basis by provincial legislation during the inter-war years, borrowing heavily from the United States Department of Commerce Standard Zoning Enabling Act.[18] The move to zoning was characterized, as Walter Van Nus shows in his chapter in this section, by a close relationship between planners and the property industry. In fact, political support for land-use restrictions through zoning was possible because it protected property values. Zoning by-laws were usually not part of a general plan, but in Vancouver zoning was an instrument in implementing a comprehensive plan.

The extent to which public authorities and planners influenced the shape of early twentieth-century cities has been the subject of research only recently. Max Foran's case study of Calgary indicates that the direction of development was determined by geography and the decisions of the railway company and speculators, but only marginally by civic planning. Subdivision was not regulated by a zoning by-law until 1932. The Civic Corporation's control was largely negative; it could, for example, discourage residential development in certain areas by withholding utility extensions. In Toronto, as Peter Moore's chapter shows, planning before 1936 was limited to the relatively minor function of improving traffic flow, while zoning was largely a neighbour-hood-based concern to prevent nuisances and protect property values. It was only in the new resource towns of the period that planners, governments, and corporations were able to put the most advanced planning ideas into practice without the difficulties inherent in working with an existing community infrastructure. Some pulp and paper towns in particular were completely preplanned; in the case of Témiscaming, Quebec, with federal government advice; in the case of Kapuskasing, Ontario, by provincial planners.[19]

During the era of reform, from 1890 to 1920, the Canadian public developed a growing urban consciousness. Cities vied with provinces for power and the largest had budgets equal to the provinces in which they were located. But from the 1920s, the direction of interest and power moved toward the provinces and national issues. Cities particularly dropped in priority during the Great Depression and the Second World War. Humphrey Carver has succinctly characterized the period:

For us the economic depression of the thirties was a vacuum and a complete break with the past.... We had no public housing programs and none of the adventurous social experiments of the New Deal.... We withered on the stem. So in 1946 we almost literally started from scratch with no plans or planners, and we immediately hit a period of tremendous city growth.[20]

The federal government had returned to the housing field during the crisis of the 1930s and formalized its intervention with a new National Housing Act in 1944. A Crown corporation, the Central Mortgage and Housing Corporation, was established in 1945 to operate the act.[21] The number of new housing units financed under this scheme increased from almost 12,000 in 1946 to 65,000 in 1955. The long-term results of this federal intervention were twofold, according to Carver. The lending policies of the CMHC literally created a Canadian house-building industry which built thousands of these new homes, but little planning accompanied this rapid growth and cities sprawled into formless suburbs.[22] During the 1950s, CMHC was reoriented from its previous emphasis on suburban mortgage lending to a concern for the interior of cities through urban renewal by contributing 50 per cent of the cost of acquiring and clearing land for low-rental housing. The first major project was Regent Park South in Toronto, followed by the Jean Mance project in Montreal and Mulgrove Park in Halifax. What began with the enthusiasm of reform, however, soon became isolated monuments, for the expected tide of urban renewal failed to gather strength, leaving low-income people segregated in public housing ghettos.[23]

The federal government's activities in the cities was paralleled by the institutionalization of local planning through the establishment of departments of planning in municipal governments. This trend tended to bring planning more directly under political control, at the expense of the older system of planning commissioners or boards, whose respectable members presumably had been above politics.[24] In searching for planners, both the CMHC and local departments recruited heavily in Britain. One result was that the "British takeover of planning in the 1940s was massive".[25] According to critic Ron Clark, the consequences of this domination by British planners was a planning profession preoccupied with the physical details of land use and a relentless desire to centralize planning power at the expense of the public's involvement in the process.[26]

While it is extremely difficult to generalize about recent trends in urban planning, at least two divergent directions are apparent. One represents a reaction to the centralizing policies of the federal agencies and city planning departments and was symbolized by the citizen-oriented fight for local control of the Trefann Court project in Toronto.[27] The issue was simply whether people who are affected by planning could have a major voice in that planning. The other direction involved planning at an entirely different scale—the regional level —which was initiated with the studies leading to the concept of the Toronto-centred region. Metro Toronto combined with several departments of the provincial government in planning a parkway belt to accommodate future transportation and industrial development for a large section of southern Ontario, focused on Toronto. Both the local and regional planning concerns reflect a renaissance of urban consciousness. Ironically, this renewal is taking place in cities which no longer have the financial or political independence to determine their own destinies.

NOTES

1. One of the few general interpretations of Canadian planning history is Kent Gerecke, "The History of Canadian City Planning", *City Magazine*, vol. 2 (1976): 12-23.

2. Some of the earliest urban planning in Canada is briefly covered in John W. Reps, *Town Planning in Frontier America* (Princeton, 1969).

3. See Norman Gidney, "From Coal to Forest Products: The Changing Resource Base of Nanaimo, B.C.", *Urban History Review*, no. 2-78 (June 1978): 18-47; and Gilbert A. Stelter, "The Origins of a Company Town: Sudbury in the Nineteenth Century", *Laurentian University Review*, vol. 3 (1971): 3-37.
   Numerous other examples could be cited, including Prince Rupert, B.C., planned in 1904 by a distinguished Boston firm of landscape architects for the Grand Trunk Pacific Railway Company. See Nigel H. Richardson, "A Tale of Two Cities", in L. O. Gertler, ed. *Planning the Canadian Environment* (Montreal, 1972).

4. Michael Doucet, "Speculation and the Physical Development of Mid-Nineteenth Century Hamilton", and Isobel Ganton, "Land Sub-division in Toronto, 1847 – 1883", in Gilbert A. Stelter and Alan F. J. Artibise, eds. *Shaping the Canadian Urban Landscape: Essays on the City-Building Process* (forthcoming).

5. See, for example, Alan F. J. Artibise, *Winnipeg: A Social History of Urban Growth, 1874 – 1914* (Montreal, 1975); and Terry Copp, *The Anatomy of Poverty: The Condition of the Working Class in Toronto, 1897-1929* (Toronto, 1974).

6. "Tomorrow's Metropolis: The Urban Reform Movement in Canada, 1880 – 1920", in Gilbert A. Stelter and Alan F. J. Artibise, eds. *The Canadian City: Essays in Urban History* (Toronto, 1977), p. 368.

7. For an excellent collection of reformers' writings, see Paul Rutherford, ed. *Saving the Canadian City: The First Phase, 1880 – 1920 – An Anthology of Early Articles on Urban Reform* (Toronto, 1974).

8. Among the useful surveys of American planning is Mel Scott, *American City Planning Since 1890* (Berkeley, 1971).

9. Good general studies of British planning include Gordon Cherry, *Evolution of British Town Planning* (London, 1974); William Ashworth, *Genesis of Modern Town Planning* (London, 1954). The original work on the Garden City idea is Ebenezar Howard, *Garden Cities of Tomorrow* (London, 1902, with numerous

subsequent editions). Followers of this approach include Frederic Osborn and Arnold Whitlick, *The New Towns: The Answer to Megalopolis* (London, 1975).

10. *The Death and Life of Great American Cities* (New York, 1961), pp. 16-25.

11. Walter Van Nus, "The Fate of City Beautiful Thought in Canada, 1893 – 1930," in Stelter and Artibise, *The Canadian City*, pp. 162-85.

12. Quoted in Vladimir Tomovcik, "The Gréber Plan for Ottawa," MA thesis, University of Waterloo (1977), p. 40.

13. Contemporary sources for this period of planning are particularly rich. These include the voluminous Commission of Conservation annual reports, 1910 – 1919; the Commission's magazine, *Conservation of Life*, 1914 – 1921; the Proceedings of the National Conferences on City Planning, usually held in the United States, but held in Toronto in 1914; the dozens of speeches Thomas Adams and others gave to Canadian Clubs in Montreal, Ottawa, Toronto, Hamilton, Winnipeg, and Vancouver, and published in annual volumes of Club *Addresses* by those respective clubs.

14. Larry McCann, "The Changing Internal Structure of Canadian Resource Towns", *Plan Canada*, vol. 18 (1978): 45-59.

15. Paul Rutherford, "Introduction" to Herbert Brown Ames, *The City Below the Hill* (new ed., Toronto, 1972), p. xvi.

16. John C. Weaver, "'Tomorrow's Metropolis' Revisited: A Critical Assessment of Urban Reform in Canada, 1890 – 1920", in Stelter and Artibise, *The Canadian City*, pp. 403-09.

17. A. E. Grauer, *Housing* (Ottawa, 1939), A Study Prepared for the Royal Commission on Dominion-Provincial Relations; John Saywell, *Housing Canadians: Essays in the History of Residential Construction* (Ottawa, 1975); Alan H. Armstrong, "Thomas Adams and the Commission of Conservation", in Gertler, *Planning the Canadian Environment*, pp. 17-35.

18. Brahm Wiesman, "The Nature and Development of Provincial Planning Legislation, 1912 – 1975", paper presented at the Canadian Urban History Conference, University of Guelph (May 1977).

19. Gilbert A. Stelter and Alan F. J. Artibise, "Canadian Resource Towns in Historical Perspective", *Plan Canada*, vol. 18 (1978): 7-16.

20. "Planning in Canada", *Planning 1960* (Chicago, 1960), p. 22.

21. The history of urban planning since the Second World War has not been examined in detail but some useful guides are available. The most readable and full account is Humphrey Carver's humanistic autobiography, *Compassionate Landscape* (Toronto, 1975). An outline of federal legislation as applied to housing and planning can be found in David Bettinson, *The Politics of Canadian Urban Development* (Edmonton, 1975), pp. 61-104. For an anti-establishment interpretation of recent events, see Ron Clark, "The Crisis in Canadian City Planning", *City Magazine*, vol. 1 (1976): 17-24. Also useful are the historical sections of papers by Brahm Wiesman and Kenneth D. Cameron in H. Peter Oberlander, ed. *Canada: An Urban Agenda* (Ottawa, 1976).

22. *Compassionate Landscape*, pp. 107-08, 157.

23. For a detailed description of the reformist expectations and the administrative and political problems, see Albert Rose, *Regent Park: A Study of Slum Clearance* (Toronto, 1959); also, Carver, *Compassionate Landscape*, pp. 134-48.

24. Gerecke, "The History of Canadian City Planning", pp. 14-15.

25. Anthony Adamson, "Thirty Years of the Planning Business", *Plan Canada*, vol. 13 (1973): 7.

26. Clark, "The Crisis in City Planning", p. 22.

27. The major study of this struggle, when it still promised to be successful, is Graham Fraser, *Fighting Back: Urban Renewal in Trefann Court* (Toronto, 1972).

7.

The Ideas and Policies of the Canadian Planning Profession, 1909-1931

THOMAS I. GUNTON

During the late nineteenth and early twentieth centuries, Canadian society underwent a significant transformation.[1] Industrialization and urbanization challenged a social order more appropriate to an agrarian society than to a complex urban one. By the 1920s almost fifty per cent of the Canadian population was urban. Problems of urban slums, poverty, disease, moral decay, and the depopulation of the countryside received increased attention. No Canadian institution escaped the impact of these changes. Churches, mourning the passing of rural Canada, responded to the problems of urbanization with the formation of such organizations as the Social Service Council. Businessmen, such as Herbert Ames and Morley Wickett, formed groups dedicated to putting "the machine in honest hands". Civic Improvement leagues, composed of community residents interested in encouraging park development, civic beauty, and efficient government sprang up in most Canadian cities. Professionals became involved with the formation of the Commission of Conservation in 1909 and the Canadian Town Planning Institute in 1918. Canadian governments at all levels responded with legislation designed to alleviate the urban dilemma.

One dimension of the response to urban problems was the growth of a Canadian planning profession that attempted to mitigate the problems of the new urban industrial order by putting forward a variety of ideas and policies. An expression of these can be found in a number of journals and reports, most notably the Commission of Conservation *Annual Report*, the *Conservation of Life Journal*, and the *Journal of the Town Planning Institute of Canada*. This chapter will focus on the ideas and policies of the Canadian planning profession as reflected in these journals.

The fact that Britain and the United States were also undergoing the trauma of urbanization at the same time provides a valuable opportunity for comparative analysis. In all three countries, professional planning organizations dedicated to the eradication of urban ills were formed. But while both American and British planners experienced similar urban problems, each responded in different ways. The British planners, concentrating on housing and public

health issues, advocated state intervention in the production of housing and the creation of new utopian communities. American planners
de-emphasized housing and public health issues and rejected state
intervention. Instead, the Americans concentrated on beautifying the
city, applying zoning by-laws, and preparing transportation plans.
How did the Canadian planners respond to the urban problems? Did
they follow the American style, the British style, or did they generate
a distinctly Canadian approach?

The ideas and policies of the Canadian planning profession can be
divided into three major categories: rural collectivism, urban liberalism, and urban radicalism. Each of these themes can be isolated from
the mass of articles, reports, and speeches found in Canadian planning literature, even though there are many instances when the views
of various individuals contain aspects of more than one category. It is
also possible to trace the source of these themes to either British or
American precedents; there were few original ideas put forward by
the Canadian planning profession in the years before 1931.

Rural collectivism was based on two fundamental principles. First,
rural collectivists argued that the preservation of the rural way of life
was central to Canada's future. The process of urbanization was
clearly undesirable. Second, they believed that the preservation of an
agrarian society was dependent on employing strong collectivist policies, including state intervention and the formation of rural co-operatives. Some Canadian planners even suggested that the Canadian
economy, and the manufacturing sector in particular, were dependent
on a thriving agrarian community. In fact, one planner concluded that
a continuation of rural depopulation and "the present unhealthy
growth of large towns" would result inevitably in the total collapse of
Canadian society.[2]

Echoing the views of a large segment of Canadian society, some
planners went on to articulate an almost romantic vision of rural life.
On both a moral and physical level, rural life was considered superior
to urban life. Farmers had a sense of co-operative commitment to
Canada and to their fellow man; the rootless urban masses were not
to be trusted.[3] In the countryside, the air was fresh, the water clean,
and the malignant city absent. As one prominent Canadian observed:

> There is a rush, no doubt, into the cities from other sources. It is an
> unhappy tendency. In the city, living is dearer, the air is not so good. The
> moral atmosphere is worse for children. Country life has a sense of com-
> munity lacking in the city.[4]

Upon its inception in 1914, the Town Planning Branch of the Commission of Conservation immediately focused on the question of rural planning.[5] According to planners such as Thomas Adams,[6] a prominent British planner hired as a planning expert by the Commission of Conservation, rural problems were both obvious and serious.[7] The massive migration from farm to city was a result of a lack of rural credit, a lack of an adequate rate of return and, most significantly, a lack of social amenities in rural areas.[8]

Planners formulated a number of policies to deal with these problems. The first solution came under the category of scientific design. Farms were too large and were laid out in a manner that ignored the fertility of the soil and the topography of the land. Scientific surveys of farm land were recommended, leading to smaller, more compact farms.[9] The resulting increase in farm density would create small service towns dedicated to the provision of social amenities.[10] A second solution called for the establishment of credit, provided by the state, to aid in the establishment of farming co-operatives.[11] A third, more radical set of solutions suggested the need for changes in land tenure. Although the use of free homesteads was seen as an attractive aspect of Canadian farming life, it led to problems of land speculation and absentee landlords. Several leading planners proposed that the state clear the land, build the homesteads, and lease the farms to prospective farmers. Fertile farmland held idle by speculators was to be expropriated or taxed in a manner that would force the owner to sell or cultivate.[12] As one well-known Canadian planner, Noulan Cauchon, stated:

> It would be wise to undertake boldly and fearlessly the reversion to the crown of such suitable arable lands.... Once expropriated, the public domain should never more be allowed to pass from the crown.[13]

What is most notable, however, is not the specific proposals but the fact that a small but significant group of planners were calling for collectivist policies. At a time when the frontier thesis, romanticizing individualism and self-reliance, was being popularized in both the United States and Canada,[14] some planners were calling into question the feasibility of private development of agricultural land. Since, they argued, individual farmers lacked both the resources and the motivation to establish viable farming communities, it was essential for the state to supply the necessary initiative to settle the rural hinterland.[15]

The second major dimension of the Canadian response to rapid urbanization was urban liberalism. Unlike rural collectivists, urban liberals viewed the process of urbanization and industrialization as a symbol of progress. In a speech before the Canadian Club, Byron Walker summarized this "booster" view of the city in the following manner:

> Toronto is the second largest city of our country: it is the largest of English-speaking people; we want to show the British what our material civilization amounts to. . . . We do not always want to remain a wooden backwards place with provincial ideas.[16]

Although problems of slums, disease, and corruption were acknowledged, urban liberals believed that the structure of society was basically sound. Solutions to problems, therefore, had to be compatible with the laissez-faire idea. Herbert Ames, a Montreal businessman and a prominent author on urban problems, typified this mentality when, after completing an exhaustive scientific analysis of a portion of Montreal, he cautioned that any solution to urban ills must operate within a capitalist framework.[17]

Urban liberalism first manifested itself in a style of planning often referred to as City Beautiful planning. The essential features of a City Beautiful plan were the creation of parks, the construction of wide boulevards, and the building of massive civic centres and public buildings. It was felt that these measures would lead to a miraculous disappearance of the pressing urban problems of slums, poverty, and poor health. As one prominent City Beautiful planner concluded:

> It has been found that there is no better way to redeem a slum district than by cutting into it a great highway that will be filled with through-travel by a city's industries like a stream of pure water. Cleansing what it touches, this tide of traffic, pulsating with the joyousness of the city's life and toil, wakes the district to the larger interests and higher purposes.[18]

Some Canadian planners, lauding the efforts of American planners to eliminate the ugliness of their towns, urged Canadian municipalities to adopt similar measures such as sidewalk construction, tree planting, and hedge cutting.[19] Major Canadian plans, including the 1906 plan for Toronto and the 1915 plan for Ottawa, were based almost entirely on City Beautiful planning principles.[20]

Initially it seemed City Beautiful planning fit the bill; it was a conscious effort to deal with urban problems without challenging any basic tenets of Canadian society such as the rights of private property. Soon, however, Canadian planners lost their enthusiasm for City Beautiful planning because of its failure to deal with problems of health and housing, but more importantly, because of its high cost of implementation. One planner noted that the public assumed town planning "is only concerned with what is called by the ugly word 'beautification'; therefore, [it] is only another scheme for spending the money of citizens."[21]

It became obvious that urban liberals had to define another style of planning that dealt with urban problems without involving the extravagant public spending associated with City Beautiful planning. The new approach, termed "City Planning" by Thomas Adams, placed a strong emphasis on efficiency, science, and zoning, in addition to giving some attention to the City Beautiful concerns of boulevards, parks, and public buildings.[22] City Planning, then, was in many ways a mature and financially accountable City Beautiful approach. And, like the City Beautiful style of planning, City Planning reflected the values of urban liberalism: an acceptance of the urban industrial order, a rejection of strong state intervention, and a de-emphasis on housing and public health issues.

The belief of city planners in efficiency and science was intense. Efficiency became an ideology by which to evaluate any planning decision. During the 1920s, for example, a series of editorials appeared in the *Journal of the Town Planning Institute of Canada (JTPIC)* defining planning simply as a means of saving money.[23] Associating a profession with scientific origins seemed a prerequisite to establishing a certain legitimacy and objectivity in the eyes of the public, no matter how tenuous the connection may have been in fact. Simply mentioning the words "planning" and "science" together seemed to be sufficient.[24] Thomas Adams stated on numerous occasions that "practical men without scientific knowledge" as well as "utopian schemes without practicality" were the enemies of planning.[25] Science, it seemed, was more than a match for any urban problem.

Canadian planners were not as vocal, however, when asked about the specific implementation of a scientific, efficient approach to planning. None the less, they gradually pieced together a step-by-step formula for city planning which the planners attempted to follow on numerous occasions.[26] According to Thomas Adams, the planner was to commence with a fact-gathering mission referred to as the civic survey. The planner then was to prepare a transportation plan with detailed breakdowns between major and minor streets. The preparation of the all-important zoning by-law was the next step, aimed at legally preventing incompatible uses of adjacent properties; residential and industrial areas, for example, were not to be too close to one another. Having prepared the zoning by-law, the planner was then to address the matter of public buildings and parks. Finally, a subdivision control scheme was formulated to prevent building on topographically unsuitable land.

At first glance, the use of zoning by-laws establishing public regulation over private property appears contradictory to the basic tenets of urban liberalism. A major impetus behind the adoption of zoning by-laws was, however, the desire to increase property values.[27] Zoning became a good way of prohibiting the intrusion of industry and low-income tenements into the more prosperous neighbourhoods. A second justification of zoning was the protection of public health. An examination of some Canadian city zoning plans reveals, however, that this concern over public health was definitely of less importance. In the Kitchener plan, for example, the city was zoned into four categories: industrial, commercial, institutional, and residential.[28] Although no industrial uses were allowed in the areas zoned residential, residential uses were allowed in the industrial areas of the city. Surely, if it was important to keep noisy and polluting industries out of existing residential areas for public health reasons, it was just as important to keep new residential construction out of the unhealthy industrial areas. The urban liberals did not seem to think so.

While urban liberal planning de-emphasized the significance of health and housing issues, it did give some attention to these two problems. But any interest in these more humanitarian concerns had to be rationalized in terms of their impact on increasing the efficiency and industrial output of workers, not in terms of improving the quality of life for working people out of a sense of justice.[29] The president of the Town Planning Institute of Canada coined the following slogan at the 1924 Annual Meeting of the Institute:

Health for Efficiency
Efficiency for Production
Production for Well Being.[30]

It was also argued that the moral and physical security of the middle class depended upon decent health and housing standards.[31] J. J. Kelso, Superintendent of the Department of Neglected Children, put the matter with some urgency:

These slums are exceedingly dangerous to the health and morals of a city because they are, to the great majority of the people, inhuman and unexplored retreats. The slums should be attacked and abolished because they are the great enemy to the home which is the foundation of the state. Bad housing conditions inevitably tend to drunkenness in parents; to delinquency in children; to immorality in the growing generation; to the spread of typhoid fever, diphtheria, scarlet fever and the ravages of the great white plague.[32]

In fact, some planners suggested that the continuation of slums and bad health might even lead to social unrest and the establishment of Bolshevism in Canada.[33] But this concern did not lead to calls for socialistic measures to solve health and housing problems.[34] In fact, some observers attributed the failure of Canadian municipalities to take full advantage of federal government post-war housing loans to an apprehension by some Canadian planners about state intervention.[35]

Urban liberals seemed more comfortable with such solutions as "philanthropy and five per cent".[36] This proposal involved the establishment of philanthropic housing associations made up of "public-spirited entrepreneurs" who would borrow government money at subsidized interest rates to build housing for low-income people at a maximum rate of return of five per cent. And, of course, there was always the vague suggestion by some planners that an "application of scientific knowledge" would miraculously eliminate the problem.[37] As might be expected, they were never very clear as to what those "scientific principles" were.

Urban radicalism, the third dimension of the planning response to the urban crisis, was fundamentally different from rural collectivism and urban liberalism. Unlike the rural collectivists, urban radicals accepted the urban setting as desirable. But, unlike the liberals, the radicals concluded that the solution to urban problems required the establishment of an aggressive system of state planning that would replace the vagaries of the unrestrained capitalist system. Further, the primary objective of state interventionist planning was to improve the lot of the average Canadian. Urban radicalism, therefore, reflected a synthesis of the collectivist elements of rural collectivism with the urban orientation of the urban liberals.

The fundamental differences between the urban liberal and urban radical approaches were apparent in the treatment of public health and housing issues. For urban radicals, public health and housing were viewed as the very foundations of planning, not as some peripheral concern. Thomas Adams summarized this distinction between urban liberal planning (which he termed "City Planning") and urban radical planning (which he termed "Town Planning") in the following way:

City planning is the control of street lines, laying out of boulevards and open space, control of sky line in buildings and other matters which are concerned with the monumental side of the town rather than with the home life of the people.

Now town planning includes the consideration of every aspect of city life. And the essence of town planning is the safeguarding of the health of the community and the provision of proper homes for the people.[38]

In making this statement, Adams expressed his clear support for Town Planning, not City Planning. A significant component of the Canadian planning movement agreed. For example, from its inception in 1909, the Commission of Conservation frankly admitted that its interest in Town Planning was only a product of an interest in public health.[39] Indeed, the Commission hired Dr. Charles Hodgetts, previously medical health officer for Ontario, and began its public health studies over four years before it hired Thomas Adams, the Town Planning expert, to set up the Town Planning Branch of the Commission of Conservation.[40] Also, whenever Canadian planners attended planning conferences, such as the 1910 International Planning Conference in London or the Annual National City Planning Conference in Toronto, they expressed their concern about public health and housing.[41] As one planner stated: "Town planning may be regarded as good only in so far as it raises the standard of public health or gives better housing conditions and as bad as in proportion as the reverse is the case."[42]

The differences between urban liberalism and urban radicalism were even more apparent in the types of policies which were advocated to solve the health and housing problems. Urban radical policies sought to replace private enterprise, rigid notions of private property, and individualism with public intervention in both land ownership and the construction of housing. As Dr. Hodgetts, medical advisor to the Commission of Conservation, put it: "If ownership is one of the foundations of society, public health is another and it also has a right to consideration."[43] Some planners, including Thomas Adams, argued that property owners who disregarded public health should have their property expropriated by the state without compensation.[44] The housing crisis, a problem created by "greedy land speculators",[45] should be solved by land expropriation and the construction of state housing.[46] These planners had little patience with the idea of leaving the housing problem to private charities. Some planners went as far as suggesting that the government should redistribute wealth as well as construct housing and own land.[47]

One of the more radical aspects of the urban radical perspective was the promotion of garden cities. The European Garden City Movement had its origins in the utopian socialism of Saint Simon, Fourier, and Owen.[48] Although there were some differences among the utopian socialists, they all generally proposed a vision of a new society based on a sense of co-operation and collectivism manifested physically in the form of small independent communities dedicated to the pursuit of "civilized goals".[49] Ebenezer Howard, the father of the Garden City idea, moulded the concepts of earlier utopian socialists into a capitivating scenario which found some support among Canadian planners. For Howard, the key to the success of these communities was the public ownership of land and the functioning of a mixed economy containing co-operatives as well as some private enterprises.[50] Howard's purpose was as follows:

> To establish a system of distribution to take the place of chaos; a just system of land tenure for one representing the selfishness which we hope is passing away; to found pensions with liberty for our aged poor now imprisoned in our work houses, to banish despair and awaken hope in the breasts of those who have fallen; to silence the harsh voice of anger; and to awaken the soft notes of brotherhood and good will.[51]

The first hint of any support for a Garden City concept in Canadian planning journals came in 1916 when a Canadian planner called for the decentralization of large cities and the encouragement of settlement in small towns.[52] Several years later, other prominent Canadian planners advocated similar programs. Editorials in the *JTPIC* treated the Garden City Movement as the symbol of a social renaissance; a new society based on an equitable social system where slums and poverty would be eliminated.[53] Its application to Canada was regarded as imminent. One planner concluded that garden cities were "the answer of scientific reason to the universal demand for a more civilized basis for urban society".[54]

Support for urban radicalism in Canadian planning was, of course, never as strong as the support for urban liberalism. Yet, radicalism existed as a well-defined approach to planning that challenged a few of the basic tenets of capitalist society. As Buckley, the editor of the *JTPIC*, remarked: "A social system that keeps a few people inordinately rich and masses of the people not only poor in money but poor in enjoyment is fundamentally a failure."[55]

Early in the Canadian planning movement, Canadian planners had suggested that they would be highly dependent upon the United

States and Great Britain for both planners and planning ideas.[56] This
prophecy proved valid. The thrust of British planning ideas, based
predominantly on the public health, housing, and Garden City Movement, showed strong similarities with the Canadian ideas of urban
radicalism.[57] Starting as early as the 1830s, British planners wrote a
series of planning reports on housing and public health issues that
advocated strong state control and called for public expropriation of
private property, nationalization of land, and state construction of
housing.[58] The British government responded with several pieces of
legislation embodying many of these principles. In fact, by the 1920s,
British planners were applauding the British government for initiating
90 per cent of all new housing when only a few short years before the
government share of the market was a mere 10 per cent.[59]

Garden Cities, the other major component of urban radical thought
in Canada, also had their origins in Britain. The intensity of support
for the Garden City idea by British planners was indicated by the
publication of the *Journal of the Garden City and Town Planning
Association*, an effort dedicated to the Garden City idea, and the
publication of numerous articles in other planning journals supporting
the garden city as the answer to the problems of urban society.[60] The
extent of support for this "new society" in British life can be seen by
the eventually large government support for New Town programs. A
second strain in British planning thought was similar to rural collectivism. Like their Canadian counterparts, some British planners called
for policies of government ownership of land and the creation of rural
co-operatives to deal with Britain's rural problems.[61]

Canadian urban liberal planning thought seemed closely akin to
American planning ideas as embodied in the "City Beautiful" and
"City Planning" approaches. The City Beautiful Movement in the
United States matured into a full fledged style of planning with the
development of the Columbian Exposition in Chicago in 1893 and the
Washington and Chicago plans at the turn of the century.[62] Daniel
Burnham, the chief figure in the American movement, summarized
his views on planning at the London International Conference by
stating that the objectives of planning must be "order and beauty".[63]

American planners began rejecting the City Beautiful approach for
the more responsible and efficient City Planning approach several
years before their Canadian counterparts.[64] Efficiency, science, zoning, parks, and transportation, the major issues of city planning, soon
became the primary topics of discussion at almost all of the Annual
National Conferences on City Planning in the United States.[65] Goals

of efficiency were so intense that one American observer stated: "Efficiency is not to be judged from preconceived notions of morality but morality is perhaps to be reconsidered and reviewed by the help of fundamentals of efficiency."[66]

The American planners were apprehensive about aspects of urban radicalism. Although there was some discussion of urban radical policies in esoteric circles,[67] urban radicalism never permeated the mainstream debates the way it did in the Canadian journals.[68] Housing and public health issues, a major focus of urban radical concern, were rarely discussed at annual planning conferences in America.[69] Even when American planners did mention health and housing, they religiously rejected strong state intervention as a solution to urban ills. Lawrence Veiller, the president of the National Housing Association of the United States, expressed a widely held view when he insisted that although the British approach of public housing construction was a highly effective program it could not be adopted in the U.S. because:

> The United States is a land of private enterprise and that government housing plays no part in the solution of its housing problems.... The observance of this principle is essential to the preservation of democracy.[70]

American planners, instead, concerned themselves with passing by-laws or with constructing Tappan Steel houses (a new house design promoted by the company's owner, Tappan, a planner and entrepreneur) or with the old standby of philanthropy and five per cent.[71] Planners such as Veiller frequently admitted that a policy of Garden Cities was an attractive solution to urban problems,[72] but they speedily dismissed the policy as being ideologically unacceptable; the idea of public ownership of land was completely foreign to American thinking.[73] And government policy seemed to confirm this.[74]

The Canadian planners' reliance on both American urban liberal and British urban radical styles of planning resulted in a rather awkward compromise. Canadian planning represented the British model moderated by American influence; decreased emphasis on health and housing and equivocal support of the Garden City and state intervention. Also, the fact that Canadian planning included some concern for housing, a belief in scientific humanism instead of merely science, and the use of zoning for public health as opposed to the use of zoning for efficiency alone, suggests some attachment to the American model as modified by British influence.

Why did Canadian planning have strong similarities to British urban radicalism and American urban liberalism and yet accept neither? The obvious and simple explanation for this phenomenon lies in what could be termed a cultural transmission theory: Canadian planners simply adopted those ideas to which they were exposed. But as the example of the United States demonstrates, this interpretation lacks credibility. The American planning movement was also exposed to many British ideas but chose to reject the principal features of the British planning movement due, in large part, to a rigid belief in liberalism.

It is probable that some British ideas were welcome in Canada for two principal reasons. They were, first, thought to be relevant to the material conditions of the Canadian environment. Although Canada was not urbanizing as quickly as Great Britain, Canadian planners seemed to feel that they were facing the same types of problems faced by British planners, and that British planning policies could help resolve those problems.[75] As one observer concluded:

> There is no earthly reason why the principle [garden cities] should not be applied in Canada, America, the Antropodes or anywhere else. It is simply applied common sense and the whole object of this thing is to provide good comfortable dwellings for everybody.[76]

But Canadian planners not only saw similarities between Canada and Britain, they felt that the British urban radical style of planning was superior to the American's urban liberal approach.[77] The liberal capitalist idea, pre-urban in origin, now had to confront a complex urban society, and it was by no means clear that it could do so successfully. It might be acceptable to preach individualism, self-reliance, and freedom from collectivist constraints on the frontier where one was self-sufficient and one's nearest neighbour had difficulty visiting, let alone impinging upon one's health and welfare. But the urban community was fundamentally different. The divisions of labour in such a community resulted in extreme interdependence and the congestion resulted in the potential for the behaviour of one citizen to have disastrous implications for others. Also, the sheer power to transform the environment led to the need for considering some strong government restraints to protect the public welfare. The successful management of the urban environment seemed dependent upon the use of urban radical policies.

A second element disposing Canadian planners to accept urban radicalism may have been the nature of the Canadian political tradition. As a number of commentators have pointed out, Tory and collectivist tendencies occupied a more prominent place in the Canadian mind than they did in the American.[78] Canadians, in consequence, showed themselves much more willing than their southern neighbours to welcome the positive state and allow a marked degree of government planning and intervention in the social and economic sphere. This should not, however, lead to the conclusion that American ideas were incompatible with the basic orientation of the Canadian mind. Although collectivist tendencies were present in Canadian society, they were not nearly as evident as in Great Britain since Canada did not have the lengthy feudal heritage of the mother country.

Why were Canadian collectivist ideas too weak to support both a strong rural collectivism and an urban radicalism? The impact of the frontier seems to be a crucial variable.[79] It must, indeed, be emphasized that the planning movement was primarily environmentalist in its interpretation. And by thinking in environmental terms, Canadian planners were unconsciously forced to begin identifying with the United States. As Morley Wickett, a prominent businessman involved in urban affairs, noted, both Canada and the United States had a new world experience.[80] As Canadians began to think in environmental terms, they, like their southern neighbours, began to emphasize the significance of the frontier in Canadian experience. The myth of the true north strong and free is, in fact, a Canadian version of the idea that the environment vitalizes those who live in its midst. Canadians, the myth suggests, would be even more self-reliant and rugged than Americans and, by implication, Canadian society would be even more individualistic than American society.

Yet Canada, thanks to its "Tory touch", could never see the frontier in precisely the same terms as did a country that viewed it through unambiguously liberal eyes. The peculiar character of the Canadian ideological tradition thus joined with the nature of the physical environment to ensure that Canadian planning thought would be a hybrid, combining important elements of both the American and the British approaches to planning. Adams, for example, wrote that housing was the key issue in planning, that state intervention was essential, that garden cities were a good idea, and that private property should be expropriated without compensation. But he also argued that private property was sacred, private enterprise crucial, and transportation, park planning, and zoning the primary concerns of the planner.[81] Noulan Cauchon, another leading planner of the period, expressed the same ambiguous attachment to both American and British planning ideas.[82] Even the definition of planning employed by the Canadian Town Planning Institute presented an ambiguous conception of planning. It was defined as both efficiency-oriented, placing it in the urban liberal category, and public-health-oriented, placing it in the urban radical category. At the same time, it was both urban and rural in scope:

> Town planning may be defined as the scientific and orderly disposition of land and buildings in use and development with a view to obviating congestion and securing economic and social efficiency, health and well-being in urban and rural communities.[83]

Canadian planners approached urban problems in three distinct ways: rural collectivism, urban liberalism, and urban radicalism. These contradictory approaches made it impossible for the planning profession to attract a dedicated following in Canadian society.[84] While the businessman was attracted to the efficiency aspect of urban liberal planning ideas, he was also suspicious of the urban radical ideas with their emphasis on a new and equitable social order. Poorly housed working people, attracted by the promise by planners to solve the housing crisis, could hardly trust planners suggesting that good planning increased profits of real estate and business interests. Homeowners, attracted by the promise to protect property values, were concerned with discussions of property expropriation. Agrarian interests were wary of the appeal to urban interests, and *vice versa*. The Canadian planning movement, by trying to appeal to all segments, appealed to none.

With the coming of the Great Depression, the need for planning was more compelling than ever before. Canadian planning floundered; a 1943 survey of Canadian cities and towns showed that not one city or town had adopted an official community plan and few were doing any planning.[85] Canada had no public housing programs and none of the adventurous social experiments of the American New Deal.[86] Both planners and Canadian society at large could reach no consensus on the nature of the planning profession; the foundations were simply not deep enough.

In the years after 1945, when planning became one of the key priorities of Canada's postwar recovery effort, urban liberalism quickly emerged as the strongest theme in the Canadian planning profession. The collectivist tradition, weak to begin with, could not adequately support two distinct styles of collectivist planning, rural collectivism, sympathetic to the rural option, and urban radicalism, sympathetic to the urban option. This, then, became the tragedy of Canadian planning; while it was able to share in the vitality and efficiency of urban radicalism and the planned society, it accepted the impotency of urban liberalism and the unplanned society. And, when the need for planning was greatest—during the tremendous urban growth of the 1950s and 1960s—the response of the planning profession was weak. Canadian planning had had its battle with the private market forces and had lost.

NOTES

1. For a general study, see R. C. Brown and R. Cook, *Canada, 1896 – 1921: A Nation Transformed* (Toronto, 1974).

2. "Agriculture and Industrial Urbanization", *Commission of Conservation Annual Report* (1916), pp. 129-34 (hereafter *Commission A. R.*); George Phelps, "Need for Government Organization of Land Settlement", *Conservation of Life: Public Health, Housing and Town Planning*, vol. 4, no. 1 (1918): 3-8 (hereafter *Conservation*).

3. "Agriculture and Industrial Urbanization," pp. 118-29; Peter Bryce, "Some After-War Problems", *Conservation*, vol. 2 no. 3 (1916): 50-53; and Phelps, "Need for Government Organization of Land Settlement", *Conservation*, vol. 4 no. 1 (1918): 3-8.

4. Goldwin Smith, "Toronto, A Turn in its History", *Canadian Magazine*, vol. 28 (1906): 525.

5. Phelps, "Need for Government Organization of Land Settlement", pp. 3-8.

6. Thomas Adams was the first president of the British Town Planning Institute and first secretary of the Garden City Association of Letchworth. He began his career in Canada in 1914 as a consultant to the Commission of Conservation and remained as Canada's most prominent planner until his departure to New York in 1923. See Alan H. Armstrong, "Thomas Adams and the Commission of Conservation", in L. O. Gertler, ed. *Planning the Canadian Environment* (Montreal, 1972), pp. 17-35.

7. Thomas Adams, "Report of the Planning Development Branch", *Commission A. R.* (1917), pp. 92-107.

8. Ibid., pp. 92-102.

9. Ibid.

10. Noulan Cauchon, "Rural Planning", *Town Planning Institute Journal*, vol. 3 no. 1 (1916): 9 (hereafter *TPIJ*).

11. "Agriculture and Industrial Urbanization", p. 9.

12. Phelps, "Need for Government Organization of Land Settlement", pp. 5-8; Cauchon, "The Economic Release of Canadian Lands", *Journal of the Town Planning Institute of Canada*, vol. 6, no. 1 (1927): 37-40 (hereafter *JTPIC*); and Adams, "Should Government Conscript Land or Regulate Its Use", *Conservation*, vol. 4, no. 3 (1918): 59.

13. Cauchon, "The Economic Release of Canadian Lands", pp. 37-40.

14. Frederick J. Turner, *Frontier in American History* (New York, 1962); and J. M. S. Careless, "Frontierism, Metropolitanism and Canadian History", in C. Berger, ed. *Approaches to Canadian History* (Toronto, 1967), pp. 63-83.

15. "Agriculture and Industrial Urbanization", pp. 4-10; and Phelps, "Need for Government Organization of Land Settlement", pp. 3-6.

16. Byron E. Walker, "A Comprehensive Plan for Toronto", in Paul Rutherford, ed. *Saving the*

Canadian City: The First Phase, 1880–1920 (Toronto, 1974), p. 225. See also Alan F. J. Artibise, "Boosterism and the Development of Prairie Cities, 1871–1913", in Gilbert A. Stelter and Alan F. J. Artibise, eds. *Shaping the Canadian Urban Landscape: Essays on the City-Building Process* (forthcoming).

17. Herbert Ames, *City Below the Hill: A Sociological Study of a Portion of the City of Montreal* (Toronto, 1972 [first published 1897]). See also Terry Copp, *The Anatomy of Poverty: The Condition of the Working Class in Montreal, 1897-1929* (Toronto, 1974).

18. Charles M. Robinson, *Modern Civic Art* (New York, 1903), p. 121.

19. "Civic Improvement Organization for Canada", *Conservation*, vol. 2 no. 1 (1915): 5.

20. Walker, "A Comprehensive Plan for Toronto", p. 223; and "Housing, Town Planning and Civic Improvement in Canada", *Conservation*, vol. 2, no. 4 (1916): 89.

21. "Town Planning in British Columbia", *Conservation*, vol. 4, no. 3 (1918): 65.

22. Adams, "Comments", *Proceedings of the Sixth Annual Conference on City Planning* (Toronto, 1914), p. 149; and Adams, "Modern City Planning", *JTPIC*, vol. 1, no. 11 (1922): 11-14.

23. James Ewing, "Ways and Means", *JTPIC*, vol. 1, no. 4 (1921): 5-9; Adams, "Modern City Planning", pp. 11–14; and "Town Planning Reduces Taxes", *JTPIC*, vol. 1, no. 8 (1922): 2.

24. A. G. Dalzell, "Housing of the Industrial Classes in Canada", *JTPIC*, vol. 7, no. 5 (1928): 126; and Ewing, "Plain Words for Montreal", *JTPIC*, vol. 4, no. 4 (1925): 12-14.

25. Adams, "Planning Greater Halifax", *Conservation*, vol. 4, no. 4 (1918): 82.

26. Dalzell, "A Contrast in City Planning", *JTPIC*, vol. 2, no. 2 (1923): 18; Cauchon, "Critique by Noulan Cauchon," *JTPIC*, vol. 4, no. 5 (1925): 14; Cauchon, "A New Federal District Commission for

Ottawa", *JTPIC*, vol. 6, no. 3 (1927): 109-12; Horace Seymour, "A Plan for the City of Kitchener", *JTPIC*, vol. 4, no. 1 (1925): 2-8; and Town Planning Institute of Canada, "Proposed Planning Act for Quebec", *JTPIC*, vol. 8, no. 4 (1929): 72-77.

27. Cauchon, "Zoning; Its Financial Value", *JTPIC*, vol. 2, no. 3 (1923): 11; "Economic Case for Zoning," *JTPIC*, vol. 5, no. 1 (1926): 23-24; J. M. Kitchen, "What it Means to Zone", *JTPIC*, vol. 5, no. 2 (1926): 38; and "Zoning of Ottawa", *JTPIC*, vol. 2, no. 5 (1923): 23.

28. Seymour, "A Plan for the City of Kitchener", pp. 2-8.

29. Adams, "Report on Housing, Town Planning and Municipal Government", *Commission A. R.* (1919), pp. 95-98; and Cauchon, "Presidential Address", *JTPIC*, vol. 3, no. 1 (1924): 7.

30. Cauchon, "Presidential Address", p. 7.

31. Ames, *City Below the Hill*, pp. 44-45; and Dr. Charles Hastings, "Modern Conception of Public Health", *Conservation*, vol. 3, no. 4 (1917): 87-91.

32. J. J. Kelso, "Unsanitary Housing," *Commission A. R.* (1910), p. 51.

33. "Urgency of Housing Problems in Quebec", *Conservation*, vol. 5, no. 1 (1919): 3-4.

34. "Housing in Canada", *JTPIC*, vol. 6, no. 3 (1928): 7-72; Frank Beer, "A Plea for City Planning Organization", *Commission A. R.* (1914), pp. 110-21; and Ames, *City Below the Hill*, p. 133.

35. "Why Toronto Housing was Held Up", *JTPIC*, vol. 9, no. 2 (1930): 34-36; and "Building Should Proceed", *Conservation*, vol. 6, no. 3 (1920): 52.

36. Alfred Buckley, "Garden City Idea", *JTPIC*, vol. 4, no. 3 (1925): 4-8; Kitchen, "What it Means to Zone", pp. 3-8, Beer, "A Plea for City Planning Organization", pp. 110-21; and Ames, *City Below the Hill*, p. 113.

37. Dalzell, "Housing of the Industrial Classes in Canada", pp. 123-26.

38. Adams, "Comments", p. 149.

39. *Commission A. R.* (1914), pp. 10-15.
40. Ibid. (1911), pp. 50-52; and ibid. (1915), p. 3. See also Kent Gerecke, "The History of Canadian City Planning", in James Lorimer and Evelyn Ross, eds. *The Second City Book: Studies of Urban and Suburban Canada* (Toronto, 1977), pp. 150-61.
41. Dr. Sidney Lawrence, "Discussion", *Transactions: 1910 International Conference on City Planning*, p. 58; and Clifford Sifton, "Address of Welcome", *Proceedings of the Sixth National Conference on City Planning* (1914), pp. 5-13.
42. "Housing Conditions in Berlin", *Conservation*, vol. 2, no. 3 (1916): 63.
43. Dr. Charles Hodgetts, *Commission A. R.* (1910), pp. 50-51.
44. Adams, "Planning of Cities in Ontario," *Conservation*, vol. 6, no. 1 (1920): 2-4.
45. Dalzell, "Housing of the Industrial Classes in Canada", pp. 123-26.
46. Dalzell, "Current Trends in Housing", *JTPIC*, vol. 9, no. 2 (1930): 34-36; and "Civic Improvement, Town Planning and Housing in Canada", *Conservation*, vol. 4, no. 4 (1918): 91-94; and Dr. Charles Hastings, "Modern Conception of Public Health", *Conservation*, vol. 3, no. 4 (1917): 87-91.
47. Alfred Hastings, "Modern Conception of Public Health", pp. 87-91.
48. Leonard Benevolo, *Origins of Modern Town Planning* (London, 1967), pp. 39-85.
49. Ibid., p. 51; and William Ashworth, *Genesis of Modern British Town Planning* (London, 1954), pp. 122-41.
50. Ebenezer Howard, *Garden Cities of Tomorrow* (London, 1965), pp. 58-95.
51. Ibid., p. 150.
52. "Settlement of Agricultural Areas", *Conservation* vol. 2, no. 2 (January 1916): 43-44.
53. Alfred Buckley, "Garden City Idea", *JTPIC*, vol. 4, no. 3 (June 1925): 4-8; and "Garden Cities and the Social Renaissance," *JTPIC*, vol. 6, no. 3 (June 1927): 89-97.

54. Buckley, "Garden Cities and the Social Rennaissance", p. 89.
55. Buckley, "Town Planning: The Science of the Social Organism", *JTPIC*, vol. 6, no. 1 (February 1927): 43-44.
56. Adams, "Road Improvements", *Conservation*, vol. 2, no. 1 (October 1915): 11; and "Editorial" *JTPIC*, vol. 1, no. 2 (1921):1.
57. Peter Hall, *Urban and Regional Planning* (London. 1974), pp. 18-19. Gordon Cherry, *Evolution of Britisn Town Planning* (London, 1974); William Ashworth, *Genesis of Modern Town Planning* (London, 1954); and Lewis Keeble, *Town Planning at the Crossroads* (London, 1961).
58. Leonard Stokes, "Address by the President", *Town Planning Conference: Transactions* (London, 1910), p. 61; Raymond Unwin, "Symposium on Municipal Ownership of Land", *Town Planning Review*, vol. 4, no. 1 (April 1913): 13-15 (hereafter *TRP*); Henry Aldridge, "Municipal Ownership of Land", *TPR*, vol. 3, no. 4 (January 1913): 233; and S. D. Adshead, "Municipal Ownership of Land", *TPR*, vol. 3, no. 4 (January 1913): 238.
59. J. S. Clarke, "Housing in Relation to Public Health and Social Welfare," *TPR*, vol. 11, no. 4 (February 1926): 261.
60. See, for example, Reade, "A Defense of Garden Cities", *TPR*, vol. 4, no. 3 (April 1913): 245-51; and Lloyd, "New Town Proposals", *TPR*, vol. 4, no. 3 (October 1913): 245-52.
61. Adshead, "Town Planning and the Rural Problem", *TPR*, vol. 4, no. 4 (January 1914), p. 30; and Patrick Abercrombie, "Preservation of Rural England", *TPR*, vol. 12, no. 1 (May 1926): 5-56.
62. Mel Scott, *American City Planning Since 1890* (Berkeley, 1971), pp. 47-110; James G. Coke, "Antecedents of Local Planning", in William I. Goodman and Eric C. Freund, eds. *Principles and Practice of Urban Planning* (Washington, D.C.: International City Managers' Association, 1968), pp. 5-29; Norman J. Johnston, "A Preface to the

Institute", *Journal of the American Institute of Planners*, vol. 31 (1965): 198-210 (hereafter *JAIP*); and Roy Lubove, *The Urban Community: Housing and Planning in the Progressive Era* (Englewood Cliffs, N.J., 1967), pp. 1-23.

63. Burnham, "City of the Future under a Democratic Government", *Town Planning Conference: Transactions* (London, 1910), p. 371.

64. Scott, *American City Planning*, pp. 110-83; and Lubove, *The Urban Community*, pp. 1-23.

65. *Proceedings of the National Conference on City Planning* (1914 – 1931).

66. Harrington, Emerson, *Efficency as a Basis for Operation and Wages*, cited in Melvin Holli, "Urban Reform", in Lewis L. Gould, ed., *The Progressive Era* (Syracuse, 1974), p. 147.

67. Roy Lubove, *Community Planning in the 1920s* (Pittsburgh, 1963).

68. Scott, *American City Planning*, pp. 110-83.

69. *Proceedings of the National Conference on City Planning* (1914 – 1931).

70. Lawrence Veiller, "Housing Problems in the United States", *TPR*, vol. 13, no. 4 (1929): 239.

71. Buttenheim, "Slum Clearance by Private Effort", *JTPIC*, vol. 8, no. 2 (1929): 29; Tappan, "The Tappan Factory Made Steel House", *JTPIC*, vol. 8, no. 2 (1929): 32-35; Edith Wood, "Is Government Aid Necessary in Housing Financing", *JTPIC*, vol. 8, no. 2 (1939): 26-38; and Veiller, "Are Great Cities a Menace", *JTPIC*, vol. 2, no. 1 (1923): 7.

72. Ibid.; and "Slum Clearance Policy", *JTPIC*, vol. 8, no. 2 (1929): 8.

73. Veiller, "Are Great Cities a Menace", p. 7.

74. Scott, *American City Planning*, pp. 110-83; and Lubove, *The Urban Community*.

75. Hodgetts, "Housing and Town Planning", *Commission A. R.* (1912), p. 130; "Dinner to Garden City Delegates," *JTPIC*, vol. 4, no. 3 (1925): 27; and "Tendencies in American Housing," *JTPIC*, vol. 8, no. 1 (1929): 10.

76. W. R. Davidge, "Comments", *Proceedings of the Sixth National Conference on City Planning* (Toronto, 1914), p. 19.

77. "Dinner to Garden City Delegates," *JTPIC*, vol 4, no. 3 (1925): 27; and "Tendencies in American Housing", *JTPIC*, vol. 8, no. 1 (1929): 10.

78. Gad Horowitz, "Conservatism, Liberalism, Socialism in Canada: An Interpretation", *Canadian Journal of Economics and Political Science*, vol. 32, no. 5 (1966): 143-72; Kenneth McCrae, "Structure of Canadian History", in Louis Hartz, ed. *Founding of New Societies* (New York, 1964), pp. 219-74; Carl Berger, *Sense of Power: Studies in the Ideas of Canadian Imperialism, 1867 – 1914* (Toronto, 1970); Seymour Lipset, *Agrarian Socialism: The CCF in Saskatchewan* (Toronto, 1950); George Grant, *Lament for a Nation: The Defeat of Canadian Nationalism* (Toronto, 1970); and Hershel Hardin, *A Nation Unaware: The Canadian Economic Culture* (Vancouver, 1974).

79. Cole Harris, "Myth of the Land in Canadian Nationalism", in Peter Russell, ed. *Nationalism in Canada* (Toronto, 1966), pp. 27-43; Carl Berger, "True North Strong and Free", ibid., pp. 3-26; Marcia B. Kline, *Beyond the Land Itself: Views of Nature in Canada and the U.S.* (Cambridge, Mass., 1970); McRae, "Structure of Canadian Society"; William Kilbourn, "Writing of Canadian History After 1920", in C. F. Klink, *et al.*, eds. *Literary History of Canada* (Toronto, 1965), pp. 496-519; J. M. S. Careless, "Frontierism, Metropolitanism and Canadian History", in Berger, ed. *Approaches to Canadian History*, pp. 63-83; and Donald Creighton, *Towards the Discovery of Canada* (Toronto, 1972), pp. 28-46.

80. Wickett, "City Government in Canada", p. 290.

81. Adams, "Government Housing During the War", pp. 25-28; "Improvement Housing During the War", pp. 25-28; "Improvement of Slum Areas", pp. 36-39; "Should Government Conscript Land", p. 59;

"Town Planning, Housing and Public Health", p. 123; and "Modern City Planning", p. 11.

82. Cauchon, "Town Planning and the Proposal for a Federal District for Ottawa", p. 25; "Economic Release of Canadian Lands", pp. 37-40; "Zoning and Town Planning Legislation", p. 177; "Critique by Cauchon", p. 14; "Presidential Address", p. 7; and "Zoning: Its Financial Value", p. 11.

83. *JTPIC*, vol. 2, no. 2 (1923): 1.

84. "Arrival of Public Opinion," *JTPIC*, vol. 6, no. 6 (1927): 191-215.

85. Gerecke, "History of Canadian City Planning", pp. 151-52.

86. Humphrey Carver, "Planning in Canada," *Habitat*, vol. 3, no. 5 (1960): 10.

8

The Principle of Utility and the Origins of Planning Legislation in Alberta, 1912 – 1975

P. J. SMITH*

When the idea of planning as a social responsibility of government was first given legal form in Alberta, in 1913, the enabling legislation was built on a single ethic—the principle of utility. Over a span of a century or more, that ethic was the foundation of much beneficial reform in the institutions of government but, as a basis for planning, and particularly as a basis for making choice judgments in conflict situations, it is fundamentally unworkable. Nevertheless, the principle of utility continues to be the ethical cornerstone of urban planning legislation, in Alberta as elsewhere. Through the inertia of its central doctrine, a once radical institution became a reactionary one.

THE INTERNATIONAL VISION: EFFICIENCY AND ORDER, PROGRESS, AND THE PUBLIC GOOD

Alberta's Town Planning Act of 1913 was passed at a time of considerable reform effort, nationally and internationally. At first glance, that may seem to be all the explanation that is needed, but Alberta was actually one of the first governments anywhere to take such a step. In Canada, only New Brunswick and Nova Scotia acted more quickly, and the tardiness of other provinces was to be a regular complaint of planning advocates for at least the next decade.[1] It must also be remembered that the Province of Alberta was only eight years old in 1913. It was remote, sparsely settled, and essentially agrarian. It had no cities worthy of the name, and its total urban population was only 150,000. Yet the Alberta legislation was undoubtedly in the mainstream of planning philosophy as it was evolving around the world, and can be understood only in the context of much larger international currents.

* Three graduate students made important contributions to this essay. Steve Martin and Lynfa Jones were of great help in searching through local records, and Bill Batey provided invaluable assistance in clarifying the central idea.

Utilitarianism and the Urban Environment

The 1913 act was modelled closely on the first planning legislation of the English-speaking world, the Housing, Town Planning, etc. Act which was adopted by the British Parliament in 1909 and which, in its turn, was merely a step in a long evolutionary process.[2]

FIGURE 8:1

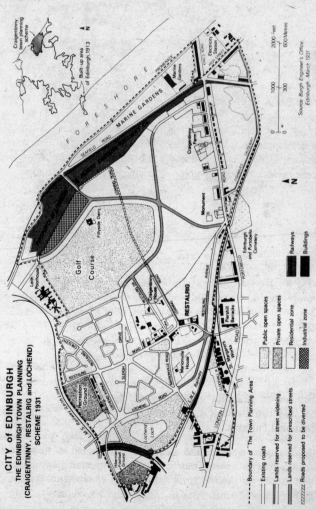

CITY of EDINBURGH
THE EDINBURGH TOWN PLANNING
(CRAIGENTINNY, RESTALRIG and LOCHEND)
SCHEME 1931

Source Burgh Engineer's Office.
Edinburgh, March 1931

FIGURE 8:2

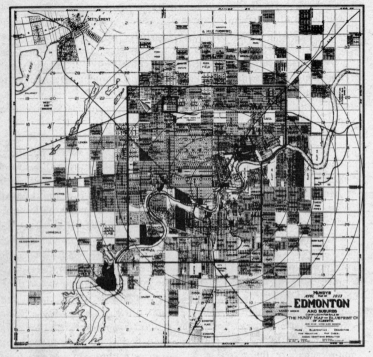

When the Liberal Government was swept into power in 1906 it was under great pressure to act positively to improve the environment. A succession of Select Committees and Royal Commissions since the 1830s had urged action to improve housing and environmental conditions in towns, and a plethora of legislation had been enacted, yet the problems seemed no nearer solution.[3]

The environmental reform movement of Victorian Britain drew strength from many sources, but one, above all, was to be pre-eminent in giving it legal form: this was the ethical doctrine known as "utilitarianism". As a philosophical concept, utility is very difficult to pin down, but it is usually equated with such awkward abstractions as good, happiness, welfare, and well-being.[4] The cardinal tenet of utilitarianism, the principle of utility, is that the greatest happiness of the greatest number is the fundamental criterion of morality. Utility, then, is anything which contributes to the general happiness, and the general happiness, in turn, is conceived to be the *summum bonum*, the highest of all goods. But, since "each individual always pursues what he believes to be his own happiness", which may not be in harmony with the general happiness, it is necessary for governments to set constraints on personal freedoms, to ensure that "the interests of the individual coincide with those of the community".[5] The utilitarian ethic therefore provides a rationale for government intervention in private affairs, from which was derived the notion of service for the public good which has sustained all utilitarian reformers for a century and a half.

The central notions of utilitarianism are old, but they were put into modern dress by three men: James Mill, John Stuart Mill, and, most notably of all, Jeremy Bentham.[6] Together, they comprised the school of philosophical radicals, so called because they were the chief theoreticians behind the reform legislation of Victorian Britain. Indeed, writes Bertrand Russell, "their importance is not so much philosophical as political",[7] and their influence on legislation and policy he describes as "astonishingly great, considering their complete absence of emotional appeal".[8] This last is a reference to their insistence on the power of reason to determine where the general happiness lay. James Mill, for example, argued that political judgments would be determined by the weight of objective evidence, underscoring the utilitarian belief that this evidence would always point to one solution which could contribute most to the general happiness.[9] The impact of this particular notion on planning thought has been profound, but, more generally, the emphasis on reason set utilitarianism apart from other intellectual currents which were contributing to urban reform, such as the evangelical movement, utopian socialism, aestheticism, or even simple philanthropy.[10] Although these all contributed to the evolution of the planning idea, they had little overt impact on the early planning legislation;[11] their effects were concentrated in other arenas.

Between Bentham's death in 1832 and the passage of the first planning act in 1909, the utilitarian reformers pressed for change on many fronts.[12] The urban environment offered special challenges for them, though, since it provided such stark evidence of the failure of the laissez-faire approach to freedom of enterprise. The environmental defects of the nineteenth-century city were an offence against many sensibilities but, in the utilitarian view of the world, they were, above all, an offence against reason.[13] Most simply, they led to enormous and intolerable waste. It has been said of Edwin Chadwick, probably the most celebrated practitioner of Bentham's doctrines, that the mainspring of his long and successful career was a "horror of waste".[14] Efficiency became the practical goal of reform,[15] spawning a flock of catchwords, such as health, economy, convenience, and order, which persist to this day as catchwords of planning.[16]

Motivated always by their view of the public good, the utilitarians sought to reform the laws and institutions by which urban life was shaped. In the name of reason, they ushered in the era of the technical expert. Many of them were themselves scientists, chiefly physicians and engineers, who found technical solutions to some of the most pressing environmental problems, particularly those related to public health.[17] Many of them, including Chadwick, made important contributions to the infant social sciences.[18] Universally, they advocated the use of scientific knowledge to cure the problems of the day, to bring order and economy out of chaos and waste. The conception of planning as a rational scientific activity was thus an inevitable extension of utilitarian doctrine,[19] but one which was to set a dead hand on the institutional form of the planning idea. The success of the utilitarians in coping with some of the physical problems of the urban environment led to the unwarranted assumption that *all* urban problems would be equally amenable. But while it is possible to accept the elimination of typhoid as an example of a general good, bearing equally on everybody, only the most elemental problems can be judged so neatly.

The utilitarian contribution to urban planning was a naïve belief in a consensual view of the general happiness and, following from that, a belief in a "best" technical solution to every problem. In fact, a crude determinism was the outcome, and it, too, can be traced directly to Bentham, in a psychological insight which he called the "association principle". "To Bentham, determinism in psychology was important, because he wished to establish a code of laws—and, more generally, a social system—which would automatically make men virtuous."[20] This notion was given clear expression in the planning movement, first in the Victorian slum clearance schemes, where social and moral improvement was expected to follow from physical improvement,[21] and later in the sociological notions of such pioneer planners as Raymond Unwin and T. C. Horsfall.[22] By creating well-planned urban environments, happy and healthy homes would be made available to working families, constructive social intercourse would be facilitated, the economic and social efficiency of the nation would be enhanced, and the general happiness would be increased. The moral purpose was self-evident.

Conservation, Progressivism and the City Efficient

In the United States, the utilitarian ethic was also to be highly influential, most notably, at first, in the conservation movement of the late nineteenth century. Its practical credo, in Hays' words, was "the gospel of efficiency":[23]

> The conservation movement was, in large measure, an effort of scientists, engineers and other technicians to substitute planned, centrally controlled resource development for the individual, inefficient, and wasteful exploitation of the past. The social ideal of the disinterested technician, the impartial servant of society, greatly influenced the thinking of conservation leaders, who viewed the expert as the key figure in a new age of planned economic growth, the saviour of a society which would no longer afford the physical and human waste of days gone by.[24]

In this vision, only the dispassionate expert, secure in the verities of scientific knowledge, could make the judgments that would lead the nation forward to a better future. This highlights another distinctive feature of American utilitarianism, the belief in progress.[25] In retrospect, progress turns out to have been a remarkably vague abstraction, but it was none the less to be the emotional underpinning of reform efforts for several decades after 1880.[26] In theory, progress could be defined as anything which brought greater happiness to a greater number of people, and thus contributed to the public good. In practice, there was no consensus on the nature of happiness or good or progress.

In the first decade of the twentieth century, the conservation movement gained a vital new impetus.

> This new interest in conservation, which dominated the movement between 1908 and 1910, came primarily from middle- and upper-income urban dwellers. Most of the new conservation organizations recruited their members and obtained their financial support from urbanites, and many of their leaders had been active in other types of urban reform.[27]

Conservation and urban improvement came to be seen as opposite sides of the same coin. Industrialization and rapid urban growth had reduced the city to an obscene and unhealthy excrescence, whereas nature was clean and pure, the resort of fundamental virtues and non-materialistic values. The strength of the country had therefore to be made accessible to the urban worker, through parks and wilderness reserves, industrial villages, and garden cities. Population and industry had also to be decentralized, to clear the way for the task of rebuilding the existing cities.[28] It all added up to an image of powerful

emotional appeal, imbued with Arcadian romanticism, and strongly
influenced by British experiments in town-building and by Ebenezer
Howard's Garden City concept.[29] At the same time, of course, nature
had to be protected from the continual overspilling of deprived urban
humanity. Urban decentralization was therefore to proceed in an
orderly and controlled manner and, for all its romanticism and utopian idealism, the Garden City concept was firmly rooted in a belief
in efficiently planned urban systems.[30] It also locked the concepts of
rural conservation and urban planning firmly together.

In the United States, this interweaving of the conservation and
urban reform movements seems to have wrought changes on both
groups. The conservation movement, although badly torn by the new
moral fervour, gained in vigour, while the urban reform movement
began to absorb some of the old-line conservationists' faith in science
and efficiency.

> Housing reformers grasped the planning movement as a young but powerful
> ally. They joined with the engineers, architects, and landscape architects
> who provided its leadership in a common effort to rebuild our cities and
> direct their future growth.... Along with conservation, the city planning
> movement symbolized the Progressive infatuation with efficient social or-
> ganization.[31]

The new emphasis was marked, most particularly, by the emergence
of the zoning power, borrowing a legal device which had been
brought to maturity in Germany in the years after 1900. Even more
than planned decentralization, zoning was seen as a "scientific" tool
for improving the quality of the urban environment. From about
1910, then, the city planning movement in the United States, which
had previously been dominated by an aesthetic vision—the City Beautiful—came to be dominated by a utilitarian vision—the City Efficient
or the City Functional.[32] The principle of utility may not have been
acknowledged overtly, other than in the belief in a public good, but to
maximize efficiency was, *ipso facto*, to maximize utility.

The Commission of Conservation

The progression of ideas in Canada was strikingly similar, although in
Canada the planning movement was nurtured more directly by the
conservation movement, through the activities of a unique Canadian
institution, the Commission of Conservation. The Commission arose
out of initiatives taken in the United States by President Roosevelt,
and it combined, in a single organization, the two mainstreams of

progressive social philosophy, environmental conservation and urban improvement. It also epitomized the adaptation of utilitarian doctrine to the Canadian setting. This was made explicit in the opening address of the chairman to the first annual meeting of the Commission in 1910,[33] and it continued to be explicit throughout all the Commission's publications.[34]

The central purpose of the Commission was to give the government the best scientific advice on conservation matters, in the name of economic progress and national well-being. In the words of Lord Grey: "The future prosperity of Canada depends on scientific research and upon the efficient application of the results of that research to the industrial and physical life of the people."[35] The belief in a bright economic future was literally boundless,[36] and it was paralleled by a desire to make sure that American mistakes in resource development should not be repeated. Above all, this meant that the wastefulness of individual cupidity could not be tolerated. Thus, in deference to the national vision, "the interests of the individual must be subordinated to the greater interests of the State".[37]

The Commission of Conservation was remarkable in many respects, and not least in the breadth with which it interpreted its mandate. Although its explicit purview was the natural resources of Canada, it took the stance that the health of the people is the greatest resource of all.[38] A direct link was forged through pollution. Careless disposal of domestic sewage was seen as one of the greatest problems of water resource management, because of the hazard to public health posed by typhoid and other water-borne sources of contagion. The concern for public health did not stop there, though. Just as typhoid provided the conceptual bridge between resource conservation and public health, so the other great environmental disease of the day, tuberculosis, provided a further bridge between public health and the condition of the built environment.[39] As early as the second annual meeting, in 1911, these bridges were being put firmly in place by Dr. Charles Hodgetts, the Commission's advisor on public health and a staunch believer in the remedial power of town planning.[40] Hodgetts was squarely in the Benthamite tradition of scientific reformers, and he saw himself as serving one overriding public good—the health of the people and, synonymously, the health of the nation.

From 1911 until its disbandment by Parliament in 1921, the Commission promoted the planning cause as one of its most notable activities.[41] And under the leadership of Hodgetts and Thomas Adams, who became the Commission's town planning advisor in 1914, an unmistakably clear view emerged.[42] Town planning was the application of scientific knowledge to secure efficiency in the urban environment; and efficiency meant, above all, that waste and chaos, disease and squalour, would give way to economy, order, and health. The utilitarian ethic was to be served in the national good, which meant, in turn, that planning was properly an activity of government and of dedicated public servants.

THE ALBERTA POLITICAL CONTEXT
Sources of the Planning Idea

Just as the Commission of Conservation was to play a vital role in crystallizing a Canadian view of urban planning, so, too, it acted as the seed-bed for the Alberta Planning Act of 1913. The link came in the person of Arthur Sifton, premier of Alberta from 1910 to 1917 and the province's representative on the Commission through all that time, and also the older brother of Clifford Sifton, the originator of the Commission and chairman during its most active years. As a member of one of Canada's most prominent political families (above all, a family which epitomized the beliefs of the progressive conservationists) Arthur Sifton was in a position of immense influence. He also had a reputation of his own as a reformer and iconoclast.[43] His personal interests were primarily in resource management, and in railway construction as a means to the controlled exploitation of natural resources,[44] but there can be little doubt that he was personally sympathetic to the principles of efficiency in the urban environment that town planning was believed to stand for.

Although there is no direct evidence that Sifton ever became an active advocate of the town planning movement, he could not help but be aware of contemporary thinking.[45] At the first Commission meeting which Sifton attended, in January 1911, Dr. Hodgetts presented a vigorous address on Canadian housing problems,[46] which he blamed squarely on "administrative inefficiency" and the failure of governments to intervene forcefully in the urban environment. He also devoted a lengthy section of his paper to town planning, reviewing recent experience in Germany, Belgium, the United States, and Britain, and advancing the plea that urban authorities be "compelled ... to build and plan on proper lines". In a similar address, a year later,[47] he developed his concept of urban efficiency more fully, and continued his review of international experience. The British Planning Act of 1909 was particularly singled out in both lectures, though

Hodgetts was careful to warn that even this "advanced" legislation might have to be modified to make it applicable to Canadian conditions.

Through Hodgetts' addresses and other Commission reports, Sifton would also be aware of the various urban reform initiatives that were being taken, erratically, across the country.[48] In Alberta, too, there was some sputtering of popular interest, chiefly in urban beautification in the classical revival tradition. The Calgary City Planning Commission, which was organized in 1911, engaged the English firm of T. H. Mawson and Sons to prepare a city plan, which turned out to be a grandiose fantasy.[49] In Edmonton, the main attention was on the development of an urban park system, and the creation of a civic centre in the best Beaux Arts manner.[50] Developers were laying out subdivisions, in a frenzy of competition, and were seizing on the trappings of contemporary planning to promote their products. Outlying suburbs became "garden cities", and the inlying ones offered gracious tree-lined streets—in the dreams of the boosters.[51] Alberta even had its place on the international lecture circuit, and the occasional visiting "experts" did their share to spark at least intermittent interests in "urban improvements".[52] In no sense, though, did this add up to a powerful local movement with political impact. At least as much was happening in other parts of the country, with little impress on provincial legislature.[53] The only unique feature of the Alberta setting was Arthur Sifton, and it is hard to escape the feeling that Alberta's early adoption of a planning Act was in response to Sifton's own predilections.

Sifton the Leader

This interpretation also fits what is known about Sifton's style as a political leader, and the political environment in which he found himself.[54] He was invited to become Alberta's second premier in 1910, and both the times and the man were remarkable. The government of Premier Rutherford had collapsed at the first whiff of its first scandal, the Alberta and Great Waterways Railway affair. The Liberal party desperately needed to re-establish its credibility by securing a new leader who was untainted by association with the Rutherford government, a man whose integrity and honesty were absolutely beyond question, a man with the leadership qualities to bring them through this first difficult trial. They chose brilliantly. As Chief Justice of the supreme courts of the North-West Territories and Alberta since 1903,

and as a member of the territorial legislature before that, Sifton stood
in the highest repute in the infant province. He was known to be
highly intelligent, decisive, and a "master of men".

> He was implicitly trusted and sometimes feared by his colleagues in the
> Cabinet. He was always master of the House. His followers on the back
> bench believed he could lead them safely through every attack of the
> opposition and he always did.[55]

The portrait is one of a strong leader whose will prevailed in all
situations.[56] Through a rare combination of personality and political
moment, Sifton was in a position of undisputed authority, and this
was never more clearly demonstrated than in the legislature's spring
session of 1913. Sifton was facing his first election campaign as party
leader, in the summer, and he had a large schedule of legislation
which he wished to see enacted. His dispatch stirred some complaints
in the opposition press,[57] but the Premier was not to be slowed. Even
so, the town planning bill was not expected to reach the House, and
only some last minute lobbying by an Edmonton alderman changed
its fate.[58] In fact, it was introduced on the last day of the session and
was rushed through all three readings in a matter of moments, slip-
ping into law without serious discussion and virtually unheralded in
the local press.[59] If Sifton himself regarded it as a significant piece of
progressive legislation, there is no evidence that the view was widely
shared.

The Legislative Models

These circumstances suggest a low level of commitment to the planning act, an impression which is supported by its lack of originality.
Like all the early planning legislation in Canada, the Alberta Act was
modelled on the town planning section of the British Housing, Town
Planning, etc. Act of 1909,[60] though not directly. Except for some
points of detail, the Alberta Act is an exact copy of New Brunswick's
Town Planning Act of 1912.[61]

Overall, the British Act suffered little change in its translocation. Its
central purposes remained intact, and the greatest part of it was
repeated verbatim, disregarding Hodgetts' warning about the unique-
ness of Canadian needs and problems. In particular, there was no
apparent sensitivity to the generations of social and political struggle
out of which the British Act was born, and no apparent thought to its
appropriateness in the very different Canadian context. The unthink-
ing ease with which the Alberta Act was adopted, for example, was not

mirrored from the parent legislation. The debate over the British Act was long and hard, and its passage was another painfully won step in the reform of the institutions of government.[62] Like all the legislation which preceded it, the 1909 planning act reflected the need to adapt the principle of utility, and the goal of the public good, to the realities of social power. This meant, most notably, a belief in the sanctity of free enterprise and self-interest, and a reluctance on the part of government to extend municipal rights over private interests. Nineteenth-century legislation on the powers and responsibilities of local government therefore tended to be permissive or, at most, to set development standards that were very low.[63] It was also hedged around with cumbersome procedural requirements, both to give maximum protection to private interests and to ensure close scrutiny by the central government.

The promoters of the 1909 act came into frontal collision with this attitude, and gained an ineffective compromise. On the positive side, they won acceptance of a vital principle: the propriety of government intervention in the urban development process. They had installed the foundation stone of planning as a legal institution, and had taken a major step in the long process of shaping public attitudes.[64] At the same time, planning advocates found much to criticize in the act's legalistic caution. Planning was not a mandatory activity for local governments;[65] recent developments in planning theory were not acknowledged;[66] and, most damaging of all from an operational standpoint, the act contained so many legal hoops and barriers, that only the most dedicated local authorities ever made their way through it.[67] Perhaps not surprisingly, then, the legal draftsmen of New Brunswick and Alberta set out to simplify the town planning process, an intention which is revealed by two main changes from the parent legislation.[68]

At the core of all three acts is the notion of the town planning scheme, a legal document which would specify the conditions under which urban development would be permitted on exactly defined tracts of land. But, in the British Act, before work could commence on a scheme, a local government, acting on its own initiative or on behalf of a group of landowners, had to obtain the central government's permission to *prepare* a town planning scheme. In the words of the act, a *prima facie* case had to be made,[69] which meant that the local authority had to establish that the land in question was suitable for urban development and was likely to be used at some indefinite time. The chief concern was that private landowners should not be forced to yield their land to development if they did not wish to do so, and the local authorities were charged to secure the co-operation of the owners "at every stage of the proceedings".[70]

In the two Canadian acts, this step was not explicitly required and it seems safe to assume that it was omitted deliberately. Local authorities were required to obtain permission to put town planning schemes "into effect",[71] but there was no prescription to seek approval at any earlier stage. In Alberta, at least, this can be related to the prevailing attitudes towards land in the urban fringe. In the spring of 1913, Alberta was in the dying throes of the most extravagant land boom in its history. The only value that was attached to land within a broad radius of any town or city was the speculative value of hoped-for urban development. Protection against urban development was the last thing that was desired.

The second change, clearer and more substantial than the first, relates to decision-making responsibility. In the British Act, the principal approving authority was the Local Government Board, a civil service agency for which there was no Canadian equivalent. Each of the Houses of Parliament also had the right to veto a town planning scheme, as a final resort. In New Brunswick and Alberta, on the other hand, decision-making authority was vested entirely in the executive branch of government. In New Brunswick, it was the Lieutenant-Governor in Council; in Alberta, in one of the few original features of the act, it was the Minister of Municipal Affairs. This was an extraordinarily bold move, and could fairly give us cause to wonder whether the Alberta members really understood what they were doing. Although it removed much of the procedural complexity for which the British Act had already been criticized,[72] it also swept away the safeguards that were built in over months of difficult debate and negotiation. The British legislators were well aware that their town planning bill gave radically new powers of government intervention in the land development process, and they had no intention of allowing those powers to escape completely from the control of Parliament. The possibility that they could be concentrated in the hands of one man, even a minister of the Crown, would simply have been unimaginable.

Why was it not unimaginable in Alberta? The best explanation is that the government was naïve as well as docile.[73] The province was young; the legislators were inexperienced; public attitudes were not clear, let alone hardened; and Premier Sifton was a man who liked decisions to be made cleanly and quickly. The executive powers of the Town Planning Act certainly provided that opportunity, though no Minister was ever put to the test.

THE NATURE AND PURPOSES OF TOWN PLANNING UNDER THE 1913 ACT

In common with planning legislation generally, the 1913 act is chiefly devoted to the legal procedures by which town planning was to be implemented. It does not define planning and says very little about its nature and purposes. In the absence of reported discussion, it is difficult to know exactly what the Alberta government thought their form of town planning would achieve, but some conclusions can be drawn from the legislation itself and from outside experience.

On one point, the act is explicit: town planning was applicable only to undeveloped land on the urban fringe.[74] It could not be extended to existing built-up areas and could not contribute to the improvement of existing urban environments. This may seem paradoxical, since the original emphasis in British urban reform was on the improvement of existing conditions, but it reflects the peculiar evolution of the British legislation. In fact, earlier versions of the housing act had already given substantial powers of intervention to local governments, including the right to carry out slum clearance and redevelopment schemes. The special contribution of the 1909 Act was to extend that right of intervention beyond the existing built-up areas.[75] Whether out of ignorance, or because they were not thought to be relevant in Canada, the planning powers of the housing section of the 1909 Act were ignored in both New Brunswick and Alberta.

All three acts specify that town planning schemes could be prepared for "any land which is in course of development or appears likely to be used for building purposes". In the case of Alberta, this has been interpreted as meaning that the government intended to use the act to check land speculation,[76] but there is no evidence to support this view. Even in Britain, it was not given as an objective of the planning act, and in Alberta's emotional environment, where rapid growth was seen as inevitable and good, restraint was simply undreamed of. "Any land ... which appears likely to be used for building purposes" set no effective limits, and was not meant to, as experience in Britain demonstrated.[77] In many other ways, the wording of the legislation makes this plain. There was no requirement to demonstrate that land was needed for development; in Alberta, there was not even the check of having to obtain permission to prepare a scheme; and there was nothing to prevent development or speculative subdivision on land that was not covered by town planning schemes. Perhaps more than anything, the notion of constraint was contrary to the central concept that was emerging in British planning: that extensive, low density suburban development was a social need, both to improve the living conditions of the working classes and to permit population to be decanted from slum areas prior to redevelopment.[78] This, more than anything, explains why the town planning legislation was seen as an extension of the existing housing legislation. If the Alberta government really intended that it should also be a tool against speculation, they had picked the wrong model.

While the economic goals of planning were left undefined, its technical purposes were perfectly clear. In the words of the Canadian acts, which differ slightly from the British Act, town planning schemes had "the general object of securing suitable provision for traffic, proper sanitary conditions, amenity, and convenience in connection with the laying out of streets and use of the land and of any neighbouring lands for building or other purposes".[79] No definition is provided for terms such as "suitable" and "proper", "amenity", and "convenience", but the influence of the utilitarian ethic is evident. Town planning was conceived to be a rational means of imposing efficiency and order on urban expansion and, in the words of Thomas Adams, "where the work is taken up in the right spirit, by the right men, and carried out on scientific lines", true social progress could be expected.[80] The "right men", the scientifically trained experts, would not need legislation to tell them what was "suitable" or "proper". Their technical competence equipped them to make the right judgements; the legislation had merely to establish the over-arching principles.[81]

In practice, based on British experience, town planning schemes were detailed regulatory devices.[82] Although they included maps which defined the boundaries of land-use zones and delineated the major street network (Figure 8:1), the development details were left to the entrepreneurs,[83] working within a framework of minimum standards. Under the guise of "scientific lines", town planning schemes actually addressed the same sorts of things as zoning did in the United States: these included density controls, height and setback regulations, and minimum building and street standards. Like zoning, town planning as defined by the early legislation was a negative power,[84] designed to prevent development from falling below certain specified standards, but unable to determine where or when it would occur.

At the same time, the town planning scheme offered opportunities that zoning has never been able to match. For example, by providing a mechanism for individual property owners to combine their land holdings for planning purposes, it was possible to prepare a single, unified design for quite large tracts of land, commonly of a thousand acres or more. The subdivision design could also be adapted to the anticipated uses, whereas the conventional North American practice was to overlay a zoning pattern on the undifferentiated grid subdivision, in the expectation that every urban function could be made to fit into a standardized physical mould. The town planning scheme was also able to incorporate non-economic features in the public good, such as parks and open space, attractive landscaping, and community centres. In short, it offered the aesthetic order of unified design rather than the mechanistic order imposed by zoning and grid subdivision.

From this, it should be evident that although the early legislative conception of planning was limited in scale and scope, it offered local governments the chance to take the initiative in improving the quality of urban design. But this task of improvement was not to be undertaken in some narrow cosmetic sense, as the word "amenity", in particular, might suggest. The concept of amenity was very powerful in late Victorian times, and seems to have been used in much the same spirit as "quality of life" is today. In its urban planning sense, "amenity" has been described as meaning "the provision of a good environment for the promotion of a healthy and civilized life".[85] At the turn of the century, this meant family life above and beyond anything else, a point that Dr. Hodgetts, for one, was emphatic about.[86] In the same vein, just days before the 1913 Act was rushed before the Alberta legislature, an English Garden City expert told his Edmonton audience that the task of town planning was to provide "the city with the greatest possible number of happy homes".[87] The planning concept of amenity therefore fitted the principle of utility and Bentham's vision of a virtuous society. High amenity environments were in the public good because they enlarged the happiness and well-being of their residents. And ultimately, if all the population could be housed in such environments, the public good would be maximized, and the most efficient form of city would have been created.

The gospel of efficiency was also to be served in a more conventional way. Urban extensions which were laid out under town planning schemes were expected to show higher property values,[88] which led, in all three acts, to the notion that the whole community had a right to share in the financial benefits of planning action. Local authorities were thus given the power to impose a betterment tax, to recapture half the value which had been added to a property by virtue of its town planning scheme.[89]

More broadly, economic arguments figured most prominently in the attempts to justify and interpret the planning legislation, in both Britain and Canada. The best catch-phrase came from Thomas Adams—"economies which can be effected by town planning schemes"—by which he meant the economies that could be achieved in public expenditure by anticipating long-term needs for such things as parks, arterial streets, and main sewers.[90] A Canadian exposition was provided by Beer:

> Neglect and lack of foresight in planning cities lead to needless expense, and, when ratepayers find that heavy expenditure is necessary to remedy the results of early neglect, the tendency is to curtail the expenditure. The effect is inevitable. A few years later, they are faced with the same problems in aggravated forms, the remedies are still more expensive and money spent upon half-remedies is found to have been largely wasted. The prevention of such waste is one of the objects of modern city planning.[91]

This economic argument could also be combined with the sanitary improvement argument which had been the practical spark for legislative reform in both Canada and Britain:

> Unregulated growth has been shown to be not only wasteful, but productive of insanitary conditions. With town planning the opportunity is afforded of preventing social and sanitary evils which are due in no small measure to bad development and which are costly to deal with once they have been allowed to be established.[92]

The reference to "proper sanitary conditions" in the legislation thus had an economic dimension as well as a health one, and we may speculate that this was the main consideration in the minds of the Alberta legislators. At all events, sanitary reform was not an issue in Alberta in 1913, as it was in the cities of central Canada, or even in Winnipeg, with its large population of poorly housed immigrants.[93] What was at issue was the desirability of attempting to control the manner in which urban expansion was carried out, with the aim of securing a more efficient environment than was possible under standardized grid subdivisions (Figure 8:2). There were some local examples of what could be achieved with more careful design, such as the Mount Royal district of Calgary and the Glenora district of Edmonton, but the legislative models had to come from elsewhere. Whatever the understanding of urban planning in Alberta in 1913—and the whole chain of circumstances surrounding the adoption of the act suggests a low level of understanding—the first institutional form of planning was indistinguishable from that which was being advocated elsewhere in Canada, which, in turn, was firmly rooted in the British precedent.

And yet, there is one hint in the Alberta act that a little more than blind imitation was involved. Section 6(2), a portion of the act dealing with compensation for injury arising from the approval of a town planning scheme, has an insertion which is unique to Alberta. It provides that there will be no compensation for vacant land taken for park or open space purposes, up to a maximum of five per cent of the area of the property.[94] This notion of compulsory dedication, which did not become a standard feature of planning legislation for another forty years, was a clear recognition of the utility value of town planning, and an attempt to distribute that utility to the greatest number.

FROM RADICAL INNOVATION TO REACTIONARY DOCTRINE: THE INERTIA OF AN IDEA

The Alberta Act of 1913 was totally ineffective, not necessarily because of inherent defects but because its timing was wrong. The opportunity for town planning schemes was already past. The real estate boom was fading into recession,[95] and the urban land supply that had been created around Edmonton and Calgary was to endure until the 1960s. The only significance of the Town Planning Act, then, is its place in the history of the idea of planning and, particularly, its contribution to the Alberta view of planning that is in place today. The central point is simple: the principle of utility continues to be served, as unswervingly and as unthinkingly, as it was in 1913. Unwittingly, Sifton's government set a doctrinaire hand on the evolution of planning thought in Alberta, and the gospel of efficiency continues to be the only explicit ethic that supports the institution of planning.

Alberta's experience is not unusual, of course; it is an international experience and it has affected all modes of planning, not just urban planning. In Canada, its persistence can be charted very easily, from Charles Hodgetts' first appearance before the Commission of Conservation in 1911 to the latest version of the by-laws of the Canadian Institute of Planners. Its basic building blocks were securely implanted between 1914 and 1919 by Thomas Adams, the Scottish surveyor who became a tireless advocate of planning across the breadth of Canada. Like many able people, Adams was drawn into the planning movement by Garden City fever, but he was a Benthamite by conviction. In 1910, he was appointed to organize the planning department of the Local Government Board, a role which epitomized the Benthamite ideal of public service and in which Adams was to begin the task of codifying British planning practice. It was this experience which he was to bring directly to Canada, and which he was to urge on Canadians with some adaptations.[96]

In 1919, largely on Adams's initiative, the Town Planning Institute of Canada was established and began to publish a regular journal. The profession of planning in Canada had become institutionalized. More than that, it had become institutionalized around a particular ethic, the principle of utility, and around a particular conception of the city, the City Efficient. The point is made on almost every page of the *Journal of the Town Planning Institute* over its ten-year life. It is also explicit in the professional definition of planning, which began to appear as a banner on the first page of the journal in 1923.

> Town planning may be defined as the scientific and orderly disposition of land and buildings in use and development with a view to obviating congestion and securing economic and social efficiency, health and well-being in urban and rural communities.

Utilitarianism was unrepentant and unrefined, and continues so to this day. The language of the modern by-laws is a little tidier, but the definition of planning is almost identical with that of fifty years ago.[97]

This national view has been paralleled in Alberta. The planning act was amended and revised several times in the 1920s, but chiefly to adapt the machinery of planning to the evolving North American techniques of planning commissions, subdivision controls, zoning by-laws, and official town plans.[98] The first provincial planning officer was appointed in 1928, and gave Alberta a direct link back to the Commission of Conservation where he had begun his career as an assistant to Thomas Adams.[99] This was also the year of the only substantial change in planning purpose, when an entirely new section, devoted to the preservation of natural beauty, was added to the act. In a sense, this can be interpreted as an attempt to re-establish the original links between conservation and town planning, and it was highly praised as the first Canadian legislation which recognized that urban planning and rural planning were essentially the same conception.[100] In fact, though, the amendment came about because Premier Brownlee had returned from his first visit to England raving about the beauty of the English countryside.[101]

In the post-war years, Alberta's planning legislation has been rewritten many times, to create an administrative system that is far more complex and elaborate than Sifton or Brownlee could ever have conceived. But all the change has been directed at the how of planning; the why of planning has persisted, unmodified, since 1913. In the contemporary language, planning's institutional purpose is "to achieve the orderly and economical development of land . . . without infringing on the rights of individuals except to the extent that is necessary for the greater public interest".[102] Not only do the catch-words of nineteenth-century utilitarianism still provide the only insti-tutional criteria for judging the merits of proposed urban develop-ments, but the legislation is still bedevilled, as was the British Act of 1909, with the attempt to reconcile the free enterprise ethic with the utilitarian ethic of the public good.[103] The catchwords, unfortunately, do not allow judgments to be made between them.

To appreciate the force of this conclusion, it is necessary to consider the status of utilitarianism among recent philosophers. To begin on purely pragmatic grounds, the principle of utility is regarded as naïve, because there is no objective value that can be attached to happiness to allow it to be used as a criterion in resolving conflicts in which the public good is expected to prevail over private good. Welfare econo-mists, who leaned heavily on utilitarian doctrine in the nineteenth and early twentieth centuries, have long since given up attempting to operationalize utility.[104] The Benthamite interpretation of equality is also criticized as naïve, because it led to the belief that "good" and "evil" would be valued by all people in exactly the same way in any given situation, so that a common view of the public good could always prevail.[105] In fact, the whole notion of public good has turned out to be unmanageable beyond the vaguest level of abstraction.[106]

More fundamentally, the principle of utility fails with contemporary philosophers because it does not incorporate a principle of justice. The central difficulty is described by Rescher:

> Justice limits utility at exactly the point of the "Reformer's Paradox": Given an imperfect existing initial distribution, any redistribution in the interests of arriving, from the standpoint of justice, at a superior distribution runs headlong into the pattern of existing claims that cannot—in the interests of the very justice that provides the rationale for the entire enterprise—be brushed aside as an irrelevant obstacle.[107]

In the context of contemporary planning, a principle of justice (spe-cifically, distributive justice) is necessary because the decisions that have to be taken in the name of planning address the comparative treatment of individuals. Planning, in its institutional form, is an allocative process in which scarce resources, notably land and public funds, have to be distributed among rival claimants.[108] Conflict among many interests is inherent in the situations with which planning must deal. To resolve conflict, there has to be an ethic, and that ethic has to incorporate a principle of justice independent of utility, since it will rarely be possible to prove, objectively, that the desires of one individual or interest group would contribute more to the general welfare than those of another.[109]

At the same time, as Frankena emphasizes, "the utilitarians have hold of an important part of the truth".[110] It is patently desirable to work towards the greatest possible balance of good over evil, as a moral end. The philosophical problem, then, is not to replace utilitarianism with something else, but to root it in a more basic principle of distributive justice which will provide a decision-making ethic in conflict situations.

Precisely this theme is at last coming to be explored in the literature of urban planning. The past decade has borne witness to a huge volume of critical writing in Britain and the United States,[111] and even some in Canada.[112] It has also brought major advances in planning theory, but neither the criticisms nor the theory have made any notable impact on planning legislation in Alberta. As far as the planning act is concerned, planning is a technical activity to be carried out by experts whose scientific knowledge equips them to judge that certain courses of action are "best" because they maximize utility. There is no acknowledgement that planners must work in an environment of high uncertainty, with a future that is essentially unknowable, or that they are acting in a pluralistic society in which conflict is inevitable, a society which is not bound by a single, universal conception of utility but is fragmented into a multitude of individual, equally just utilities. Even the catchwords behind which planners have shielded themselves—order, economy, efficiency—turn out not to be absolutes; they are as value-loaded as good or happiness or beauty, and no more practical as operational criteria.

The irony of this situation bites deep. The original planning legislation, for all its limitations, was squarely in a proud tradition of radical reform. By acting as it did, in 1913, the government of Alberta was reshaping public attitudes as well as public institutions; it was giving form to ideas that were still formless in most people's minds. But in the planning act of 1970, and the proposed new act of 1977, the radical has become reactionary. Because of the inertia of the central idea of the purpose of planning, the legislation is falling further and further out of the mainstream of contemporary planning thought. Fortunately, there is a brighter side. The things that planners are doing in Alberta in the 1970s are closer to the precepts of planning theory than they are to the prevailing legislation. Many examples could be cited, but one must suffice. Some years ago, the staff of the Peace River Regional Planning Commission began work on their preliminary regional plan. Initially, in the name of efficiency, they conceived a strategy of centralization, in which growth and improvement would be concentrated in a few, favoured towns. But it turned out that the small towns of the region are far from dead, and their people have no intention of letting them die. The planning strategy had to be turned completely around, to reflect the lifestyle values of the population.[113] The gospel of efficiency was dethroned; the justice of existing claims prevailed.

Of course, following Frankena, none of this is intended to suggest that cities should not be as efficient as planning can make them, or that the comfort, health, and well-being of the population should not be served, as general ends of planning. But as long as planning acts are designed on the assumption that there is only one reasonable way of looking at the world, they will continue to present an outmoded and naïve view of the planning function. In terms of providing Canadian planning with an institutional ethic, the legislation has not advanced an inch from Jeremy Bentham, who died 147 years ago, in an entirely different world. Nor has it advanced from that other different world of 1913, when progress seemed tangible, science still held the promise of a rational future, and it was possible to believe that democratic institutions could really serve a single general welfare. Today's world may not really be any more complex than that of 1832 or 1913, but the perceptions of its complexity are certainly more realistic. How sad, then, that our institutions cannot be adapted more quickly to the new perceptions. In the particular context of urban planning, it is now clear that the principle of utility, standing alone, does not work: that is the real lesson of the Alberta Town Planning Act of 1913.

NOTES

1. Between 1915 and 1925, all the remaining provinces except Quebec passed planning legislation of some kind; the tenor of the complaints then shifted from the lack of legislation to the lack of use of the legislation. See, for example, Nolan Cauchon, "Retiring President's Address", *Town Planning*, vol. 5, no. 2 (1926): 1-5.

2. William Ashworth, *The Genesis of Modern British Town Planning* (London, 1954); and Gordon E. Cherry, *The Evolution of British Town Planning* (London, 1974), pp. 6-62.

3. John Minett, "The Housing, Town Planning etc. Act, 1909", *The Planner*, vol. 60, no. 5 (1974): 676.

4. Nicholas Rescher, *Distributive Justice: A Constructive Critique of the Utilitarian Theory of Distribution* (Indianapolis, 1966), pp. 5-22.

5. Bertrand Russell, *History of Western Philosophy* (London, 1946), p. 803.

6. *The Utilitarians: An Introduction to the Principles of Morals and Legislation (Jeremy Bentham), and Utilitarianism and On Liberty (John Stuart Mill)* (Garden City, 1973).

7. Russell, *History of Western Philosophy*, p. 801.

8. Ibid., p. 805.

9. Ibid., p. 804.

10. These are described in a huge literature, but useful overviews are provided by Gordon E. Cherry, *Urban Change and Planning: A History of Urban Development in Britain since 1750* (Henley-on-Thames, 1972); Leonardo Benevolo, *The Origins of Modern Town Planning* (London, 1967); and Francoise Choay, *The Modern City: Planning in the 19th Century* (London, c. 1970).

11. This was notwithstanding the fact that the promoters of the legislation might be motivated by more than the utilitarian ethic. The notable case was that of John Burns, MP, who nursed the 1909 Act through the British Parliament. At a conference in 1910 he advanced a vision of the role of planning which took his audience "beyond all the petty trivialities of his Act". *Town Planning Review*, vol. 1, no. 3 (1910): 183.

12. David Roberts, *Victorian Origins of the Welfare State* (New Haven, 1960), pp. 26*ff.*

13. Ibid., pp. 26-27.

14. S. E. Finer, *The Life and Times of Sir Edwin Chadwick* (London, 1952), p. 3.

15. Ibid., p. 13.

16. Urban planning "is designed to fulfill local objectives of social economic and physical well-being": F. Stuart Chapin, *Urban Land Use Planning* (Urbana, 1965), p. vi. On page 41 he identifies health, safety, convenience, economy, and amenity as the purposes of the public interest in planning.

17. For a pair of case studies see P. J. Smith, "Pollution Abatement in the Nineteenth Century: The Purification of the Water of Leith", *Environment and Behavior*, vol. 6, no. 1 (1974): 3-36, and P. J. Smith, "The Foul Burns of Edinburgh: Public Health Attitudes and Environmental Change", *Scottish Geographical Magazine*, vol. 91, no. 1 (1975): 25-37.

18. M. W. Flinn, ed., *Report on the Sanitary Condition of the Labouring Population of Great Britain, by Edwin Chadwick, 1842* (Edinburgh, 1965), pp. 38*ff.*

19. For an explicit acknowledgment of the planning movement's debt to Bentham see Henry R. Aldridge, *The Case for Town Planning* (London: The National Housing and Town Planning Council, 1915), p. 333. For a misinterpretation, see Lewis Mumford, *The City in History* (New York, 1961), pp. 452-55. Mumford dismisses utilitarianism as the *reductio ad absurdum* of laissez faire, a misunderstanding which appears to have been common in the nineteenth century (Flinn, *Report on the Sanitary Condition of the Labouring Population*, p. 38.)

20. Russell, *History of Western Philosophy*, p. 802.

21. The following extract is typical. It was written by a Benthamite reformer, Edinburgh's medical officer of health, in justification of public slum clearance. "No one can visit the poorer districts of the city without being impressed with the close connection which exists between outward filth and inward depravity.... In attempting to raise the poor in our towns from their degraded position, we must attack that which lies on the surface. Until the dwellings of the poor are rendered more habitable, and the poor themselves are taught the wholesome lesson of outward cleanliness it is not to be expected that their deeper nature can be effectually stirred". Henry D. Littlejohn, *Report on the Sanitary Condition of the City of Edinburgh* (Edinburgh, 1865), p. 120.

22. See, for example, Walter L. Creese, ed., *The Legacy of Raymond Unwin* (Cambridge, 1967), pp. 110-11, and T. C. Horsfall, "On the Interaction between Dwellings and their Occupants in Germany and in England", *Town Planning Review*, vol. 2, no. 4 (1912): 281-302.

23. Samuel P. Hays, *Conservation and the Gospel of Efficiency: The Progressive Conservation Movement, 1890–1920* (New York, 1975).

24. Roy Lubove, *The Progressives and the Slums: Tenement House Reform in New York City* (Pittsburgh, 1962), p. 215.

25. This is not to suggest that a belief in progress was unique to Americans. Beginning with the concept of the improvement scheme in the nineteenth century, British planning legislation was clearly conceived in a progressive spirit. This spirit imbues all the contemporary writing, as can be seen, for example, in the early issues of the *Town Planning Review* which began publication in 1910.

26. John D. Buenker, *Urban Liberalism and Progressive Reform* (New York, 1973), pp. vii-viii.

27. Hays, *Conservation*, p. 142.

28. Ibid., pp. 141-46.

29. Lubove, *The Progressives*, pp. 217-29. See also Gillian Darley, *Villages of Vision* (London, 1975), and Walter L. Creese, *The Search for Environment: The Garden City Before and After* (New Haven, 1966).

30. Ebenezer Howard, *Garden Cities of Tomorrow* (London, 1949). See also Creese, *The Search for Environment*, pp. 144-57. Although Howard's personal philosophy was more akin to the utopian socialists than it was to the utilitarians, and he acknowledged his debt to such social critics as John Ruskin and Edward Bellamy, he shared the utilitarian dismay at waste and inefficiency. To the socialists, though, the prevailing system was more than wasteful and inefficient; it was also unjust. Russell, *History of Philosophy*, pp. 807-09, therefore describes utilitarianism as a transitional school which gave birth to socialism.

31. Lubove, *The Progressives*, p. 215.

32. Roy Lubove, *The Urban Community: Housing and Planning in the Progressive Era* (Englewood Cliffs, 1967), pp. 1-22, and Mel Scott, *American City Planning since 1890* (Berkeley and Los Angeles, 1969), pp. 47-182.

33. Canada, Commission of Conservation, *Report of the First Annual Meeting* (Ottawa, 1910), pp. 1-27.

34. These are chiefly the annual reports which were published between 1910 and 1920, but various special reports and monographs were also prepared for the Commission.

35. Canada, Commission of Conservation, *Report*, pp. 27–28.

36. From Clifford Sifton's opening address: "Now our time has come. Population is flowing in; development of resources is proceeding rapidly; trade is growing. In all human probability a period of great expansion and prolonged prosperity lies before us". Canada, Commission of Conservation, *Report*, p. 26.

37. Canada, Commission of Conservation, *Report*, p. 28.

38. Again from Sifton's opening address: "The physical strength of the people is the resource from which all others derive value. Extreme and

scrupulous regard for the lives and health of the population may be taken as the best criterion of the degree of real civilization and refinement to which a country has attained". Canada, Commission of Conservation, *Report*, p. 12.

39. Address by Peter H. Bryce, Chief Medical Officer, Department of the Interior, in Canada, Commission of Conservation, *Report*, pp. 114-34. It comes as no surprise that Dr. Bryce should make admiring reference to Edwin Chadwick (p. 132), and his address concludes with a classic summation of the North American progressive interpretation of the utilitarian ethic: "If anyone is inclined to question the value of municipal, provincial or State intereference in matters affecting the public health, it would appear that the illustrations taken from England, Germany and even the United States go abundantly to prove that *laissez-faire* methods are no more logical in the face of foes active against the public health than they are when a foreign foe in arms attacks our shores. National prosperity in every field is demanding more and more the daily application of the scientific method in every field of human energy. . . . Public health is no longer to be classed as an *imponderable* but as a *ponderable* entity, to be dealt with along lines as exact as the . . . getting of the highest mechanical efficiency out of a well-constructed steam engine" (p. 134).

40. Canada, Commission of Conservation, *Second Annual Report* (Montreal, 1911), pp. 50-84, 105-06 and 118-219. The last citation is a report on the Dominion Public Health Conference of 1910; this was devoted to environmental health, with particular reference to the problems of typhoid and tuberculosis.

41. For a general review of the work of the Commission of Conservation see C. Ray Smith and David R. Witty, "Conservation, Resources and Environment: An Exposition and Critical Evaluation of the Commission of Conservation,

Canada", *Plan Canada*, vol. 11, no. 1 (1970): 55-71, and vol. 11, no. 3 (1972): 199-216.

42. For a review of the contributions of Hodgetts and Adams see Alan H. Armstrong, "Thomas Adams and the Commission of Conservation", *Plan Canada*, vol. 2, no. 1 (1959): 14-32.

43. John Blue, *Alberta Past and Present: Historical and Biographical* (Chicago, 1924), p. 135. For an overview of the development of progressive ideology in the prairie provinces see W. L. Morton, *The Progressive Party in Canada* (Toronto, 1950), particularly pp. 3-60.

44. Blue, *Alberta*, pp. 118-119, and Charles G. D. Roberts and Arthur L. Tunnell, eds., *A Standard Dictionary of Canadian Biography*, vol. I (Toronto, 1934), p. 470.

45. Blue, *Alberta*, p. 135 offers the comment that Sifton was "familiar by long residence in the country [i.e., western Canada] with its deepest problems". Sifton was born in Ontario but moved with his family to Manitoba in 1875. He practised law with his brother Clifford, in Brandon, from 1883 to 1885, and then on his own in Prince Albert and Calgary. See Roberts and Tunnell, *Standard Dictionary*, p. 470, and A. O. MacRae, *History of the Province of Alberta* (1912), vol. II, p. 1000.

46. *Second Annual Report*, pp. 50-84.

47. Canada, Commission of Conservation, *Report of the Third Annual Meeting* (Montreal, 1912), pp. 130-48.

48. Commission publications included a number of pamphlets: for instance T. Aird Murray, *The Prevention of the Pollution of Canadian Surface Waters* (1912); Charles N. B. Camac, *The Epidemics of Typhoid Fever in the City of Ottawa* (1912); and C. A. Hodgetts, *Refuse Collection and Disposal* (c. 1913). In the annual reports up to and including 1913, in addition to the transcript of the Public Health Conference of 1910, the Nova Scotia and New Brunswick planning acts are printed in full, and there are numerous references to such things as the proposed improvement commission for the

Ottawa federal district, the City Improvement League of Montreal, the Civic Guild of Toronto, the Winnipeg Town Planning Commission and the First Canadian Conference on Town Planning held in Winnipeg in 1912. There is also much discussion of urban environmental legislation, particularly with respect to housing and public health. It might also be noted, as some indication of national interest that Premier Sifton could scarcely escape, that 1913 was the first year in which *The Canadian Annual Review* devoted a special section to housing and town planning, "a most interesting economic-social development of the year": J. Castell Hopkins, *The Canadian Annual Review of Public Affairs, 1913* (Toronto, 1914), pp. 722-24.

49. T. H. Mawson, *Calgary: A Preliminary Scheme for Controlling the Economic Growth of the City* (published under the auspices of the City Planning Commission of Calgary by T. H. Mawson and Sons, London, 1914).

50. Edmund H. Dale, "The Role of Successive Town and City Councils in the Evolution of Edmonton, Alberta, 1892 to 1966", PH D thesis, University of Alberta (1969), pp. 117-40.

51. A. W. Rasporich and Henry Klassen, eds., *Frontier Calgary: Town, City and Region, 1875-1914* (Calgary, 1975), essays by J. P. Dickin McGinnis, "Birth to Boom to Bust: Building in Calgary, 1875 – 1914", p. 17, and Max Foran, "Land Speculation and Urban Development in Calgary, 1884 – 1912", pp. 209-20.

52. Thomas Mawson was reported to have addressed "a crowded meeting" in Calgary, in 1912 (*The Town Planning Review*, vol. 3, no. 3 [1912]: 218), and Ewart G. Culpin, secretary of the Garden City Association, delivered a lecture in Edmonton which was said to be "largely attended" (*The Edmonton Journal*, March 5, 1913, p. 7).

53. In Manitoba, despite a considerable amount of enthusiasm on the part of a few Winnipeg residents, a planning act was not adopted until 1915: Alan F. J. Artibise, *Winnipeg: A Social History of Urban Growth, 1874 – 1914* (Montreal, 1975), pp. 267-80. In Saskatchewan, the Minister of Municipal Affairs in 1914 was strongly opposed to an act on the British model, and one was not passed until 1917: *Journal of the Town Planning Institute of Canada*, vol. 1, no. 3 (1921): 2. This was notwithstanding a local interest in planning that took shape at least as early as 1908: *Town Planning*, vol. 10, no. 1 (1931): 1. British Columbia provided an even more extreme case. Although Mawson was working on a Vancouver plan at the same time as his Calgary plan, no act was passed until 1925: Thomas H. Mawson, "Vancouver: A City of Optimists", *The Town Planning Review*, vol. 4, no. 1 (1913): 7-12. Mawson also prepared a plan for "parks and boulevards" for Regina in 1914: J. Castell Hopkins, *The Canadian Annual Review of Public Affairs, 1914* (Toronto, 1915), p. 721.
Blue, *Alberta*, pp. 125-29, and L. G. Thomas, *The Liberal Party in*

54. Blue, *Alberta*, pp. 125-29, and L. G. Thomas, *The Liberal Party in Alberta: A History of Politics in the Province of Alberta, 1905-1921* (Toronto, 1959), pp. 58-133.

55. Blue, *Alberta*, p. 135. Blue also provides a graphic account of Sifton's characteristic behaviour in the House (pp. 135-36).

56. A similar character sketch is provided by Roberts and Tunnell, *Standard Dictionary*, p. 471: "Sifton's intellect was very great, and his penetration and lightning decisions frequently astonished lawyers and litigants alike during his days on the bench. Though reputed a brilliant conversationalist with a caustic and lively wit, he was too reserved and cold in outward bearing ever to be widely popular."

57. "Sifton to Bring Down Estimates with a Rush", *Edmonton Journal*, March 3, 1913.

58. "Legislature Prorogues: Town Planning Act is Passed at Last

Moment", *Edmonton Journal*, March 26, 1913.

59. The *Edmonton Journal* expressed mild astonishment that the rules of the House could be waived, when "everyone understood the bill was to be thrown out this session" (March 26, 1913), but offered no comment on the need for the legislation or its intended purposes. The *Edmonton Bulletin*, March 26, 1913, merely recorded the passage of the bill. In his review of legislative accomplishments in the spring session of 1913, Thomas, *The Liberal Party*, pp. 134-37, does not even mention the Town Planning Act.

60. 9 King Edward VII, chapter 44, 1909.
61. Statutes of the Province of Alberta, 4 George V, first series, chapter 18, 1913; and New Brunswick, Acts of the Legislative Assembly, 2 George V, chapter 19, 1912. The Nova Scotia act of 1912 also followed the British act, but its wording is so strikingly different that it could not have been the model for Alberta. It might also be speculated that New Brunswick was chosen as the model because it was more faithful to the parent legislation.

62. Minett, "The Housing, Town Planning etc. Act", pp. 676-80. See also F. W. Platt, "Presidential Address", *Journal of the Town Planning Institute*, vol. 17, no. 1 (1930): 2-3.

63. For a general review see T. M. Cooper and W. E. Whyte, *Law of Housing and Town Planning in Scotland* (Edinburgh, 1920), pp. 1-14.

64. Thus, the Town Clerk of Edinburgh, reflecting on the 1909 Act ten years later: "There are few great legislative enactments of recent years which have caught the imagination of the local authorities and public alike to a greater extent than the town planning provisions of Part II of the Act of 1909. The Act opened up a most attractive vision for the future" (*Edinburgh Council Record*, May 6, 1919, p. 307).

65. For example, Cherry, *The Evolution of British Town Planning*, p. 64 quotes the reaction of George Cadbury, the famed philanthropist

and builder of the industrial village of Bournville.

66. The main concerns were derived from the work of Patrick Geddes, particularly his emphasis on the planning survey and the need for a comprehensive view of city and region: Patrick Geddes, "Two Steps in Civics: Ghent International Exhibition", *The Town Planning Review*, vol. 4, no. 2 (1913): 78-94. For examples of criticisms see Patrick Abercrombie, "International Contributions to the Study of Town Planning and City Organisation", *The Town Planning Review*, vol. 4, no. 2 (1913): 109; S. D. Adshead, "The Town Planning Act: Its Administration and Possibilities", *The Town Planning Review*, vol. 1, no. 1 (1910): 44-50; L. P. A., "The Progress of the Town Planning Act", *The Town Planning Review*, vol. 1, no. 4 (1911): 323-24; and "Chronicle of Passing Events", *The Town Planning Review*, vol. 2, no. 1 (1911): 72.

67. H. C. Dowdall, "The Procedure Regulations of the Town Planning Act", *The Town Planning Review*, vol. 1, no. 2 (1910): 129-31. The widespread interest of British local authorities is attested to by a stream of articles in *The Town Planning Review*, the *Journal of the Town Planning Institute* and *The Architectural Review*, but few ever managed to complete town planning schemes: G. L. Pepler, "Twenty-one Years of Town Planning in England and Wales", *Journal of the Town Planning Institute*, vol. 17, no. 3 (1930): 51-52, Platt, "Presidential Address", p. 3, and the Town Clerk of Edinburgh, *Edinburgh Council Record*, May 6, 1919, p. 307.

68. In this they anticipated the British Government by several years. When the 1909 planning act was revised in 1919, one of the chief concerns was to make it easier to implement: Gordon E. Cherry, "The Housing, Town Planning etc. Act, 1919" *The Planner*, vol. 60, no. 5 (1974): 681-84.

69. Section 54(2).
70. Section 56(2)(a). Interpreters of the 1909 Act were at pains to

demonstrate its protective attitude towards private interests: "Town planning does not mean that the local authority should acquire and themselves develop the land; nor does it mean that the local authority can compel an owner to develop his land before he wishes to do so, or before, in his opinion, he can develop it with profit. Town planning simply empowers the local authority to lay down and regulate the lines which development will follow when that development is ready to take place": William E. Whyte, *Town and Country Planning in Scotland* (Edinburgh, 1934), pp. 7-8.

71. Section 1(3) in both acts.

72. Thomas Adams, "The Housing and Town Planning Act, 1909", *The Architectural Review*, vol. 27 (1910): 118.

73. In a different context, Blue (*Alberta*, p. 129) describes the Alberta members of 1910 as "ingenuous novices".

74. Section 1(1).

75. Platt, "Presidential Address", pp. 2-3.

76. The author of this interpretation is Noel Dant, past Director of Planning for the Province of Alberta. He has expressed it in a number of unpublished papers on Alberta planning law, and it has been picked up in at least one published work: David G. Bettison, John K. Kenward and Larrie Taylor, *Urban Affairs in Alberta* (Edmonton, 1975), p. 18.

77. To cite just one example, the Corporation of Edinburgh gained the approval of the Local Government Board for the preparation of ten town planning schemes between 1910 and 1918. If development had followed, the built-up area of the city would have been increased by 150 per cent, yet all the land was described as "mature" for building: P. J. Smith, "Urban Site Selection in the Ferth Basin", PH D thesis, University of Edinburgh (1964), p. 287.

78. See, for example, J. S. Nettlefold, "Birmingham: City Extension and Town Planning", *The Town Planning Review*, vol. 2, no. 2 (1911): 108-12.

Although this concept was not effectively implemented until the housing acts of the 1920s and 1930s, it had been urged by housing reformers since mid-Victorian times: see, for example, James Begg, *Happy Homes for Working Men and How to Get Them* (London, 1866), pp. 21-22.

79. Section 1(1) in both acts.

80. Adams, "The Housing and Town Planning Act", p. 119.

81. Who was to prepare town planning schemes? "I would say without hesitation in the first place the municipal engineer. But having regard to the immensity of the issues involved, his work must at times be supplemented by specialists from outside. The land surveyor and the valuer will need to be called in, and the architect, more especially in advising upon the details of the scheme and the laying out of the secondary streets, should be consulted": Adshead, "The Town Planning Act", p. 50. The Canadian equivalent, as defined in a model town planning act prepared by J. H. Burland for the Commission of Conservation, was a local housing and town planning board made up of the mayor, the municipal engineer, the medical health officer and two ratepayers, preferably an architect and a financier: Canada, Commission of Conservation, *Report of the Sixth Annual Meeting* (Toronto, 1915), p. 248. Hodgetts also stressed, on several occasions, the need for "expert" assistance at the provincial level.

82. For the fullest description of British town planning schemes see Aldridge, *The Case for Town Planning*, pp. 157-670. There are also many descriptions in the early issues of *The Town Planning Review*.

83 "Elasticity" was the favourite word to describe this characteristic. The general conception was explained in the following way by Abercrombie: "The drawing out of a complete and fully developed plan with hard and fast zoning was at one time thought to be essential, but turns out in practice quite unobligatory. Main traffic routes must be laid down, but

all infilling of residential roads can proceed as development takes place, according to principles laid down in the Provisions [of the scheme], giving the authority full control. The town plan, in fact, need never be finally made until the area is built upon": Abercrombie, "International Contributions", pp. 109-10.

84. Whyte, *Town and Country Planning in Scotland*, p. 8.

85. David L. Smith, *Amenity and Urban Planning* (London, 1974), p. 2.

86. Canada, Commission of Conservation, *Second Annual Report*, pp. 50-84.

87. "Town Planning Expert Points to City's Need", *Edmonton Journal*, March 4, 1913, p. 5.

88. Adams, "The Housing and Town Planning Act", p. 52.

89. Section 58(3) in the U.K. Act, and Section 5(3) in the New Brunswick and Alberta acts.

90. Adams, "The Housing and Town Planning Act", p. 118. See also, for example, Nettlefold, "Birmingham", pp. 99-112, and W. Thompson, "The Ruislip-Northwood and Ruislip-Manor Joint Town Planning Scheme", *The Town Planning Review*, vol. 4, no. 2 (1913), pp. 133-44.

91. G. Frank Beer, "A Plea for City Planning Organization", in Canada, Commission of Conservation, *Report of the Fifth Annual Meeting* (Toronto, 1914), p. 112.

92. Whyte, *Town and Country Planning in Scotland*, p. 4.

93. See, for example, Dr. Hodgetts' report to the Commission of Conservation in 1911 and 1912. See also Artibise, *Winnipeg*, pp. 177-94, and Paul Rutherford, ed., *Saving the Canadian City: The First Phase, 1880–1920* (Toronto, 1974), particularly the extracts in Part 2.

94. The idea seems to have originated with the Calgary City Council in 1910, in a suggestion that the owners of new subdivisions should surrender 10 per cent of the subdivided land for park purposes: Foran, "Land Speculation and Urban Development in Calgary", p. 218.

95. *The Canadian Annual Review of Public Affairs, 1913*, pp. 29-42.

96. Adams' first report to the Commission of Conservation was published in 1915, his last in 1919.

97. "Planning means the planning of the scientific, aesthetic and orderly disposition of land, with a view to securing physical, economic and social efficiency, health and well-being in urban and rural communities": section 1.6, By-law Number 4 (New Series), Canadian Institute of Planners, October 21, 1976.

98. Revisions were made in 1922 and 1928, and a totally new Town Planning Act was passed in 1929: *Revised Statutes of Alberta*, 1929, chapter 49.

99. "Mr. Horace L. Seymour Goes to Alberta", *Town Planning*, vol. 7, no. 6 (1928): 156-57.

100. See, for example, "The New Alberta Town Planning Act", *Town Planning*, vol. 7, no. 3 (1928): 63-64. The importance of linking urban and rural planning was emphasized repeatedly by Thomas Adams, most notably in his monograph, *Rural Planning and Development* (Ottawa: Commission of Conservation, 1917). It is also noteworthy that the British legislation was not changed to the *Town and Country Planning Act* until 1932.

101. "Premier Brownlee, Alberta", *Town Planning*, vol. 6, no. 6 (1927): 192-93.

102. *Revised Statutes of Alberta*, 1970, chapter 276, section 3.

103. For a case study of the planning implications of the free enterprise ethic see P. J. Smith and D. G. Harasym, "Planning for Retail Services in New Residential Areas since 1944", in B. M. Barr, ed., *Calgary: Metropolitan Structure and Influence*, University of Victoria, Western Geographical Series, vol. 11 (Victoria, 1975), pp. 157-91.

104. Rescher, *Distributive Justice*, p. 10.

105. Russell, *History of Western Philosophy*, pp. 803-07.

106. For a recent review see William J. Meyer, *Public Good and Political Authority* (Port Washington, N.Y., 1975), pp. 3-15.

107. Rescher, *Distributive Justice*, p. 121.
108. "Land planning is the right and balanced allocation of land between rival claimants": L. Dudley Stamp, *Applied Geography* (Harmondsworth, 1960), p. 65. Stamp does not define "right and balanced". For a critique of allocative planning see John Friedmann, *Retracking America: A Theory of Transactive Planning* (Garden City, N.Y., 1973), pp. 52-59.
109. John Rawls, *A Theory of Justice* (Cambridge, 1971).
110. William K. Frankena, *Ethics* (2nd ed., Englewood Cliffs, 1973), p. 45.
111. See, for example, David Harvey, *Social Justice and the City* (London, 1973); Robert Goodman, *After the Planners* (Harmondsworth, 1972); Jacob L. Crane, *Urban Planning—Illusion and Reality* (New York, 1973); and J. M. Simmie, *Citizens in Conflict: The Sociology of Town Planning* (London, 1974).
112. Ron Clark, "The Crisis in Canadian City Planning", *City Magazine*, vol. 1, no. 8 (1976): 17-24; and Kent Gerecke, "The History of Canadian City Planning", *City Magazine*, vol. 2, nos. 3/4 (1976): 22-23. Both authors address the professional tensions that arise from the gap between the institutional reality of Canadian planning and its reform roots and radical aspirations.
113. Ian Wight and Grahame Allen, "Evolving Settlement Strategy in the Peace River Region of Alberta", paper presented at the Environment Conservation Authority's Conference on the Urban Environment, Edmonton (October 1976).

9.

Towards the City Efficient: The Theory and Practice of Zoning, 1919 – 1939

WALTER VAN NUS

The two preceding chapters have a common theme: the historically weak commitment within the Canadian planning profession to social justice for the urban collectivity. Both condemn planning based exclusively on a cult of efficiency. This chapter carries the critique a step further, by showing that in practice early Canadian planners were incapable of applying even the ideal of efficiency to the city as a whole. One should not, however, conclude that the ideal of an optimally efficient urban organism was (to use Tom Gunton's terms) merely a "liberal" rather than a "radical" one. In fact, it was precisely the sweeping restrictions on property rights required to achieve this ideal that encouraged so many planners to shrink from its imposition.

The planning professionals of Canada were first organized nationally at a meeting in Ottawa in May 1919, when a group of architects, engineers, and surveyors founded the Town Planning Institute of Canada, in which only members of their three professions were eligible for "full membership".[1] During the next twenty years, the young profession, and particularly its engineers and surveyors, tended to forsake the ideal of relatively permanent plans and zones for the gradual development of optimally efficient cities in favour of a more passive, managerial sort of planning which sought little more than the co-ordination of the desires and development policies of private interests. It will be argued that while the planners' retreat from rigid zoning was necessitated by the political impracticability of the severe restrictions on property rights involved, it was also facilitated by their own doubts (eminently justified) as to whether they were competent to devise a relatively permanent general plan. The elastic zoning which emerged in practice served not to maximize overall efficiency, but to stabilize the value of certain urban property.

THE RETREAT IN PLANNING THEORY FROM FIXED DESIGN TO ADMINISTRATIVE PROCESS

The first point to examine is the origins and gist of the belief that an optimally efficient city could be achieved only by adhering to a long-term, relatively inflexible urban general plan, which in turn required rigid zoning. This ideal was never implemented for any large Canadian city in the inter-war period, of course, but even at the theoretical level, it tended increasingly to be replaced by a view of planning as continuous administrative adjustment. Planners embraced this less difficult duty because they doubted their ability to draw up a workable long-range plan: their self-confidence was sapped as they considered the vast quantities of necessary data which lay uncollected or uncollated, their own lack of interdisciplinary training, and the inordinate difficulty of predicting the rate of growth for a specific city. It can also be suggested that the adoption of this more modest role was reinforced by planners' political dependence on local businessmen.

Unlike City Beautiful theorists, who were concerned about the psychological effect of the appearance of the urban environment on its inhabitants, many engineers and surveyors thought first of the need to build the city's physical plant at the lowest possible cost. This tendency was consistent with the engineer's view of the fundamental aim of engineering. As John Empey told the Association of Ontario Land Surveyors in 1934: "Back of all engineering thought stands [*sic*] the high ideals of our profession. These ideals include thoroughness of construction, soundness of planning, efficiency in the use of labour, and of the nation's resources of power and material."[2] It followed that the measure of progress in engineering was the increase in efficiency and economy.[3] That the basic aim of applied science should also motivate city planning was made explicit as early as 1912 by G. W. Hayler:

> Modern Science has used all its endeavours to prevent waste. Improved methods of manufacture, labor saving devices, advanced education, etc., have all tended to concentrate effort and eliminate the element of non-production whether in the machine or in the man. All true progress is towards this end and the city, which is only a centralization of industry, should in itself be an efficient arena for the life which it embodies.[4]

Most engineers and surveyors held "the development of a healthy and efficient social and industrial organization which will give us the maximum of production" to be the cardinal purpose of town planning.[5] "Good city planning", emphasized A. E. K. Bunnell, "is not primarily a matter of aesthetics, but of economics. Its basic principle is to increase the working efficiency of the city."[6] Engineers and surveyors also tended to view the city as a totality, and they saw their task as ordering and co-ordinating the activities of its many social and economic interests in such a way that the city as a whole might become an optimally efficient unit.[7] This perception grew, in part, out of the experience of municipal engineers who tried to integrate public works projects into city-wide systems.[8] The preoccupation of these professionals with the waste incurred by planning public and private development in isolation, without city-wide co-ordination, led to the frequent comparison of the city with a single "organism". Each of its organs, the metaphor ran, must be healthy and synchronized with the rest, and all its arteries must be free of congestion. As engineer James Ewing put it:

[A] city is not a mere indiscriminate collection of bricks and stones; it is a living, breathing, pulsating organism, like a human body, and a well-planned city is one which performs its various complex and interdependent functions with ease and efficiency.[9]

The bungling of laissez-faire city building was so blatant[10] that none of the planning professionals doubted that the control of city development by means of plans would mean greater overall efficiency. The use of plans was central to the daily work of these men, and their view of the city as a single unit or organism led them to advocate general, city-wide plans for future development. The ideals of and experience in municipal engineering lay at the root of planners' commitment to the city efficient.

An urban general plan, the argument went, would show how urban development could be shaped over the course of a specified period of years. The municipality was expected to adopt by-laws compelling future public and private development to conform to it. Like City Beautiful plans, the general plan was expected to set aside land for parks and for a network of arterial roads. In addition, however, it was to employ zoning in order to segregate conflicting land uses into the most suitable areas and to control the height of buildings and the proportion of the lot they might occupy. A general plan would base the road pattern (and thus that of the services installed underneath the streets) on the topography of the city site and on the needs of traffic. Once the nature and intensity of land use were established for every section of the city, it would be easy to calculate the maximum future demands on roads and on every other public project. With every sort of land use placed in the most efficient location and served by public works of optimal capacity, relatively permanent zoning would minimize the costly replacement of water and sewerage pipes and the continual widening of streets and bridges necessitated by the uncontrolled intensification of land use. Every producer in the city

would have his costs reduced, and every taxpayer would hail the
council that had slashed the cost of public works by its investment in
a general plan.[11]

Most professionals who shared this ideal recognized that enormous
difficulties were involved. Few would have agreed with surveyor T. B.
Speight, who in 1912 pictured town planning as a developed science
which only needed application.[12] Many more would have echoed
Horace Seymour's more modest assertion that "as a science, it [town
planning] is in its infancy".[13] They recognized that planners had yet to
collect a vast amount of basic data before they could prepare general
plans. Thomas Adams, the Town Planning Advisor to the Commission
of Conservation, described the existing "scientific data required to
afford guidance to the planner" as "very inadequate". "The true
logical order" in developing the science of town planning, he added,
required that any creative work be preceded by "investigation, by
means of observation and experiment, to discover facts and their
mutual relations".[14] The *Journal of the Town Planning Institute of
Canada (TPICJ)* agreed. Using Herbert Spencer's definition of science
as ordered knowledge, it confessed that "we are still in the embryonic
state of the development. . . . Such research work as the Commission
of Conservation has done only reveals the poverty of our knowledge
compared with the greatness and complexity of the task to be undertaken."[15] Planners outside the Commission were led to a similar conclusion when they tried to collect data on current conditions. The
most fundamental information had either not been gathered by anyone, or was scattered among government and business offices. The
Saskatoon Town Planning Commission, for example, found that no
one had tried to count the number of vehicles entering the downtown
core, nor had anyone determined the proportion of business frontage
currently in use.[16] Most cities did not hire the permanent staff needed
to collect, synthesize, and keep up-to-date the copious quantities of
data which planners claimed they required. Indeed, by Horace Seymour's criteria, it would appear that in no Canadian city before the
Second World War should planners have felt confident to move from
the stage of gathering facts to the business of comprehensive planning.
On the basis of his work on the Vancouver plan of 1930[17] (the most
comprehensive general plan made for any city in Canada between the
wars), Seymour presented to the 1929 convention of the Association of
Ontario Land Surveyors a list of fity-eight "Maps and Studies to be
Made in Connection with a Comprehensive Town Plan". The list
ranged from studies of population growth, building trends, and traffic

counts, to studies of natural resources in tributary areas, recreational facilities, and prevailing winds. He warned, however, that his enumeration had included only "a few of the more important studies suggested from a consideration of the Vancouver plan that might be of value for other municipalities". He hastened to assure the delegates that "if all the facts can be collected . . . then a solution of any town planning problem becomes comparatively simple".[18] If even Vancouver's planners had not been supplied with enough data to test this assumption, then assuredly it was not tested for any Canadian municipality in these years.

A number of planning engineers recognized that the complexity of the urban organism required an interdisciplinary approach extending beyond such proposals as that for the reintegration of engineering,[19] or even for a synthesis of engineering, surveying, and architecture.[20] "Town planning," wrote engineer and housing expert A. G. Dalzell in 1929, "is supposed by many to be a new and special branch of engineering. But, as Professor Patrick Geddes points out, it is not a new specialism added to existing ones, but it is the . . . co-ordinating of them all towards civic well-being."[21] Not only the engineer and architect, declared engineer Norman Wilson, but also the social worker, health authority, economist, and legislator must co-operate in planning work.[22]

The desire that planners be generalists, synthesizing many disciplines, was manifest in both the calls for and the content of planning courses in Canadian universities during the 1920s. Advocating such training in 1921, the *TPICJ* pointed out that engineers, surveyors, and architects had not been taught the social and economic factors of urban development.[23] Discussing "Town Planning at the University", Adrian Berrington, Professor of Architecture at the University of Toronto, observed that planners should understand not only engineering and architecture, but also demography, ethnography, history, economics, crowd psychology, and folklore.[24] Certainly the organizers of the two-week extension course in town planning held at the University of Toronto in February 1923 considered economics and scoiology part of the complete planner's repertoire, judging from the list of twenty-six lectures. For example, R. M. McIver spoke on "The Economics of Town Planning", and C. R. Fay discussed "The Co-operative Tenants System".[25] Though McGill University inaugurated a short course in planning during the early 1920s,[26] and the Faculty of Applied Science and Engineering at the University of Toronto offered a new optional fourth year course in "Town Planning and Municipal Administration" beginning in the 1922-23 session,[27] and while the University of

Alberta did in 1930 make town planning a compulsory subject in the final year of architecture and engineering,[28] Canada offered nothing to compare with the program at Harvard's School of City Planning (founded in 1929). One doubts that many members of the three planning professions received an effective interdisciplinary education at the formal level.

Certainly engineers and surveyors needed more expertise than they possessed to draw up a general plan. How, for example were they to determine the rate of a city's future growth, recognized as the basic input for any general plan? A few planners went beyond the simple recognition of the need for such information, and discussed the means of predicting the rate of growth. Of these, none expressed unqualified confidence in the ability of any combination of experts to forecast urban expansion. Norman Wilson came closest to such optimism:

> The laws of the growth of cities, while empirical and affected by various local conditions, are on the whole remarkably fixed. Any live community may expect to increase its population one-quarter each decade, and to approximately double its commerce each decade. This may be the reason that its assessable value increases much faster than the growth of population. From research made by J. R. Bibbins, of the Arnold Co., Chicago, it is found that the average basic land value of a great number of cities increases as the 1.7th power of the population....
>
> Thus it may be said that a town reasonably well situated will in one generation of thirty years double its population, increase its general commerce seven or eight times, and triple its basic land value, which latter is the measure of its ability to tax itself for improved conditions.

Elsewhere in the same article, however, Wilson conceded that the rate of future growth was "the unknown factor in any problem of town planning". Admitting that there might arise unpredictable circumstances that would retard or accelerate city growth, or shape that growth abnormally, he emphasized that a plan must be "capable of amplification and amendment from time to time with the growth of the community".[29] Such caution was typical. *The Canadian Engineer* noted such factors as rural migration and differing rates of industrialization in centres of similar size, and was pessimistic about the reliability of long-term population forecasting.[30] Those professionals who wrote about the forecasting problem usually agreed with Edmonton's Town Planning Assistant, B. P. Scull: "It is impossible to anticipate the future with any degree of certainty beyond a very limited span of years."[31]

If local peculiarities made growth predictions based on a composite of the experience of other cities risky, could any university economics program then available have taught planners a reliable forecasting method? Even general falls in the North American business cycle, such as those of 1913 – 15 and 1930 – 33, had not been accurately predicted by most economists. The crisis in municipal finance which had begun in 1913 helped make professionals wary of city works projects whose long-term efficiency depended on a continuation of current growth rates. Take, for example, the provision of underground installations before paving in areas adjacent to a municipality where building of homes seemed imminent. In a period of sustained growth, such a policy might seem reasonable, as it obviated the later ripping up of pavement. In some instances, large trunk sewers had been installed before 1913, and thereafter no money was available for laterals. Where laterals had been added on the basis of overly optimistic growth forecasts, they were damaged by electrolytic action after two or three years' disuse. There were, of course, few if any local homeowners to help pay for these premature installations.[32]

Lack of confidence in long-term forecasting helps explain why only a minority of Canadian planners by the 1920s still advocated the drawing up of relatively rigid comprehensive plans which would provide for every city "a clear objective towards which we can gradually work".[33] As engineer J. M. Kitchen repeatedly stressed, "permanence in the development of the city" could be secured by comparatively inflexible zoning.[34] To a large extent, the continued insistence by this minority group on a plan difficult to amend grew from fear of "subsequent alterations which would destroy its usefulness".[35] But for a few of them, it also arose from a desire for an urban environment like that of the great European cities, which linked the inhabitant with his past and which was not subject to continual demolition. The editor of the TPICJ longed "to capture the mellowed glory of the older lands". "Nothing," he added, "will so certainly cure the nomadic restlessness of a new country as planning for mellowed permanence. . . . "[36] This view paralleled the emphasis in German zoning theory on preserving one's city as a heritage,[37] though there is no evidence of its direct influence in Canada.

The majority of planners by the 1920s tended to view planning as a continuous administrative process, rather than the gradual completion of a largely fixed design. This approach assumed (if often only implicitly) that the greatest control which planners could expect to gain over the efficiency of urban development was that of co-ordinator of the various economic interests which affected development.[38] Those who thought in this way bowed before the steady rise in land values, which meant that buildings of greater earning power must replace smaller ones, so as to carry the charges on those increased values. In 1919, Noulan Cauchon estimated that 90 per cent of all urban building in Canada would be replaced within thirty years.[39] City growth, agreed Norman Wilson, always meant change in existing land uses, and "the acme of city planning" was "the foreseeing the competent directing of that change".[40] Planners, however, felt as unsure about predicting long-term land use changes as they did overall population growth. As G. G. Powell, Deputy City Engineer of Toronto, pointed out, development might differ from that forecast by planners, especially where all urban land was not publicly owned, and zoning might have to be revised drastically.[41] Powell's argument was typical in conceding the initiative in urban development to private interests. Planning thus became the prediction and co-ordination of the urban development effected by property owners. To foresee the long-term aggregate result of the decisions of numerous developers was so difficult that many professionals were led to abandon the idea of relatively inflexible, long-range plans. This trend may have been encouraged by those local officials who by the late 1920s did not have confidence in long-range forecasts of urban growth, and said so.[42] Transition from the notion of a fixed, ideal plan was evidently considered a setback by some, who hoped that alterations would be required only occasionally. B. P. Scull, for instance, wrote in 1932:

> It is impossible to anticipate the future with any degree of certainty beyond a very limited span of years. Therefore, although it is necessary in the original plan to make provision for the probable ultimate development of an urban centre, the plan must be susceptible to alteration from time to time, so that it may progress with the development of the community and be sensible and practical.... [43]

Others, however, opted frankly for a largely managerial role; planners were to regulate land-use changes by allowing steady and orderly distension of expanding kinds of land use (as opposed to scattered intrusions into other areas), at a rate slow enough to prevent such an increase in the amount of land available for a certain use that the type of property would decline in value.[44] As Wilson explained, "Only to a relatively limited degree can we foresee the future...." Therefore, "town planning means the continuous anticipation of growth and the intelligent control of the changes which that growth entails."[45]

The rejection of the idea of permanency through zoning was almost always only implicit. One of the few direct attacks on the concept was delivered in 1936 by Tracy le May, formerly Toronto's City Surveyor and by then its Planning Commissioner. "Theoretically, zoning is grand," he began, "you just predetermine the future location of residence, commercial and industrial areas and govern yourselves accordingly, once residential always residential, and so on. . . . " He proceeded to stress "the difference between theory and practice", especially in a country of rapid development. If, for instance, one laid out an industrial area with a capacity greater than current need, a large part of it might lie waste, producing nothing but taxes until required for its particular purpose. For other parts of the city, meanwhile, the burden of public services would be unduly heavy because they had to pass through unproductive stretches of land. As well, rigid zoning constituted a refusal to permit obsolescence in housing and to compel the replacement of old homes as advances in living standards and habits rendered existing dwellings undesirable. Rather than preventing industrial areas from expanding into old residential ones, it would be better to establish buffer strips to permit gradual transition from residential to industrial use. "Zoning without elasticity," he concluded, "must fail. . . . "[46]

The view that the planner was to provide management rather than a rigid plan is explained not only by lack of confidence in long-term forecasting, but also by sympathy for the property industry: a flexible, on-going planning process could much more readily accommodate changing growth patterns caused by decisions of private developers and industry than could a fixed plan. Horace Seymour, for example, observed in 1924 that the development of the automobile and of the steelframe skyscraper "show the necessity for elastic rather than stereotyped planning". In his next sentence, Seymour unwittingly revealed the extent to which planning was coming to mean accommodation to the desires of developers. "The solution of the problems created by modern methods of urban growth," he wrote, "is not to change existing developments or make new developments so that they may conform to a pattern, but to make these developments conform to a system or plan that can be modified and adjusted to meet the needs of growth and the changes incidental to growth."[47] Such an obliging attitude to the aims that business set for the city may be explained in part by the admiration felt by planners for the efficiency of successful (and non-speculating) businessmen. The co-ordinated efficiency believed to characterize large corporations provided a model for City Efficient orators. "It is time," Adams declared in 1921, "to apply the scientific and business principles that have made a success of industrial organization, to the social organization of the city."[48] Not only did some big businessmen embody the ideal of efficiency, but the support of local businessmen was also considered essential by many professionals in order to overcome political apathy concerning planning. Businessmen, argued the TPICJ, could organize more readily and effectively for political support or resistance than could any other group.[49] As Seymour indicated in 1921, planning would not accomplish much unless it held out the promise of profit to local businessmen. Planners must, he confided candidly, appeal to "the commercial urge".[50] Since the average citizen was indifferent to long-range planning for urban efficiency, Professor Frank Buck of Vancouver told the TPIC in the 1928 Presidential Address, the planner should appeal to the business community rather than to the general public.[51]

Few spoke as bluntly as Professor Buck, but most agreed on the practical necessity to gain business support. The housing reform movement, so important in popularizing planning in the 1910s, declined in the 1920s, perhaps because of the general post-war disillusionment with social reform and also because of the stabilization of workers' living costs in the early 1920s.[52] After the war, local businessmen supplanted that movement in providing the major "impulse to action" in planning.[53] In 1918, the Canadian Manufacturers' Association, in a brief to the federal government, had urged the immediate expansion of the work of the Commission of Conservation's Town Planning Branch.[54] In 1918 as well, a committee of the (Montreal) South Shore Board of Trade had tried to inaugurate work on a comprehensive planning scheme for the area encompassing St. Lambert, Greenfield Park, Montreal South, and Longueuil. Its activities led to the appointment of a South Shore Joint Town Planning Board, which hired the consulting engineering firm of Ewing, Lovelace, and Tremblay to prepare the scheme.[55] In 1921, the Downtown District Association of Toronto, in an effort to maintain the position of the city's retail centre by means of zoning, called for a City Planning Commission, and invited Horace Seymour to address them.[56] In 1919 and again in 1929, the Peterborough Board of Trade advocated a planning commission for the town, and in London, the Chamber of Commerce salvaged Adams' planning efforts there by a donation which permitted Seymour to continue the work.[57] In addition, a number of resource corporations were in the 1920s erecting planned towns, the most notable of which was Arvida, founded in 1926 by the Alumi-

num Company of Canada. Examples of business support were hailed
in the planning and professional journals, which in the 1920s boasted
that, as in the United States, planning would come to be regarded as a
"business proposition".[58] The passivity of planners towards businessmen occasionally extended to hope for charitable donations from
them. Seymour, for example, suggested that they or their associations
fund the preparation of town plans,[59] and Cauchon wondered
whether "some Canadian millionaire" might not, in his "benevolent
wisdom", emulate those American millionaires who had financed
demonstration towns.[60] All in all, most Canadian planners by the
1920s were unlikely to rebel against the view that planning would
control property developers only in the sense of co-ordinating their
activities so that, as engineer Morris Knowles put it, the business
community as a whole might be shown how to make the most of the
city's opportunities.[61]

THE PRACTICE OF ZONING, 1919 – 1939

In light of the preceding discussion of the theoretical framework for
planning between the wars, it comes as no surprise that the actual
preparation of zoning by-laws for built-up areas became largely the
confirmation of existing development trends. Commenting on a draft
zoning by-law which he had helped draw up for Ottawa in 1924, J. M.
Kitchen described its intention as "to control future permissibility as
far as possible from the status of existing home and work conditions
. . . they being considered a forecast upon which to base future permissibility."[62] Regarding the Regina Town Planning Association's tentative zoning by-laws for that city, Colonel A. C. Garner indicated the
Association's solicitude for property owners when he declared, "The
by-laws could be applied now without injury to anyone and yet
protection would be assured to citizens' property interests."[63] The
authors of the Vancouver plan of 1930 located the boundaries of the
various zones according to the predominance of existing uses.[64] The
passivity of zoning in the face of private development trends, implicit
in the writings of the managerial school, and many professionals' lack
of confidence in long-range forecasting, both became obvious in practice.

  In accounting for the tendency to use zoning to confirm the status
quo, it is only fair to stress that the opportunity to develop expertise
in long-term forecasting as a basis for zoning was severely limited by
the inadequate funding of planning efforts. J. M. Kitchen noted the
simplicity of the draft Ottawa zoning by-law, compared to those of

other cities, and gave as one reason the small amount of money available to draw it up.[65] Because of strict budget limitations, H. J. Doughty-Davies was given only a few months in late 1929 and early 1930 to formulate an interim zoning by-law for Calgary.[66] In 1932, the year before the adoption of the Edmonton zoning by-law, the city's Town Planning Commission had a total budget of only $4,300.[67] Even the authors of the Vancouver plan of 1930, the most generously financed and best researched of our period, had to admit lack of detailed study for their zoning proposals.[68] One suspects that lack of money discouraged zoning based on research other than that into prevailing land uses.

One must also remember that in most Canadian cities in these years, the franchise was so restricted that property owners, as the *TPICJ* repeatedly complained, dominated municipal politics.[69] The principal basis of political support for zoning was the desire to prohibit the intrusion of uses which could reduce neighbouring property values. When they set out to sell zoning to the public, planners appealed above all to the determination to maintain property values. They pitched this appeal in particular to real estate interests.[70] Zoning, explained Ottawa Town Planning Commission Chairman Noulan Cauchon in 1923, stabilized the value of residential properties by prohibiting noxious uses. By restricting the expansion of commercial areas to a level justified by current economic conditions, it sustained the value of business property as well. In Canada today, he added, practically all investment in unprotected urban land was liable to a depreciation of 25 per cent, whereas zoned property afforded safe investment. He appealed to the trust companies, which had loaned vast sums upon realty, to endorse zoning and to encourage the investing public to press for zoning by granting smaller loans at higher interest rates on land that had not been zoned.[71] In the pre-war speculative boom, explained A. G. Dalzell in 1920, sale of real estate was facilitated by the uncertainty of future land use. Investors had since been so badly hurt by jumble building that the same uncertainty now discouraged land buying.[72] "There is much groaning among land dealers because land will not sell," echoed the *TPICJ* in 1926; sooner or later, the real estate fraternity must realize that the cause of their woes lay in an "insecurity of property values ... because nobody knows how soon those values will be destroyed by neighbouring atrocities".[73] In the mid-1920s, some realtors—already familiar with maintaining values through private land-use restrictions—were responding to this argument.[74] It has not been possible to determine the extent to

which business support in any given city was really only support for
protective zoning, but certainly the zoning efforts during the later
1920s in Saskatoon[75] and Vancouver[76] were supported by important
elements in the local real estate business. By 1925, at least some
realtors in Toronto and Windsor were supporting zoning,[77] and by
1927, a number of real estate men had joined the TPIC.[78] Planners
welcomed such support, and rarely addressed themselves to the possibility of conflict between the ideal of zoning for an optimally efficient
urban unit on the one hand, and zoning as "a stabilization of the
merchandise the realtor sells", as one TPIC member put it,[79] on the
other.

The experience of the authors of the Vancouver plan of 1930 suggests that planners could not even be assured of exercising their best
judgment freely in the task of achieving the "stabilization of the
merchandise the realtor sells". Influential retail merchants in Vancouver wanted to speculate on the value of residential main street lots,
hoping that they would one day have commercial value. Being politically aware, the Vancouver team of planners calculated the total
allowable retail business frontage most generously. They used the
figure of seventy-three feet of frontage per unit population, instead of
the actual current figure of sixty-seven, and assumed moreover that
the city's population had already reached the 370,000 maximum possible under the zoning by-law. The reaction of local businessmen to this
already excessive largesse was summarized frankly in the plan:

> If, however, commercial districts are restricted in this scientific and reasona-
> ble way, they do not meet with the wishes of owners of property who have
> anticipated certain streets as future business streets. For this reason the
> entire frontage of Davie, Denman and Robson Streets have [sic] been zoned
> as six-storey commercial districts, although such classification is in excess of
> the estimated requirements for the district.[80]

The Vancouver case illustrates how limited planners were by their
political dependence on local businessmen. It also points to the un-
reality of the distinction planners drew between speculating businessmen, whom they denounced, and productive, socially useful ones, the
efficiency of whose operations they wished to enhance. In fact, important businessmen indulged in both kinds of profit making.

The dilution by business of the efficiencies possible by means of
zoning did not, of course, stop once the final draft of a zoning by-law
was adopted. The erection of new structures which did not conform to
the by-law was often permitted because it suited the needs of a

developer, and not because it formed part of a careful program of transition from one land-use zone to another. In 1928, the *TPICJ* accused builders of "blackmail" against municipalities which attempted to enforce zoning or height restrictions. It complained of developers "who are threatening to take their buildings elsewhere if they are not allowed to build on 100 per cent of their lot, with the sky for a limit".[81] With the exception of Kitchener, where alterations to the zoning by-law were subject to Municipal Board approval, zoning by-laws in Canadian cities during the 1920s and 1930s made spot zoning relatively easy. Under Vancouver's by-law, for example, property owners might petition a Zoning Board of Appeal against literal enforcement which resulted in unnecessary hardship. The Board was permitted to "make such relaxations as may be required to meet special cases", and was to endeavour to ensure "that the interests of any individuals are not unduly or unnecessarily sacrificed for the benefit of the community".[82] Writing in 1935, J. A. Walker, Engineer Secretary to the Vancouver Town Planning Commission, revealed the political importance of such flexibility. "The Zoning Board of Appeal," he explained, "has proved to be a real 'safety valve' in the administration of the zoning by-law. Without the existence of this Board it is extremely doubtful if the zoning by-law would have much public support."[83]

Students of the subject disagree as to whether in Vancouver, where zoning served as an instrument in the implementation of a general plan of development, such exceptions were limited in their cumulative impact.[84] More often than not, however, a zoning by-law was passed without a general plan. Those planners who helped prepare this sort of by-law often recognized that their approach was not the ideal one, but rather the best they were permitted to take by the local council. In 1927, Victoria hired J. H. Doughty-Davies to produce a zoning scheme, but he frankly told the local Real Estate Board that the most scientific procedure involved deciding first on a comprehensive plan, of which zoning would be a part. As it was, he was able to base his zone boundaries merely on what appeared to be the logical future development of the existing street system, in the hope that logic would prevail in this connection.[85] Edmonton was discouraged from adopting a general plan by the Alberta Town Planning Act of 1929, under which the Minister of Municipal Affairs had to approve every amendment to an official plan. In 1933, when Edmonton adopted its zoning by-law without a general plan, the budget of its Town Planning Commission was reduced to $500, and thereafter, with no overall plan to guide it, the Zoning Appeal Board accepted so much uncoordinated spot zoning as to vitiate the original by-law.[86]

Planners had been made aware of the dangers of zoning without a general plan by considerable writing and discussion by their colleagues on the matter. Adams recalled in 1921 that earlier City Beautiful plans had failed to safeguard their proposed road and park systems by prohibiting nearby land uses which threatened the systems' usefulness. Now, he continued, some centres had gone to the opposite extreme, by zoning industry, business, and homes without relating the zones to transportation and parks plans.[87] The *TPICJ* agreed that the location of industrial and residential zones must be co-ordinated with a plan for future transportation and parks development, observing that if a zoning plan were prepared before a general plan, it might require considerable alteration after the general plan was completed. If, therefore, a municipality could not afford the immediate preparation of a comprehensive general plan, it should have the work done in logical sequence. First, a survey should be conducted and maps prepared showing existing conditions; from these studies, the city's general needs could be inferred. Second, a plan of future transportation and parks systems would be drawn up. Only then should city-wide zoning take place, based on the results of the first two steps.[88] In much of the United States during the 1920s, "zoning not only came before planning but very rapidly seemed to become equated with it." By the end of that decade, only about twenty per cent of the American cities which had zoning ordinances also had completed comprehensive plans.[89] Canadian planners were able to discern this weakness early, in part because they were aware of the contrasting British approach. During a discussion on zoning held by the Toronto Branch of the Engineering Institute of Canada in late 1920, W. S. B. Armstrong described the American type of town planning as "inferior to that followed in England; in the United States, they are disposed to consider zoning as town planing [*sic*], whereas it is only part of that science, although no doubt a necessary part".[90] The *TPICJ* contrasted the imperfect American concept of zoning without a general plan with the British theory of a comprehensive plan covering everything from road, rail, and harbour facilities, to scenic preservation and school location.[91] Any municipal official in the 1920s who read the *TPICJ* or *The Canadian Engineer* had been warned repeatedly against zoning without a general plan.

A few planners, frustrated at the limitations on using zoning to transform existing cities into efficient organisms, toyed with the application of zoning in two other areas: the urban fringe and small towns. As Adams wearily admitted, the zoning of areas already occupied by permanent structures "has to be governed by existing conditions to such an extent that only very imperfect results are attainable".[92] To American zoning, which tended to ignore areas of likely future development, Adams preferred the English practice, which concentrated on the urban fringe and did not include land that had been built upon to any large extent. It was in the control of new suburban development that the greatest opportunity lay for successful zoning, he argued, because vested interests in existing buildings had not yet been created.[93] But by what criteria was the urban fringe to be zoned? How could one zone such an area before the transition from agricultural use? Basically, the only method of zoning used by contemporaries for established cities was the confirmation of current development trends, and these were not distinct enough in the urban fringe to permit that easy solution. Perhaps as a result, almost no one discussed how to zone the urban fringe. G. G. Powell thought such prediction so uncertain that the results might be no better than those obtained without zoning.[94] Seymour seemed to suggest that all uses except heavy industry should be permitted initially within the fringe area. (Heavy industry would be allowed only within 1,320 feet of a railway and at least 500 feet away from any other use.) As soon as any part of the area exhibited a pronounced land-use tendency, he suggested, it could be zoned as a particular district, so that development might become increasingly uniform within it.[95] This approach hardly fulfilled Adams' hope for suburban zoning. Rather, it extended planners' passivity in the face of private development trends into their dealing with the urban fringe.

Some planners, observing that to reshape existing cities involved prohibitive cost, argued that they would have been efficient had they been planned properly when still small. From this assumption they drew the lesson that today's small towns must adopt development plans, so that the future cities of Canada might benefit from the experience of older centres.[96] The *TPICJ* urged villages and small towns to avoid the replanning difficulties of larger places by setting aside zones in advance of building development. The *Journal* formulated the doctrine that "the smaller the municipality the more it will benefit by orderly development . . . ".[97] In making this sweeping recommendation, with no allusion to its practical limitations, these writers may have been influenced by the popularity of the idea among such pre-war municipal reform leaders as Dr. Charles Hodgetts, Medical Advisor to the Commission of Conservation, Mayor Hopewell of Ottawa, and Harry Bragg, editor of *The Canadian Municipal Journal*.[98]

Other planners, though, argued that to predict the rate and nature of the growth of a new townsite was even more difficult than to do so for an established city. In their *Preliminary Report on a City Plan for North Bay* (1928), Wilson, Bunnell, and Borgstrom stated bluntly that "it is seldom possible in the formative stage of any community to foresee its future with accuracy and the varying influences which determine the location of its first streets and buildings must usually be left to work out their own results".[99] Tracy le May dismissed the idea of establishing zones of future development for new centres. "A little thought," he wrote, "will show that to zone even a new town successfully you must also limit growth." If one laid out a nucleus of industrial and commercial zones surrounded by residential areas, for example, one would incur the heavy expense of installing public services through the largely unoccupied nucleus.[100]

Such doubts were justified in light of the experience of those few company towns which were planned before 1930 for a substantial ultimate population. In 1906, site clearing had begun for Prince Rupert, which the Grand Trunk Pacific expected to become the main port for a great trade with Alaska and the Far East, since it had a large harbour and was situated about five hundred miles closer to the Orient than any competing port. The railroad engaged an American firm of landscape architects to lay out a townsite for a population of one hundred thousand. As late as 1961, it was still a fishing port with a population of eleven thousand.[101] In 1926, when the Aluminum Company of Canada began to build Arvida, it was planned to accommodate fifty thousand people. In 1956, its population was still under thirteen thousand, and great gaps of open land and forest remained between the developed sections of the town.[102] In view of these disastrous forecasts, the planning of small towns simply to be efficient small towns, rather than the beginning of something greater, may indeed have been the extent of planners' competence in these years. This more modest aim was in fact embodied in the Saskatchewan and Alberta townsite planning regulations of the 1920s.[103] By the later 1930s, at least, planners might have asked themselves how predicting the growth of an ordinary small town could be possible, if a company which controlled the economy of a one-industry town could not do so for its own location.

CONCLUSION

It is clear that Canada's infant planning profession of the inter-war period was justifiably uncertain about its competence to draw up relatively permanent urban general plans. As well, the decline in the 1920s of the housing reform crusade removed much of the counter-weight to businessmen's influence on the newly organized profession. As has been explained elsewhere, a small minority of Canadian planners in the 1920s did support Ebenezer Howard's Garden City concept, which promised to solve the fundamental problem of planning cities whose future growth patterns were unknown, by having most future urban growth take place by means of satellite cities whose final size and layout were known in advance.[104] In practice, however, most Canadian planners in these years exchanged the goal of an optimally efficient urban organism for that of an optimally profitable one for the property industry.

NOTES

The following abbreviations are used:

ADLSR   Association of Dominion Land Surveyors, *Annual Report*

AOLSP   Association of Ontario Land Surveyors, *Proceedings*

CE   *The Canadian Engineer*

CMJ   *The Canadian Municipal Journal*

MRC   *The Municipal Review of Canada*

TP&CL   *Town Planning and Conservation of Life*

TPICJ   *Town Planning Institute of Canada, Journal*

1. CE, vol. 36 (May 15, 1919): 452-53. The revised TPIC constitution of July 5, 1920, extended the scope of professional membership to include artists, sculptors, and sociologists. The founding professions continued dominant, however. Within two months of the Institute's founding, its membership increased from the original 18 to 52, reaching 130 by the end of 1922. Between 1919 and 1930, a total of 367 professionals had joined the TPIC. CE, vol. 36 (June 26, 1919): 571; ADLSR (1923): 107; J. M.

Kitchen, "Town Planning Institute of Canada", MRC, vol. 46, (1950): 8. A copy of the revised TPIC constitution may be found in Volume 9 of the Noulan Cauchon Papers, Public Archives of Canada.

2. J. M. Empey, "President's Address", AOLSP (1934): 15.

3. A. G. Dalzell, "Engineers' Town Planning Attitude", CE, vol. 56 (June 25, 1929): 627.

4. G. W. Hayler, "The Economics of City Planning", CMJ, vol. 8, no. 7 (1912): 254. See also Noulan Cauchon, "Town Planning", CE, vol. 21 (November 9, 1911): 551.

5. Thomas Adams, "The Planning of Land in Relation to Municipal and Social Problems", CE, vol. 37 (November 20, 1919): 472. See also Noulan Cauchon, "The Essentials of Town Planning", CMJ, vol. 15, no. 11 (1919): 370.

6. A. E. K. Bunnell, "Resources for Town Planning", CE, vol. 45 (September 18, 1923): 324.

7. H. W. Meech (Commissioner of Public Works, Lethbridge), "Town Planning", CE, vol. 43 (November 14, 1922): 542.

8. Ibid., 542-43. See also George R. MacLeod, "The City Engineer's Work in Relation to Town Planning", *MRC*, vol. 34, no. 7 (1938): 17-18; and James Ewing's remarks in *TPICJ*, vol. 4, no. 4 (1925): 14.

9. James Ewing, "The Engineer and the Town Plan", *CE*, vol. 42 (June 4, 1922): 675. See also Ewing's comments in *TPICJ*, vol. 1, no. 9 (1922): 13; and Noulan Cauchon, "Economic Case for City Zoning", *CE*, vol. 50 (April 27, 1926): 520.

10. The bungling of suburban development is briefly summarized in the author's "The Fate of City Beautiful Thought in Canada, 1893-1930", in G. A. Stelter and A. F. J. Artibise, eds., *The Canadian City: Essays in Urban History* (Toronto, 1977), pp. 162-85, and is discussed more fully in his "The Plan-makers and the City: Architects, Engineers, Surveyors, and Urban Planning in Canada, 1890-1939", PH D diss., University of Toronto (1975), Chapter I and *passim*.

11. Noulan Cauchon, "Town Planning", *CE*, vol. 21 (November 9, 1911): 551; Thomas Adams, "Town and Country Planning in Quebec", *TP&CL*, vol. 6, no. 4 (1920): 77 and "Town Planning Notes", *MRC*, vol. 24, no. 2 (1928): 66; C. J. Yorath, "Municipal Finance and Administration", *TP&CL*, vol. 3, no. 4 (1917): 75-76; George MacLeod, "Municipal Engineering", *MRC*, vol. 27, no. 8 (1931): 17-18; A. G. Dalzell, "Saskatchewan Town Planning", *CE*, vol. 54 (June 19, 1928): 624; Cauchon, "Economic Case for City Zoning", 520; H. L. Seymour, "Town Planning Reduces City's Taxes", *CE*, vol. 76 (April 25, 1938): 4-5.

12. T. B. Speight, "A Few Observations on City Surveying", *AOLSP* (1912): 145. But see a similar claim by Professor F. E. Buck made before the TPIC in 1928. *CE*, vol. 55 (September 18, 1928): 319.

13. H. L. Seymour, "Housing and Town Planning: A Survey", *AOLSP* (1920): 149.

14. Adams, "The Planning of Land in Relation to Municipal and Social Problems", 472.

15. Editorial, *TPICJ*, vol. 1, no. 3 (1921): 1.

16. B. P. Scull, "Town Planning Progress in Saskatoon", *CE*, vol. 62 (February 9, 1932): 10, 42.

17. Vancouver Town Planning Commission, *A Plan for the City of Vancouver, British Columbia, Including Point Grey and South Vancouver and a General Plan of the Region* (1930).

18. H. L. Seymour, "Town Planning Surveys", *AOLSP* (1929): 133-35.

19. *CE*, vol. 49 (December 1, 1925): 600. See also MacLeod, "Municipal Engineering", 17.

20. *CMJ*, vol. 8, no. 7 (1912): 274.

21. Dalzell, "Engineers' Town Planning Attitude", 628.

22. N. D. Wilson, "Town Planning and Civic Development", *CE*, vol. 40 (March 24, 1921): 322

23. Editorial, *TPICJ*, vol. 1, no. 2 (1921): 2.

24. *TPICJ* vol. 1, no. 9 (1922): 12-13.

25. *ADLSR* (1923): 103-04.

26. *TPICJ*, vol. 1, no. 3 (1921): 9-10.

27. *CE*, vol. 43 (August 1, 1922): 217; vol. 43 (December 26, 1922): 672; vol. 45 (October 23, 1923): 440.

28. *CE*, vol. 58 (March 25, 1930): 432. Seymour's lectures in this course during the fall term, 1930, are preserved among his papers at the Public Archives of Canada.

29. Wilson, "Town Planning and Civic Development", 319, 321.

30. Editorial, "Rate of Growth of Population", *CE*, vol. 41 (December 29, 1921): 6. See also the comments of A. J. Latornel, City Engineer of Edmonton, in *CE*, vol. 28 (February 25, 1915): 295.

31. Scull, "Town Planning Progress in Saskatoon", 10.

32. Editorial, "Laying Down Pavements and Tearing Them Up Again", *CE*, vol. 28 (April 29, 1915): 511; A. G. Dalzell, "Problems of Sewer Design in Canada", *CE*, vol. 48 (May 12, 1925): 476.

33. James Ewing, "The Montreal Situation with Reference to Town Planning", *CE*, vol. 42 (March 21, 1922): 325.

34. *TPICJ*, vol. 3, no. 3 (1924): 24; *CE*, vol. 50 (February 23, 1926): 258. See also

W. E. Hobbs' emphasis on the desirable permanency given to general plans by zoning, in his remarks to the Association of Manitoba Land Surveyors in 1929. *Canadian Surveyor*, vol. 3, no. 4 (1929): 17.

35. George MacLeod, "Montreal's Main Thoroughfares", *CE*, vol. 41 (October 6, 1921): 1.

36. *TPICJ*, vol. 6, no. 1 (1926): 52. Compare W. A. Langton's remarks in, Ontario Association of Architects, *Proceedings* (1906), p. 51.

37. Seymour I. Toll, *Zoned America* (New York, 1921), pp. 134-35.

38. Morris Knowles, "Community Planning", *CE*, vol. 40 (January 13, 1921): 128.

39. Noulan Cauchon, "Ethical and Practical Sides of Town Planning", *CE*, vol. 37 (December 4, 1919): 512.

40. Wilson, "Town Planning and Civic Development", 320.

41. *CE*, vol. 39 (November 25, 1920): 558.

42. This point was made by at least three municipal officials during a discussion of zoning at the 1929 convention of the Union of Canadian Municipalities. They were Samuel Baker (City Clerk, London), E. T. Sampson (City Clerk, Outremont), and Controller Peebles of Hamilton. *MRC*, vol. 25, no. 9 (1929): 367.

43. Scull, "Town Planning Progress in Saskatoon", 10. See also H. L. Seymour, "Planning of Kitchener and Waterloo, Ont.", *CE*, vol. 47 (July 8, 1924): 129.

44. Noulan Cauchon, "Zoning", *CE*, vol. 46 (May 6, 1924): 490. See also J. M. Kitchen, "What It Means to Zone", *TPICJ*, vol. 5, no. 4 (1926): 6-7.

45. Wilson, "Town Planning and Civic Development", 319.

46. *AOLSP* (1936): 61-62.

47. Thomas Adams and H. L. Seymour, "Study in Problems of Urban Growth", *CE*, vol. 47 (November 25, 1924): 547-48. The content suggests that this part of the article was written by Seymour. If Adams agreed, he had changed his views markedly since campaigning for garden cities.

48. *CE*, vol. 40 (April 7, 1921): 363. See also National Conference on City Planning, *Proceedings* (1914): 313 and *AOLSP* (1912): 153-54.

49. *TPICJ*, vol. 6, no. 6 (1927): 198.

50. Seymour, "Zoning", *AOLSP* (1921): 170-71. See also his address before the Civic Bureau of the Vancouver Board of trade, *CE*, vol. 52 (February 1, 1927): 176.

51. *CE*, vol. 55 (September 18, 1928): 319.

52. Terry Copp, *The Anatomy of Poverty* (Toronto, 1974), p. 136.

53. *TPICJ*, vol. 8, no. 5 (1929): 96. See also *TPICJ*, vol. 3, no. 1 (1924): 1-2.

54. *TP&CL*, vol. 4, no. 3 (1918): 72.

55. *CE*, vol. 36 (June 12, 1919): 545; *CMJ*, vol. 15, no. 7 (1919): 235.

56. *AOLSP* (1921): 170-71; *CE*, vol. 42 (January 3, 1922): 118.

57. *CE*, vol. 37 (November 20, 1919): 479; *TPICJ*, vol. 8, no. 5 (1929): 96; Ibbotson Leonard, "Brief History of Town Planning in London, Ontario, Canada", *TPICJ*, vol. 7, no. 6 (1928): 147.

58. *TPICJ*, vol. 8, no. 5 (1929): 96. See also *TPICJ*, vol. 4, no. 1 (1925): 1 and the remarks of Horace Seymour in *CE*, vol. 53 (October 25, 1927): 481.

59. *TPICJ*, vol. 6, no. 3 (1927): 88.

60. *TPICJ*, vol. 5, no. 6 (1926): 26.

61. Knowles, "Community Planning", 128.

62. J. M. Kitchen, "Preparing Zoning By-laws for the City of Ottawa", *TPICJ*, vol. 3, no. 3 (1924): 24.

63. *CE*, vol. 46 (April 1, 1924): 388

64. *A Plan for the City of Vancouver . . .*, p. 225.

65. Kitchen, "Preparing Zoning By-laws for the City of Ottawa", 23.

66. *TPICJ*, vol. 9, no. 4 (1930): 73.

67. Edmund H. Dale, "Decision-Making at Edmonton, Alberta, 1913-1945: Town Planning Without a Plan", *Plan Canada*, vol. 11, no. 2 (1971): 141.

68. *A Plan for the City of Vancouver . . .*, p. 232.

69. *TPICJ*, vol. 5, no. 6 (1926): 29; *TPICJ*, vol. 6, no. 1 (1927): 67; *TPICJ*, vol. 9, no. 1 (1930): 7.

70. See Seymour's remarks in *AOLSP* (1923): 50; and in his paper on "Zoning", *AOLSP* (1921): 171.

71. Noulan Cauchon, "Zoning – Its

Financial Value", *TPICJ*, vol. 2, no. 3 (1923): 11.

72. A. G. Dalzell, "Town Planning and Real Estate", *TP&CL*, vol. 2, no. 3 (1920): 63-64.

73. *TPICJ*, vol. 5, no. 4 (1926): 1.

74. B. Evan-Parry, "Zoning for the Health of the Community", *CE*, vol. 49 (July 21, 1925): 151.

75. *TPICJ*, vol. 6, no. 1 (1927): 56.

76. *TPICJ*, vol. 1, no. 11 (1922):3; *CE*, vol. 43 (September 26, 1922): 389; *TPICJ*, vol. 1, no. 2 (1921): 5; *TPICJ*, vol. 4, no. 1 (1925): 9; *TPICJ*, vol. 6, no. 6 (1926): 198; *CE*, vol. 46 (May 20, 1924): 541.

77. According to Norman Wilson, *CE*, vol. 48 (March 17, 1925): 322.

78. *TPICJ*, vol. 6, no. 3 (1927): 94.

79. Evan-Parry, "Zoning for the Health of the Community", 151.

80. *A Plan for the City of Vancouver . . .* , p. 223.

81. *TPICJ*, vol. 7, no. 3 (1928): 83.

82. *A Plan for the City of Vancouver . . .* , p. 287.

83. J. A. Walker, "Town Planning in Vancouver", *MRC*, vol. 31, no. 6 (1935): 9.

84. For a positive assessment of the working of the by-law, see Vancouver Town Planning Commission, *Preliminary Report upon Economic Background and Population* (1945), pp. 9, 64-65. For a critique, see John C. Weaver, "The Property Industry and the Fate of Town Planning: The Vancouver Experience, 1900-1950", unpublished manuscript. My thanks to Professor Weaver for sending me a copy of his article in advance of publication.

85. *TPICJ*, vol. 6, no. 2 (1927): 76, 78.

86. David G. Bettison, *et al., Urban Affairs in Alberta* (Edmonton, 1975), pp. 52-53; Dale, "Decision-Making at Edmonton . . .", 139-42.

87. Thomas Adams, "Relation of Zoning to City Planning", *CE*, vol. 40 (January 13, 1921): 127.

88. *TPICJ*, vol. 1, no. 3 (1921): 10. See also Seymour's remarks during the discussion of zoning by the *EIC*'s Toronto Branch (November 1920). *CE*, vol. 39 (November 25, 1920): 557.

89. Toll, *Zoned America*, pp. 261, 204.

90. *CE*, vol. 39 (November 25, 1920): 557.

91. *TPICJ*, vol. 4, no. 6 (1925): 12. See also Thomas Adams, "Zoning and City Planning", *CE*, vol. 40 (January 20, 1921): 142.

92. Adams, "Town Planning in Relation to Public Safety", *TP&CL*, vol. 4, no. 4 (1918): 92.

93. Adams, "Zoning and City Planning", 143 and "Relation of Zoning to City Planning", 127.

94. *CE*, vol. 39 (November 25, 1920): 558.

95. Seymour, "Regional Zoning", *TPICJ*, vol. 4, no. 3 (1925): 8-9.

96. James Ewing, "Town Planning That Pays", *CMJ*, vol. 16, no. 3 (1920): 83. See also le May's remarks in *AOLSP* (1913): 94-95.

97. *TPICJ*, vol. 9, no. 3 (1930): 65; *TPICJ*, vol. 4, no. 5 (1925): 2.

98. Canada, Commission of Conservation, *Annual Report* (1913), pp. 3-4; *CE*, vol. 21 (September 7, 1911): 289; *CMJ*, vol. 11, no. 2 (1915): 52.

99. Quoted in *TPICJ*, vol. 7, no. 2 (1928): 37. See also Wilson, "Town Planning and Civic Development", 319.

100. *AOLSP* (1936): 61.

101. Ira M. Robinson, *New Industrial Towns on Canada's Resource Frontier* (Chicago, 1962), pp. 19-20.

102. Ibid., p. 66.

103. *ADLSR* (1923): 104; *TPICJ*, vol. 1, no. 9 (1922): 2; *MRC*, vol. 21, no. 12 (1925): 436; Seymour, "Town Planning in Alberta", *TPICJ*, vol. 10, no. 1 (1931): 9-10.

104. "The Plan-makers and the City . . .", pp. 247-54.

10.

A Confluence of Interests: Housing Reform in Toronto, 1900–1920

SHIRLEY SPRAGGE

Although concern with housing reform was nation-wide, Toronto is a convenient area in which to study the pattern of reform because in a twenty-year period the city mounted two major efforts to house workers: the quasi-public Toronto Housing Company in 1913 and the public Toronto Housing Commission of 1920. Both efforts had a public-policy component, a framework of legislation, and public funding. Both efforts were mirrored elsewhere in the country; before the Great War there were a rash of housing associations in Montreal, Ottawa, Halifax, Hamilton, and Winnipeg, although few produced any housing.[1] Toronto's 1920 effort also paralleled the efforts of the Federal-Provincial Housing Loan scheme across the country.[2] An examination of the groups involved in reform in Toronto—the public health advocates in the Toronto Department of Health and the Ontario Provincial Board of Health, the businessmen and manufacturers of the Civic Guild, the Board of Trade, and the Toronto branch of the Canadian Manufacturers' Association, the women increasingly vocal through organizations such as the Council of Women, and the idealists backing the co-operative movement or the Garden City movement—reveals some of their aims and explains what impact housing reform had on urban development.

BACKGROUND TO HOUSING REFORM

The background to Toronto's efforts in the area of housing reform is complex and includes the city's rapid growth rate, transportation problems, its geography, and the pressures of an inflationary economy. In 1901, 62 per cent of Canadians lived in rural areas; by 1921 half of Canada's population was urban.[3] Urbanization was regional; the West grew from almost nothing, Ontario and Quebec consolidated their advantages, and the Maritimes dropped behind.[4] From 1900 the nation was at last experiencing net growth in migration; in effect Canada was no longer a stopping-off place en route to the United States. Canada was growing in population faster than Ontario, and

Toronto faster than Canada. Civic growth came not only from migration, internal or external; the period up to 1912 was one of rapid
annexation of suburban areas by cities[5] until the increased tax rate
required to provide services, and the recession of 1913, called a halt to
the expansion and the accompanying "land boom".[6]

Related to the suburbanization of the city was the development of
public transportation. Toronto had had horse-drawn streetcars since
1862; electrification began in 1892 with Sir William Mackenzie's Toronto Street Railway—and so did the city's thirty-year struggle with
Mackenzie for the extension of the single-fare zone beyond the 1891
limits of the city. Transportation costs remained high with nine separate systems in 1921 collecting nine fares to serve the city.[7]

Geography also posed difficulties for Toronto. Crossing the Don
Valley to the east of Toronto was a problem, for although the city
built car lines east in 1912 – 13,[8] Toronto tended to expand to the
northwest and west.[9] The suburbs might beckon but the problem was
how to get there. The pressure on the city housing stock was rising,
not only with the increased population but also because industrial
expansion in the heart of downtown resulted in a decrease in the
number of older dwellings.[10] This pressure was most severe at the
lower price levels of accommodation because the immigrants who
arrived with little capital to invest in housing were in competition for
the cheaper dwellings. Added to these factors, the aftermath of a
disastrous fire in the downtown area in 1904 was followed by increased building by-law standards especially regarding the rough-cast
(stucco) construction that had been used for low-rent dwellings.[11]

As significant for housing demands as the absolute increase in
population was the creation of new households. The growth of new
households is measured by net family formation, a concept based on
calculating the number of new families formed by marriage, plus the
number of married female immigrants, less the number of families
dissolved by death, plus the number of married female emigrants.
Using this concept, the economist O. J. Firestone drew up a table that
compared on a national level net family formation and the number of
dwellings completed. The table shows that the periods of greatest
concern for housing needs in Toronto (i.e., 1907, 1912 – 13, and 1919 –
20) coincide with an excess of family formation over dwellings completed.[12]

The natural result of the pressure on the housing stock was that
rents increased at a time when all costs of living were rising rapidly.
The inflationary spiral that had begun when the newly discovered

supplies of gold hit the market in the 1890s finally prompted a national inquiry in 1913.[13] The analysis by R. H. Coats, later to become Dominion Statistician, showed that in terms of the percentage of income spent from 1900 to 1913, food had risen little but the increase in rent was marked—a jump from 20.9 per cent to 24.7 per cent of the family income.[14] At one end of the economic scale, the lack of low-cost housing led to overcrowding while for the well-to-do the number of larger houses (for which there was more profit to the builder) increased. Coats concluded: "Speaking in terms of the working class, while the skilled mechanic has perhaps improved his standard, the unskilled and immigrant class in the larger cities are crowded together to a degree that is new in the experience of the country."[15] Apparently unknown to Coats, these conclusions had already been documented for Toronto in an early cost-of-living survey by Professor James Mavor using budgets of forty-three families in central Toronto in 1907. Published in the *Weekly Sun* in April 1907, the survey showed that from 1897 the cost of food had risen 28 per cent while rents had increased a staggering 95 per cent. A study of Montreal during this period also shows how the relative prosperity of the workers was declining.[16]

A trough of depression began in 1913 that lasted well into 1915 and 1916, but the economic revival then brought about by war orders did nothing to ease the housing situation. In order to finance the war effort the government relaxed monetary controls, producing inflation. In turn this concentrated money in the wealthy business community, to whom the government turned to float domestic war loans.[17] During the war years housing construction dropped off precipitously.[18] Because of the war, marriages and new family formation had to be postponed and a sudden and sharp demand for housing was expected at the war's end. Added to this was the spectre of "Bolshevik" agitation and the fear of unemployment problems when returned soldiers flooded the labour market. The pressure for housing reform was on again.

THE FIRST EFFORT: THE TORONTO HOUSING COMPANY, 1913

Against this physical and economic backdrop of city development, various groups responded to the crisis in housing. Montreal and Toronto had their share of wealthy philanthropists wishing to provide model dwellings.[19] In 1907 a group of members of the Toronto branch of the Canadian Manufacturers' Association, led by jewellery manufacturer Thomas Roden, proposed the formation of a limited-dividend

company to be called the Cottage Home Builders' Association to build
workers' homes.[20] Roden had a potent argument for his "philanthropy
and five per cent" scheme—not only would the workers benefit but a
supply of adequate housing would overcome the shortage of labour
while lower rents would also mean fewer wage demands. The short,
sharp depression of 1907 killed that venture. Unemployment wors-
ened the situation of the worker and at the insistence of a reform-
minded controller, Horatio Hocken, the City of Toronto appointed its
first Housing Commission in the winter of 1907. The committee of
controllers and aldermen listened to the Medical Officer of Health
and the Property and Assessment commissioners and held a number
of citizens' meetings. It recommended that the city be empowered to
build and rent workers' homes to a hostile City Council and the issue
quietly faded away—but not for long.[21]

The first group to arouse concern over housing conditions were
those in the public health movement. Public health advocates and
sanitarians from the time of the discovery of the germ theory of
disease and the civic "sanitary police" inspectors of the 1880s had
been prime activists and increasingly successful legislators. From nuisance laws to the regulating of privy pits, to the entering and checking
of lodging houses for overcrowding, they progressed with an administrative machine that developed from a provincial body in the boards
of health to a federal organization in the Commission of Conservation
and with a group of officials growing steadily more expert and professional.

Ontario led the the provinces in establishing the first permanent
Board of Health in 1883 and, directed by the energetic Dr. Peter
Bryce as Permanent Secretary, the province forged ahead in health
matters.[22] Public attention was turned to housing by the fear of disease, typhoid or the more insidious tuberculosis, spreading from the
city slums of downtown Montreal, Winnipeg, Ottawa, or Toronto, or
the suburban "shanty towns" of makeshift dwellings. One of the
earliest national figures in the public health movement who was directly interested in housing was Dr. Charles Hodgetts.[23] Dr. Hodgetts,
Public Health Director of the Commission of Conservation, toured
Europe and wrote on unsanitary housing in 1911.[24]

Toronto had its own activist Medical Officer of Health in Dr.
Charles Hastings whose photographic record of Toronto's slums shook
the burghers in 1911.[25] Toronto had been worrying about its pockets
of slums as far back as 1873,[26] but by 1911 the existence of the
notorious "Ward" (bounded by Yonge, College, University, and

Queen streets), where the tenancy rate was high, turnover rapid, and the recently arrived immigrant population visible and audible, was alarming the more established populace.[27] Especially frightening was the high population density in the immigrant areas.[28] Hindsight indicates that the lodging house was a reasonable device to house temporarily the single immigrant who arrived to work to save for his family's passage, and that some of the view of overcrowding was based on Anglo-Saxon misunderstanding of the extended families of other cultures. In the early 1900s, however, bad plumbing and crowded housing were more easily fixed on as the culprit in the spread of disease and crime than the complete framework of poverty.

Dr. Hastings stirred up the citizens of Toronto in 1911 and 1918 with reports cataloguing slums and privy pits, and with solutions for the housing situation.[29] Despite his promotion of the role of the Medical Officer of Health in housing projects, Hastings was not prominent in the 1912 or 1918 Toronto attempts to house the worker. But health officers had extensive powers of control over the housing stock. By the Ontario Public Health Act of 1912, a medical officer of health could enter, close, and placard overcrowded lodging houses and this was further extended in 1916 to apply to any premises. In 1912 an attempt was made in Ontario to put regulations of tenements[30] existing or created under the Public Health Act,[31] but the bill was abandoned in favour of a clause in the 1912 amendment of the Municipal Act regulating the location of tenements. As with the heightened building standards of 1904 these building regulations tended to be applied with varying uniformity or "discretion".[32] The public health professionals functioned as the watchdogs of housing, but as others remarked, regulations did not build houses.[33]

Dr. Hastings' positive recommendations of garden suburbs for workers and co-operative housing ventures were current panaceas which Canadians sought to apply to their situation. Here the theorists saw solutions to the housing problem. Co-partnership housing, a facet of the co-operative system, had been preached to Canadians coast to coast in 1910 by Henry Vivian, British trade unionist, MP, carpenter, and secretary of Co-partnership Tenants Ltd. Vivian had met Governor General Earl Grey in the planning of Hampstead Garden Suburb where a partnership of tenants subscribed the capital for a housing development, chose and planned the site together, and agreed to pay rent sufficient to cover repairs and to permit a controlled dividend on invested capital. Earl Grey had already spoken on Vivian's co-partnership housing ideas before the Commons Special Committee of

1907 to consider permissive legislation for co-operative associations. The Committee, which had heard much evidence recommending co-operative associations in agriculture, expressed scepticism about its suitability for Canadian housing and listened to the Deputy Minister of Labour, William Lyon Mackenzie King, patronizingly describe the movement as "exceptionally beneficial from the point of view of educating the mass of the people" and "teaching the working classes something of the responsibility of capital".[34] It was the "self-help" aspect, that epitome of Victorian moralism preached by Samuel Smiles, that made co-operative housing so appealing and so "right".

The Toronto Housing Company was originally to be incorporated as the Toronto Co-Partnership Garden Suburbs Company and while it dropped that title in the act of incorporation it was empowered as "(a) a land and building company, (b) builders and contractors, (c) vendors of refreshments, (d) maintaining building and recreations grounds, carrying on social and educational work, and (e) to carry on the business of storekeeper and buy and sell goods for the company".[35] Not only did the Toronto Housing Company never sell groceries, but instead of operating as a tenants co-partnership company, it functioned as a limited-dividend, joint-stock company open to public subscription. It would appear that theory did not meet the test of economic feasibility.[36] Co-operatives took firm root in Canadian agriculture but while there have been isolated successes in housing co-operatives, neither that nor the related idea of limited-dividend companies had a sizable impact on city building.

The second part of the original title of the Toronto Housing Company contained another popular, but greatly misunderstood concept, recommended by Dr. Hastings. The terms "garden suburb" and "garden city" are often used interchangeably, but this is an error. The term "garden cities", from the title of the book *Garden Cities of Tomorrow* published in 1898 by the Englishman Ebenezer Howard, was a scheme for decentralization of the city by creation of urban nuclei: an estate of agricultural land developed with houses, shops, services, and industries[37] surrounded by a "green belt" of agricultural land. The green belt was inviolable; when the area within was developed a new "garden city" would be started. Howard had hoped garden cities would draw the population away from London, but industries had other criteria for location besides better housing for workers. However, as better transportation and cheaper land fostered suburban development the trend to planned design of streets and housing found in garden cities met and mingled with suburbanization to create the garden suburb. The garden suburb was in no way a self-contained, self-supporting unit, but it proved so popular that by 1914 there were fifty-two garden suburbs underway in England.[38]

The idea was rapidly exported to North America where few understood the distinctions.[39] Canada had many advocates of the romantic idea and one man, Dr. Emil Nadeau of the Quarantine Hospital at Quebec, tried to establish a Canadian reality. At the meeting of the American organization, the National Conference on City Planning, held in Toronto in 1914, Dr. Nadeau produced his sketch for a garden suburb called "Confederation", to be constructed outside Quebec City. Using Howard's design of a circle with intersecting diagonals, he set aside certain areas for housing, parks, and commerce, with Canada Square at the centre to house the public buildings, of which the main one would be a miniature facsimile of the Ottawa Parliament buildings called the "Temple of Public Health".[40] Nadeau got closer to realizing his ideals than most theorists. When Quebec entered the Federal-Provincial Housing Loan scheme in 1919, Dr. Nadeau was appointed Director of Housing for the province. He established the Technical Commission, headed by Frederic Todd, the Montreal landscape architect and town planner, and decreed that two and one-half per cent of the housing loans would go to finance the work of the Technical Commission whose town planning advice along Garden City lines would be obligatory for all housing schemes. Montreal led the opposition to this and other aspects of the Quebec scheme, ending in the abolition of the Technical Commission and the resignation of Dr. Nadeau.[41]

Canadians might admire the Garden City idea but they were not going to have it rammed down their throats. The Toronto Housing Company in its first rush of enthusiasm bought a two-hundred-acre farm in York County northeast of Toronto to be the site of its garden city, but was never able to develop it and the land was a liability to the company until it was sold.[42] Not only did the proposed Canadian Northern line that would serve the property never materialize, but the City of Toronto refused to guarantee the company's mortgage to build in the county.[43] Except for a few one-industry towns like Kipawa (Témiskaming, P.Q.) that had some design relationships to garden cities, no garden cities developed in Canada and no city decentralization was accomplished this way.

In the words of G. Frank Beer, the first president of the Toronto Housing Company, Dr. Hastings' 1911 Toronto report on housing was "so convincing that we found it impossible to satisfy ourselves by

sympathetic resolutions passed at public meetings or by letters expressing our deep distress published in the daily press".[44] Late in
1911, a committee was formed on "the housing problem" headed by
Mayor Geary and made up of representatives of the Toronto Board of
Trade, the Canadian Manufacturers' Association, and the Toronto
Civic Guild, an architecturally oriented group of business and professional men who promoted City Beautiful ideas. The Toronto District
Labour Council who might have represented the worker for whom
housing was sought was conspicuous by its absence. In May 1912, the
Toronto Housing Company emerged from the meetings of this group
as a joint stock company with dividends limited to six per cent. What
distinguished this housing venture was the backing by the public
purse the company sought and achieved through the Act to Encourage Accommodation in Cities and Towns,[45] which enabled the city of
Toronto to guarantee the company's bonds to 85 per cent of the value
of its holdings, an asset in seeking mortgage money.[46] The British
government had been increasing the amount of money available to
private or public housing companies through loans in the Housing of
the Working Class Acts; the Massachusetts Homestead Commission of
1908 had secured public money, and the province of Nova Scotia in
its Town Planning Act of 1912 allowed the guarantee of limited-
dividend housing company bonds up to 50 per cent of the company's
worth. These examples undoubtedly did not pass unnoticed by the
Toronto group in seeking a firm foundation for their project, but they
did not achieve this backing without a struggle. Sir James Whitney,
Conservative Premier of Ontario, was not in favour of the act and
when visited by a deputation pleading for the bill he responded wryly
that he wondered if the scheme was not altogether in the interest of
the manufacturers and that six per cent was a good investment.[47]

Was Whitney's accusation just? An examination of the backgrounds
of the fourteen founding directors[48] of the Toronto Housing Company
indicates that the interest of the majority in housing the workingman
was, if not self-serving, at least based on the immediate knowledge of
the importance of the issue. As the size of the manufacturing unit
grew, the employers' need for a pool of cheap labour also increased.
Availability of low-cost housing was one component in keeping wages
low. Given the prevailing philosophy that the lowest wage was economically and morally the best wage, the employer had to look for a
solution to the cost of living pressures on housing costs. Furthermore,
employers believed that a well-housed and healthy worker was not
only more productive but less prone to participate in labour unrest.

The concerns of eleven of the founding directors of the Toronto Housing Company probably had an influence on the decisions and development of the company. One woman director cannot be traced and the two married women may be discounted as appointed, in the context of the day, because of their husbands' social positions.[49] Of the remaining directors, six were manufacturers, two bankers, and three professionals. Three of the manufacturers were in the garment trade (gloves, millinery, and women's underwear), a rapidly expanding area of business at the time. All six directors had manufacturing establishments in the downtown area.[50] At the time Toronto had its factories and shops concentrated at the centre of the city[51] and the Company acknowledged in its minutes its concern with "the needs of the wage earning population which had to reside close to the centre of the city".[52] This acknowledgment apparently dictated the Company's choice of building sites. Of the 334 units that the Toronto Housing Company eventually built, only parcels of land within the city were used: Spruce Court, west of the Don, was built on land rented from the Toronto General Hospital; and Riverdale Court, east of the Don on Bain Avenue, was built on land bought from the City. Their final effort to launch another housing scheme was a proposal to build English cottages on the "ugly park ends" of city parks. *The Telegram* supported the idea as housing was needed "near work, not out in the blue mountains somewhere",[53] but local residents and the Toronto Civic Guild defeated the proposal.

Thomas Roden, a founding director and chief investor in the Toronto Housing Company, had already declared his conviction in 1907 that lower rents would mean fewer wage demands. The prevailing participation of manufacturers in the Toronto Housing Company, and the location of the company's projects near their respective industries argues that manufacturing interests were well looked after.

The first report of the Toronto Housing Company stated that "The lady members of our board gave valuable assistance in planning these houses".[54] It was expected of them. It has been suggested that it is the role of middle- and upper-class women to ameliorate the harsh workings of industrial capitalism in society. In the nineteenth century the work was based on sectarian groups, church and religious societies. But gradually the progression was toward non-sectarian groups of wider and even national scope, such as the Young Women's Christian Association, the Women's Christian Temperance Union, the Imperial Order of the Daughters of the Empire, and the National Council of Women. With organization came articulation and these groups entered the public sphere to press for action on their interests. Their focus was the role of women as mothers and homemakers.[55] Lady Aberdeen, who introduced the National Council of Women to Canada and remained a star in the Club's firmament, promoted housing schemes during the Aberdeens' vice-regal sojourn in Ireland, and organized an international Housing and Town Planning Conference in Dublin in 1914.

It is significant for the era that four of the fourteen founding directors of the Toronto Housing Company were women, but the roles of three of them are somewhat of a cipher. The fourth, Dr. Helen MacMurchy, was different; she was the new professional woman. Originally trained in the traditional female role of teacher, she returned to university for a medical degree and became an expert in infant mortality, a burning issue in Edwardian public health circles. Government appointments came her way: in 1913 she was appointed Inspector of the Feeble Minded for Ontario; in 1915 Inspector of Auxiliary Classes; and in 1920 she was appointed head of the Child Welfare Division of the newly organized federal Department of Health. She had great influence in this position, both administratively and through her writings. This, then, was a new type of woman attracted by the housing movement.

The developments of the Toronto Housing Company also attracted the new type of woman as tenant. In 1915 the famous evangelist, Major Lucretia (Lutie) Desbrisay of the Salvation Army, was living at the Maples, Riverdale Court, and Alice Chown, feminist and promoter of communal living and women's residences at Queen's,[56] was living at the Oaks. The home was important for the single woman as well as the mother. The National Council of Women had been receiving directives from the international organization since 1908 urging them to interest themselves in housing conditions. Finally the Toronto Council of Women, in 1913, made arrangements with the Toronto Housing Company to rent one unit to be known as the Aberdeen Club, to house working girls. Their intentions were good but their rent was continually in arrears.

Possibly the greatest contribution to housing betterment the Toronto Housing Company made was in design. The Company's Spruce Court and Riverdale Court, designed by a pair of English architects,[57] traces its lineage from the Lutyen's cottages seen in Hampstead Garden Suburb to the designs used by the American architects Clarence Stein and Henry Wright in the 1930s in Sunnyside Gardens and Chatham Village. The design produced high-density city living at a

FIGURE 10:1

The Oaks, Riverdale Courts, Bain Ave., Toronto.   The Toronto Housing Company, Ltd.

FIGURE 10:2

An Interior, Riverdale Courts, Bain Ave., Toronto.   The Toronto Housing Company,

FIGURE 10:3

One of the Aberdeen Club Residences for Business Women, Riverdale Courts, Bain Ave., Toronto.

The Toronto Housing Company, Ltd.

FIGURE 10:4

A Garden Gate, Riverdale Courts, Bain Ave., Toronto.

The Toronto Housing Company, Ltd.

human scale with the provision of communal amenities. The two-storey brick buildings with wood trim, so designed that each flat had its own front door and desirable privacy, were laid out in a U-shape, open to the street and enclosing a communal grass court. Garage areas are out of sight at the rear and brick walls and gates create pleasant vistas.

Real estate interests and speculative builders can be viewed as the logical opponents of publicly assisted housing. The Toronto Housing Company participated in the suburban land boom with its speculation in York County land, but in other land transactions bought from the city or rented from a charitable foundation. It is difficult to see the 1913 effort as a target of land and building interests, but the same cannot be said for the 1920 Toronto Housing Commission, Toronto's second venture into publicly assisted housing.

THE SECOND ATTEMPT: THE TORONTO HOUSING COMMISSION, 1920

While Dr. Hastings was rousing the citizens of Toronto with another medical report on housing in 1918, the Ontario government, under the leadership of Sir William Hearst, was concerned about housing and employment for returning servicemen and was worried about the possibility of Bolshevist unrest in the post-war period. Britain and the United States had both invested public money in housing war workers. Hearst's idea of a government loan to municipalities for housing was met and matched by the federal government early in 1919, creating the Federal-Provincial Housing Loan of twenty-five million dollars to be distributed across the country. Housing was to be made available for any worker, but the cost of land and construction was limited under the scheme. To Hearst's surprise there was opposition in his own city; Toronto claimed the financial limits were impossible in urban areas and brought forth legislation to allow the city of Toronto to fund its own housing. Privately, Sir William Hearst and Sir John Willison, Chairman of the Ontario Housing Committee, agreed that it was the real estate and construction interests who kept Toronto out of the Federal-Provincial Housing scheme.[58]

After flirting with the idea of municipal housing in response to every housing crisis since 1905, the city of Toronto was prepared to take the plunge and appointed a five-man Toronto Housing Commission of "businessmen who would conduct the operations of the Housing Commission so as to enable men and women of limited means to secure a home, and so that the city would not lose money by their operations".[59] After building 236 single and semi-detached houses in

west and east Toronto near railway lines,[60] the Commission chaired
by H. H. Williams, known as the head of the largest real estate firm in
Canada, decided the two aims were not compatible and gave up the
project.[61] The city could not persuade any other citizen group to take
over and so reverted to a commission of city officials to administer the
housing that had been built.[62]

Probably the Honorary Commission of 1920 which, unlike the Toronto Housing Company, had a real estate component in two of its
five members, was correct in its assessment of the inadvisability of
house construction at the height of post-war inflation. The history of
the Federal-Provincial Loan scheme is a sorry one, ranging from huge
deficits on many projects to the secretary's defalcation of the funds for
Ottawa's "Lindenlea", which had been planned by the Garden City
and Town Planning expert, Thomas Adams.[63] Montreal's complaints
about the cost restrictions of the federal scheme being unrealistic for
large urban areas paralleled Toronto's.[64] But the operative phrase in
the Toronto Commission's report was that "the City will not lose a
dollar" from its housing program.[65] Civic housing had not promised a
dividend but neither a wealth transfer nor competition with the private sector was contemplated.

The city's effort also lacks the innovative design of the Toronto
Housing Company's projects; the rows of substantial detached and
semi-detached housing were laid out with some variation in setback
but there was no attempt to create a community.

The co-operative movement was flourishing in agrarian, not housing, circles. Appeals to Garden City ideals dwindled except for the
efforts of Thomas Adams in *Conservation of Life*.[66] Instead, fears of
industrial and political unrest filled the public mind. The publication
of the Canadian Manufacturers' Association, *Industrial Canada*, carried advertisements urging, "Kill Bolshevism by Erecting Homes",[67]
again linking manufacturers' interests to housing reform.

The 1920 venture of the Toronto Housing Commission included no
women, nor did the Ontario Housing Committee appointed by Hearst
to survey the housing situation. In the 1920s the National Council of
Women grew increasingly vocal about the merits of town planning
and housing, but accomplished less.[68] As might be expected, women
in the emergent profession of social work expressed interest in housing problems: the periodical *Social Welfare*, founded in 1919, contains
numerous articles by women on housing. Sara Libby Carson, Ameri-
can-born head of the Presbyterian Church settlement work in Toronto, was reported to have "conducted several surveys in Toronto
and Montreal" in 1913.[69] Canada produced no Edith Elmer Wood

whose *Housing of the Unskilled Wage Earner*,[70] written in 1917, became a classic and made her an international figure in housing reform, but it is only fair to point out that neither did Canada produce a Lawrence Veiller who could organize the housing movement on a national scale.

CONCLUSION

If the failure of the housing reform groups of the first decades of this century to achieve is so apparent, if it is so obvious that their efforts have so completely sunk from national consciousness, it may be asked why bother to pick over the bones of their efforts? But the various groups whose interests merged to produce a housing reform movement did make some progress toward their goals. The co-operative and Garden City theories were an articulation of idealism. New housing was undoubtedly more sanitary and less congested than the over-built areas. Adequate housing relieved some of the strain on family life. Available housing whose proximity to work and low cost would add neither transportation nor rent pressures for wage increases was a boon to manufacturers.

Efforts at assisted housing can be compared with public health reforms and early town planning efforts. Houses were built, and action was taken that involved the public sector. In contrast, grandiose

FIGURE 10:5   A 1921 Advertisement

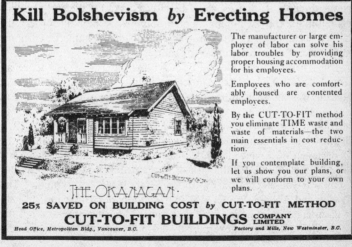

SOURCE: *Industrial Canada*, vol. 2 (October 1921):1.

schemes such as the Toronto Civic Guild plan for Toronto, Thomas
Mawson's plan for Calgary, Thomas Adams' Vancouver Civic Centre,
the Winnipeg city plan, and the Holt Commission plan for Ottawa
were all quietly laid away without action.[71] Toronto did not get off
scot free from its housing ventures; the city had to pay the interest on
the Toronto Housing Company bonds during the 1930s when the
company defaulted, and had to administer the houses of the Toronto
Housing Commission until the mortgages were paid off in the 1940s.[72]
With the collapse of the federal-provincial loan scheme, housing did
not remain the concern of a federal or provincial department or
agency.[73] When the Ontario Housing Accommodation Act was repealed in 1927, there was no longer any government support for low-
cost housing. No private sector of the economy found itself served by
publicly assisted housing as it is suggested zoning aided the property
owners and realtors.[74]

Cheap land, cheap transportation, and cheap mortgage money
could have and should have reduced the cost of housing. But the
reformers were not able to realize these three requisites in sufficient
scale to effect the results they wanted. The question is not why did the
reformers expend insufficient effort, money, and political influence to
achieve their program, but rather how could they measure how much
was necessary? Perhaps they were misled by the contemporary model
of public health reforms; programs in disease prevention, pure milk
and water provision, and immunization had rapid and tangible results. It would appear that given the proper technology and sufficient
power to apply it, changes could be effected. And if the early reformers fell into a trap by hoping a better house could be built for less, the
hidden social costs of concrete ghettos built in the name of economy
may indicate their view of the equation was more far-seeing.

These early efforts may be dismissed as paternalist and naïve attempts to solve a complex problem. Public investment in low-cost
housing was not seen at this period either as a fiscal instrument or as
a means of lowering unemployment. After the demise of the federal-
provincial loan scheme in the federal Department of Health of 1925,
the next time housing became a government concern it was under the
Department of Finance in 1935, a significant shift. These early efforts
are also remarkable for the lack of participation by Canadian unions
—this was commented on by contemporary American writers.[75] The
Trades and Labour Conference in Hamilton did come out in 1919
with an eight-point policy for a government housing program, but the
provincial and federal governments did not respond.[76] In neither the

British nor the American experience had limited-dividend housing such as the Toronto Housing Company efforts provided enough low-cost housing to affect the housing situation significantly,[77] nor did it do so in Canada. Government involvement in workers' housing in Britain and the United States had immediately been repudiated at the end of the war.[78] The Canadian scheme did not suffer this fate but it did not leave a legacy that could be built on. These abortive Canadian efforts at solving Canada's problem in housing citizens are a forgotten chapter in Canadian history, yet they have a place as indicators of social consciousness on the Canadian scene.

What effect did the housing reformers' efforts to increase the supply of low-rent housing have on the development of the city? The answer is none; the city defeated the reformers. If cheap land was needed to lower housing costs it was not to be found in the suburbs because speculation and the costs of servicing drove land prices and taxes up. If new sanitary housing could be built in the suburbs, with or without government backing, cheap transportation for workers did not materialize and the cost advantage was lost. True, the Toronto housing built in 1913 and 1920 was well constructed, but the cost of building a better house put it beyond the workers' budget. The limited government backing, either by bond guarantee or through loans, was not sufficient either to reduce the costs of building or to entice private capital into building low-cost housing.

NOTES

1. References to these associations can be found in the following: Montreal, *Conservation of Life*, vol. 4, no. 1 (1918): 12; Ottawa, Public Archives of Canada, *Cauchon Papers*, Subject files, vol. 7, Housing 1912-23 (MG30 A49); Halifax, *Conservation of Life*, vol. 3, no. 1 (1917): p. 94; Hamilton, *Labour Gazette*, vol. 13 (July 1912): 14 and (August 1912): 143; Winnipeg, *Canadian Housing and Town Planning Congress* (Winnipeg, 1912), p. 44.

2. The Federal Provincial Housing Loan scheme, funded by the federal government, organized by the provinces, and administered through the municipalities, was set up in December 1918 to assist in providing housing not just for returned servicemen but also for working men and women. See "Federal and Provincial Housing Scheme", *Conservation of Life*, vol. 5 (1919). The loan scheme of $25,000,000 from war appropriations was administered federally successively by the Housing Committee of the Cabinet, the Housing and Town Planning Branch of the Commission of Conservation (abolished 1921), and finally the newly formed Department of Health until the appropriations ceased in 1923–24. See Canada, Parliament, Sessional paper No. 19, *Report of Department of Health* (1925), p. 29.

3. S. A. Cudmore, H. G. Caldwell, *Rural and Urban Composition of the Canadian Population*, Census monograph, 7th Census, 1931, vol. 13 (Ottawa, 1942), p. 468.

4. Ibid., p. 477.

5. Toronto annexed North Rosedale in 1906, Deer Park and East Toronto in 1908, West Toronto and Midway in 1909, Dovercourt and Earlscourt in 1910, and North Toronto and Moore Park in 1912.

6. The western cities of Calgary, Edmonton, Winnipeg, and Saskatoon particularly evidenced frantic expansion. For example, in Saskatoon so many building lots returned to the city for tax defaults that they became the basis of the public land ownership in that city. G. L. Spragge, "Public Involvement in Land Development: London, Ont. and Saskatoon", MRP thesis, Cornell University (1969).

7. Toronto Transportation Commission, *Wheels of Progress* (c. 1940), p. 16. *Construction* ["A Journal for the Architectural, Engineering and Contracting Interests of Canada"] described Toronto's transportation as "thoroughly inadequate car service" in 1912 (vol. 5 [June 1913]: 70), and repeated this complaint.

8. Toronto Civic Railway lines on Gerrard in 1912 and Danforth in 1913.

9. Jacob Spelt, *Toronto* (Toronto, 1973), p. 82.

10. Toronto, City Council Minutes, 1918 App. A, p. 709. Monthly report of the Medical Officer of Health: "232 dwellings were destroyed by the General Hospital Board on the site of the new hospital, 50 by the T. Eaton Company for the purpose of erecting manufactures and 150 in the Eastern Avenue District by the Canadian Northern".

11. Toronto City By-law 4408 (1904) required asbestos paper under-roofing and a brick or partly concrete fireproof wall between frame or rough cast houses. The impact of the by-law was softened by the amendment the next year (by-law 4581) which allowed the City Architect to apply the building standard "with discretion". No estimate has been made of how widespread the inexpensive rough-cast construction was, but August Bridle in an article in the *Canadian Magazine*, vol. 22 (1903-04). "The

Homes of Workingmen", uses illustrations entitled "The Rough-cast House of the Poorest Workingman" and "Brick Fronts and Mansard Roofs, with Rough-cast Sides, Is a Step in Advance".

12. O. J. Firestone, *Canada's Economic Development* (London, 1958), pp. 54-62, 245-47, 301-02.

13. Canada. Board of Inquiry into the Cost of Living, *Report*, vol. 2 (1915).

14. Ibid., p. 80.

15. Ibid., p. 1012.

16. Terry Copp, *The Anatomy of Poverty; The Condition of the Working Class in Montreal, 1897-1929* (Toronto, 1974).

17. J. J. Deutsch, "War Finance and the Canadian Economy 1914 – 1920", *Canadian Journal of Economics and Political Science*, vol. 5, no. 6 (1940): 525.

18. Toronto, Assessment Dept. *Reports* (1915 – 20). Toronto Dwelling Construction: Total of new residences: 1915, 3,304; 1916, 829; 1917, 539; 1918, 743; 1919, 878; 1920, 1,975.

19. In Montreal, Herbert Ames and Col. Geoffrey Burland built model tenements; in Toronto in 1904 Goldwin Smith attempted to launch a limited-dividend housing company, the Artisans' Dwelling Company.

20. Thomas Roden, "The Housing of Working Men", *Industrial Canada*, vol. 5, no. 7 (1907): 654.

21. "More Small Houses Now", "Build Civic Houses for Poor Workingmen," *Evening Telegram* (December 6, 10, 1907).

22. Dr. Peter H. Bryce (1853 – 1936) was Secretary of the Ontario Provincial Board of Health (1882 – 1904) and then moved to Ottawa as Chief Medical Officer, Department of the Interior and later also Chief Medical Officer of the Department of Health and Indian Affairs.

23. Epidemics were still all too prevalent in the twentieth century. In 1911 an American expert was called in to advise on the typhoid outbreak in Ottawa caused by improperly treated drinking water. Commission of Conservation, Committee on Public Health, 1911.

24. Charles Hodgetts, "Unsanitary Housing", in Commission of Conservation, *Second Annual Report* (1911), pp. 50-84.

25. Toronto, City Hall Archives.

26. D. C. Masters, *The Rise of Toronto* (Toronto, 1947), p. 126.

27. The actual ethnic composition of the population of Toronto did not change much in this period; in 1901 ninety-two per cent of the population was of British origin, and in 1921 the percentage was eighty-five. However, as J. S. Woodsworth's books of the period indicate, Canada was struggling with physical and cultural assimilation.

28. According to the report of the Toronto Bureau of Municipal Research, *What is "The Ward" Going to Do With Toronto*? (Toronto: The Bureau, December 1918), p. 32, the 1916 assessment records showed seventy-one people per acre in the Ward where the majority of residents were foreign born compared to twenty-one persons per acre in the rest of the city.

29. Toronto, *Report of the Medical Health Officer Dealing with the Recent Investigations of Slum Conditions in Toronto, Embodying Recommendations for Ameliorations of the Same* (1911), and Toronto, City Council *Minutes*, Appendix A (June 1918), Monthly Report of the Medical Officer of Health, pp. 799-28.

30. Tenements were defined in Ontario Bill 159 (1912) s. 2 as "any house or building . . . which is rented, leased, let or hired out, or is occupied as the home or residence of two or more families, living independently of each other, but having a common right in the halls, stairways, water closets or privies or some of them . . .".

31. Bill 159 (1912) An Act respecting Apartment or Tenement Houses.

32. See Toronto *Telegram*, August 24, 1906, "By-law Too Stringent Architect to Revise It", and the somewhat cynical comments of *Construction*, vol. 5, no. 8 (1912): 62. See also, Toronto City Council *Minutes* (June 1912), *cf.* p. 693.

33. City of Toronto Controller J. O.

McCarthy, Social Service Congress, Ottawa, 1914, *Report* (Toronto), p. 125.

34. Canada, House of Commons, "Special Committee on . . . Industrial and Co-operative Societies", *Journals of the House*, App. 3 (1907), pp. 71, 79.

35. Ontario *Gazette*, vol. 45, pt. 1 (1912): 859; and *Construction*, vol. 5, no. 9 (1912): 44.

36. It proved difficult to subscribe the required capital on the market; tenant-investors probably could not be found.

37. The industries and increased land values were to pay for the investment and make the garden city self-supporting.

38. William Ashworth, *Genesis of the British Town Planning Movement* (London, 1954), p. 163.

39. The editorial in *Construction*, vol. 5, no. 5 (1912): 65, explained the difference to architects and builders.

40. *Canadian Municipal Journal*, vol. 10, no. 6 (1914): 234.

41. *Contract Record*, vol. 33, no. 32 (August 6, 1919): 747; vol. 34 [sic], no. 34 (August 13, 1919): 774; vol. 35, no. 8 (February 25, 1920): 167; no. 12 (March 24, 1920): 266.

42. The sale began in the 1920s and the final lots were expropriated in 1955 (Ontario. Ministry of Treasury, Economics and Intergovernmental Affairs, Dept. of Financial and Commercial Affairs, Toronto Housing Co. file).

43. Toronto, City Council *Minutes* 1913, items 1044, 1046, 1082, 1122.

44. Archives of Ontario, Beer Papers, "Economic Housing in Toronto", TS, nd., p. 1.

45. 3 – 4 Geo. v., c. 57, 1913, known as the Hanna Act after W. J. Hanna, Provincial Secretary.

46. In return, the City had to approve the company's plans and kept one member from City Council on the Company's board.

47. Ontario, Legislative Assembly, *Newspaper debates*, March 20, 1913 (microfilm).

48. Toronto Housing Company Incorporating Directors, May 1912. Geo. R. Geary, lawyer; G. Frank

Beer, Secretary-Treasurer, Eclipse
Whitewear; Alfred R. Clarke,
President, A. R. Clarke, Leather
Goods; Thomas Roden, Roden
Bros., Silverware; Edward Kylie,
Lecturer; Thos. D. Findley, Assistant
General Manager, Massey Harris
Co.; Gabriel T. Somers, President,
Sterling Bank; Robert S. Gourlay,
Gourlay, Winter and Leeming, Piano
Manufacturers; Arnold M. Ivey,
Managing Director, J. D. Ivey Co.,
Wholesale Millinery; Alexander
Laird, General Manager, Bank of
Commerce; Helen MacMurchy,
Physician; Emma K. Strathy,
Married Woman; Katherine F.
Grassett, Married Woman; Sarah K.
Currie (no listing).

49. Sarah K. Currie has not been traced;
Mrs. H. S. Strathy was the wife of a
first-family banker; and Mrs.
Grasset, at sixty-five the grande
dame of the group, was the wife of
the Chief Constable.

50. South of Queen Street.

51. G. F. Beer, "Housing Experience in
Toronto", *Town Planning and
Conservation of Life*, vol. 3, no. 2
(1917): 25.

52. Toronto, City Hall Archives, Toronto
Housing Company extract from
Minutes, January 28, 1913.

53. "May Build Cottages to Cure Ugly
Park Ends", Toronto *Telegram*
(September 23, 1913).

54. Reprinted in Canada, *Board of
Inquiry into Cost of Living*, vol. 2, p.
898.

55. T. Morrison, "'Their Proper Sphere',
Feminism, the Family", *Ontario
History*, vol. 48, nos. 1 – 2 (1976).

56. Alice Chown, "The Women's
Residence", *Queen's Quarterly* (July
10, 1902), pp. 80-83.

57. Sydney V. Kendall and Leonard
Martin of London, England won the
design competition; Eden Smith was
the supervising architect.
Construction, vol. 5, no. 10 (1912):
56.

58. Archives of Ontario, Hearst Papers,
Housing Question (April 24, 25,
1919).

59. Toronto Housing Commission,
Report (1920), p. 5.

60. Spears-Annette development near
Runnymede and at Coxwell near
Danforth in the east.

61. The Commission consisted of H. H.
Williams, president of the H. H.
Williams and two other realty
companies and director of a bank,
trust company, and insurance
company; Sir John Eaton, president
of T. Eaton department stores; Frank
Rolph, director of a mortgage
company and president of a
lithography company; J. A. Ross,
manager of William Wrigley Co.;
and Sir James Woods, president of
dry goods firm.

62. Toronto, City Council *Minutes*
(1920), item 510, July 19, 1920; App.
A, pp. 620, 682; App. B, p. 726.

63. *Conservation of Life*, vol. 5, no. 2
(1920): 25; and Canada, Parliament,
House of Commons, Special
Committee on Housing, *Minutes of
Proceedings and Evidence* (Ottawa:
1935), p. 58.

64. *Contract Record*, vol. 33: 327, 747,
1159, 2661.

65. Toronto Housing Commission,
Report (1920), p. 5.

66. Thomas Adams, *Conservation of Life*
(January, 1918).

67. Canadian Manufacturers'
Association, "Kill Bolshevism by
Erecting Homes", *Industrial Canada*,
vol. 21 (October 1921): 1.

68. Veronica Strong-Boag, "The
Parliament of Women: The National
Council of Women 1893-1929",
PHD thesis, University of Toronto
(1975), pp. 207, 256, 365, 367.

69. Methodist Church, *Report of the
General Board of Temperance,
Prohibition and Moral Reform*, 1913,
p. 48. These reports could not be
located in the United Church
Archives.

70. Edith Elmer Wood, *Housing of the
Unskilled Wage Earner: America's
Next Problem* (New York, 1919).

71. References to these planning
schemes may be found as follows—
Toronto: Civic Guild plan *Canadian
Municipal Journal*, vol. 2 no. 7
(1906): 248-50; Calgary: Thomas
Mawson, *Calgary, A Preliminary
Scheme for Controlling the Economic*

Growth (London & New York, 1914); Vancouver: Alan Armstrong, "Thomas Adams and the Commission of Conservation", *Plan Canada*, vol. 1, no. 1 (1959): 26; Winnipeg: A. F. J. Artibise, *Winnipeg: A Social History of Urban Growth 1874-1914* (Montreal, 1975), pp. 267-80; Ottawa: Canada, Department of Finance, *Report of the Federal Plan Commission on a General Plan for the Cities of Ottawa and Hull* (Ottawa: The Commission, 1915).

72. Toronto, City Hall Archives . . . Toronto Housing Commission accounts; Records of City Accountant.

73. The Federal Department of Health administered the Federal Provincial Housing Loan until the appropriation of housing funds was voted to cease in 1923-24. Canada, Parliament, Sessional Paper No. 19, Department of Health, *Report* (1925), p. 29.

74. Seymour Toll, *Zoned America* (New York: Grossman, 1969).

75. Wood, *The Housing of the Unskilled Wage Earner: America's Next Problem* pp. 204-07.

76. T. G. Stortz, "Ontario Labour and the First World War", MA thesis, University of Waterloo (1976), p. 225.

77. William Ashworth, *The Genesis of Modern British Town Planning* (London, 1954), p. 93; Roy Lubove, *The Progressives and the Slums* (Pittsburgh, 1962), p. 175.

78. L. F. Ohrbach, "'Homes for Heroes': Study in the Politics of British Social Reform, 1915 – 1921", PH D thesis, Columbia University (1971); Roy Lubove, "Homes and a 'Few Well Placed Fruit Trees': An Object Lesson in Federal Housing", *Social Research*, vol. 27 (1960): 469.

11.

The Influence of Thomas Adams and the British New Towns Movement in the Planning of Canadian Resource Communities

OIVA SAARINEN

Resource communities are an essential feature of the Canadian urban landscape. This chapter examines the role played by Thomas Adams in bringing to Canada the ideas of the British New Towns Movement, particularly as these ideas were applied to resource towns. A general description of the nature of the British movement is followed by an outline of Adams' work as a practitioner and publicist of these planning concepts. The major focus is a detailed case study of the significance of Adams and the British movement in the planning of two forest-based resource towns, Iroquois Falls (Ontario) and Témiscaming (Quebec).

THE BRITISH NEW TOWNS MOVEMENT

The British New Towns Movement evolved in response to the lack of any firm policy directives related to land and community development in Great Britain during the early parts of the nineteenth century. As the century progressed, the negative effects associated with the misuse of land, town congestion, and suburban sprawl gradually led to the realization that some form of planning was essential. This realization culminated in the rise of the Town Planning Movement. The movement expressed itself nationally through legislation which featured a high degree of centralized planning power and control.[1] The legislation, which included the Housing, Town and Country Planning Act of 1909, and subsequently the Town and Country Planning Acts of 1947, was particularly notable for its emphasis on the physical aspects of land development.[2] At the community level, the movement resulted in the initiation of new industrial towns and garden cities. Of the new industrial towns, those of Port Sunlight and Bournville were especially important. Port Sunlight was brought into being by the W. H. Lever Soap Company near Liverpool in 1887 and Bournville by the Cadbury Chocolate Company near Birmingham in 1889.[3] In turn, the success of these two urban experiments stimulated Ebenezer Howard in 1898 to conceive the idea of the Garden City.[4]

Howard's influence on the British Town Planning Movement was enormous. Through his efforts, the Garden City idea became an integral part of the British planning tradition. These planned communities were originally proposed by Howard for reasons of health and social advantage; he reacted against the overcrowded conditions of the industrial towns in Britain and advocated the growth of new self-contained settlements in the countryside where housing, jobs, and all the other necessities would be provided. These self-contained settlements were based on two major spatial considerations: the concept that land uses were organically interrelated, and the introduction of a green belt surrounding the community to determine the limits of settlement and to promote some form of marriage between "town and country". Other important planning features included the limitation of town size and population, the control of land in the public interest, and the need for varied social and economic opportunities.

Howard's book, *Garden Cities of To-morrow*, had as a practical outcome the foundation of two "garden cities". The first was established at Letchworth in 1903 and the second at Welwyn in 1920.[5] The town layouts affiliated with Letchworth and Welwyn were informal in contrast to the rigid or geometrical forms of earlier town plans. The main aspects of planning were centred on the introduction of tree-lined radial or curvilinear roads with no sharp corners, open-spaced superblocks having a wide diversity of forms including cul-de-sacs, an emphasis on landscaping, and high architectural and housing standards. It remained, however, until 1946 before these Garden Cities were given formal sanction by means of the New Towns Act of 1946. Between 1946 and 1975, thirty-three new towns were designated in Great Britain with a supporting population approaching two million.[6]

THOMAS ADAMS AND THE BRITISH NEW TOWNS MOVEMENT IN CANADA

The impact of the British New Towns Movement in Canada after the turn of the century was considerable. The diffusion of British New Town planning principles and ideology into the Canadian setting involved a variety of channels, the most important of which was the Commission of Conservation and the work of its town planning advisor, Thomas Adams. Other important threads in the diffusion process included the official influences of the governors general of Canada, notably Sir A. H. G. Grey, the Duke of Connaught, and the Duke of Devonshire, and the writings of the Hon. W. L. Mackenzie King. The experience of the British in New Town planning was likewise instrumental in attracting a wide number of Canadian planners to the country. Due to the achievements identified with the planned industrial towns of Port Sunlight and Bournville and the garden cities of Letchworth and Welwyn, many of these individuals returned to Canada with a strong New Town orientation. As Norman Pressman has suggested, this New Town orientation subsequently found expression in Canada within two distinct geographical frameworks: the "quasi-satellite" new town in the more populated parts of the country, and the planned single-enterprise community associated with the opening up of new primary resource areas.[7]

The Commission of Conservation was established as an advisory body to the Government of Canada in 1909.[8] The purpose of the Commission was to advise the Government of Canada on all matters relating to the conservation and better utilization of the country's natural resources. Through its membership, the body was representative of a wide range of resource interests. In order to facilitate the task of gathering data and of advancing policies for resource development, seven committees were created: fisheries, game and furbearing animals; forests; land; minerals; water and waterpowers; public health; and press and co-operating organizations. The Commission and its seven committees met on an annual basis.[9] The activities of the Commission were terminated in 1921.

The link between Thomas Adams and the Commission of Conservation arose from the conviction of the Committee of Health that "the physical strength of the people is the resource from which all others derive value".[10] This conviction gradually led the Committee to a consideration of all those factors which affected the lives and health of the population. At the start, special accord was given to the need for better housing and related issues such as dwelling heights, orientation, and densities as well as town planning in general.[11] From the early reports of the Committee, it is clear that its interest in housing and town planning was framed within a strong economic context. For example, the Committee expressed the opinion that "the importance of the town planning and housing question commands a foremost place; not only is it necessary from the purely health standpoint, but it is of economic importance that the physical standard of our people should be of the highest character".[12] The broad mandate of the Committee was also justified on the basis that it would better the individual on "moral" grounds.[13]

Under the guiding influence of Dr. Charles Hodgetts, the former Medical Health Officer for the Province of Ontario, the relationship between public health, housing, and town planning became more explicit. Elsewhere in this volume, Thomas Gunton and P. J. Smith have referred to the work of the Commission as being an expression of Canadian urban radical planning based firmly on the two elements of public health and housing. The initial interest in housing and health was expanded to include a concern for harmonious arrangements among land uses, the provision of wide thoroughfares, the division of residential districts according to the class of housing, and the need for public parks, playgrounds, and open spaces. At the same time, the Committee emphasized the importance of planning and housing legislation at the provincial level.[14]

In 1913 the Commission of Conservation decided to further its activity in the town planning field by requesting the services of Thomas Adams from Great Britain.[15] This decision was apparently fostered by Adams' impressive performance at the National planning Conference held in Philadelphia in 1911.[16] By this time, Adams had become known as a follower of Ebenezer Howard and an advocate of the garden city. In connection with the latter, he had served as the Secretary of the First Garden City at Letchworth. At the time of this Canadian request, Adams was serving as an Inspector of the Local Government Board which was responsible for the administration of the British 1909 planning act.[17] The Commission eventually succeeded in obtaining the services of Thomas Adams in 1914. After his arrival, he quickly proceeded to exert his influence on town planning and housing development in Canada. This influence manifested itself by means of four distinct, yet interrelated, threads of personal activity related to education, legislation, administration, and consultation.

Education

One of the first steps taken by Adams in Canada was the initiation of a new journal titled *Conservation of Life*. The publication was started in August 1914 and it continued in existence until March 1921. It was used extensively by Adams to spread information concerning town planning and good housing practices along the lines of the British model.[18] Another important aspect of his work involved the presentation of planning lectures at leading universities throughout Canada and at various municipal and regional conferences.[19] In order to stimulate citizen interest in the process of community improvement, Adams assisted in the formation of the Civic Improvement League for Canada. The League was inaugurated in 1916 and was soon followed by the establishment of numerous leagues at the municipal level.[20] In 1917 Adams also completed a major book titled

Rural Planning and Development: A Study of Rural Conditions and Problems in Canada which succeeded in attracting a great deal of international attention.[21]

Legislation and Administration

In his first two annual reports presented to the Commission in 1915 and 1916, Adams stated the need for planning statutes at the provincial level and the establishment of supporting administrative machinery. Through his efforts, considerable progress was made in this regard during the war years. He succeeded in revising the original draft of a model planning act for Canada which was adopted by all but two provinces (British Columbia and Prince Edward Island) and worked to improve the three existing acts; in addition, he successfully promoted the creation of several provincial departments of municipal affairs.[22]

Consultation

The final aspect of Adams' work in Canada centred around his role as a planning consultant to the various levels of government and private companies. When the Federal Housing Project was initiated, Adams was invited as a consultant to the Housing Committee of the Cabinet. He likewise assisted the Department of Public Works in the planning of public buildings and the Department of the Interior in laying out some townsites in national parks.[23] Provincially, he was called upon by the Ontario Housing Committee to elaborate on some of the differences between housing conditions in Great Britain and Canada.[24] As Table 11:1 indicates, his consultative role with respect to Canadian municipalities was extensive. In this connection, Adams followed the practice of assisting municipalities only in the preliminary stages of local planning, leaving the preparation of detailed planning to private consultants.[25] Among the more notable of Adams' achievements in the municipal planning field may be included his draft official plan for Halifax, a large town extension scheme for Saint John, and his advisory role with respect to the layout of two new towns: Ojibway near Windsor and Kipawa (Témiscaming) at Lake Temiskaming.[26] By arrangement with the Commission, he was able to devote a certain part of his time to private consulting work.[27] With one exception, none of this private work was done for private individuals or corporations in Canada. That exception involved the Abitibi Power and Paper Company townsite located at Iroquois Falls.

Following the demise of the Commission of Conservation in 1921, the Town Planning Division was transferred to the National Parks

TABLE 11:1 Linkages Between Thomas Adams and Canadian Urban Centres

ALBERTA	NOVA SCOTIA	ONTARIO (continued)
Banff	Amherst	Port Credit
Calgary	Dartmouth	Renfrew
Edmonton	Halifax	Sandwich
Fort Macleod	Liverpool	Sarnia
Lethbridge	New Glasgow	Sault Ste. Marie
Medicine Hat	Pictou	Simcoe
Stavely	Springhill	Stratford
	Stewiacke	St. Catharines
BRITISH COLUMBIA	Truro	St. Thomas
Fort Fraser	Yarmouth	Sudbury
New Westminster		Toronto
Penticton	ONTARIO	Trenton
Point Grey	Belleville	Walkerville
Trenton	Berlin (Kitchener)	Welland
Prince George	Blenheim	Windsor
Prince Rupert	Brampton	
Squamish	Chatham	PRINCE EDWARD ISLAND
North & South	Cochrane	Various centres
Vancouver	Cornwall	
Vancouver	Fergus	QUEBEC
Victoria	Ford	Chicoutimi
Williams Lake	Fort William	Hull
	Galt	Kipawa (Témiscaming)
MANITOBA	Haileybury	Montreal
Brandon	Hamilton	Quebec City
Steinbach	Hawkesbury	St. Lambert
Winnipeg	Iroquois Falls	Sherbrooke
	Kapuskasing	Sorel
NEW BRUNSWICK	Kenora	
Carleton	Kingston	SASKATCHEWAN
Fredericton	Lindsay	Estevan
Moncton	London	Moose Jaw
Saint John	New Liskeard	Prince Albert
Sussex	Niagara Falls	Regina
	Ojibway	Saskatoon
	Oshawa	Swift Current
	Ottawa	
	Pembroke	
	Port Arthur	

SOURCES: Commission of Conservation, *Annual Reports 1909-1918* (Commission of Conservation, 1910-1919) and Thomas Adams, *Rural Planning and Development: A Study of Rural Conditions and Problems in Canada* (Ottawa: Commission of Conservation, 1917).

Branch of the Department of the Interior. Adams continued to serve as a town planning advisor to the branch until 1923, at which time he was appointed Director of the Regional Plan of New York and its Environs.[28] He maintained this position until 1930 when he became Associate Professor of City Planning at Harvard University. During the 1930s, he devoted much of his attention to the writing of books on planning.[29] In 1940 he passed away while residing in England.

The spread of the British Town Planning Movement into Canada was assisted greatly by a number of other factors including the official influences of the governors general of Canada and the Hon. W. L. Mackenzie King, and the impact of personal visits by Canadian planners to British new townsites. During the early years of the present century, the governors general of Canada provided a strong impetus for the spread of the New Towns movement in Canada. Sir A. H. G. Grey, for example, was quite familiar with the Garden City idea as he had presided over the first Garden City Conference held at Bournville Garden Village in 1901. After his appointment as Governor General in Canada, he invited Henry Vivian, a member of the British Parliament and a pioneer of planning and the Garden Suburb concept in England, to come to the country and lecture on the subject in 1910.[30] Later, the Duke of Connaught delivered addresses at the Town Planning Conference held in Toronto in 1914 and the Civic Improvement Conference held in Ottawa in 1916.[31] Finally, the Duke of Devonshire arrived in Canada with a strong planning background which involved the opening of the Cottage Exhibition held at Letchworth Garden City in 1905. In addition, the Devonshire family was highly regarded for the planning of towns and villages on its English estates such as Eastbourne.[32]

Another proponent of the Garden City idea in Canada included the Hon. W. L. Mackenzie King. In 1918 he published an important book titled *Industry and Humanity: A Study in the Principles Underlying Industrial Reconstruction.* In the book, which dealt with a broad range of industrial and social issues, he praised the Garden City idea as propounded by Ebenezer Howard and stressed the need for a similar line of thinking in Canada. While the national influence of this book has been the subject of considerable debate, it undoubtedly had the effect of focusing attention among academics and planners in the country on the positive results to be achieved through the implementation of Howard's basic principles.[33] It should be noted that Mackenzie's interest in planning was stimulated by his personal acquaintance with Patrick Geddes, another well known advocate of the British New Towns Movement.[34]

The significance of the British planning experience for Canada was reinforced by the development of a tradition of municipalities and companies to send their planners to Great Britain in order to inspect the layouts of selected planned communities. In this connection one study has made the following observation:

> Other early new-town influences on the physical planning of the larger Canadian single-enterprise communities were two British Company communities: Bournville ... and Port Sunlight. Because these communities were successfully established by industrial firms they became models for similar developments in the United States and Canada. Before embarking on construction of a new town, it was the custom of several North American companies to send their potential townsite managers on a tour of previously created single-enterprise communities. These tours often included visits to Bournville and Port Sunlight.[35]

THE TOWN OF IROQUOIS FALLS

The origin of the Town of Iroquois Falls extends back to 1912 when the Minister of Lands, Forests and Mines of the Province of Ontario called tenders for the right to cut pulpwood in the Abitibi River watershed situated in northern Ontario. On August 15 of the same year, the timber rights were granted to Shirley Ogilvie and Frank Anson subject to the provision that a pulp mill employing 250 persons would have to be erected on a site near Iroquois Falls.[36] These rights were later transferred to the Abitibi Pulp and Paper Mills Company, a firm incorporated on December 4, 1912. The name of the company was changed on December 24 to the Abitibi Pulp and Paper Company and again, on February 25, 1914, to the Abitibi Power and Paper Company. The firm is now known as the Abitibi Paper Company.[37]

From the outset, it was the intention of Anson, the company's first president, to create a "garden city" around the woodworking operations to serve as a model of its kind.[38] The model community was to be located near the Iroquois Falls power site adjacent to the Abitibi River and close to the main line of the Temiskaming and Northern Ontario Railway. In 1913 clearing of the townsite began and a railway spur line to Iroquois Junction (now Porquis Junction) completed.[39] It was at this stage that the first steps were taken to plan the townsite. In this connection, it has frequently been asserted that Thomas Adams was responsible for the planning of the Iroquois Falls settlement; however, that does not appear to have been the case. The author was first drawn to this conclusion by the curious fact that Adams, in his published works, made only one brief reference to his planning role in relation to Iroquois Falls. The reference, contained in his book *Rural Planning and Development: A Study of Rural Conditions and Problems in Canada*, revealed that on one occasion he had written a short critique of a partial plan for the townsite which had been submitted to him for his commentary. The partial plan is shown in Figure 11:1. In his critique, Adams stated only that it "was excellent from the point of view of street direction, but has about twice as much street area as is necessary or can be constructed on an economic basis".[40] Interestingly, the above statement was prefaced by another remark that this was a mining townsite being developed by the Temiskaming and Northern Ontario Railway. This misleading remark indicates that his involvement in the planning of the Iroquois Falls townsite was really very limited and probably restricted only to the writing of the above critique. Additional support for this viewpoint comes from the personal recollection of H. S. Crabtree, an engineer formerly employed with the land surveying firm of Routly and Summers in Haileybury. According to Crabtree, the original sketch plan for the townsite was prepared in Chicago.[41] The sketch plan, in turn, was then reworked into its final form by Crabtree and G. F. Summers, an Ontario Land Surveyor, and submitted as a plan of survey to the Province of Ontario on April 5, 1915.[42] Further, in a biography prepared by the Association of Ontario Land Surveyors, Summers is given credit for the laying out of several townsites in northern Ontario, including that of Iroquois Falls.[43] On the basis of the above evidence, it can be concluded that Adams' role in the planning of the original Iroquois Falls townsite has been exaggerated.[44]

An outline of the plan as prepared by the firm of Routly and Summers in 1915 is shown in Figure 11:2. In the figure, the emphasis given to the curvilinear street pattern and the selection of names such as Essex, Devonshire, Cambridge, Buckingham, and Argyle indicates that the plan derived some impetus from the British New Towns Movement. With the exception of the residential area near the Temiskaming and Northern Ontario Railway property, all of the main avenues were curved, and sensitive to the natural contours of the land. Another important aspect of the plan was the large size of the residential lots, which measured in the order of 50 by 125 feet. The lot sizes permitted each residential dwelling to have its own lawn and garden.

FIGURE 11:1   Proposed Plan for Iroquois Falls Townsite Reviewed by Thomas Adams

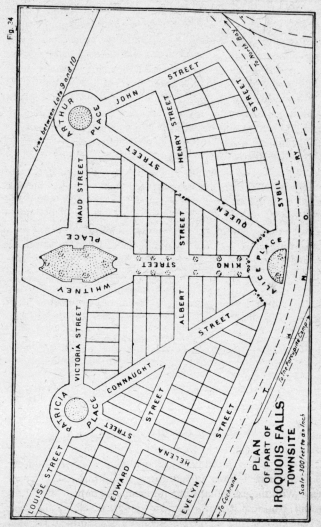

SOURCE: Thomas Adams, *Rural Planning and Development: A Study of Rural Conditions and Problems in Canada* (Ottawa: Commission of Conservation, 1917), Figure 34.

FIGURE 11:2 Outline of Original Survey Plan for the Iroquois Falls Townsite (1915).

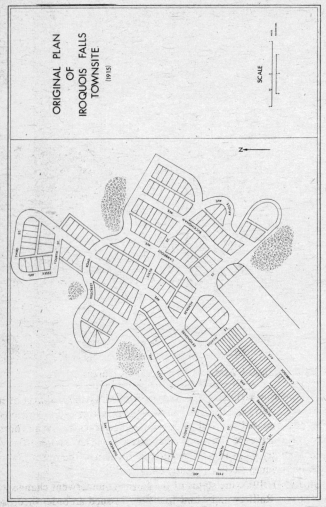

SOURCE: Derived from: Land Registry Office District of Cochrane, *Plan of the Subdivision of Parts of Lot 12 Concessions IV and V Teefy and Parts of Lot 1 Concession IV and V Calvert, District of Témiskaming*. This plan, known as M-10-T, was signed by the Minister of Lands, Forests and Mines on August 18, 1915.

FIGURE 11:3   Aerial Photograph of Town of Iroquois Falls

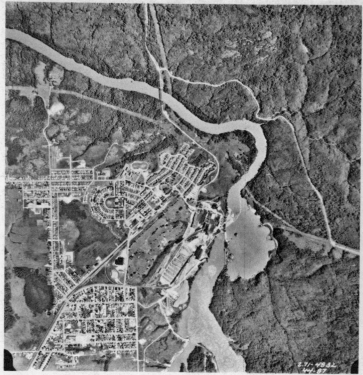

SOURCE: Ontario Ministry of Natural Resources.

These planning elements were complemented by the addition of back lanes which were used for the installation of sewers and electric lines. With the increased use of the automobile, the lanes have since become lined with garages. As the back lanes and garages have come to serve as the main entry points for the residential dwellings, the open quality of the main avenues has been greatly enhanced.

On June 5, 1915, the status of the townsite underwent change when the Ontario Railway and Municipal Board issued an order incorporating parts of the unorganized townships of Calvert and Teefy in the District of Temiskaming into a new municipality known as the Town of Iroquois Falls. The new municipality, though, did not include the wood-processing operations. The attainment of municipal status was followed, in the years between 1915 and 1919, by the first steps to transform the townsite into the "wonder town of the north land".[45] During this interval, the main focus of attention included the construction of streets, 210 residential dwellings, a hotel and town hall, sports and religious facilities, a school, one bank, and a department store operated by the company.[46] The latter was noteworthy as it underscored the emergence of Iroquois Falls as a "company-owned" town. L. R. Wilson, then Secretary of the Abitibi Power and Paper Company, affirms this status in his memoirs where he states, "In fact everything in the town was owned and operated by the company with the exception of the Royal Bank."[47] The association of Iroquois Falls as a company town continued as a fundamental aspect of community life until the 1950s when the Abitibi Paper Company finally introduced a policy of granting its employees the option to purchase their own homes.

Starting in 1919, Anson decided to promote the Garden City aspect of the Iroquois Falls townsite. As part of this promotion, L. E. Schlemm, a landscape gardener from Montreal, was hired to beautify the townsite. Under his direction the appearance of the community was greatly enhanced during the 1920s through the laying out of parks, the planting of shrubs and foliage along the main thoroughfares, and the development of the golf course situated between the mill and the townsite proper.[48] According to S. G. McCoubrey, the first Mayor of the Town of Iroquois Falls, the resulting effect was the creation of another "Garden of Eden".[49] Thus, much of the credit for the evolution of the Iroquois Falls townsite into a garden-type setting can be attributed directly to Anson and Schlemm. In the meantime, the townsite layout had been expanded to include an innovative semicircular residential subdivision to the west of the original townsite (Figure 11:3).[50]

While the above developments were taking place in the Town of Iroquois Falls, unplanned settlement was occurring along its municipal fringe. This fringe settlement was due, in part, to the fact that the original townsite plan made no specific allowance for the growth of the community. When questioned about this inflexibility in the plan, Crabtree responded simply that no growth of the community was anticipated.[51] Also, the nature of the agreement between the Province of Ontario and the Abitibi Pulp and Paper Mills Company in 1912 may have contributed to this planning deficiency because of the stipulation referring to the hiring of 250 workers. Thus it is clear that the criticism which has been levelled against Adams regarding the failure to provide against uncontrolled development beyond the boundaries

of Iroquois Falls by means of a green belt is unjustified and should
properly be directed to the firm of Routly and Summers and the
author of the original sketch plan.

Peripheral settlement around Iroquois Falls first started to take
place as early as 1915 when thirty unserviced dwellings were erected
in the unorganized territory south of the Temiskaming and Northern
Ontario Railway line. Because of the configuration of the railway line,
this residential area was known as the "Y". In like manner, a similar
development occurred in the area to the west of the townsite which
was locally known by a variety of names including West Iroquois,
Victoriaville, Petit Canada, and finally, Montrock.[52] In contrast to the
townsite, these two fringe communities were characterized mainly by
francophones residing on small privately owned lots within a gridiron
street system. The spatial cleavage of the population along ethnic lines
was notable as it foreshadowed similar developments which were to
emerge in other single-enterprise communities in northeastern Ontario
after the First World War.[53]

In 1918 the two fringe settlements were officially incorporated as
the Township of Calvert (which also included the railway junction
village of Porquis Junction and the rural villages of Kelso and Nellie
Lake). Within two years, the Township of Calvert had a population
which exceeded that of the Town of Iroquois Falls (Table 11:2). The
parallel evolution of the Iroquois Falls townsite and the peripheral
settlements gave rise to a number of difficulties related to schooling,

TABLE 11:2 Population Growth of Iroquois Falls and the Township of Calvert
(1921-1971)

YEAR	TOWN OF IROQUOIS FALLS	TOWNSHIP OF CALVERT
	Population	
1921	1,178	1,192
1931	1,476	3,131
1941	1,302	3,296
1951	1,342	4,742
1956	1,478	5,233
1961	1,681	5,494
1966	1,834	5,402
1971	7,271	

SOURCE: *Census of Canada, 1921-1971.* Note: The Township of Calvert annexed part of the Town of Iroquois Falls in 1967 and the remainder
in 1969. The name of the municipality was then changed to the
Town of Iroquois Falls as of January 1, 1971.

transportation, and the provision of public services. These problems
were unfortunately compounded by the existence of a social rift between the two municipalities.[54] The deep nature of this rift was evidenced by the fact that it remained until 1969 before the planned
Town of Iroquois Falls was amalgamated with its unplanned fringe
into an enlarged Township of Calvert. In 1971, however, the Township of Calvert changed its municipal status and a new Town of
Iroquois Falls was again born. As can be inferred from the spatial
layout depicted in Figure 11:3, this new municipality remained only
as a weak testimonial to the high aspirations of Anson, the original
founder of the Iroquois Fall townsite.[55]

TOWN OF TÉMISCAMING (KIPAWA)

During the First World War, the Kipawa Fibre Company, a subsidiary of the Riordan Pulp and Paper Company, decided to establish a
new woodworking operation in the vicinity of Lake Temiskaming situated between the provinces of Ontario and Quebec.[56] After rejecting a proposed site at Haileybury in Ontario, the company finally
selected another location in Quebec found between Kipawa Junction
on the Canadian Pacific Railway line and Lake Temiskaming.[57] The
selection of the site was based on a number of factors including its
proximity to timber resources, the availability of waterpower from
Lake Kipawa, good floating possibilities for the movement of timber,
suitable water for processing purposes, and the presence of the Canadian Pacific Railway line which linked the area to Mattawa.[58] Following this decision, C. B. Thorne, the Vice-President and Manager
of the Kipawa Fibre Company, conceived the idea of erecting a new
community at the site which would serve as a model of its kind.[59] In
Thorne's opinion, such a model industrial community was absolutely
necessary as it was the only means by which the company could attract and hold a suitable labour force.[60] As a preliminary step in this
direction, a special town department was created under the direction
of A. K. Grimmer for the purpose of organizing and executing the
entire undertaking. According to Grimmer, "similar developments in
Canada, in the United States, and in Europe, were examined with a
view to benefiting by the experiences of all."[61] In 1916, the Kipawa
Fibre Company approached the Commission of Conservation for advice regarding the layout of the proposed townsite.

The Commission of Conservation acted upon this request and during 1917 Adams devoted considerable effort to the project.[62] Part of
this effort included a personal visit to the site. Upon his arrival, he
discovered that the most favourable land had already been set aside

for the woodworking operations and that the only possible locations for the townsite consisted of two hilly and rock-strewn slopes found to the north and south of the mill site. Due to topographical considerations, the north slope was selected as the preferred option.[63] Following

FIGURE 11:4   Original Plan of the Town of Témiskaming

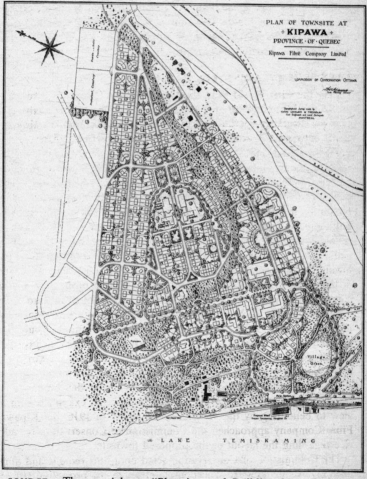

SOURCE: Thomas Adams, "Planning and Building New Towns in Canada: Kipawa", *Conservation of Life*, Vol. 5, No. 1 (1919), pp. 12-13.

this decision, Adams proceeded to sketch a preliminary plan for the townsite; at the same time, the firm of Ewing, Lovelace and Tremblay from Montreal was hired to prepare a detailed contour map.[64] Aside from the street network, the only land-use elements in the sketch plan dealt with the location of the Roman Catholic church, the positioning of the Canadian Pacific Railway station, and the selection of a hotel site overlooking Lake Temiskaming.[65] A new factor, however, was then introduced in the planning process when the Kipawa Fibre

FIGURE 11:5   Proposed Layout Plan for the Town of Témiskaming

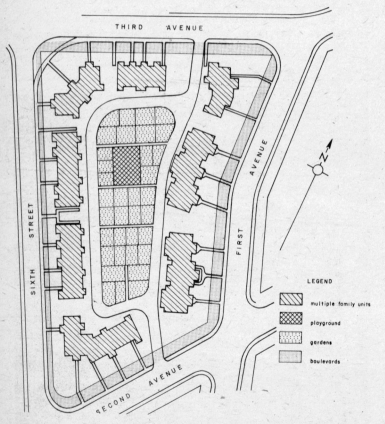

SOURCE: A. K. Grimmer, "The Development and Operation of a Company-Owned Industrial Town", *The Engineering Journal* (May, 1934), p. 220.

Company concluded that the only possible route for the water conduit linking Kipawa Lake to the east of the townsite with the power station at the edge of Lake Temiskaming would have to run through the centre of the proposed townsite. This forced Adams to modify his sketch plan considerably as the conduit was eight feet in diameter and necessitated the construction of bridges to maintain the concept of an integrated community. As can be ascertained from Figure 11:5, the inclusion of the conduit had the subsequent effect of removing some of the "model" character of the townsite layout in the final plan.

Despite the above constraints, the final plan prepared by Adams managed to reflect many of the spatial features associated with the British New Towns Movement. For example, the rectangular layout

FIGURE 11:6   Aerial Photograph of the Town of Témiskaming (1975)

SOURCE: Ontario Ministry of Natural Resources.

was eliminated as much as possible in favour of a combined curvilinear and radial pattern; because of the nature of the terrain, however,
Adams felt that the townsite did not exhibit as much flexibility in this
regard as he would have wished. The Garden City appearance of the
townsite was to be enhanced through the inclusion of trees along the
streets and the main avenue, the introduction of a central square and
village green, and the establishment of a large park preserve along the
edge of Lake Temiskaming to complement the hotel setting. The
relationship of the townsite to the natural environment was enhanced
further by the preservation of small open spaces characterized by
distinctive physical and vegetative features. These elements in the
plan were indicative of Adams' sensitivity to landscaping as an integral aspect of the planning process.

With the completion of the final plan, Adams' involvement with the
townsite was essentially completed. The task of designing the residential subdivision was entrusted to the architectural firm of Ross and
McDonald from Montreal, subject only to the provision that the
grouping, types, and locations of dwelling units would have to adhere
to the building lines and the position of the public buildings. In
developing the residential part of the plan, an attempt was initially
made to introduce the block-layout plan as outlined in Figure 11:5.
This distinctive layout, along with its back lanes, garden plots, and
enclosed children's playgrounds was not used to any great extent due
to topographical limitations. The residential scheme also included
provision for some four basic housing types to accommodate the main
employment groups associated with the mill operations: officials, mechanics, mechanics' helpers, and labourers. In the implementation of
the residential plan, the majority of the dwellings consisted either of
semi-detached or row houses. Meanwhile, the status of the townsite
underwent change in 1920 when it was incorporated as the Town of
Kipawa. In the following year, the name of the municipality was
changed to the Town of Témiscaming. For all practical purposes,
however, the community continued to function as a company town in
much the same manner as Iroquois Falls.

With the passage of time, the role of the town department became
more important in the planning process, especially after the mill
operations were taken over by the Canadian International Paper
Company in 1925.[66] The increased role of the company in town
planning was particularly evident with respect to recreational land
use. In this regard, it is pertinent to note the limited emphasis accorded by Adams to active recreational pursuits outside of those
provided by the open green spaces scattered throughout the townsite.

The weak provision for active recreational pursuits within the townsite was noteworthy considering the isolated location of the community.[67] Thus, the company itself took on most of the responsibility of providing a wide variety of recreational facilities such as an athletic field for baseball and football, four tennis courts, a ski jump, a nine-hole golf course, one skating and hockey rink, a wading pool, a motor-boat land, and a theatre hall.[68] The active involvement of the town department in planning affairs continued until 1955 when the Canadian International Paper Company first began to relinquish its role as the community landlord. In this year the Canadian International Paper Company gave up all of its community assets, started a program to sell all homes to its employees and placed its commercial properties in the townsite for sale to the highest bidder.[69] Later, in 1973, the Témiscaming mills were purchased by a co-operative body known as Tembec Forest Products, Inc.[70] As the organization was partly owned by the workers and residents of the Town of Témiscaming, the resulting effect was the transformation of the townsite from a community run by a company into a company run by a community.

TABLE 11:3   Population of the Town of Témiscaming (1921-1971)

YEAR	POPULATION	YEAR	POPULATION
1921	1,021	1956	2,694
1931	1,855	1961	2,517
1941	2,168	1966	2,799
1951	2,787	1971	2,428

SOURCE: *Census of Canada, 1921-1971.*

In contrast to Iroquois Falls, the Town of Témiscaming did not experience any problems related to unplanned settlement (see Figure 11:6). The nature of the topography virtually precluded any such development from occurring on a significant scale; also, the requirements of the mill were such that the population of the townsite never did exceed the original estimate of three to four thousand inhabitants.

CONCLUSION

During the early years of the present century, Thomas Adams served as a major thread in the diffusion of British New Town ideology into the Canadian setting. The study suggests, however, that his role in this respect was complemented by a number of other influences. From the broad Canadian perspective, there can be no doubt that his role in promoting the New Town idea was impressive; at the same time, it is clear that more attention should be accorded to other important advo-

cates of the New Towns Movement such as the governors general of
Canada, the Hon. W. L. Mackenzie King, and numerous land survey-
ors, engineers, and architects who were inspired by direct visits to
British new towns.[71]

With respect to the Canadian resource communities of Iroquois
Falls and Témiscaming, it is clear that Adams' overall role needs to be
assessed more fully. In the case of Iroquois Falls, the evidence indicates that his contribution to the planning of the townsite was peripheral and that most of the planning for the design and subsequent
development of the townsite was done by land surveyors and a landscape engineer. While his involvement with the townsite of Témiscaming was more substantial, much of the planning in the townsite beyond the initial design stage was done by architects and the town
department of the Kipawa Fibre and Canadian International Paper
Companies. Also, the personal philosophies of resource entrepreneurs
such as F. Anson and C. B. Thorne, who recognized the need for
model industrial towns in the Canadian frontier, warrants more consideration than has hitherto been the case. Consequently, the historical angle of vision should be extended to include the cumulative effect
of other diverse and creative planning impulses in the moulding of the
Canadian urban landscape.

NOTES

1. Central Office of Information, *Town and Country Planning in Britain*, Pamphlet R5355 (London: Central Office of Information, 1975), pp. 1 and 2.
2. The physical principles underlying much of British planning are clearly expressed in Lewis Keeble, *Principles and Practice of Town and Country Planning* (London, 1969), pp. 1–4.
3. See, for instance, Gerald Burke, *Towns in the Making* (London, 1971), p. 147; and Paul D. Spreiregan, *Urban Design: The Architecture of Towns and Cities* (New York, 1965), p. 31.
4. This idea was outlined in *To-Morrow: A Peaceful Path to Reform*. This publication was revised and reissued in 1902. See Ebenezer Howard, *Garden Cities of To-Morrow*, F. J. Osborn, ed. (London, 1965).
5. The history of Letchworth and Welwyn is outlined in Sir Frederic Osborn and Arnold Whittick, *The New Towns: The Answer to Megalopolis* (London, 1975), pp. 14-16.
6. Central Office of Information, *Town and Country Planning*, pp. 14-16.
7. Norman Pressman, *New Towns* (Waterloo: Division of Environmntal Studies, University of Waterloo Occasional Paper No. 1, 1972), p. 12, and Pressman, *Planning New Communities in Canada* (Ottawa: Information Canada, 1975), p. 9.
8. An evaluation of the work of the Commission of Conservation is found in C. Ray Smith and David R. Witty, "Conservation, Resources and Environment: The Commission of Conservation, Canada", *Plan*, vol. 11 (1970): 55-71; and vol. 11 (1973): 199-216.

9. A summary of these annual meetings is contained in Commission of Conservation, *Annual Reports 1909– 1918* (Commission of Conservation, 1910–1919).

10. "Public Health", *First Annual Report of the Commission of Conservation* (Ottawa: Commission on Conservation, 1910), p. 12.

11. See, for example, "Measures for the Improvement and Maintenance of the Public Health", *First Annual Report of the Commission of Conservation*, p. 130; and C. A. Hodgetts, "Unsanitary Housing", *Second Annual Report of the Commission of Conservation* (Montreal: Commission on Conservation, 1911), pp. 50-84.

12. "Town Planning and Housing", *Third Annual Report of the Commission of Conservation* (Montreal: Commission on Conservation, 1912), p. 5.

13. C. A. Hodgetts, "Housing and Town Planning", *Third Annual Report of the Commission of Conservation*, p. 138.

14. Beginning in 1911, the annual reports of the Commission summarized provincial housing and town planning legislation.

15. "Committee on Public Health", *Fourth Annual Report of the Commission on Conservation* (Toronto: Commission on Conservation, 1913), pp. 8-11. The work of Thomas Adams with the Commission of Conservation is summarized in Alan H. Armstrong, "Thomas Adams and the Commission of Conservation", in L. O. Gertler, ed., *Planning the Canadian Environment* (Montreal, 1968), pp. 17-35.

16. "Committee on Public Health", p. 9.

17. "Town Planning Advisor to the Commission of Conservation", *Conservation of Life*, vol. 1 (1914): 27 and 28.

18. See, "Garden City: Its Origin and Purpose", *Conservation of Life*, vol. 1 (1914): 33 and "Garden Cities", *Conservation of Life*, vol. 1 (1915): 60-65.

19. Refer to "Civic Improvement, Town Planning and Housing in Canada",

Conservation of Life, vol. 5 (1919): 24 and "Annual Business Meeting", *Journal of the Town Planning Institute of Canada*, vol. 1 (1921): 4.

20. Commission of Conservation, *Civic Improvement* (Ottawa: Commission of Conservation, 1916), pp. 1-11.

21. Thomas Adams, *Rural Planning and Development: A Study of Rural Conditions and Problems in Canada* (Ottawa: Commission of Conservation, 1917), and Harold Peake, "Commission on Conservation, Canada: Rural Planning and Development", *Town Planning Review*, vol. 7 (1916): 271-73.

22. The concern of Thomas Adams for Planning at the provincial level is detailed in Thomas Adams, "Housing and Town Planning in Canada", *Sixth Annual Report of the Commission of Conservation* (Toronto, 1915), p. 63 and "Provincial Departments of Municipal Affairs", *Conservation of Life*, vol. 2 (1916): 45-47.

23. "The Housing and Town Planning Work of the Commission of Conservation", *Journal of the Town Planning Institute of Canada*, vol. 1 (1921): 3.

24. See, for example, Thomas Adams, "Housing and Town Planning in Great Britain", in *Report of the Ontario Housing Committee including Standards for Inexpensive Houses Adopted for Ontario and Typical Plans* (Toronto, 1919), pp. 111-21.

25. "The Housing and Town Planning Work of the Commission of Conservation", p. 3.

26. Thomas Adams, "Reconstruction and Redevelopment at Halifax", *Conservation of Life*, vol. 4 (1918): 22 and 23; "Planning the Greater Halifax", *Conservation of Life*, vol. 4 (1918): 82-88; "Reports from the Provinces: New Brunswick", *Journal of the Town Planning Institute of Canada*, vol. 3 (1924): 17 and "Planning New Towns in Canada— Ojibway", *Conservation of Life*, vol. 14 (1918): 73-80.

27. "Mr. Thomas Adams Resigns Position Under Canadian Government", *Journal of the Town*

Planning Institute of Canada, vol. 12 (1923): 12.

28. Ibid. and "Re-arrangement of Town Planning Division", *Journal of the Town Planning Institute of Canada*, vol. 1 (1921): 10.

29. Thomas Adams, *Recent Advances in Town Planning*; (New York, 1932); Adams, *The Design of Residential Areas* (Cambridge, 1934); and Adams, *Outline of Town and City Planning: A Review of Past Efforts and Modern Aims* (London, 1935).

30. "The Governors General of Canada and Town Planning", *Conservation of Life*, vol. 3 (1916): 1-4.

31. Ibid., 3; and "Speech of the Governor General", in *Civic Improvement*, pp. 1-3.

32. "The Governors General of Canada and Town Planning", 3 and 4; and "New Governor General is Fluent Speaker in Public", *The Daily Nugget*, October 15, 1916, p. 6.

33. W. L. Mackenzie King, *Industry and Humanity: A Study in the Principles Underlying Industrial Reconstruction* (Toronto, 1918), pp. 358-61; and "Town Planning as the Premier Sees it", *Journal of the Town Planning Institute of Canada*, vol. 6 (1927): 1.

34. Personal Communication with Shirley Spragge, May 13, 1977.

35. Reference is made to such visits in Institute of Local Government, Queen's University, *Single-Enterprise Communities in Canada* (Ottawa: Central Mortgage and Housing Corporation, 1953), p. 24.

36. Department of Lands, Forests and Mines, *Report of the Minister of Lands, Forests and Mines of the Province of Ontario for Year Ending 1912* (Toronto, 1913), p. vi and App. No. 33, pp. 77-83.

37. E. G. Faludi and Associates Limited, *A Study and Advice on the Desirability of Altering the Boundaries Between the Township of Calvert and the Town of Iroquois Falls, (District of Cochrane)* (Toronto, 1968), pp. 21 and 22.

38. Hortus, "One House: One Garden", *The Broke Hustler*, May 1, 1920, p. 8. In this article reference is also made to the planned communities of

Bournville and Port Sunlight in Great Britain. *The Broke Hustler*, a publication of the Abitibi Pulp and Paper Company in Iroquois Falls, first appeared in print on August 25, 1917 and continued as a local weekly until January 29, 1929, when it was replaced by the Toronto-based monthly known as the *Abitibi*.

39. Temiskaming and Northern Ontario Railway Commission, *Twelfth Annual Report of the Temiskaming and Northern Ontario Railway Commission, for the Year Ended October 31st 1913* (Toronto, 1914), p. 23.

40. Adams, *Rural Planning and Development*, Figure 34.

41. Personal telephone communication with H. S. Crabtree, March 9, 1977.

42. Land Registry Office, District of Cochrane, *Plan of the Subdivision of Teefy and Parts of Lot 1 Concessions IV and V Calvert, District of Temiskaming*. This plan, known as M – 10 – T, was signed by the Minister of Lands, Forests and Mines on August 18, 1915.

43. Association of Ontario Land Surveyors, Committee on Biography, *Biography of Gordon Foster Summers* (Toronto: Association of Ontario Land Surveyors, Toronto, n.d.), pp. 135 and 136.

44. See, for example, Institute of Local Government, *Single Enterprise Communities in Canada*, p. 24; "New, Improved Town Gets Same Name as Old One", *The Broke Hustler Enterprise Special*, November, 1972, p. 9; Faludi, *A Study and Advice*, p. 26.

45. Ontario Railway and Municipal Board, *Tenth Annual Report of the Ontario Railway and Municipal Board to December 31st, 1915* (Toronto) pp. 111-15. An underlying factor behind this incorporation was the friction which had already developed between management and employees on the company-controlled townsite. See Frank Lendrum, "Fall Incorporated 1915: McCoubrey Its First Mayor", *The Daily Press*, January 14, 1950, pp. 3 and 4. "The Wonder Town of the

North Land", *The Broke Hustler*, October 2, 1920, p. 2.

46. "Abitibi Directors Visit Iroquois Falls", *The Broke Hustler*, October 4, 1919, p. 2.

47. L. R. Wilson, *A Few High Spots in the Life of L. R. Wilson* (n.p.; n.d.), p. 27. The domination of Abitibi is clearly revealed in Corporation of the Town of Iroquois Falls, *Minutes of the Council of the Corporation of the Town of Iroquois Falls (July 24, 1915 – September 25, 1933)*, Iroquois Falls, (1915-1933).

48. "Abitibi Directors Visit Iroquois Falls", p. 1 and "Touch of Magic Wand Turned Ugly Mud into this Beautiful Town", *The Broke Hustler*, June 12, 1928, pp. 1 and 8.

49. See "Premier Drury and Colleagues Visit Iroquois Falls", *The Broke Hustler*, December 13, 1919, pp. 1 and 2; and "Mr. Anson's Greatest Monument: The Love of the Men Working for Him", *The Broke Hustler*, November, 1923, n.p.

50. "Twenty-five Moderate Priced Houses to be Built this Summer: Townsite Plan to be Completed", *The Broke Hustler*, June 19, 1923, p. 1. This subdivision, known as the Circle and Piccadilly, was intended to provide housing accommodation for all the married employees.

51. Personal telephone communication with H. S. Crabtree, March 9, 1977.

52. K. Boyd, S. Grist and N. Sandrin, *Search into our Past* (Iroquois Falls, 1973).

53. See, for instance, S. D. Clark, "The Position of the French-speaking Population in the Northern Industrial Community", in Richard J. Ossenberg, ed., *Canadian Society: Pluralism, Change, and Conflict* (Scarborough, 1971), pp. 62-85.

54. This social rift is exemplified by a motion passed by the Council of the Town of Iroquois Falls in 1926 which objected strenuously to an advertisement by an Ansonville hotel placed in the Porcupine *Advance* which gave its location as Iroquois Falls. Corporation of the Town of Iroquois Falls, *Minutes of the Council of the Corporation of the*

Town of Iroquois Falls, vol. 5 (January 25, 1926), p. 295. The spatial cleavage and resulting social rift between the townsite and its two fringe settlements may have been a factor contributing to Premier Drury's insistence that Kapuskasing should never acquire a "closed" or "company" form of status. Premier Drury visited Iroquois Falls on two occasions in 1919 and 1921.

55. Planning in the Town of Iroquois Falls is now being undertaken in co-operation with the consulting firm of Proctor, Redfern, Bousfield & Bacon. See Proctor, Redfern, Bousfield & Bacon, *The Official Plan of the Town of Iroquois Falls Planning Area* (Iroquois Falls: Town of Iroquois Falls, 1972).

56. "Founding of Town of Temiscaming", *The North Bay Nugget*, June 30, 1967, Section 5, p. 4.

57. The proposed site at Haileybury is discussed in "Another Big Paper Mill Town for North", *The Porcupine Advance*, September 19, 1917, p. 7.

58. The Canadian Pacific Railway line was built earlier, in 1895, and it served as part of the Temiscaming Colonization Road. "Founding of Town of Temiscaming", p. 5.

59. "How 'Company' Town Gained Independence", *The North Bay Nugget*, June 30, 1967, Section 5, p. 5.

60. Thomas Adams, "Report of Planning and Development Branch", *Report of the Eighth Annual Meeting of the Commission of Conservation* (Montreal: Commission of Conservation, 1917), pp. 103 and 104.

61. A. K. Grimmer, "The Development and Operation of a Company – Owned Industrial Town", *The Engineering Journal*, vol. 17 (1934): 219.

62. Thomas Adams, "Town Planning and Land Development", *Report of the Ninth Annual Meeting of the Commission of Conservation* (Ottawa, 1918), p. 198.

63. "The Town of Kipawa", *Report of the Tenth Annual Meeting of the*

Commission of Conservation, (Ottawa: Commission of Conservation, 1918), App. VII, p. 110.

64. "Planning and Building New Towns in Canada: Kipawa", *Conservation of Life*, Vol. v (1919), p. 11. See also "Big New Town will be Built on Temiskaming Lake on Latest Model", *The Daily Nugget*, September 14, 1917, p. 2.

65. As the mill site was located on a former mission operated by the Oblate Fathers, the Roman Catholic Church was granted a prominent position in the new townsite. See "Lumber Village Started Settlement", *The North Bay Nugget*, June 30, 1967, Section 5, p. 6.

66. "Founding of Town of Temiscaming", p. 4; and "Giant CIP

Operation Just Keeps on Growing", *The North Bay Nugget*, June 30, 1967, Section 5, p. 7.

67. It remained until 1938 before the Town of Temiscaming acquired a road link with North Bay. "Lumber Village Started Settlement", p. 6.

68. Grimmer, "The Development and Operation of a Company-Owned Industrial Town", p. 222.

69. "Founding of Town of Temiscaming", p. 4.

70. Tembec, *Annual Report 1975* (Montreal: Tembec, 1975), pp. 1 and 6.

71. This need to give more emphasis to "non – professionals" has been noted in Kent Gerecke, "The History of Canadian City Planning", *City Magazine*, vol. 12 (1976): 12-23.

12.

Land Development Patterns in Calgary, 1884 – 1945

MAX FORAN

Calgary mirrored the western Canadian experience before 1950 in that its land-use patterns developed with little regard to the formal planning which has characterized more recent urban growth. Yet it would be erroneous to assert that land patterns evolved aimlessly, for the guiding, if inexpert, hand of civic policy-making was a definite influencing factor. Indeed, the idea of planning and of provision for specialized districts had been entertained in Calgary since it was incorporated in 1884. Policy implementation, however, was another matter entirely, but here the operating concept was that of feasibility. Those agencies which contributed to Calgary's physical growth, whether in the public or the private domain, were governed in their actions by factors of feasibility. These factors included the scope of legal power, available funds, existing technology, and the limitations imposed by specific topographic conditions.

LAYING THE FOUNDATIONS: THE FRONTIER YEARS, 1884-1909

In this pioneer stage the basic foundations for later land-use were laid. The main contributing agents were the CPR and a few private landholders. Lacking the expertise, financial means, and the will to influence land development, the various local governments followed the only feasible path, and abrogated a responsibility that was hardly theirs by statute or prescription. The limitations imposed by Calgary's site also resulted in patterns of settlement which had later impact in differentiating and directing residential expansion.

The Calgary townsite as fixed by the CPR in 1884 was located in a saucer-like depression between the Bow and Elbow rivers (see Map 12:1).[1] The North-West Mounted Police had chosen this spot in 1875 as the site of its third post in present-day Alberta. The NWMP were doubtless influenced in their choice by strategic considerations, and with respect to defence purposes the fort was ideally placed. The railway company's decision to locate its station and townsite on the flat flood plain west of the fort was only partly influenced by the

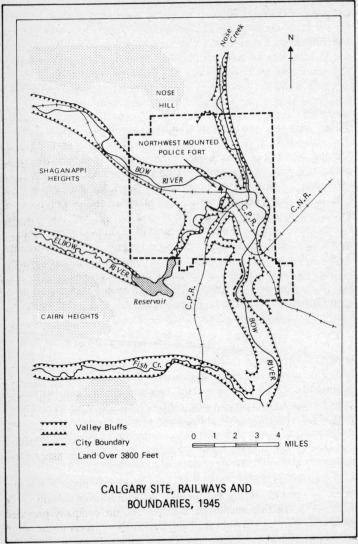

CALGARY SITE, RAILWAYS AND
BOUNDARIES, 1945

SOURCE: Adapted from Figure 3 in P. J. Smith, "Change in a Youthful City: The Case of Calgary, Alberta", *Geography*, Vol. 56 (1971): 1-14; and boundary maps in Planning Department, City of Calgary.

existing nucleus of settlement[2] which had clustered under the protective wing of the law. The CPR surveyors were loud in their praise in the merits of the townsite at Fort Calgary. John Egan, CPR General Superintendent, described the Calgary townsite as being "far ahead of any location that we have on the line of the Bow".[3] Egan's statement was reasonable considering the CPR's priorities in choosing townsites along its mainline. Situated in a natural depression and on an odd-numbered section, the Calgary townsite was easily surveyed and laid out; fresh water was available from two sources while the rising ridges afforded a degree of protection from the biting north winds.

In terms of long-range expansion however, the CPR's choice of townsite was less than ideal. The Elbow River snakes in from the southwest to join the Bow before it makes a sharp swing to the south. The flat land to the east of the fort was thus interrupted by two streams. Immediately north of the Bow directly opposite the town rose a six-hundred-foot ridge which then opened up onto gently undulating prairie. The area of flat land upon which the original town was built was broken up by ridges and ravines to the south and west less than two miles from the railway station. This configuration of rivers, ravines, and ridges was an effective barrier to physical expansion in that it complicated utility extensions and facilitated grades prohibitive to horse-drawn vehicles. In retrospect the CPR would have better served the purposes of uniform and aesthetically desirable development had it chosen for its townsite either a spot well to the east, or even the windy north hill above the Bow River.

The CPR mainline from Medicine Hat approached Calgary from the southeast and made a sharp swing to the west near the fort, bisecting the townsite as it followed the Bow towards the Rockies. The CPR's idea of compact towns probably was the reason why the railway station was fixed north of the line (see Map 12:2). In any case, the close proximity of the rails to the river effectively isolated the business community and produced definite patterns of commercial development.

The nature of Calgary's business and wholesale districts was decided by the CPR during this period. By withdrawing certain lands from sale at the first auction of townsite lots, the company provided for a retail core entirely north of the tracks. Even access to the south was across bumpy level crossings chosen arbitrarily by the CPR. The latter was interested in reserving the area directly south of the tracks for wholesale purposes. City Council inadvertently aided in this development when it donated a sum of $25,000 to the CPR in 1898 for the erection of freight sheds in the city.[4] The CPR's decision to build these

facilities right in the downtown area east of its terminal virtually
ensured the development of the area near the tracks for wholesale
purposes. The resulting band of wholesale activities with its need for
spur-line trackage was a buffer to future retail and business expansion. When manufacturing establishments such as International Mill-

FIGURE 12:2

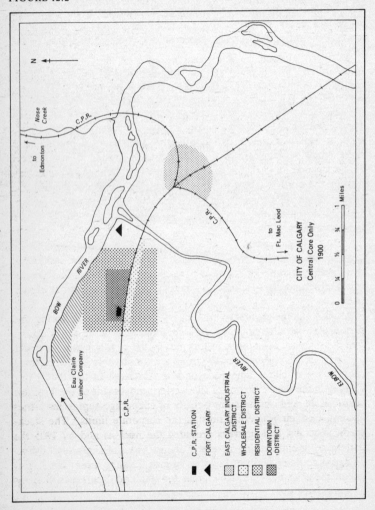

ing took advantage of available trackage and the city's need for industries to locate themselves in the area, the differentiation of Calgary's commercial growth north and south of the tracks was assured.

When Calgary was incorporated in 1884, its boundaries included those areas of Sections Fourteen, Fifteen, and Sixteen south of the Bow River. Difficulty of access made expansion north of the Bow neither feasible nor desirable. Utility extensions, for instance, were complicated by the river, and although the view from the top of the ridge was easily Calgary's finest, there were few who thought of braving the precipitous incline observable in early photographs of the north hill.

Following the completion of two bridges across the Bow River, clusters of settlement grew up on the narrow flats below the ridge. These were usually small, unserviced, and rude dwellings erected by owners who wished to avoid paying taxes. The presence of "shack towns" outside the corporate limits of major urban centres was common in western Canada, and it probably had its local precedent in these small settlements. When the privately owned Centre Street bridge opened in 1907, for example, an instant "tent town" materialized on the north bank of the Bow River.[5] On the top of the hill, the small village of Crescent Heights consisted of inexpensive houses situated on land sold cheaply by a local landowner.[6] Early in the twentieth century ethnic groups congregated at Bridgeland near the Langevin Bridge.[7] Farther east were the brothels of the Nose Creek area as well as a few odoriferous meat works. By the time settlement was feasible in terms of access and function the north hill had already assumed second class status as an area of potential residential expansion.

Another significant feature of Calgary's physical growth during this period was the emergence of a manufacturing area in east Calgary. The convergence of railways in this part of the city, however, provides only part of the reason since the trend was observable before railroad construction to either Edmonton or Fort Macleod. In the 1880s, east Calgary landholders, fearful of the western movement of the business centre, embarked on conscious policies of encouragement to industries locating on their properties outside the corporate limits.[8] The stockyards, abattoirs, and brewery provided the nucleus and by 1905 the pattern of manufacturing in east Calgary was definitely established. The continuing erection of factories in east Calgary meant the loss of one of the city's most desirable areas for residential purposes in terms of natural beauty.

Residential growth during this period was confined to the area adjoining the business and wholesale establishments. The result was heterogeneous land usage particularly between the railroad and the river where private houses blended with small manufacturing establishments and retail stores. To the south, beyond the wholesale houses, Calgary's wealthiest residents erected large houses. This southern movement was an early indication as to the future direction of residential growth; the north hill was not yet feasible or even desirable, while east Calgary seemed destined for future manufacturing land usage. By 1909 the differentiation of retail, wholesale, and manufacturing districts had originated in response to decisions made by private interests. Already these decisions, together with factors of topography, had implications for residential growth.

Local government possessed neither the motivation nor the power to be vitally concerned with directing the town's physical growth. It was chiefly interested in gross expansion and gave little thought to its differentiation. The absence of a building by-law meant a wide diversity of building use without respect to location. Town Council had no power to control manufacturing land use outside the corporate limits. In this period, anyway, the town councils were only too happy to have industries come to the community, and were more prepared to offer concessions than to impose regulations governing location.[9] Lacking also the financial resources to control development through the extension of utilities, the civic authorities were in no position to prescribe growth policies even if they had wished.

A good example of Council's lack of power and desire to direct growth is the case of the Eau Claire Lumber Company. In 1886 the company received the right from the federal government to use the Bow River for logging purposes and to erect mill facilities in Calgary.[10] Town Council subsequently gave its approval to the lumber company's application to build a mill on the river right in downtown Calgary, in the vicinity of the present-day Centre Street bridge. Other small related manufacturing enterprises located themselves nearby with the result that the area between the river and the business area became associated with manufacturing. The identification of waterways with industry and transportation is linked with the notion of functional land use in port cities, and so the civic authorities were essentially following precedent in terms of feasible land development in granting the Eau Claire Lumber Company the right to operate. Also, there was a question of legality as to the precise ownership of riverbank boulevards. Illustrative of this point is the fact that William

Pearce, the resident Superintendent of Lands and Mines, reserved the north bank of the Bow for boulevard purposes in the 1890s. By allowing the Eau Claire Lumber Company substantial rights in 1886, the civic authorities, albeit acting feasibly, forfeited the right to direct development along the south bank of the Bow. Before 1909 this attitude of indifference was reinforced by periodic floods, log jams, and the tendency by nearby residents to use the south bank of the Bow as a dumping ground for refuse.[11] In this light the actions of the conservation-minded Pearce in reserving the north bank of the Bow was understandable.

The first twenty years of Calgary's corporate existence produced some definite trends in land usage. The precise location of railway facilities was of immediate importance in determining the placement of the business district as well as manufacturing enterprises. The close proximity of river and railway to the business district contributed to a netherland of heterogeneous development that has remained to the present day. The inability of contemporary technology to conquer the north hill ensured the latter's second-class status by 1909. An east Calgary industrial base was also identifiable well before 1909. Residential and commercial expansion in this direction was forestalled by this development. By 1909, too, it was apparent that the railway had contributed to differing patterns of commercial development north and south of the station which, combined with the freight sheds immediately to the east, ensured a future westward expansion of the business district. It was in the face of these established patterns that the post-1909 period began.

THE EMERGENCE AND CONSOLIDATION OF DIFFERENTIATED DISTRICTS, 1909 – 1945

In the first decade of the twentieth century Calgary grew rapidly, reaching a population of 45,000 in 1911. With this marked population influx came substantial physical expansion. The business district was extended to accommodate the intensified demand for retail and wholesale facilities. Factory areas blossomed into manufacturing districts. Perhaps the most dramatic manifestation of gross expansion lay in the degree of residential development. New districts emerged north and south of the business centre to give Calgary a true suburban appearance by 1912. These years were of profound importance in determining Calgary's land-use patterns, for the extent of physical growth delineated by 1912 was to remain virtually unchanged until the 1950s (see Map 12:3).

In this period, local government was the chief decision-making agency. These elected bodies possessed good intentions respecting planned development, particularly after 1911 when some adverse effects of unregulated growth became apparent. However, when civic authorities were unable to follow through on their notions of planned development they were forced to implement feasible alternatives. In providing for manufacturing districts, for example, Councils were able to apply a specific workable policy with consistency and good results. It was when they were unable to pursue a definite policy that feasibility and short-term considerations became guiding forces. The emergence and development of differentiated districts between 1909 and 1950, then, reflected the relationship between perceived ends and practical implementation.

Specific Land-use Areas: Manufacturing

The city's greatest success in directing land-use patterns after 1909 was through its industrial policy. Introduced in 1911, this policy prescribed procedures that were followed with reasonable consistency. The overall result of the industrial policy has been the consolidation of manufacturing enterprises in suitable locations with adequate provision for future expansion.

Provision for manufacturing land usage provided fewest problems for civic authorities in that it was relatively easy to control. Calgary's industrial policy called for the municipal purchase of suitable industrial sites. Industries were then induced to locate in these areas through the extension of uniform concessions.[12] Because the city was also able to provide utility and transportation services, the municipally owned areas were in an advantageous position in comparison with other privately owned properties. Indeed, the loudest objections to the city's policies came from those individuals who had held land hoping to profit from sales to prospective manufacturers.[13] Given the rate at which new industries were coming to Calgary in the 1910–12 period, there was certainly reason for such speculation. Owners of factories already located in acquired areas complained that the city's uniform concession policy had the effect of depreciating the value of their properties.[14] Nevertheless, the end result of the industrial policy of 1911 was the gradual removal of manufacturing concerns from high-rent areas to either municipal or adjacent privately owned sites. The fact that the policy was not always popular indicated that there was scarcely a perceived need on the part of the public for special industrial districts.

The city's choice of locations for its industrial sites dictated future trends. Wisely, large areas were selected along the railways heading north to Edmonton and south to Fort Macleod. The main area, Manchester, is in an unsightly trough of land east of the busy Macleod Trail, and with access to trackage facilities. As Calgary expanded, the industrial areas reached farther towards the city limits. Not all were municipally owned. Properties were bought on an individual basis and converted into private industrial parks. In this sense, the city's purchase of industrial sites contributed to land speculation. In 1912, for example, Pat Burns sold lands in the designated industrial areas to private developers for $1.7 million.[15] However, most industries were attracted to municipal sites. Well into the post-Second World War period, Manchester was easily the largest industrial area in Calgary.[16]

The industrial policy was possible only in the light of expanding municipal powers which enabled cities to purchase land outside the corporate limits for industrial purposes. Indeed, the old practice of locating manufacturing concerns outside the city limits had been a major obstacle to early local control over areas later incorporated within city boundaries.[17] The local government was, therefore, reluctant to allow street railway services to extend into areas of potential industrial development.[18] Typical was the village of Forest Lawn east of the city. This area was on the entrance route to Calgary of the Grand Trunk Pacific Railway, and much acreage fell into the hands of private speculators. Huge industrial complexes were projected. The city authorities, however, were not interested in extending necessary street railway services to the district, preferring instead to wait for tangible results. In the meantime they continued to exercise their own prerogative, and advertised the merits of their own industrial district in Manchester.

The city was also able to encourage the erection of workmen's houses in close proximity to industrial areas. Sometimes, the purchase of property by the city for industrial sites was contingent upon subsequent land being made available by the owner for residential purposes.[19] There were precedents for this policy as city planners of the day were convinced of the need to design residential subdivisions which would harmonize with the industrial areas they served.[20] So even though commuting was made feasible by the street railway, the pattern was established that located small residential enclaves in areas which were later zoned entirely as industrial. Typical are the districts of Manchester and Bonnybrook. In the case of the former, the city has expended substantial sums in order to facilitate relocation. The residents of Bonnybrook have not been so fortunate. Due to the remoteness of the district, utilities were not extended to residences with the result that as recently as 1946 the continuing presence of surface privies, cesspits, and contaminated drinking wells were sources of grave concern to city health officials.[21] In 1945, twenty-six families requested relocation from their present location near the British American Company's oil refinery in east Calgary.[22]

The period after 1909 was characterized by a consolidation of established attitudes toward land use along the south bank of the Bow River. Given the intensified activity in railway construction, the city exercised feasible prerogatives in encouraging the use of river banks for railway purposes. For example, City Council approved when the Grand Trunk Pacific bought the North-West Mounted Police barracks, the site of the original Fort Calgary, and ran its rails along the river's edge to the proposed terminal. To City Council's way of thinking, costly and time-consuming right-of-way problems were thus avoided. In 1910 it was announced that the proposed market site should be beside the river "because of trackage considerations".[23] Declining property values in the area influenced official thinking. Certainly the decision to allow the Chinese to establish their Chinatown in 1910 was linked to a belief in the continuation of falling land prices. Property values in the area continued to decline after 1912 with the collapse of the land boom. The failure of the various railway ventures, and the movement of industrial areas towards the southeast resulted in the steady deterioration of the area along the south bank of the Bow into a mishmash of heterogeneous land usage. Given the financial difficulties of the period, it was not surprising that suggested beautification schemes were not implemented. Traditional attitudes were thus maintained. On one occasion Council was requested to establish a firm policy of residential land use in the area. The Commissioners refused to act on the grounds that the district was traditionally commercial and industrial.[24] In 1946, for example, the city purchased the Eau Claire property for a moderate $38,235. A move was initiated in Council to have certain lands set aside for park purposes.[25] The Town Planning Commission's subsequent report squelched the proposal on the grounds that "such a park is neither realistic nor desirable and might be dangerous".[26] The City Transit bus sheds were erected there instead.

Industrial land use followed precedents set in the frontier period, being oriented in suitable areas, close by railways and main roads, in the east and southeast. Sites were chosen judiciously with a view towards functional efficiency and later expansion. However, the early provision for residential areas within industrial districts has resulted in peculiarly isolated, underprivileged communities. A traditional concept of the role of river banks in determining land-use patterns had its effects. The south bank of the Bow River remained underdeveloped in terms of optimum land use or scenic potential.

Specific Land-use Areas: Commercial

The population influx, with its demand for increased wholesale and retail space, resulted in the extension of the downtown area. Pre-1909 patterns were followed. Expansion was in a westerly direction along the three main avenues, but was generally contained laterally within half a dozen blocks. With the advent of the streetcar, a belt of semi-commercial land use began to appear along the main routes surrounding the main business area. Yet, in terms of commercial development, the most observable trend from 1912 to 1945 was the continued dominance of the downtown core. Part of the reason was the excellent service provided by the streetcars. Also, Calgary's slow growth after 1912 brought an end to the spiralling demand for rental space. Finally there were the policies of the municipal government which appeared unsympathetic towards expanding commercial land use.

Most streetcars entered the downtown area, and the corner of Eighth Avenue and First Street West became the focal point of streetcar convergence and hence of retail activity. Fares were very reasonable and were actually subject to reductions in the early 1920s.[27] In the good commercial year of 1929, approximately one-third of the population used the streetcars daily.[28] In 1944 the percentage was maintained when over 67,000 passengers took daily advantage of the public transportation system.[29] Although the automobile was increasing in popularity it had not begun to divert commercial activity away from the business centre. In 1925, for instance, no gasoline filling station was located south of Twenty-fifth Avenue Southwest.[30]

Slow economic growth after 1912 was also a contributing factor to the continuing dominance of the downtown business area. Although it is probably true that some retailers moved away from the downtown district to take advantage of lower rentals, the post-First World War period saw a virtual stagnation in building development. For thirteen consecutive years, between 1915 and 1928, less than one thousand building permits were issued annually, and even in the boom year of

1929, the figure was about half that for 1912. Falling land prices led to a stabilization of rents with the result that small businessmen could retain their downtown locations. Indeed, during the Depression land-lords actually competed with each other for paying tenants. Only in the premium areas along Eighth Avenue were rents comparatively high as compared with areas away from the business centre. Rent on the tiny Nut House on Eighth Avenue, for example, was more than double that paid by larger confectionery stores on First Street West or in the Roxborough Block on Twenty-sixth Avenue South.[31] In the early 1940s, rental space along busy Ninth and Eleventh avenues was sometimes less than half that along Eighth Avenue.[32] The shortage of business and residential space engendered by the population influx during the Second World War forced rentals up and drove developers to the cheaper land areas well beyond the downtown centre. Only with the advent of subsequent shopping plazas did the central retail district begin to relinquish its long-held dominance.

Civic policy appeared to militate against commercial expansion outside the central business area. The imprecise nature of the building by-law produced conflicts in which the homeowner enjoyed preferen-tial treatment at the expense of the intruding businessman. Outside the main business district, the establishment of commercial enterprises was contingent upon the approval of neighbouring residents.[33] Even when this was obtained the city reserved the right of disallowance. When commercial expansion was not vigorous it was fairly easy for surrounding homeowners to petition successfully for adjoining blocks to be designated residential.[34] In other areas, commercial expansion was prevented by homeowners who refused to sell. By enjoying the lower residential assessment they could well afford to wait for demand for commercial space to force land prices up.[35] Thus, the cluster of business establishments along the streetcar routes, being unable to consolidate themselves, remained small and non-competitive with the downtown core.[36] For example, the busy thoroughfare on Sixteenth Avenue North between Centre Street and the Edmonton Trail was not zoned commercial until 1945.[37]

As commercial growth necessitated the least regulation in terms of land usage, City Council was content to allow the laws of supply and demand to take their course. The main emphasis lay in the downtown area where building restrictions were tightly regulated. Also, as long as population pressure on the main business district remained fairly constant, there was no urgency to widen roads or improve access to the downtown core. Yet it was the very dominance and concentrated nature of the business district which isolated it and prevented creeping expansion towards the suburbs. In this sense, one could argue that deficiencies in the structure of the main retail district, as well as falling land prices in the outer area, forced commercial development in the suburbs by the 1950s.

Specific Land-use Areas: Residential, 1909 – 12

Between 1909 and 1912 differentiated residential districts emerged with astonishing rapidity. Easily the most important influencing factor was the presence of the street railway. City Council possessed neither the power nor inclination to direct residential development in terms of regulating either the extent or nature of building. In their commitment to absolute growth, elected officials also did not seem to realize, let alone utilize, the value of the street railway or utility extensions as instruments of civic policy in controlling physical growth.

The growth of residential districts after 1909 reflected the marked influence of the street railway. Areas most popular with prospective homebuilders were close to streetcar routes. The CPR's decision to construct extensive repair facilities at Ogden in 1911 was contingent upon streetcar construction.[38] Although a working-class residential area was established adjacent to these shops many workers commuted from other areas in the city. The streetcar route to Bowness, well beyond the city limits, ran north of the Bow River and opened up the areas of Parkdale and Westmount.[39] Land speculators were very conscious of the value of the street railway in promoting their subdivisions. The districts of Tuxedo Park, Pleasant Heights, Shaganappi, Killarney, and Elbow Park gained early prominence as residential areas because of streetcar extensions.[40] Even the village of Forest Lawn outside the city owed its existence to the street railway. Originally intended for intensive industrial activity along the entrance route to the city of the Grand Trunk Pacific, Forest Lawn attracted the interest of developers who sold lots on the guarantee of street railway facilities.[41] In fact it was maintained that these speculators promoted land sales by laying railway ties even though they had no franchise or agreement with the city to provide street railway services.[42]

Although the street railway was crucial in determining the extent of residential expansion, two other factors contributed to differentiation. The first was the degree to which building restrictions could be enforced, while the second involved the extension of utility services. The city was not in a position to enforce the former, and seemed to have no overall policy regarding the latter.

Before 1912, Calgary had no building by-law, while zoning was not introduced until the 1930s. The Building By-law of 1912 was loose and imprecise, particularly with respect to residential construction. Moreover, the legal prerogatives of Council were often unclear with the result that residential expansion in the city occurred under loose civic supervision.

Variations in lot shapes contributed to differentiated districts. Before 1912 the twenty-five foot frontage lot was common, and indeed was popular with purchaser, developer, and the city. The building by-law was specific only on absolute lot size,[43] and thus the deep, narrow-frontage lot prevailed despite later attempts to encourage wider frontages.[44] The overall result was the presence of small bungalows, and the emergence of closely packed neighbourhoods.

There were other inconsistencies. Although many subdivisions were poorly laid out, approval was generally secured from city councils that were concerned with easing the acute housing shortage, and acquiring needed taxation revenue.[45] Often, construction commenced before the issuance of building permits.[46] Houses were placed at varying distances from the street line, while others were constructed with poor quality materials and were little more than shacks.[47] These vague and poorly enforced civic regulations resulted in widely differentiated districts depending on the policy of the individual developer.

Before 1912 private developers determined the type of residential area, by contracting with buyers on the type of dwellings to be erected. Because many of these "contracts" were unenforceable, either by the developer or the city, haphazard growth patterns occurred in areas sometimes intended for exclusive residences. Development on the Lindsay Estate provides a good case in point. Scenically located on a rise south and east of the Elbow River, this subdivision was intended by its owner, Dr. N. J. Lindsay, to cater to a better class of resident. Instead, buyers refused to honour their commitments with the result that substandard buildings were erected. When Dr. Lindsay tried to persuade the city to withhold building permits, he was informed of the city's legal impotence in the matter.[48]

Some developers were successful in enforcing building restrictions. Easily the best results were in the subdivision known as Mount Royal, owned by the CPR[49] and handled by the prominent firm of Toole Peet and Company. Prescribed building restrictions were enforced strictly with the result that Mount Royal became Calgary's first truly exclusive subdivision. Huge mansions were set in spacious lots on the specially contoured thoroughfares. Residents guarded their interests through the Mount Royal Improvement Association.[50] This organization was headed by the most powerful real estate men in the city, who, having built residences in Mount Royal, were determined that it remain a haven for the privileged few. To the south along the Elbow River Calgary's most innovative developer, Freddie Lowes, utilized building restrictions and extensive land improvements to make his subdivisions among the most desirable in the city.[51]

Utility services could not keep pace with residential expansion during this period. The city had no policy respecting utility extensions and had borrowed considerably in efforts to meet the growing demand for essential services. Indeed, land in most subdivisions was sold on the guarantee of available utilities. By 1912, however, utility extensions lagged far behind residential development, with those favoured districts being those close to the business area, particularly to the southwest where construction was easiest.

Thus by 1912, differentiated residential districts had emerged in Calgary. The street railway delineated the placement of these districts. However, their differentiation was predicated upon two additional factors. One was the degree of adequately enforced building restrictions, the other was the availability of utilities. Only in the southwest were all three requirements operable with the result that fashionable districts were restricted to this area of the city. Lacking both the legal power and inclination to provide an overall policy, City Council's contribution to the birth of suburban Calgary was essentially vicarious.

Trends in Residential Land-use, 1912 – 45

The years 1912 – 40 marked a period of consolidation in Calgary's urban development. The collapse of the land boom was accompanied by a drastic falling off in immigration and a scarcity of investment capital. Faced with a heavy bonded indebtedness, the city was obliged to implement policies designed to restrict physical growth. These policies, by encouraging a closer concentration of population, contributed to multiple land-use in the inner city, and depressed prices in the outer suburbs.

One effect of the land boom has been the over-extension of residential districts. Houses were scattered far and wide throughout the city virtually isolated from main roads and utility trunk lines. In 1922 a report by a special Council committee referred to twenty-eight of Calgary's thirty-six sections as being mainly unimproved,[52] while eight years later it was estimated that over 80 per cent of the city's area was

FIGURE 12:3

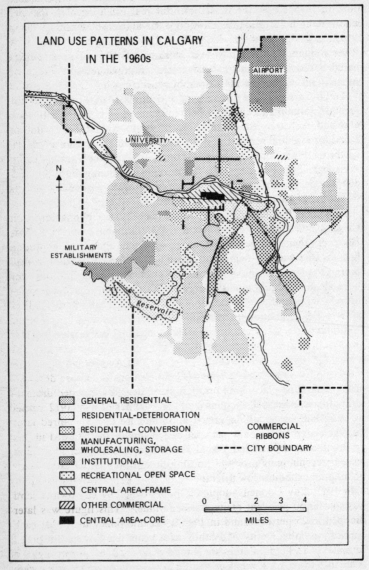

LAND USE PATTERNS IN CALGARY
IN THE 1960s

AIRPORT

UNIVERSITY

N

MILITARY
ESTABLISHMENTS

Reservoir

GENERAL RESIDENTIAL
RESIDENTIAL-DETERIORATION
RESIDENTIAL- CONVERSION
MANUFACTURING,
WHOLESALING, STORAGE
INSTITUTIONAL
RECREATIONAL OPEN SPACE
CENTRAL AREA-FRAME
OTHER COMMERCIAL
CENTRAL AREA-CORE

COMMERCIAL
RIBBONS
CITY BOUNDARY

0   1   2   3   4

MILES

SOURCE: Adapted from Figure 4 in Smith, "Change in a Youthful City: The
Case of Calgary, Alberta", *Geography*, Vol. 56 (1971).

unoccupied.[53] Construction activity was slow during the period before 1940. In 1946, Calgary had 28,506 occupied dwellings. Fully 30 per cent were built before 1911, and only 6,055 erected between 1911 and 1940.[54]

The continued reversion of land to the city in lieu of unpaid taxes placed additional strains on the limited financial resources of civic governments. Over $200,000 worth of property reverted to the city in 1914.[55] By the following year over $4.3 million were owing in tax arrears.[56] Over the years the trend continued. In 1933 the city took title to some 1,600 pieces of property.[57] Nine years later the value of disposable land owned by the city was in the vicinity of $5 million.[58]

Faced with a scattered population, and with land increasingly being removed from the assessment rolls, Council initiated a formal policy of growth restriction in 1920. Essentially this policy involved curtailing streetcar services, the restriction of utilities beyond a designated inner-city area, and the levying of high assessments in outlying areas on non-agricultural land. Encouragement programs were built into this policy. Owners of lots in outer areas were encouraged to exchange them for corresponding pieces of property closer in.[59] A special house-moving fund was established and levied against the city utilities "for the purpose of encouraging and assisting the moving of buildings from the outer areas into the inner areas".[60] A year later in 1930 a by-law was passed prohibiting the sale of property in outlying areas for construction purposes unless adjacent to existing buildings.[61] As late as 1935 the city's "dust laying" programs on city thoroughfares did not extend beyond 38th Avenue South and 21st Avenue North.

This policy had several effects and implications for future development. In the first place, land prices in the outer area dropped dramatically. In some areas reductions were over 80 per cent of 1912 values by 1916.[62] Much acreage reverted to agriculture to be acquired later by developers for very low prices. Council inadvertently aided in this process during the Second World War when, in an effort to acquire needed revenue and promote housing, it disposed of its large land-holdings at extremely low prices.

In 1941, City Council adopted a policy whereby city-owned land was sold at 50 per cent of its assessed value.[63] This figure was later dropped to 25 per cent, and in 1944 it became policy to "judge each application on its merits".[64] Within three years the City had disposed of much of its land holdings for a total of $377,000.[65] A parcel of 1.6 acres in Spruce Cliff was sold for $240,[66] while nineteen acres were sold in Glendale for $500 cash.[67] Building lots went for as low as $20.[68] Prime space in commercial areas was also obtained at bargain rates.[69] By 1945 official alarm was expressed at the speculative evils that had once more been launched on the city, and in 1946 a City Lands Committee recommended that the policy be discontinued.[70]

Calgary's inner area absorbed the population increase of over 100 per cent between 1911 and 1946, and this had its effects on residential land use particularly in areas contiguous to the business district. Although apartments appeared increasingly in close-in areas, existing water and sewerage services were insufficient to enable the erection of large, high-density units. Instead there was the increasing use of former large single dwelling houses as multiple dwelling residences. In 1929 an investigation into housing conditions in Calgary revealed that the area between the CPR mainline and Seventeenth Avenue South was the most congested in the city.[71] Fully one-third of families investigated lived in one or two rooms sublet in large houses.[72] Moreover, inadequate toilet and washing facilities created health hazards.

In addition to contributing to residential congestion, the official restricted growth policy resulted in multiple land use in the close-in areas. The Zoning By-law reflected this trend by allowing for a multiple use district. Containment was virtually impossible especially in the early 1940s when an acute housing shortage forced the civic authorities to relax regulations. Site area was reduced for duplexes, and approval was easily secured to convert almost any dwelling into suites anywhere in the city.[73] The result was an acceleration of heterogeneous land use along the streetcar routes and near existing business and factory areas.

The policy of restricted growth served to consolidate pre-1914 residential patterns. Mount Royal retained its pre-eminence as did the southwest portion of the city. Only in this area were the three requirements present for optimum residential growth. Adequately serviced by utilities and the street railway, and with districts subject to building restrictions, the southwest became unchallenged as the most desirable residential area in the city. Expansion to the north and east, on the other hand, was slow and modest. Falling land prices in the 1920s resulted in lower assessments which scarcely invited the heavy expense associated with utilities. In 1929, for instance, the residents of Capitol Hill in northwest Calgary were forced to accept septic tank facilities instead of the sewerage they had requested.[74] Only in the 1960s, when the three criteria mentioned above lost their significance, did areas in the northwest and the southeast begin to rival the residential supremacy of the southwest.

The emergence of deprived residential districts during this period was not due solely to factors of age or multiple-use zoning as was the case in the post-1950 years. In outlying areas, poorer residential districts were those favoured with streetcar routes but without full utility service or building restrictions. Bowness and Forest Lawn were two such communities. Both were situated outside the city limits but were within Calgary's urban purview. Both owed their origins to real estate speculators and their grandiose schemes in the 1910 – 12 land boom. In 1929 large unserviced lots were offered in Bowness for $100 on the guarantee that annual taxes would not exceed $1.00.[75] Residents of Forest Lawn, many of them European immigrants, were in reasonable commuting distance from the east Calgary factories via the street railway which ran to adjoining Albert Park. Bowness was connected directly to Calgary by the street railway and became something of a "shack town" in the 1930s. The governing rural municipalities were unable to regulate growth in these villages despite requests and offers of aid from concerned officials in Calgary.[76] Thus it is not surprising that when the communities of Bowness and Forest Lawn were incorporated into the City of Calgary in the early 1960s, they continued to function as low-priced residential areas.

CONCLUSION

Calgary, like most urban centres, grew and developed amid prodigal attitudes towards land use. In times of economic buoyancy and heavy population influx, these attitudes were given full rein. Concomitantly, in periods of economic uncertainty, the trend towards retrenchment represented more a response to prior extravagances than it did a change in philosophy. Official policies, therefore, reflected current economic conditions and involved short-term priorities.

The extravagant land-development practices between 1909 and 1912 were based on the assumption that Calgary was destined for big-city status. For instance, sufficient land was reserved for manufacturing purposes to accommodate the needs of a city of almost half a million people.[77] Also, it was believed that subdivisions in advance of immediate requirements represented sound planning techniques. Certainly the heavy municipal borrowing which occurred during this period was based on the notion that population and assessment would continue to rise.

It is also true that under the pressure of growth, a need was felt to control future development. In this respect, municipal bodies exhibited an awareness of the importance of long-range planning, although it should be added that local government's two attempts to plan for expansion were in response to provincial legislation. In 1912, the British Town Planner, Thomas Mawson, was commissioned by the city to prepare a comprehensive plan for Calgary's future growth. His elaborate plans were never implemented,[78] for the financial ruin which faced the city by 1916 called for austerity in which expensive planning programs had no place. Similarly, the movement towards zoning in 1929 was accompanied by studies of housing conditions as well as the preparation of a major street and arterial highway plan.[79] Again, these schemes were shelved because of economic distress.

Civic land-development policies were never clearly stated. It is doubtful whether they could have been, given the Council's position of legal uncertainty on many issues. For example, the City's right to force property owners back an additional five feet from the street line was challenged and referred to the courts in 1936.[80] Enacted policies were usually ones of retrenchment and revealed a need to control expenditures. On other occasions they were more in response to existing situations than instruments to regulate desirable growth. A good example was the Zoning By-law, with its emphasis on multiple-use districts and its lack of policy for the outer-city area. The tendency towards multiple use dwellings was observable long before the zoning by-law made provision for it.

Calgary's land-use patterns may have originated in spontaneous decisions but they did not develop spontaneously. In the frontier period, they grew in response to factors associated with site, the railroad, and the policies of east Calgary landholders. During the boom period, land speculators and developers, using the street railway and building restrictions, succeeded in differentiating residential districts, while City Councils firmly established manufacturing land use. The policies of consolidation engendered by slow economic growth and financial limitations after 1914 had their effect in delineating commercial districts and determining the nature of residential development. In good times, City Council facilitated growth by providing the essential services which encouraged private enterprise. In lean years, municipal officials pursued policies of retrenchment which resulted in evolving patterns of local government to control growth, and the financial structures under which it generally operated, and its notions of optimum growth could not possibly have been translated into practical policies. For while civic officials and land speculators alike may have entertained ambitious dreams for Calgary's physical development, it was the implementation of feasible policies designed to bring immediate results which determined the nature of land use in the city.

NOTES

1. While the rails reached Calgary in August 1883, the townsite was not laid out by railway officials until December when the dispute with the federal government was settled over ownership of the section upon which the NWMP post was located. In essence Calgary was a creation of the CPR. Section 15 on which the townsite was actually located was an odd numbered section and therefore CPR land under terms of the contract.

2. This nucleus included the I. G. Baker Company (Montana), the Hudson's Bay Company post, as well as a few cabins belonging to the freighters who used Fort Calgary as a stop-over point on the oxen-Red River cart route from Fort Benton to Fort Edmonton.

3. From a letter copy in possession of the author, James Egan to William Van Horne, August 1, 1883.

4. Glenbow Historical Library and Archives, Calgary (hereafter cited as Glenbow), City of Calgary Council *Minutes* (hereafter cited as CCM), March 28, 1898.

5. *The Calgary Herald* (hereafter cited as *Herald*), August 10, 1907.

6. See *Herald*, August 13, 19, 1909; also Glenbow, City of Calgary Papers (hereafter cited as CCP), Box 22, file folder 182.

7. These were mostly German immigrants. In fact the area was referred to as Germantown with religious denominations such as the Moravians prominent. There were also Italians and Galicians in this area.

8. For a fuller discussion, see M. L. Foran, "Early Calgary 1875-1895: The Controversy Surrounding the Townsite Location and the Direction of Town Expansion", in A. R. McCormack and I. MacPherson, eds., *Cities in the West: Papers of the Western Canadian History Conference-University of Winnipeg, October 1974* (Ottawa, 1975), pp. 26-45.

9. See Glenbow, Wesley Orr Papers, Orr to Mary Scheiber, March 30, 1892.

10. For information on this and other agreements, see Glenbow, Calgary Power Papers, Box 8, file folder 77.

11. Glenbow, Files from the Office of the City Clerk (hereafter cited as CCF), Box 37. Correspondence dated May 7, 1916. Also Box 429 "Annual Report of the Parks Superintendent, 1915." NOTE: the above cited collection has recently come into possession of the Glenbow Archives and has not as yet been catalogued or indexed. Hence the only citation given is the Box number.

12. These essentially provided for fixed purchasing prices and assessment rates plus tax exemptions on improvements, machinery and stock. Utility services were supplied at reduced rates.

13. CCF, Box 104, letter dated October 31, 1911.

14. Ibid., letter dated November 9, 1911.

15. Glenbow, Patrick Burns Papers, Box 2, file folder 13. These sales were made between February and April, 1912.

16. City of Calgary Industrial Department, *Annual Report, 1959*, pp. 16-17.

17. CCF, Box 45 contains a copy of an agreement made with Pat Burns respecting taxation.

18. Ibid., Box 128, letter dated December 10, 1912.

19. Ibid., Box 104, letter dated July 5, 1911.

20. See Thomas Mawson, "Report of Town Planner," in *The City of Calgary Past, Present and Future* (Published under the auspices of the City Planning Commission of Calgary, 1914), pp. 50-51.

21. See CCP, Commissioner's Report, November 1, 1946. When the question of extending utilities to Bonnybrook was raised by residents, the city officials refused on the grounds that "the total cost is unjustified for so few residents and a precedent would be set where the city would be spending large sums extravagantly in areas which are not residential areas. A ruling should be made that residents move from the area". CCM, October 28, 1946.

22. CCM, May 14, 1945.

23. Ibid., April 23, 1910.
24. CCF, Box 78 undated letter, 1910; Box 1639 correspondence dated September 13, 1945.
25. CCM, August 19, September 30, 1946.
26. Ibid., Town Planning Commission's Report, October 17, 1946.
27. CCM, March 3, 1923.
28. Probably not quite accurate. Figures show that over seventeen million passengers used the streetcars in 1929. When divided by the population, this figure comes out at 50 per cent. However, most would be using the cars on a two-way basis.
29. Glenbow, "Financial Statements of the City of Calgary, 1944".
30. CCM, May 2, 1925.
31. Glenbow, Toole Peet Papers, Box 2, file folder 15.
32. Ibid.
33. CCF, Box 45. Specific provisions were contained in By-law 763, section 19. For example see CCF, Box 590, correspondence dated January 21, 1918.
34. For example, see the petition involving residents on Kensington Road, CCM, January 14, 1931.
35. CCF, Box 2092, June, 1956.
36. Sections of Seventeenth Avenue South, Eleventh Street South, Fourteenth Street South, Tenth Street North, Sixteenth Avenue North, Edmonton Trail, and the Macleod Trail contained the busiest commercial activity.
37. CCF, Box 1639, September, 1945.
38. See Herald, Nov. 21, 1916. The agreement with the CPR was called the Ogden Agreement.
39. Westmont is contained within the area traversed by Kensington Road between Fourteenth Street North and Twenty-Fourth Street North.
40. For a typical example of this type of negotiation see CCF, Box 12 correspondence dated March 9, 1910.
41. Glenbow, Chestermere Lake Historical Society Research, Box 1, file folder 1, article by J. B. Poppitt, December, 1969, p. 3.
42. Ibid.
43. Frontages did not have to exceed the minimum of 25 feet if the lot area equalled 3,000 square feet.
44. Frontages of 37.5 feet and 50 feet were encouraged. See CCM, Jan. 21, 1929.
45. For example see CCF, Box 12, correspondence dated February 18, 24, 1910.
46. CCM, September 30, 1929.
47. Ibid. Also August 16, 1929.
48. CCF, Box 66, correspondence dated July 21, 1909.
49. The CPR inserted caveats into sales of land in this subdivision.
50. Calgary Optimist, December 18, 1909.
51. CCF, Box 78, correspondence dated February 14, 1910.
52. CCP, Box 3, Report of Special Council Committee on City Lands, 1922.
53. CCF, Box 176, Zoning Report (undated, probably, 1930).
54. Census of the Prairie Provinces, 1946, vol. III, Table 10.
55. Glenbow, Financial Statement of the City of Calgary, 1914.
56. Herald, September 3, 1915.
57. Annual Report of the Board of Trade, 1933.
58. CCM, July 23, 1941.
59. Ibid., March 15, 1928.
60. Ibid., "Report of the Special Housing Committee of City Council", July 19, 1929.
61. CCF, Box 689.
62. See CCF, Box 132, correspondence dated October 21, 1916.
63. CCM, October 23, 1941.
64. Ibid., July 18, 1944.
65. Ibid., February 19, March 3, 1945.
66. Ibid., April 16, 1945.
67. Ibid., May 6, 1941.
68. See "List of City Owned Lots" published by City of Calgary Land Department, 1941.
69. See CCM, February 26, 1941; April 26, 1944.
70. Ibid., October 22, 1946.
71. CCF, Box 1088, "Report of the Special Housing Committee", July 19, 1929.
72. Ibid.
73. CCM, March 4, May 30, 1941.
74. Ibid., August 16, 1929.
75. Herald, July 13, 1929.
76. CCF, Box 176, correspondence dated October 30, 1930.

77. Ibid., Note from Doughty Davies, Town Planner for the City of Calgary, 1930.

78. See Mawson, *The City of Calgary*.

79. CCF, Box 176 "Major Street and Arterial Highway Plan" (undated, *circa* 1930).

80. *Herald*, June 3, 1936.

13.

Zoning and Planning:
The Toronto Experience,
1904 – 1970*

PETER W. MOORE

INTRODUCTION

Planners have always viewed zoning as just one tool, albeit an important one, with which to achieve the goals of a comprehensive plan. Others see zoning in a different light. For some it is a means of protecting neighbourhood quality and property values, others see it as an impediment to their freedom to use private property, and still others treat it as something to be manipulated for political gain. All of these views are part and parcel of the zoning experience in Toronto, but the concern here is with the relationship between planning and zoning in that city. The central argument is that, in Toronto, planning and zoning developed from different sets of values, and their relationship can only be understood in light of these values.

In discussing zoning and planning as political functions, some ideas developed by Harold Kaplan will be used. He distinguishes between "Tories" and "Populists" in relation to political input and decision-making procedures. "The Tories' central values are order, rationality, centralization, and hierarchy in decision-making ... [and they have] ... an image of the community as a corporate entity, so that one could search for and discover measures that were in the public interest of the entire community."[1] In municipal politics, the reform movement held Tory values. On the other hand, municipal populism "has extolled the virtues of the average man on the street and has sought to protect him from the experts, the 'interests', big government, big business, and big labour. Decentralization and small scale means keeping things close and responsive to the people. Thus groups and political leaders with deep roots in a specific neighbourhood were closer to the people than civic groups with a city-wide constituency. Order and rationality in decision-making were less important than providing a number of different access points for citizens with a

---

* I wish to thank Jim Simmons and Jim Lemon for comments on an earlier draft of this chapter.

316

grievance."[2] Populism, based on a belief in direct democracy, dominated muncipal politics in the first half of the twentieth century, so that city councils proceeded on a case-by-case basis, rather than formulating general guidelines or policies.

This chapter begins with a brief review of the development of zoning and planning in North America, to set the Toronto story in its broader context. It turns then to an examination of planning and zoning in Toronto before 1936, and this is followed by an examination of the enactment of Toronto's Zoning By-law and its relationship to the planning movement in the city. Finally, the implementation and enforcement of the Zoning By-law after 1954 is briefly examined, once again in terms of its relationship to planning in the city.

ZONING AND PLANNING IN NORTH AMERICA

Zoning is a use of the police power[3] which divides a community into zones or districts according to permitted uses of land in order to control and direct the use and development of properties in the city. Its legal origins can be found in the law of nuisance, and in restrictive covenants, both of which offered individuals limited and generally ineffective control over externalities generated by other properties. Precursors to zoning can be found in the use of the police power to restrict the location of noxious and dangerous activities such as tanneries, slaughter houses, and powder houses. In the late nineteenth and early twentieth centuries the restrictions became more and more common, and the uses prohibited more and more general, as zoning as we know it began to take shape. In 1885 laundries in Modesto, California, were limited to a certain section of the city, and other cities followed suit with an ever-growing list of "nuisances", such as dance halls, livery stables, saloons, and pool halls. In 1904 Ontario's cities were given the right to control stores, laundries, butcher shops, and factories. In 1909 Los Angeles was divided into twenty-seven industrial districts and one residential district, and soon variations in permitted residential character became common. In 1912 large Ontario cities were permitted to control the location of apartment and tenement houses by districts. Although the police power was ostensibly used to promote order, safety, health, morals, and the general welfare of society, there can be little doubt that in these early forms of zoning it was used to protect property values by controlling the effects of negative externalities.

As well as use districts, height districts, in which limits were placed on the heights of buildings, were instituted in many cities, partly to control population density, partly to allow sunlight to reach between buildings, partly to control traffic congestion, partly for symbolic reasons, and partly for reasons of fighting fire. Use restrictions and height restrictions constituted the basic components of comprehensive zoning.

In the 1880s, zoning combining both use and height restrictions had developed in Germany from the building by-laws.[4] Zoning formed part of a city plan and was co-ordinated therewith in a coherent whole, which treated urban life as an organic unity, not as a series of separate problems. It was to Germany, and its examples of this zoning scheme, that planners in the early 1900s looked in a search for solutions to problems of neighbourhood deterioration and congestion and chaos in central areas. Low-density and restricted residential areas would provide a better environment for urban dwellers, and the proper arrangement of commercial and industrial areas would make the city more efficient. For these early city planners, such as Bassett, Nolan, Marsh, and Ford, zoning had to be part of an overall plan, in order to achieve the best solution to the problem of arranging land uses and circulation in the city.

When comprehensive zoning ordinances were developed in North America they were seldom part of such a plan, but continued the traditional preoccupation with property values, and to a lesser extent downtown congestion. The first comprehensive ordinance in North America, that of New York, in 1916, exemplifies this, for it resulted from a general concern with the traffic congestion produced by skyscrapers, and from the particular problem of the merchants on Fifth Avenue whose property values were depreciated by the invasion of their district by the loft factories of the garment industry. These factories, in turn, were leaving behind a blighted area of low property values which reduced tax revenues for the city and threatened the investments of financial institutions. During the 1920s, zoning was adopted in many cities and towns in the United States, especially after the publication of the Commerce Department's Standard State Zoning Enabling Act. Although this act mentioned the importance of a comprehensive plan, it did not define it, and Scott concludes that the model act "encouraged overall zoning unsupported by a thoughtfully prepared general plan for the future development of the City".[5] Edward M. Bassett, one of the zoning pioneers in New York, reckoned that 99.9 per cent of zoning was "what the average informed real estate owner of that district will stand for".[6]

In the 1940s and 1950s, again following the lead of New York, many cities were rezoned in order to deal with the problems of "overzoning" which had often characterized earlier ordinances. Too much land had been zoned for commercial or high-density residential uses, with the result that these uses were encouraged to "invade" many districts, initially driving property values up, to be followed by declines on the remaining single-family dwellings, leading to deterioration and blight. Although these zoning revisions might have borne some relation to the provisions of a general plan, they, too, were largely an attempt to stabilize property values.

Finally, the exclusionary zoning which has become a feature of suburban and exurban life in North America is also in large part an attempt to protect property values, even though it is often justified on aesthetic or environmental grounds. The real fear is low-income workers and blacks and their impact on property values and lifestyles, not the effect of overcrowding or the consumption of land or the assimilative capacity of the environment. The fact that zoning ordinances and official plans in these areas coincide results from the common goals of both rather than the subordination of one to the other.

Although planners have envisioned zoning as part of the implementation of the city plan, property owners, politicians, developers, real estate dealers, and financial institutions have maintained its use as an instrument for the creation and maintenance of property values, with only coincidental connections with city planning.

City planning is defined as the manipulation of the development of the physical elements of a city by an agency of the state in order to achieve general goals for the whole community. It is concerned with the arrangement of land uses, the provision of parks, roads, transit facilities, and public places according to predefined goals of welfare, orderliness, efficiency, and the like. Other chapters in this volume have discussed its Canadian and North American origins in depth, so only a brief historical glance is required here.

At the turn of the twentieth century, city planning in North America concerned itself with the City Beautiful, with Paris as its model. The chaotic, congested, utilitarian cities of the new world produced architects, philanthropists, and others, who sought relief in the design of great boulevards and malls, parks, public buildings, monuments, fountains, and civic squares. With its preoccupation with aesthetics and civic art, this movement was criticized by those who saw it as wasteful and profligate in the face of more urgent urban problems, particularly the housing conditions of the poor. The City Beautiful Movement soon gave way to one with a more practical base—that of making the city more efficient and more functional. City planning became a science, concerned with gathering information, analysing it, and according to the goals of the community, solving its problems with a plan for the future—precisely the kind of scientific management that was becoming accepted in business at the same time. It was this kind of planning which envisaged zoning as one of its tools.

As Smith observes in his paper in this volume, this conception of planning has remained prevalent to today, with variations in scale and the object of concern. With the widespread growth of automobile usage in the 1920s, a preoccupation with highway planning became firmly embedded, and this later produced demands for regional planning. In the years following the First World War, urban renewal constituted a new theme in planning, and in the 1960s, it was the process of planning as much as its object that came under scrutiny with demands for citizen participation and advocacy planning. However, planning in the 1960s bore little relation to either zoning or planning in Toronto at the turn of the century.

ZONING AND PLANNING AS SEPARATE TRADITIONS, 1900-1936

Until 1954, no comprehensive zoning ordinance operated in the City of Toronto. Instead, a large number of "residential restrictions", dealing with districts of varying size, were instituted in the city, beginning in 1904 and continuing until 1954. Two broad categories of restrictions can be identified; those separating residential and non-residential areas; and those establishing variations within residential districts.

The first kind of restrictions, "non-residential" restrictions, originated in 1904, when at the request of the City of Toronto, the Ontario Legislature amended the Municipal Act to allow cities to control "the location, erection, and use of buildings for laundries, butcher shops, stores, and manufactories".[7] After 1904, further businesses, trades, and noxious uses were added to the list of those prohibited as the Ontario Legislature passed successive amendments to the clause. These uses included stables, tanneries, rag, bone, or junk shops, blacksmith shops, forges, dog kennels, hospitals or animal infirmaries, plumbers' shops, machine shops, tinsmith shops, movie theatres, private hospitals, public dance halls, undertakers' establishments, warehouses, gasoline or oil filling stations, the sale of goods, wares, and merchandise on private lands, tents, awnings, and other coverings for business purposes, buildings for the housing of motor trucks or cartage apparatus, tents for human habitation, and the storage for sale of coal, coke, or other fuel.

Large areas of the city were covered by these regulations, with most of the resulting "residential districts" being established before

1924 (see Figure 13:1). Many districts were established as a response to a proposal for a non-residential development within them, such as a laundry, corner store, or factory. The resulting restrictions usually covered only a small district such as two blocks, a street, or a block face. These districts generally lay south of Bloor between Dufferin and the Don, in an area where non-residential development was most likely to occur as the city grew. Another large area of the city was covered by larger districts which were established to maintain resi-

FIGURE 13:1

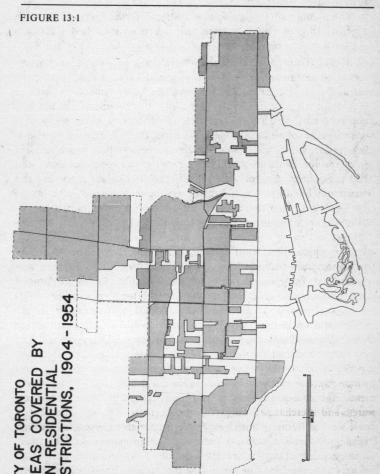

CITY OF TORONTO
AREAS COVERED BY
NON RESIDENTIAL
RESTRICTIONS, 1904 - 1954

dential districts where no proposal for non-residential change had been made. These districts were "zoned" as they were developed, or soon after, in order to guarantee environmental quality. Finally, it is possible that some of the older residential areas in the city were restricted as a response to a general sequence of change which had begun in the neighbourhood. The rationale for the regulations was similar to that for the first kind of district identified—it was an attempt to maintain past environments and property values, rather than to shape future ones.

Within some of the residential districts, further restrictions were applied. Three variations on this theme can be identified, each progressively more exclusive, and applying to a smaller area of the city.

In 1912, Toronto began prohibiting the use and erection of apartment and tenement houses in most residential areas in the city. Apartment houses were defined as any dwelling house containing three or more separate dwelling units. Generally, these districts already had non-residential restrictions, and after 1912, the two sets of restrictions were usually introduced at the same time. In 1912, most of the existing "residential districts" were covered in one by-law, which resulted from specific demands made by a group of real estate dealers, who had noticed the effect on single-family property values of the low rise apartment buildings which became common in the city after about 1905. After the first two by-laws, the motive for these restrictions was to prevent possible future changes rather than to stop proposed development.

Beginning in 1921, some areas in Toronto were restricted to private residences only. Instead of listing prohibited uses, allowable ones were spelled out. These restrictions covered most of the city east of Bathurst and north of Bloor, as well as many other areas, particularly West Toronto (Figure 13:2). Many of these districts were established in the 1940s, and besides private residences, permitted other uses, such as converted dwellings, medical offices, churches, and playgrounds. The districts established by these restrictions were a response either to a specific proposal for change, or a response to changes observed elsewhere which were likely to occur in the neighbourhood. Whatever the cause, the motive was the same: to protect property values by protecting the residential environment.

A final set of restrictions specified certain minimal conditions which residential development on the restricted properties had to fulfil. These concerned the lot size, the position of the house on the lot, the value of the dwelling, the size of the dwelling, its construction materials, and so on. These areas were predominantly located in North

Toronto, where the first set of these regulations was applied to Lawrence Park in 1927. They were simply a continuation of the restrictive
covenants on properties in that suburb, which were due to expire in
1929, and the application from the residents left no doubt about their
motives:

> that the residential character of the park should be preserved and the value
> of their property should not be depreciated or destroyed by ... semi-de-
> tached houses, duplex houses, apartments, stores. ... [8]

FIGURE 13:2

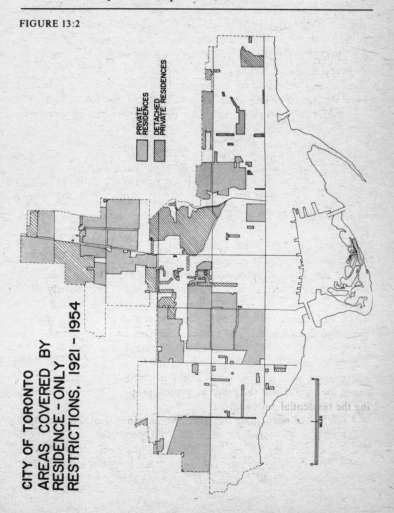

PRIVATE
RESIDENCES

DETACHED
PRIVATE RESIDENCES

CITY OF TORONTO
AREAS COVERED BY
RESIDENCE – ONLY
RESTRICTIONS, 1921 – 1954

The processes by which these varying kinds of residential districts were established, and by which the regulations were enforced and amended, had their roots in the neighbourhoods themselves. Whether as a response to a perceived threat of change or a specific instance of land-use development, the initial demand for the establishment of the district came from its residents in the form of a petition or deputation to City Council, or a request to the aldermen. Similarly, when an individual sought an amendment to the restrictions to allow the establishment of a previously prohibited use, a poll was conducted by the Property Department among nearby property owners to gauge their attitude to the change. The results of this survey of neighbourhood opinion usually, but by no means always, played an important role in determining the outcome of the application. Also, the enforcement of the restrictions relied on complaints from affected or nearby residents, especially when the conversion of existing dwellings to other uses, both residential and non-residential, was involved.

These restrictions were enacted and administered in the populist tradition identified by Kaplan, for in essence, they were neighbourhood-based, case-by-case attempts to control nuisances or externalities, to protect and maintain the residential environment or "character", and above all to protect property values. Zoning in this form was a collective device used for individual benefit, rather than the collective benefit that characterized planning.

Just as the residential restrictions in Toronto were similar to the districting common in many North American cities before 1920, so too planning in Toronto in many respects reflected the broader movement of planning in North America. The City Beautiful in Toronto was proclaimed by the Civic Art Guild which was established in the late 1890s, and produced a plan for the city in 1909. This plan contained three main proposals: a pair of diagonal thoroughfares from the city centre to the northeast and northwest, a program for expanding the system of parks and playgrounds, and a scheme to develop the waterfront area to the east of the Don. It also identified a central theme in the need for more beauty in the streets.

This plan was not implemented and, in 1911, the Civic Improvement Committee produced an early attempt at a comprehensive plan which was predominantly derived from City Efficient ideas, but contained some elements of the City Beautiful. This plan proposed an extensive system of street railways and railroads, and a program for facilitating the efficient movement of vehicular traffic. It also proposed extending the park system and developing the waterfront, and in addition proposed a civic centre. This plan, too, was largely ignored. After this the planning movement in Toronto was carried on largely by the Civic Guild which emphasized convenience, utility, economy, and health, as well as beauty. The major concerns of the Guild were with circulation and transportation, open spaces and parks, and the development of lands outside the city. It was instrumental in the passage of the City and Suburbs Plans Act of 1912 which required that future subdivisions within five miles of the city be approved by the Ontario Railway and Municipal Board, and the creation of a City Surveyor's Office in the Assessment Department to administer the provisions of the act for the city. This represented the beginning of official planning in Toronto.[9]

In 1928 and 1929 an Advisory City Planning Commission, consisting of four businessmen and an engineer, produced a plan for the extension of University Avenue south from Queen, the development of a plaza and radiating avenues in the same area, and a whole range of street widenings, extensions, and arterial connections. This plan, which combined elements of the City Beautiful and the City Functional, was to be implemented over a period of fifteen years; however, it was rejected by the voters of the city in 1929.

In 1930, a further Advisory City Planning Committee, made up of city officials, produced a plan firmly in the City Functional tradition for the improvement of circulation and transportation in the city. This plan was concerned exclusively with street extensions and widenings, and some of its proposals were adopted by City Council. Also in 1930, a City Planning Department took over the duties of the City Surveyor's office, as well as the role of advising council and examining conditions in the city. Its duties did not include the preparation of an official plan. Tracy D. le May, who had been City Surveyor since 1912 became the City Planning Commissioner, a position he held until 1954.

Thus, between 1900 and 1936, planning in Toronto was preoccupied initially with civic beauty, and then with the efficient movement of men and vehicles. It was not involved with the system of land-use controls in the city.

The planning movement during the period was a child of the reform movement and its Tory values, which sought to change the structures and procedures of city politics in the era prior to the First World War. The basic reform ideology treated the city as a community with an identifiable public interest, which should determine decisions, so that the "politics" would be taken out of local government.

In this tradition the plans of the period before 1936 assumed a public interest, and by assembling large amounts of information on population, traffic, and the like it attempted to satisfy that public interest in the most rational and efficient manner, primarily by improving highways. The quasi-independence of the planning bodies and commissions ensured that the "politics" was kept out of planning. Planning leadership came from business groups and the daily press, and its public interest was largely that of the business community as represented by the Board of Trade or other bodies with a city-wide base.

The politics of planning contrasts strongly with the politics of zoning, for the latter identified no community-wide public interest, but only that of individuals, and groups of property owners. Restrictions, and amendments to them, were passed, in the Populist tradition, in response to local demands and opinions, and not according to the rational, Tory goals of efficiency and order. The restrictions were analagous with potholes, rather than expressway systems.

ZONING AND PLANNING IN TRANSITION, 1936 – 1954

To set the context for a discussion of the relationship between planning and zoning during this period it is necessary to outline briefly the course of events that led to the implementation of the Zoning By-law in 1954, and to the confluence of zoning and planning.

In 1942 the City Planning Board of Toronto was established, the culmination of the previous forty years of planning and reform. It was a quasi-independent board, with strong backing from the Board of Trade and newspapers, but only an advisory relationship with City Council. Its first report stressed that planning, and a master plan in particular, were in the interest of the whole community:

> ...a city plan does not aim at localized improvements only, but the improvement of the whole city for the economic and social benefit of all, and is to be achieved step by step over a period of years.[10]

Zoning would constitute one element of the city plan.

Work on the first zoning by-law began long before the establishment of the City Planning Board. In 1927 and 1934, City Council decided not to embark on a comprehensive zoning by-law, but in 1936 a move to consolidate and revise the residential restrictions was viewed more favourably, and the City Planning Commissioner and Property Commissioner were ordered to perform this task. These officials decided that this consolidation should take the form of a comprehensive zoning by-law, and this idea was approved by City Council in 1937 along with a proposal for seven types of districts. By 1939 the officials had completed their work and produced a draft zoning scheme which essentially stabilized existing land uses in the city. City Council then appointed an Independent Committee on Zoning (ICZ) to review the draft and to conduct public hearings. This Committee consisted of two architects, two engineers, and a real estate agent, and as such was a panel of experts not citizens. After conducting its public hearings and completing its review of the provisions of the proposed by-law, the ICZ presented its report to the Property Committee ofCity Council in September 1942. The Property Committee promptly submitted the by-law to the City Planning Board for its consideration, and this Board spent a further year or so making revisions, before recommending its adoption in December 1943, following the publication of the Board's Master Plan for the city. In response to the changes in the city produced by the demands of a wartime economy, further revisions were made in 1944, until By-law 16253, the Zoning By-law, was passed on December 19, 1944.

The 1944 Zoning By-law was not implemented, because it lacked legislative authority. Some of its provisions required additions to the enabling powers in the Municipal Act, and these were applied for in 1945, but not passed because of the early dissolution of the legislature. Most of the powers were granted in 1946, but not those which would allow the city to control off-street parking requirements or to set up a Board of Appeals to interpret and adjudicate minor variations in the regulations, so the 1944 By-law languished without approval. Nevertheless, a special committee consisting of Controller Smith, the Commissioners of City Planning, Property, and Building, and the City Solicitor, was set up to review and revise the by-law, for its maps had first been drawn in 1937 and 1938.

Also in 1946, the Ontario government passed the Planning Act, partly at the behest of the City of Toronto, which immediately established the City of Toronto Planning Board. The City Planning Board had resigned in 1945 in anticipation of the Planning Act. The revision of the Zoning By-law continued under the auspices of the new Planning Board which was also preparing an official plan, as required by the act. This official plan was released in 1949, and approved in 1950. Its most important elements were a generalized land-use map and a highways map.

The Planning Board continued its revision of the Zoning By-law, and in 1950 held a series of public meetings to allow local and city-wide groups to offer their criticism and comments. In 1951, the Prop-

erty Committee began its consideration of the Planning Board's proposals, and held a series of special meetings in early 1952, concluding
with two public meetings at which representations from local groups
and other interested organizations, such as the Board of Trade, were
heard. In May 1952, the Board of Control made further changes,
followed by the City Council before it finally passed the Zoning By-
law, No. 18642, on June 10, 1952. As had been previously agreed, the
Ontario Municipal Board gave the by-law temporary approval so that
a series of local hearings could be held throughout the city under the
auspices of the Property Committee. Twenty-one such meetings were
held, following which the City Planning Commissioner and City Solicitor drew up a report listing all requested changes along with their
recommendations. The Property Committee then held a further nine
meetings in March and April 1953, to consider this report and hear
further property-owner presentations. Following these deliberations,
the full report along with the Committee's recommendations were sent
to City Council which held a special meeting to discuss them. The
Council passed By-law 18878 to give effect to the recommendations it
adopted as well as some other changes. Following the passage of these
amendments to the Zoning By-law, the Ontario Municipal Board held
its hearings and issued its report which required a few more minor
changes. City Council then passed an amendment to give effect to
these changes on March 8, 1954. The Zoning By-law could now be
enforced and implemented, some eighteen years after work on it had
begun.

The development of the Zoning By-law after 1936 can be viewed as
an attempt to replace the Populist values and traditions of the residential restrictions with the Tory values and procedures of the reform and
planning movements. This was not an open conflict, but more in the
nature of an evolution, as the attitudes of city councillors slowly
changed, and they were able to accommodate the new procedures
with the old. This process of accommodation is now examined in
greater depth.

The Zoning By-law originated as a scheme to revise and consolidate
the existing set of residential by-laws, of which there were over five
hundred with thousands of amendments. This consolidation had no
connection with the overall planning of the city as embodied in a
master plan, nor with any components of planning such as highway
widening or the provision of parks. The purpose of the consolidation
was administrative efficiency, and as such lay in the reform tradition.
At the same time, however, the implementation, enforcement, and
amendment of the restrictions were to remain neighbourhood-based.

In 1934 City Council had specifically rejected a proposal by the major civic officials to bring in a "comprehensive and co-ordinated scheme for the regulation of the use of land in the city",[11] and earlier in 1936 two proposals to adopt a comprehensive zoning system and simultaneously examine the possibility of establishing a City Planning Commission were not acted upon. In a limited sense the 1936 origins of the Zoning By-law were reformist, but the traditions and procedures established over the previous thirty years of residential restrictions were to remain paramount.

Tracy D. le May, the Commissioner of City Planning, and dominant member of the committee of civic officials which prepared the original draft of the by-law was a planner in the reform tradition, who clearly felt the need for a co-ordinated system of land-use regulation in the city. Although he appears to have been responsive to the demands of the established political structures at city hall, with their populist emphasis and neighbourhood basis, he was also critical of the way the restrictions were administered, and blamed city government for the blighted condition of some neighbourhoods. In their report to the Property Committee, the Commissioners of Planning and Property claimed that the map of existing land uses illustrated

> in a graphic way the wholesale and indiscriminate infiltration of non-conforming uses into the middle and lower value residential districts, bringing with them the speculative values and residential depreciation that are the forerunners of blight or slum conditions. The fact that there are about 2,000 amendments to existing residential bylaws places the responsibility for this condition generally upon the government of the city.[12]

Having delivered this broadside at the politicians and their populist traditions they then sought a solution in the reform ideology:

> If the proposed new by-law is to achieve its purpose, it must be definitely protected with provisions that make its amendment impossible except where it can be shown to be in the general public interest to do so.[13]

The original reformist urge for the Zoning By-law came from the civic administration rather than the city council.

Like the original demand for a zoning by-law, the Independent Committee on Zoning also contained elements of the populist and reform ideologies with the latter dominating. The concept of a panel of experts who could review the proposals, and adjudicate citizen demands for changes in the general public interest, is reformist. On the other hand, the populist tradition was recognized in the need to listen to individual and neighbourhood objections to the provisions of the by-law, and to implement changes where necessary. Even this need was justified by reform principles that citizens should be fully acquainted with the advantages to the general public interest if the by-law was passed, and that if objections were not headed off at this stage, they may delay indefinitely the approval of the by-law by the Ontario Municipal Board. The ICZ would take the "politics" out of zoning.

The precise nature of the relationship between planning and zoning was debated by the ICZ. The majority of the ICZ recognized that the original demand had not been for a zoning by-law, but for a consolidation of the existing restrictions. They saw a close relationship between planning and zoning with their opinion that the adoption of the Zoning By-law would provide a good foundation on which to build by stabilizing the existing pattern of land uses and property values. "You have got to stabilize conditions and then do your planning because planning isn't a matter of a year,"[14] they commented. Also, they suggested that the duties of the Board of Appeals be entrusted to the City Planning Board which would be interested in all matters relating to the use of the land. In all other ways their report was consistent with the contemporary planning values such as the identification of a general public interest, the stabilization and control of change, and if nothing else, the elimination of the confusion and uncertainty surrounding existing restrictions. For the majority of the Committee, the Zoning By-law was a holding operation and an essential forerunner to a city plan.

One member of the ICZ, J. S. Galbraith, felt that zoning should follow a city plan, an opinion which he expressed at the ICZ's public meetings in 1941, before the City Planning Board was established. He felt that the enactment of a zoning scheme which was not part of planning was exceedingly dangerous, and based his view on a conception of planning which itself was based on a conception of change in the city which separated physical change from social and economic change:

> Changes constantly take place in the physical structure of a progressive community. The changes in the physical structure automatically create changes in the community's social and economic structures. Planning is the means employed to find out the effects of these changes and to work out the relationship which ought to exist *in and among* the physical, social, and economic structures of the community.[15]

He considered zoning to be a part of planning, which if used alone might force changes in the physical structure that would have damag-

ing effects on the city's social and economic structures. By planning
and zoning together it was "possible to predetermine and create a
design to direct and control future changes in the city's physical
structure, so that they will conform to a pattern that is also socially
and economically sound".[16] Galbraith was a civil engineer, and as
such he saw zoning as a response to a problem in the overall physical
design of the city rather than a response to a problem produced by
externalities in the property market.

Galbraith's view prevailed and the ICZ's draft by-law was referred
to the Planning Board which then revised it in conjunction with the
preparation of its Master Plan. In its 1943 Plan, the Board recommended immediate adoption of the Zoning By-law to which it had
made about fifty minor amendments. Nevertheless, although the Zoning By-law might be enacted, and the Master Plan approved in principle, the latter could have no official or legal status because the Planning Board had not been granted power by the province. If the
Zoning By-law were implemented its subordinate role to a city plan
would largely disappear.

Although the Planning Board's consideration of the ICZ's report was
consistent with planning values, it also enabled the City Councillors to
defer consideration of the Zoning By-law for a further eighteen
months, and so to postpone the discussion of a measure which would
have produced an upheaval in their established traditions. Furthermore, when Council eventually passed the Zoning By-law it was not
subordinate to a legal master plan and would be quite amenable to
the demands of the neighbourhood-based traditions of the residential
restrictions. This clash of the Reformist and Populist ideologies in the
implementation of the Zoning By-law was postponed for a decade,
however.

The accommodation of the contrasting Tory and Populist values
continued after the passage of the Planning Act in Ontario in 1946. It
was in large part a response to the City Planning Board of Toronto's
lack of power to implement its master plan, and demands for this
power came not only from the planners themselves as they sought to
extend their control,[17] with its Tory ideology, but also from the politicians of the city who were anxious to take advantage of the National
Housing Act's grants for slum clearance in cities which were adequately planned with appropriate zoning regulations. At the same
time, the city's proposals for urban renewal were based on the recommendations of the City Planning Board's Master Plan, and its 1944
Report.

The Planning Act gave appointed planning boards the power to prepare official plans, which were defined, in part, as:

> showing a programme of future development, including the regulation of the use of land, buildings or structures or the location of buildings and structures in the planning area and any other feature designed to secure the health, safety, convenience, and welfare of the inhabitants.[18]

This provision demanded a ruling on the relationship of the Zoning By-law to an official plan. The City Solicitor determined that the plan and the by-law could be separate, so that the plan would be confined to matters not dealt with in the by-law, which would be administered by the City Council. On the other hand, he advised, if the Zoning By-law were incorporated in the official plan, it would be subordinate to that plan, and administered by the Planning Board.[19] City Council was faced with a clear choice: to enact and administer by itself a Zoning By-law separate from the official plan, which would continue the neighbourhood-based, Populist traditions of the restrictions, or to pass control of zoning to the Planning Board and so remove a vital link between City Hall and the neighbourhoods. Controller Smith, who was on the Committee then reviewing the Zoning By-law, recommended the former course, because the Planning Board should be concerned with matters of general policy rather than detailed "day-by-day" administration, and because the public would prefer zoning regulations to be administered by elected representatives of the people.[20] The Planning Board, understandably enough, disagreed because "the best interest of the city" would be served by the incorporation of all land-use regulations in the official plan, largely because the powers of the Planning Act were far broader than the zoning enabling legislation in the Municipal Act.[21]

The City Council compromised by passing the task of revising the Zoning By-law to the Planning Board, which would co-ordinate the zoning regulations with the official plan, but making the by-law separate from the plan and under the Council's jurisdiction. The locus of control would remain with the Council.

The enactment of the Zoning By-law in 1952 enabled City Council to assert its dominance in the control of land-use regulations in the city, and maintain many of the Populist traditions associated with the residential restrictions. As might be expected, the 1949 official plan envisaged the immediate enactment of a Zoning By-law which would implement in detail the generalized land-use plan. By setting out only broad divisions of use, such as residential, commercial, and industrial, the Board gave the City considerable discretion over the division of uses and densities within these categories. This discretion in implementation was rational from a planning point of view, but it weakened the political position of the Planning Board.

When the Planning Board submitted the Zoning By-law to the Property Committee it was accompanied by a letter from le May outlining the purpose of the by-law. Although this letter stressed the importance of the by-law's role as an essential element in the City's official plan, it also contained elements of continuity with the old residential restrictions. The ultimate value of the plan and the by-law was couched in terms of property values:

> it needs no argument to prove that selfish or speculative interests in individual parcels of land can destroy the amenities of residential areas and produce a heterogeneous mixture of conflicting uses that not only depresses land values and assessments, but also paves the way for the destruction of moral and social values through the value of the home. Security is the right of every property owner against the devaluating effect of some use of adjoining property that is inconsistent with the character of the area.[22]

This was the kind of argument with which property owners of the pre-Zoning By-law era were perfectly familiar, because the interests at stake were those of individuals and neighbourhoods, not those of the "general public". Le May also reiterated a theme which had dominated the Zoning By-law since 1936. No drastic changes in land use would result. The by-law was

> in effect a catalogue of existing predominant land uses supported by stringent regulations designed to not only prevent further deterioration, but also to create a confidence in respect to future conditions that will justify improvement.[23]

Like the residential restrictions the Zoning By-law would stress existing and past conditions, rather than the direction of future change.

The density provisions of the Planning Board's draft Zoning By-law were not based on the residential restrictions, although they were roughly consistent with existing development. The provisions were criticized by the Buildings Commissioner, especially as they related to commercial buildings and apartment houses. He felt that in their proposed form the density regulations would reduce the building program in the city.[24] They were also criticized by the Board of Trade, which in previous years had been instrumental in institutionalizing planning in the city. The City Council responded to these criticisms by raising the floor area ratio for the highest density zones from nine to twelve times permissible coverage, before passing the Zoning By-law. Also, when the amendments were passed in 1953, City Council, with no recommendation from the Planning Board, the Property Committee, or the City officials, changed the density provisions for apartment buildings to allow up to seven times coverage regardless of the density zone the building was in. These changes were not a response to neighbourhood demands, but to city-wide interests whose major goal was economic growth rather than the general health and welfare of the community with which the Planning Board was concerned.

The residential restrictions continued to operate while the Zoning By-law was being prepared after 1936, ensuring that the neighbourhood basis of these restrictions was always visible. Although the Planning Commissioner and the Planning Board sometimes made recommendations about applications for changes in the restrictions, according to the proposals of the draft zoning by-laws, the decision outcomes were largely based on local opinion as shown in polls. Neighbourhood control over land-use regulations remained intact.

A further Tory influence threatened the restrictions in 1941, when the City Solicitor ruled that zoning changes could only be made in accordance with the general public interest, after changes in the Municipal Act that year. This brought, in theory at least, an end to the spot rezoning of specific properties for individual benefit, which had prevailed in the previous thirty-seven years. City Council reacted to this requirement by unsuccessfully attempting to have the provision changed, especially during the war years, when additional housing was urgently required, but the wholesale breakdown of the existing restrictions was felt to be too great a price to pay. Council then adopted other strategies. It defined the general public interest in very restricted spatial terms, so that only block faces, or portions thereof, were rezoned. Also, the new uses permitted were stated very specifically, so that most proposed changes from residential to non-residential uses, still required an amendment to the restriction.

In summary, in the 1940s, the planning movement in Toronto attempted to use zoning as an instrument of the master plan to regulate land use in the public interest, but this meant taking an existing set of regulations and changing their purpose, from the protection of neighbourhoods and property values therein, to the control of the proportions and arrangement of land uses in the whole city according to the plan. "The goal of the planning movement . . . was not to create a new programme, but to redirect thinking about an established one, to encourage council to see zoning as the enforcement arm of the official plan, rather than a line programme pursuing its own distinctive goals."[25] The realization of this goal was not easily produced, if it was at all. On one hand, the City entrusted the Planning Board with the task of revising the 1944 By-law both before and after its passage, and preparing the 1952 By-law, so its potential input to the regulations was large. On the other hand, several factors militated against the change being realized. First, the City Council assigned the administration of the zoning regulations to the Property Committee rather than the Planning Board. Second, the 1944 By-law originated as a consolidation and revision of the existing restrictions, and the overall preservation of existing patterns of land use was a dominant theme of the production of the Zoning By-law. Third, the high level of neighbourhood input into the administration of the residential restrictions continued during this period. Fourth, even though it was justified in planning terms, the goal of the Zoning By-law was the protection of property values, the same as the residential restrictions.

Although it was centralized for administrative efficiency in one by-law, and theoretically connected to the official plan, both in its provisions and administration, the Zoning By-law also represented a continuation of the residential restrictions. The extent to which it would become an old tool with a new purpose would be determined in its implementation.

ZONING AND PLANNING: A NEW RELATIONSHIP, 1954–1970

In the early 1950s, following the long construction drought of the depression and the war, the high-rise apartment boom came to Toronto. These buildings were a visible sign of growth and progress, and a source of increased assessment revenues. For both symbolic and fiscal reasons, City Council promoted high-rise development, even if it overrode the interests of neighbourhoods as the Zoning By-law intended them to be preserved, in the tradition of the residential restrictions. Instead of neighbourhood interests being supported by the Council, they were now supported by the Planning Board,[26] so that in the conflict over high-rise development, the old Populist – Tory distinction became irrelevant. Where zoning was not concerned with high-rise development, this distinction and the merging of the two traditions was still apparent, and in the discussion that follows these two separate themes (high-rise and non-high-rise) will be pursued.

The 1952 Zoning By-law permitted, if certain conditions were complied with, the erection of apartment buildings in R.1, R.1A, and R.2

areas, and in 1954 and 1955 many applications were made to build
them. Ratepayer groups in affected areas, basically north of Bloor
between Bathurst and the Don, banded together in protest, and City
Council responded with some amendments to the bulk of building
regulations in R. districts. The Ontario Municipal Board gave these
amendment temporary approval so that the Planning Board could
report and propose new standards for all R. districts. Eventually, the
Board produced proposals for new residential standards which increased the parking requirements in apartment houses, and revised
the density and maximum permissible floor area of buildings. The
new regulations were generally approved by the neighbourhood
groups which first demanded them, for apartment development was
excluded from R.1 areas and much higher standards were required in
R.1A and R.2 zones. The only opposition to the new standards at the
Ontario Municipal Board hearings came from the Toronto Real Estate
Board and the Metropolitan Toronto Apartment Owners' Association,
and the substance of their opposition was largely discounted by the
Board. Although these were general regulations, the demands for their
change had arisen from a group of neighbourhoods, which had supported the Planning Board, and used it to protect their interests and
undoubtedly the value of their property. At the same time as the
revised restrictions tightened up on apartment construction in R.1 and
R.2 areas, they permitted the development of very tall buildings on
large lots, particularly in downtown R.4 areas. In this sense, the
growth goals of the Council were not thwarted.

Although the revised residential standards offered "protection" in
theory, in practice pressures for the development of high-rise buildings continued, and developers continued to apply for amendments to
the regulations. Instead of uniformly supporting the by-law and rejecting these applications—a practice which had been completely foreign
to the administration of the residential restrictions—the city used the
application as an opportunity to control details of development, such
as layout and general appearance. "The use of the by-law thus
evolved into a form of development control, with the specific by-law
amendment becoming a kind of individual development permit."[27] In
a sense, zoning simply "froze" the use of the land until a future
decision on its use was made. Zoning used in this way did not provide
the certainty over future use and property values of the residential
restrictions. City Council made full use of the flexibility inherent in
the broad definitions of land uses in the official plan and the discretion accorded to the Zoning By-law. By allowing development to

occur it was acting according to what it defined as the interests of the city as a whole, rather than those of the localities which had previously been so important.

Besides apartment development, there were many other zoning amendments applying to small areas, according to the procedures developed after 1941. The Planning Board also played an integral role in the amendment process by making a report on most applications, while neighbourhood polls were less common. The experience of one small neighbourhood in the city, the East Annex, shows that in seventeen out of eighteen applications which the Planning Board reported upon, its recommendation was followed by City Council.[28] Sixteen of these were refusals. The area had a strong ratepayers' association, which also opposed zoning changes, so it is difficult to determine the influence of one or the other. In general, the role of the Planning Board in the rezoning process became firmly institutionalized for the first time, so further breaking down the Populist tradition of the restrictions before 1954.

The evidence of the East Annex decisions suggests that the neighbourhood residents, as might be expected, still adopted local interests as a guideline, and property values were the best indicator of that interest. Inevitably, this produced a split between those who wanted a low-to-medium density neighbourhood and others who wanted to sell to developers for high-density residential and commercial uses. The former "protected" all existing residential values; the latter would have caused some to rise but others to fall. The protectors were initially more successful because they had the support of the Planning Board, and without concrete proposals for redevelopment City Council was not prepared to make the changes.

Since the late 1950s, as part of the planning process in the city, the Planning Board has produced a series of district plans, which required an amendment to the Zoning By-law to take effect. The first of these plans, that for the Annex, exemplifies this process. It originated after a group of residents and owners attempted to have a small area in the southeast of the neighbourhood rezoned from R.2 to R.4A. The Planning Board produced a "district appraisal" with its proposals, which were then studied and discussed by ratepayers' groups and residents. Initially, many residents and the Annex Ratepayers' Association disagreed with some recommendations, particularly those which either increased densities or rezoned areas to permit a wider range of uses. Eventually, when the Buildings and Development Committee considered the proposals, a compromise was reached, partly it seems because of the ratepayers' respect for the city's chief planner, Lawson. The Chairman of the ARA summarized his Association's feelings:

[the ARA] . . . fully endorses and supports the zoning plan for the Annex as approved in its final version by the Committee on Buildings and Development. While the plan does not satisfy all of our original hopes for the maintenance of residential standards in this community, we feel it is a fair and workable compromise among the many viewpoints put forward.[29]

Although major public works (subways, expressways) were considered in the plan, in this case planning was largely zoning. The official plan, with its organic view of the city, could afford to relegate zoning to a subsidiary role (even though in the 1950s and 1960s zoning largely superceded the plan), but in neighbourhood or district plans, virtually all planning was land-use planning, and land-use planning at this level of detail was zoning. Neighbourhoods could afford to neglect or ignore the official plan's land-use provisions, but not those of the district plan, and in the case of the Annex, the residents played an important role in determining the final outcome. Although the role of the Planning Board in the zoning process had increased, that of the neighbourhood had not diminished. While the old links between the neighbourhood and the City Council had remained, new ones between the neighbourhood and the Planning Board had developed, partly as a neighbourhood response to the institutionalization of the Board in the rezoning process, and partly as a result of the Board's efforts to protect and stabilize low-density neighbourhoods.

Between 1966 and 1969, a new official plan was developed and adopted by the City of Toronto. It distinguished between high- and low-density residential areas, and an important element of the plan concerned the provision of apartment accommodation for the anticipated growth in population by 1981. The delineation of areas of proposed apartment construction and associated densities was a formal recognition by the Planning Board of the reality of Toronto's residential development in the previous decade. Although the proposals were made by the Board in 1966 and justified in terms acceptable to the planners, they were in large measure an institutionalization of the City Council's policies since the early 1950s.

In some areas the plan proposed changes which required an immediate change in the Zoning By-law, but by and large changes in the neighbourhoods were largely left to be determined by district plans, so that for most areas the existing zoning would continue. Planning became much more of a determinant of zoning than in 1949. While the district plans and the citizen participation movement were ensuring neighbourhoods continued control over zoning, the official plan was removing some of that control and shaping land-use regulation into a coherent whole in the city.

During the 1950s and 1960s, planning as a program became more institutionalized and accepted in Toronto. Although zoning retained elements of the residential restrictions (it was still used to protect property values, and it was still partly neighbourhood based) it became more subservient to planning. In the 1969 official plan the role of the zoning regulations in facilitating the provision of apartment housing was spelled out in detail, but at the same time the district plans left some discretion in the neighbourhoods. In general the role of zoning as a neighbourhood-based device for the protection of property values and residential "character" was retained, as the revised residential standards, the rezoning process, and the district plans indicate. However, the increased institutional strength of planning and the use of development-control zoning broadened the role of zoning. The Planning Board used it to protect neighbourhoods as it had always intended while the City Council used it to promote high-density development. In the 1969 plan these two uses were combined, in a manner satisfactory to both the Board and the Council, and to the neighbourhoods. Zoning had been integrated with the planning process; the old tool had retained its original purpose, but also gained new ones.

CONCLUSION

The origins of both planning and zoning in Toronto can be placed in the broader context of urban North America around the turn of the twentieth century. They were not related in Toronto for the first forty years of the century, for both had different purposes, served different interests, and developed from different political traditions. Populist, protective, and neighbourhood-based, zoning contrasted strongly with the rational, reformist planning movement which "served" the general public. After 1940, the planning movement in Toronto attempted to remodel the zoning institution to serve its own purposes, by developing a comprehensive Zoning By-law to implement the generalized land-use pattern of the official plan. The City Council, and ultimately the province, refused to cede control of zoning to the Planning Board, and until 1954 the old system of residential restrictions continued as the major mechanism of land-use control. The traditions and procedures associated with these restrictions were not abandoned when they were superseded by the Zoning By-law in 1954, but the increased institutional strength of planning used zoning more and more for its own purposes, so that by 1970 zoning was being used to serve both neighbourhood interests and those of the "general public" including developers of high-rise apartment buildings. The extent to which it served either depended upon the strength of neighbourhood interests, those of the Planning Board, those of City Council, and the kinds of changes occurring in the neighbourhood. By 1970, zoning in the City of Toronto represented a synthesis of the historic system of residential restrictions and the growing strength of the planning function.

NOTES

1. H. Kaplan, "Origins of Planning Programmes in Montreal, Toronto, and Winnipeg: A Study in the Culture, Structure and Evolution of Municipal Political Systems", paper presented at a seminar held by Ministry of State for Urban Affairs (Ottawa, September, 1973), pp. 15 – 16.

2. Ibid., p. 16.

3. The police power is "the exercise of the sovereign right of government to promote order safety health morals and the general welfare of society within constitutional limits". Corpus Juris Secundum Sec. 174, quoted by R. H. Platt, The Open Space Decision Process, University of Chicago, Department of Geography, Research Series, No. 142 (Chicago, 1972), p. 85. Platt observes (p. 85), "The test of 'reasonableness' is . . . the constitutional standard for the exercise of the police power".

4. German zoning is discussed more fully in, T. H. Logan, "The Americanization of German zoning", Journal of the American Institute of Planners, vol. 42 (1976): 377-85.

5. M. C. Scott, American City Planning Since 1890 (Berkeley, 1969), p. 195.

6. S. I. Toll, Zoned American (New York, 1969), p. 280.

7. Statutes of Ontario, 4 Edw. VII, c. 22, s. 19.

8. Toronto City Council, 1927 Minutes, App. A, p. 1609. Mr. F. C. Carter, on behalf of the Lawrence Park Property Protective Association, to Property Committee.

9. For details on early city planning in Toronto, see C. F. Knappe, "The Development of Planning in Toronto, 1893 – 1922: A Survey". MA research paper, University of Toronto (1974).

10. City Planning Board of Toronto, Annual Report (1942), p. 7.

11. Toronto City Council, Property Committee, 1934 Minutes, Minute No. 621.

12. Toronto City Council, 1939 Minutes, App. A, p. 1043.

13. Ibid.

14. Toronto City Council, Property Committee, 1943 Minutes, Minute No. 176 App. E, Report of the Independent Committee on Zoning.

15. Ibid., App. F. Minority Report of J. S. Galbraith.

16. Ibid.

17. The role of professional planners in lobbying for the Act is briefly outlined in A. J. Dakin, Toronto Planning: A Planning Review of the Legal and Jurisdictional Contexts from 1912 to 1970, University of Toronto, Department of Urban and Regional Planning, Papers on Planning and Design, No. 3 (Toronto, 1974), p. 13-14.

18. Statutes of Ontario, 10 Geo. VI, c. 71, s. 1(g).

19. City Solicitor to Commissioner of City Planning, September 25, 1946. Held in City of Toronto Archives, File 2.1.8 – 05, No. 26(2).

20. Toronto City Council, Board of Control, 1946 Minutes, Minute No. 2932, Memorandum from Controller

Smith. Held in City of Toronto Archives, File 2.1.8 – 05, No. 26(2).

21. City of Toronto Planning Board, *1946 Report*, p. 17.

22. le May to Property Committee, June 18, 1951, p. 2. Held in City of Toronto Archives, File 2.1.8 – 05, No. 26(2).

23. Ibid., p. 3.

24. Toronto City Council, Property Committee, *1951 Minutes*, Minute No. 586.

25. Kaplan, "Origins of planning programmes", fn 1, p. 35.

26. One writer comments: "To a great extent, the fact that Toronto is still a city of houses, with tree-lined neighbourhoods near the downtown, is due to [the Planning Commissioner's] refusal to yield to the pressure from Council to approve every development proposal". See G. Fraser "Planning *vs.* Development: Placing Bets on Toronto's Future", in A. Powell, ed., *The City: Attacking Modern Myths* (Toronto, 1972), p. 107.

27. Dakin, *Toronto Planning*, fn 17, p. 32.

28. Data from the Rezoning Application Files, 1954 – 1970. Held in Central Records Office, City Hall, Toronto.

29. A. Wood, Chairman ARA, to Mayor and City Council, March 28, 1960, in ARA Papers, held in City of Toronto Municipal Reference Library, City Hall, Toronto.

IV.

A Brief Guide to Canadian Urban Studies

a) Reading and Research

1. INTRODUCTION

2. NEWSLETTERS AND JOURNALS

   A. *Urban History Review/Revue d'histoire urbaine*
   B. *Urban Focus*
   C. *City Magazine*
   D. *Plan Canada*
   E. *Urban Forum/Colloque urbaine*
   F. *Contact: Journal of Urban and Environmental Affairs*
   G. *Urban History Yearbook*
   H. *Journal of Urban History*
   I. *Urbanism – Past and Present*
   J. *Urban Canada Index*

3. MINISTRY OF STATE FOR URBAN AFFAIRS

   A. Information Resource Service
   B. Publications and Editorial Services
   C. Urban Profile Series
   D. Urban Prospects Series

4. OTHER RESOURCES

   A. Urban Research Council
   B. Community Planning Association of Canada
   C. Institute of Urban Studies
   D. History of Canadian Cities Series
   E. Institute of Local Government
   F. Urban Profile Slide Series
   G. Urban Studies Series
   H. Centre for Urban and Community Studies
   I. Canadian Federation of Mayors and Municipalities
   J. Bureau of Municipal Research

1. INTRODUCTION

This guide is designed to introduce students to the vast field of urban studies. The following sections cover much of the material available to the student of the Canadian city. It is obvious, however, that in a topic as broad as is urban studies a good deal of the resources available could not be covered here. Readers are, therefore, directed to two more comprehensive guides to the field. They are:

1. *Directory of Canadian Urban Information Resources*. This guide is an annual publication of the Ministry of State for Urban Affairs and is available, free of charge, from the Information Resource Service, Ministry of State for Urban Affairs, Ottawa, K1A 0P6. The Directory has four main sections: Urban Literature; Libraries, Archives, and Information Centres; Urban Organizations; and Universities.

2. Alan F. J. Artibise, "Canadian Urban Studies", *Communiqué: Canadian Studies*, vol. 3, no. 3 (April 1977): 1-130. This special issue of *Communiqué* is available from the Association of Canadian Community Colleges, 651 Warden Avenue, Scarborough, Ontario, M1L 3Z6. The issue includes sections on Newsletters and Journals; Ministry of State for Urban Affairs; Public Archives of Canada; Archives, Libraries, and Information Centres; Audio-Visual Resources; Other Resources; and an extensive select bibliography of Canadian Urban Studies organized both topically and by city and region.

2. NEWSLETTERS AND JOURNALS

The rapid growth of the field of urban studies in Canada and in other countries is nowhere more apparent than in the growing number of periodicals devoted to urban themes. The following list of journals is obviously a selective one; it contains only those journals and newsletters that are devoted almost exclusively to urban topics. Urban-studies specialists should be familiar with all of them since they provide the best means of keeping abreast of this rapidly developing field. At the same time, other journals should not be neglected since they often contain material dealing with the broad field of urban studies. An examination of the Bibliography in this guide will indicate those journals that do carry urban material.

A.   *Urban History Review/Revue d'histoire urbaine* (1972 –)
     Publisher: National Museums of Canada,
                  360 Lisgar Street,
                  Ottawa, Ontario,
                  K1A 0M8

     Editor: Alan F. J. Artibise

     Frequency: three issues per year

     Subscription Rate: $5.00 per year

     Comments: This bilingual journal is the best single source of
     information on urban studies in Canada. It contains informa-
     tion on a variety of subjects regarding the development of
     urban Canada. The *Review* includes both long and short arti-
     cles, book reviews, book notes, archival notes, conference infor-
     mation, notes on photographic collections, etc. Despite its title,
     the *Urban History Review* is not restricted to historical material
     since the issues contain much that is of value to everyone
     interested in urban Canada. The *Review* also publishes theme
     issues. The ones published to date include "The Canadian City
     in the Nineteenth Century" and "Urban Reform in Canada".

B.   *Urban Focus* (1972 –)
     Publisher: Institute of Local Government,
                  Queen's University,
                  99 University Avenue,
                  Kingston, Ontario,
                  K7L 3N6

     Editor: T. J. Plunkett

     Frequency: five issues per year

     Subscription Rate: $5.00 per year

     Comments: The purpose of *Urban Focus* is to provide a vehicle
     for the discussion and development of viewpoints regarding the
     problems of urban government in a federal system. It is pub-
     lished under the joint sponsorship of the Institute of Local
     Government and the Institute of Intergovernmental Relations.
     The format of *Urban Focus* is that of a newsletter; it is usually
     6-10 pages in length and consists of short articles, notes, and
     comments. Some issues also contain material on the historical
     development of urban Canada.

C. *City Magazine* (1974 –)

   Publisher: Charlottetown Group Publishing Inc.,
               35 Britain Street,
               Toronto, Ontario,
               M5A 1R7

   Editorial Board: G. Baird, K. Bladen, R. Clark, K. Gerecke, D. Gutstein, J. Lorimer, E. Ross, A. Stewart, and V. Wyatt.

   Frequency: eight issues per year

   Subscription Rate: $7.00 per year

   Comments: This is the best magazine dealing with current urban affairs in Canada. Besides reporting on city politics, architecture, planning, community organizing, housing, and land development in its main articles, *City Magazine* has regular features such as book reviews and "City News" and "City Diary" which provide capsule comments on developments in cities across Canada.

D. *Plan Canada* (1959 –)

   Publisher: Canadian Institute of Planners,
               Suite 30, 46 Elgin Street,
               Ottawa, Ontario,
               K1P 5K6

   Editor: Gerald Hodge

   Frequency: three issues per year

   Subscription Rate: $15.00 per year

   Comments: Plan Canada is the journal of the Institute of Planners. Most of the articles carried in the journal deal with planning and related areas but *Plan Canada* also carries articles on other topics broadly connected with urban development. Regular features also include a book review section, lists of recent Canadian municipal documents, listings of articles in other journals, and an historical section entitled "From Our Past".

E. *Urban Forum/Colloque urbaine* (1975 –)

   Publisher: Urban Research Council of Canada,
               251 Laurier Avenue West,
               Ottawa, Ontario,
               K1P 5J6

> *Editor:* Vernon Lang
>
> *Frequency:* four issues per year
>
> *Subscription Rate:* $3.00 per year
>
> *Comments:* The *Urban Forum* is published by the Urban Research Council of Canada and supersedes the *Urban Research Bulletin*. Besides carrying a number of feature articles, the *Urban Forum* contains interviews, book reviews, a calendar of events, and a section on studies in progress. Recent articles have dealt with land use, planning, architecture, conservation, and urban growth.

F. *Contact: Journal of Urban and Environmental Affairs* (1968 –)

> *Publisher:* Faculty of Environmental Studies,
> University of Waterloo,
> Waterloo, Ontario,
> N2L 3G1
>
> *Editor:* N. E. P. Pressman
>
> *Frequency:* four issues per year
>
> *Subscription Rate:* $12.00 per year
>
> *Comments: Contact* is published by the Faculty of Environmental Studies and the School of Urban and Regional Planning, University of Waterloo. Its aim is to provide current information to those who are engaged systematically in relating humankind to its environment and resolving environmental dilemmas. Issues include feature articles, book reviews, a section on international developments, and reports on other journals, conferences, and symposia.

G. *Urban History Yearbook* (1974 –)

> *Publisher:* Leicester University Press,
> University of Leicester,
> Leicester, England,
> LE1 7RH
>
> *Editor:* David Reeder
>
> *Frequency:* one issue per year
>
> *Subscription Rate:* $10.00 per year (approx.)
>
> *Comments:* The *Yearbook* is a more formal and extensive elaboration of the *Urban History Newsletter*, begun more than a decade ago by Professor H. J. Dyos. It includes articles, notes

on urban history meetings, synopses of experiments in urban history, reviews of books on the urban past, an extensive current bibliography, and a massive annual survey and register of research in progress. The *Yearbook* has correspondents from around the world and makes a successful effort to deal with developments in the field on an international scale. The Canadian correspondent is Professor Gilbert A. Stelter, Department of History, University of Guelph, Guelph, Ontario, N1G 2W1.

H.   *Journal of Urban History* (1974 –)
     Publisher: Sage Publications,
                P.O. Box 776,
                Beverly Hills, Calif. 90212
     Editor: Blaine A. Brownell
     Frequency: four issues per year
     Subscription Rate: $12.00 per year
     Comments: The *Journal of Urban History* is the major scholarly journal in the field of urban history in North America. In the introductory editorial, the editor pointed out that "urban history is a big tent" and went on to point out that whether potential articles dealt with specific cities, the relationship of cities to broader regions, new research techniques or methodologies, interdisciplinary approaches, comparative studies, or historiography, they would all be included in the *JUH*. Based on issues published to date, this broadly inclusive policy has been followed. The *JUH* also has an excellent book review section that encompasses works done in the field of urban history throughout the world.

I.   *Urbanism—Past and Present* (1975 –)
     Publisher: Department of History,
                University of Wisconsin—Milwaukee,
                P.O. Box 413,
                Milwaukee, Wisconsin, 53201
     Editor: Bruce Fetter
     Frequency: two issues per year
     Subscription Rate: $5.00 per year
     Comments: Urbanism—Past and Present supercedes the Urban History Group *Newsletter* which was published between 1954

and 1975. The new journal contains articles presenting topical analysis of basic urban problems, theoretical interpretations of urbanism, and the results of specific urban-related research. A major objective is to present scholarly material to aid in understanding contemporary urban problems. A regular feature of the journal are comments about the articles by other specialists. Through such comments the editors hope to encourage cross-fertilization of urban studies among the various social sciences and humanities. *Urbanism—Past and Present* also contains an international bibliography of urban studies in each issue.

J. *Urban Canada Index* (1977 –)
    Publisher: Micromedia Limited,
                 Box 502, Station S,
                 Toronto, Ontario,
                 M5M 4L8

    Editor: Linda Petherick

    Frequency: four issues per year

    Subscription Rate: $75.00 per year

    Comments: The *Urban Canada Index* covers publications issued in Canada in the field of urban and regional planning and development. It is produced quarterly with an annual cumulation. The *Index* deals with government and non-government, and monograph and serial publications. The *Urban Canada* service began with monographs issued in 1976 and serials issued from January 1977.

3. MINISTRY OF STATE FOR URBAN AFFAIRS
    A. *Information Resource Service*
        The Information Resource Service is the information and documentation centre for the Ministry. The current holdings of the Service include 5,000 books, 2,500 government documents, and 300 serials. The collection includes works on urban and regional planning, housing, transportation, urban economics, sociology, urban indicators, environment, land use, political and administrative structures, and intergovernmental relations. It also includes municipal documents from a number of Canadian cities consisting of official plans, land-use plans, enabling legislation, etc.

The Service responds to public inquiries made to the Ministry. Queries should be directed to:

> Information Resource Service,
> Ministry of State for Urban Affairs,
> Ottawa, Ontario,
> K1A 0P6

B. *Publications and Editorial Services*

The Ministry has a growing number of reports, books, and articles available to urban specialists. Many of these are available free of charge. By writing the Ministry, individuals, organizations, and libraries can be placed on the mailing list and will receive news releases, lists of publications, etc.

C. *Urban Profile Series*

In 1973, the Ministry provided a research grant to a group from the Université du Québec à Montréal for a factual study of ten Canadian urban regions. The ten regions were chosen on the basis of 1971 Census data. The common thread to the governing of these ten centres is the presence of some two-tier form of government, ranging from the urban community model in Montréal and Québec, to the regional planning commissions of Alberta, to the regional government system introduced in Ontario over the past few years.

Publication of the Profiles was prompted by the enthusiasm and recommendations of those local elected and administrative officials who assisted the research team as well as the recognized need to make municipal information more generally available. The series was published over a period beginning in November 1974 and ending in July 1975.

A researcher is presently undertaking the preparation of an update booklet for each Profile, reviewing the most important changes which have occurred in each region as well as incorporating new statistical information and including a bibliography of recent reports and studies.

The ten volumes published in the Profile series are listed below. All were compiled by a team consisting of André Bernard, Jacques Léveillé, and Guy Lord. They are available from the Publications Branch of the Ministry. All titles are also available in separate French editions.

Profile: Halifax – Dartmouth. The Political and Administrative Structures of the Metropolitan Region of Halifax – Dartmouth. 1974.

Profile: Québec. The Political and Administrative Structures of the Metropolitan Region of Québec. 1975.

Profile: Montréal. The Political and Administrative Structures of the Metropolitan Region of Montréal. 1974.

Profile: Ottawa – Hull. The Political and Administrative Structures of the Metropolitan Region of Ottawa – Hull. 1974.

Profile: Toronto. The Political and Administrative Structures of the Metropolitan Region of Toronto. 1975.

Profile: Hamilton – Wentworth. The Political and Administrative Structures of the Metropolitan Region of Hamilton – Wentworth. 1975.

Profile: Winnipeg. The Political and Administrative Structures of the Metropolitan Region of Winnipeg. 1975.

Profile: Calgary. The Political and Administrative Structures of the Metropolitan Region of Calgary. 1975.

Profile: Edmonton. The Political and Administrative Structures of the Metropolitan Region of Edmonton. 1974.

Profile: Vancouver. The Political and Administrative Structures of the Metropolitan Region of Vancouver. 1975.

D. *Urban Prospects Series*

The Urban Prospects Series, published by Macmillan of Canada for the Ministry of State for Urban Affairs, is intended to provoke discussions and debate on important urban issues. As the name implies, the Urban Prospects series focuses primarily on current issues facing Canadian urban society and the volumes are prospective, concerned with the future rather than the past. The goal of the series is to provide an opportunity for authors to present their ideas and views on the wide range of urban issues which are of concern to decision makers and policy planners in Canadian government.

The series contains twelve volumes, all published in either 1975 or 1976. A complete list of the volumes follows:

Jackson, C. I., ed. *Canadian Settlements—Perspectives*. 1975.

Burke, C. D. *The Parasites Outnumber the Hosts: A Review of Some Economic Trends and Their Impact on Public Policy for Urban, Regional and National Economic Development*. 1975.

Coleman, A. *Canadian Settlement and Environmental Planning*. 1976.

Burke, C. D. and D. J. Ireland. *An Urban/Economic Development Strategy for the Atlantic Region*. 1976.

Coopersmith, P., and R. C. Hall. *Heritage By Design*. 1976.

Nelson, R. F. W. *The Illusions of Urban Man*. 1976.

Lash, H. *Planning in a Human Way: Personal Reflections on the Regional Planning Experience in Greater Vancouver*. 1976.

Hamilton, S., and G. Maffini. *The Superior Oracle*. 1976.

Burke, C. J., and D. J. Ireland. *Holding the Line: A Strategy for Canadian Development*. 1976.

Rawson, M. *Ill Fares the Land: Land-Use Management at the Urban/Rural/Resource Edges: The British Columbia Land Commission*. 1976.

Kettle, J. *Hindsight on the Future*. 1976.

Thompson, R. *People Do It All the Time: How Community-Based Enterprises Across Canada are Successfully Meeting the Needs of Their Communities*. 1976.

All twelve volumes are available in separate French editions. To order copies, write the Publications and Editorial Services Division of the Ministry of State for Urban Affairs.

4. OTHER RESOURCES

A. *Urban Research Council*
251 Laurier Avenue West,
Ottawa, Ontario,
K1P 5J6

The Urban Research Council, formerly known as the Canadian Council on Urban and Regional Research, has three major objectives. They are as follows:

1. To identify gaps in knowledge in urban and regional affairs and encourage research in these areas.

2. To facilitate the flow of research information.

3. To bring together concerned organizations, administrators, elected officials, and the academic community to identify issues and areas requiring further research.

The activities of the Urban Research Council include grants-in-aid to research, the organization of conferences, and a publication program which includes a journal called *Urban Forum* and an annual bibliography entitled *Urban and Regional References*.

For details concerning membership, write to the Council at the above address.

B. *Community Planning Association of Canada*
National Office,
415 Gloucester Street,
Ottawa, Ontario,
K1R 5E9

The CPAC was established in 1964. Its objective is to foster cooperation among laymen, professionals, and politicians in directing the growth and planning of Canadian communities. It is a non-governmental association with a membership of over six thousand persons. Membership is open to everyone.

The members of CPAC receive the following services:
1. *CPAC Review*, a national periodical containing current and forthcoming events, book reviews and notices, reports on activities in the urban field, and "case studies" of particular situations or events.
2. Detailed information on events in your particular region from one of nine CPAC divisions spread across the country.
3. Special reports, studies, and publications.
4. *Checklist of Books*, a catalogue of urban titles, specifically Canadian, but with some foreign publishers included. All books are available by mail-order from the CPAC Bookshop. Additional services, such as collection development, central ordering, and advice on books, are also available from CPAC.

C. *Institute of Urban Studies*
University of Winnipeg,
515 Portage Avenue,
Winnipeg, Manitoba,
R3B 2E9

The Institute was established in 1969. It conducts research in a number of areas: policy research in housing and urban affairs, planning in older neighbourhoods, new housing initiatives, performance of the new scheme of local government in

Winnipeg, citizen participation, urban growth, senior citizen housing, and social housing management training.

The Institute also supports citizen-based organizations such as the People's Committee for a Better Neighbourhood and Winnipeg Home Improvement Project; encourages local neighbourhood institutions; undertakes various contract studies including Meals on Wheels Service in Winnipeg, a study of women's concerns about the quality of life in the city, and a study of inner city conditions as related to native people and the police force.

A list of the Institute's programs and publications is available on request.

D. *History of Canadian Cities Series*

In response to a continuing demand for more popular publications, the History Division of the National Museum of Man has undertaken to publish a series of books on a wide range of cities. The purpose of the series is to offer the general public a stimulating insight into the country's urban past. During the next decade, the Museum plans to have published as many as thirty volumes dealing with such varied communities as Montreal and Vancouver, Chicoutimi and Brandon, London and Sydney.

While the series is primarily designed to meet the Museum's commitment to provide informative and attractive publications for the general public, there are obviously a number of other reasons for the project. The projected volumes in the series will fill needs at the university and college levels in urban history and urban studies, and will also be useful for high school students working on their own community in particular and urban Canada in general. Also, since all authors in the series will be following a set pattern in regard to format and presentation, the series should prove to be a major addition to Canadian historiography and to urban studies. At the very least, the series will be a progressive step along the path to a general and comparative history of the Canadian city.

To date, two volumes have been published. They are Alan F. J. Artibise, *Winnipeg: An Illustrated History* (Toronto, 1977) and M. Foran, *Calgary: An Illustrated History* (Toronto, 1978). The volumes are co-published by the National Museum of Man and James Lorimer and Company, and are available from the latter. Other volumes either in press or being prepared include: Toronto, Montreal, Halifax, Saint John, Whitehorse, Kitchener, Fredericton, Ottawa, Vancouver, and Windsor. Further volumes are planned.

For more information, contact:

> Professor Alan F. J. Artibise,
> General Editor,
> History of Canadian Cities Series,
> University of Victoria,
> P.O. Box 1700
> Victoria, B.C.
> V8W 2Y2

E. *Institute of Local Government*
Queen's University,
99 University Avenue,
Kingston, Ontario,
K7L 3N6

The Institute of Local Government was established in 1945 as a centre for research, education, and publication on urban local governments. Current and future programs of the Institute focus on the following:

1. Development of continuing education for individuals concerned with local government, politics, and administration.
2. Development of a continuing program of research and publication with particular emphasis on an inter-disciplinary approach.
3. Participation in programs of instruction by agreement with any department or faculty which considers an understanding of urban government essential to its requirements.
4. Counselling students interested in a career in urban government and assisting in course selections that would aid students in pursuit of such a career.

In recent years these broad objectives have been met through such activities as annual week-long seminars for municipal administrators; three-year correspondence courses for municipal officials in Ontario; seminars for selected groups to deal specifically with urban policy and management issues. The institute has also published a number of occasional papers on specific topics in urban local government, and in conjunction with the Institute of Intergovernmental Relations published *Urban Focus*.

For further information write T. J. Plunkett, Director, at the address above.

F. *Urban Profile Slide Series*

This series is produced by and is available from:

> Education Committee
> Canadian Association of Geographers
> Burnside Hall
> McGill University
> 805 Sherbrooke Street West
> Montreal, Quebec,
> H3A 2K6

Each "kit" in the series contains twenty slides and a booklet with descriptions of the slides and a short essay. This is an on-going series. Sets either available or in preparation include Montreal, Hamilton, Halifax, Toronto, Winnipeg, Thunder Bay, Calgary, Edmonton, and Sherbrooke.

G. *Urban Studies Series*

Clarke, Irwin and Company has published three volumes and a teacher's guide in this series. The published volumes in order of publication are as follows:

Baine, R. P., and A. L. McMurray. *Toronto: An Urban Study.* Toronto and Vancouver. 1970. Maps. Illustrations.

Harvey, E. Roy. *Sydney, Nova Scotia: An Urban Study.* Toronto and Vancouver. 1971. Maps. Illustrations.

Baine, R. P. *Calgary: An Urban Study.* Toronto and Vancouver. 1973. Maps. Illustrations.

Baine, R. P., A. L. McMurray, and E. Roy Harvey. *Urban Studies Series Teacher's Guide.* Toronto and Vancouver. 1974.

According to the general editor of the series, Richard P. Baine, the format followed by these urban studies is a "a major departure from the format of a standard textbook". They are a compilation of selected material in the form of photographs, maps, charts, diagrams, and statistics. There is little expository writing. Each item has something to say about one city (Toronto, Calgary, Sydney) in particular and about cities in general. The volumes are obviously designed for intensive use in urban studies courses.

For further information write:

Educational Department,
Clarke, Irwin and Company,
Clarwin House,
791 St. Clair Avenue West,
Toronto, Ontario,
M6C 1B8

H. *Centre for Urban and Community Studies*
University of Toronto,
150 St. George Street,
Toronto, Ontario,
M5S 1A1

The Centre, established in 1964, has an active program of
research and publication in the following areas: urban development and growth, forecasting urban growth, urban renewal, the
physical environment as attraction and determinant, social effects in housing, urban contact systems, land-use structure and
change, transportation studies, co-operative housing, and urban
data systems. It currently has several bibliographies, major reports, and over ninety research papers published.

The Centre for Urban and Community Studies also has a
program of seminars, lectures, and visiting speakers.

A complete list of publications is available on request.

I. *Canadian Federation of Mayors and Municipalities*
220 Laurier Avenue West
Suite 600
Ottawa, Ontario,
K1P 5J8

This federation of more than twenty regional and provincial
associations is concerned with all areas affecting municipalities,
including finance, economics, social planning, transportation
and communication, environmental protection, community development, cultural affairs, recreation and leisure. The CFMM
organizes conferences; distributes, exchanges, and disseminates
federal and provincial legislation reports, municipal statistics,
and municipal research reports; and co-ordinates, supports,
and undertakes research on municipal affairs. The CFMM also
publishes a monthly information bulletin called *Municipal Report*.

J. *Bureau of Municipal Research*
2 Toronto Street,
Suite 306,
Toronto, Ontario,
M5C 2B6

The Bureau's objectives are to inform the public about governmental policy-making, to stimulate public debate, and to provide constructive evaluation of programs. To this end, it undertakes research in such areas as planning, land use, transportation, urban development, housing, government organization and staffing, taxation, assessment, municipal finance, intergovernmental relations, and environment.

Besides publishing special studies and monographs, the Bureau publishes BMR *Comment*, an occasional newsletter, and *Civic Affairs*. The latter is published three times per year and provides in-depth analysis of key issues.

b) A Selection of General Works on Canadian Urban Development

This list is restricted to general works of a national scope, with an emphasis on twentieth-century politics and planning. Some of the most relevant non-Canadian material is also included.

For references on particular cities or regions, see Alan F. J. Artibise, "Canadian Urban Studies," *Communiqué: Canadian Studies*, Vol. 3 (April, 1977), pp. 51-124.

OUTLINE:

A. General
B. Government and Politics
C. Planning and Architecture
D. Bibliographical and Methodological

A. General

Axworthy, L., and Gillies, J. M., eds. *The City: Canada's Prospects, Canada's Problems*. Toronto: Butterworths, 1973.

Bellan, R. C. *The Evolving City*. Toronto: Copp Clark, 1971.

Blumenfeld, Hans. *The Modern Metropolis: Its Origins, Growth, Characteristics and Planning*. Montreal: Harvest House, 1967.

Bollens, J. C., and Schmandt, H. J. *The Metropolis: Its People, Politics and Economic Life*. New York: Harper and Rowe, 1965.

Bourne, L. S., and R. D. MacKinnon, eds. *Urban Systems Development in Central Canada: Selected Papers*. Toronto: University of Toronto Press, 1972.

Bourne, L. S., J. Siegel, and J. W. Simmons, eds. *Urban Futures for Central Canada: Perspectives on Forecasting Urban Growth and Form.* Toronto: University of Toronto Press, 1974.

Bourne, L. S. *Urban Systems: Strategies and Regulation: A Comparison of Policies in Britain, Sweden, Australia, and Canada.* Toronto: Oxford, 1976.

Bryfogle, R. C., and R. R. Krueger, eds. *Urban Problems.* rev. ed. Toronto: Holt, Rinehart and Winston, 1975.

Cameron, K. D., ed. "National Urban Policy". *Plan Canada*, vol. 12, no. 1 (1972) [Special issue].

Careless, J. M. S. "Frontierism, Metropolitanism, and Canadian History". *Canadian Historical Review*, vol. 35, no. 1 (March 1954): 1-21.

———. "Metropolitan Reflections on 'Great Britain's Woodyard'". *Acadiensis*, vol. 3, no. 1 (Autumn 1973): 103-09.

———. "Urban Development in Canada". *Urban History Review*, No. 1-74 (June 1974): 9-13.

———. "Metropolis and Region: The Interplay between City and Region in Canadian History Before 1914". *Urban History Review*, No. 3-78 (February 1979): 99-118.

Carver, H. *Cities in the Suburbs.* Toronto: University of Toronto Press, 1962.

Chambers, E. J., and G. W. Bertram. "Urbanization and Manufacturing in Central Canada, 1870-1890". In S. Ostry and T. K. Rymes, eds. *Papers on Regional Statistical Studies.* Toronto, 1966.

Clark, S. D. "Canadian Urban Development". *Urban History Review*, No. 1-74 (June 1974):14-19.

Colthart, A. J. "The Metropolis – Hinterland Thesis and Regional Economic Development". MA thesis, University of Alberta, 1974.

Commission of Conservation. *Urban and Rural Development in Canada: Report of Conference Held at Winnipeg, May 28-30, 1917.* Ottawa, 1917.

Crawford, K. G. "Urban Growth and Boundary Readjustments". *Canadian Public Administration*, vol. III, no. 1 (March 1960): 51-58.

Dyos, H. J., and M. Wolff, eds. *The Victorian City: Images and Realities.* 2 vols. London and Boston: Routledge and Kegan Paul, 1973.

Faris, Robert E. L. "Interrelated Problems of the Expanding Metropo-

lis". *Canadian Journal of Economics and Political Science*, vol. 5, no.
3 (August 1939): 341-47.

Federal Publications Service. *Urbanisme et Environnement/Urbanism
and Environment*. Ottawa: Federal Publications Service, 1974.

Gertler, L. O. *Urban Issues*. Toronto: Van Nostrand Reinhold, 1975.

Gertler, L. O., and R. W. Crowley. *Changing Canadian Cities: The
Next Twenty-Five Years*. Toronto: McClelland and Stewart, 1977.

Gillespie, W. I. *The Urban Public Economy*. Ottawa: CMHC, 1971.

Grossner, C. "Specialization in Canadian Cities". MA thesis, Queen's
University, 1970.

Gutstein, D. I. "Towards a Model of the Urban Development Process". MArch. thesis, University of British Columbia, 1972.

Hartwick, J. M., and R. W. Crowley. *Urban Economic Growth: The
Canadian Case*. Ottawa: Ministry of State for Urban Affairs, 1973.

Hellyer, P., *et al. Report of the Federal Government Task Force on
Housing and Urban Development*. Ottawa: Queen's Printer, 1969.

Hodge, G. "Urban Systems and Regional Policy". *Canadian Public
Administration*, vol. 9, no. 2 (June 1966): 181-93.

———. "Comparisons of Urban Structure in Canada, the United
States, and Great Britain". *Geographical Analysis,* vol. 3, no. 1
(1971): 83-90.

Jackson, J. N. *The Canadian City: Space, Form, Quality*. Toronto:
McGraw-Hill Ryerson, 1973.

Jacobs, Jane. *The Death and Life of Great American Cities*. New York:
Random House, 1961.

———. *The Economy of Cities*. New York: Random House, 1969.

Johnson, H. *Urbanization and Economic Growth in Canada, 1851-1971*.
Dept. of Economics, Research Report No. 7321. London: University of Western Ontario, 1973.

Johnston, R. J. "Regarding Urban Origins, Urbanization and Urban
Patterns". *Geography*, vol. 62, no. 1 (January 1977): 1-7.

Kasahara, Y. "A Profile of Canada's Metropolitan Areas". *Queen's
Quarterly*, vol. 70 (Autumn 1963): 303-13.

Kerr, D. "Metropolitan Dominance in Canada". In J. Warkentin, ed.
Canada: A Geographical Interpretation. Toronto, 1968.

Leman, A. B., and I. A. Leman, eds. *Great Lakes Megalopolis: From*

Civilization to Ecumenization. Ottawa: Ministry of State for Urban Affairs, 1976.

Lighthall, W. D. "War-Time Experiences of Canadian Cities". *National Municipal Review*, vol. 7, no. 1 (January 1918): 19-23.

Lithwick, N. H., and G. Paquet, eds. *Urban Studies: A Canadian Perspective*. Toronto: Methuen, 1968.

Lithwick, N. H. *Urban Canada: Problems and Prospects*. Ottawa: Central Mortgage and Housing Corporation, 1970.

——. "The City: Problems and Policies". In L. H. Officer and L. B. Smith, eds. *Canadian Economic Problems and Policies*. Toronto, 1970.

——. "An Economic Interpretation of the Urban Crisis". *Journal of Canadian Studies*, vol. 7, no. 3 (August 1972): 36-49.

——. "The Process of Urbanization in Canada". In R. M. Irving, ed. *Readings in Canadian Geography*. Toronto, 1972.

Lorimer, J., and E. Ross, eds. *The City Book: The Planning and Politics of Canada's Cities*. Toronto: J. Lorimer, 1976.

——. *The Second City Book: Studies of Urban and Suburban Canada*. Toronto: J. Lorimer, 1977.

Lower, A. R. M. "The Metropolitan and the Provincial". *Queen's Quarterly*, vol. 76 (Winter 1969): 577-90.

——. "Metropolis and Hinterland". *South Atlantic Quarterly*, vol. 70 (1971): 386-403.

Lucas, Rex A. *Minetown, Milltown, Railtown: Life in Canadian Communities of Single Industry*. Toronto: University of Toronto Press, 1971.

McMullin, S. E., and P. M. Koroscil, eds. "The Canadian Urban Experience". *Canadian Issues*, vol. 1, no. 1 (Spring 1975): 1-145.

Marshall, J. U. "City Size, Economic Diversity, and Functional Type: The Canadian Case". *Economic Geography*, vol. 51 (January 1975): 37-49.

Maxwell, J. W., J. A. Greig, and H. G. Meyer. "The Functional Structure of Canadian Cities: A Classification of Canadian Cities" In R. M. Irving, ed. *Readings in Canadian Geography*. Toronto, 1972.

Mumford, Lewis. *The City in History: Its Origins, Its Transformations, and Its Prospects*. New York: Harcourt Brace, 1961.

Nader, G. A. *Cities of Canada. Volume 1: Theoretical, Historical and Planning Perspectives*. Toronto: Macmillan, 1975.

—— . *Cities of Canada. Volume 2: Profiles of Fifteen Metropolitan Centres.* Toronto: Macmillan, 1976.

Oberlander, H. Peter, ed. *Canada: An Urban Agenda.* Ottawa: Community Planning Press, 1976.
O'Connor, K. "Industrial Structure and Urban Growth of Canadian Cities, 1951-1961". PHD thesis, McMaster University, 1974.

Pearson, N. "A Case for New Towns in Canada." In R. Krueger and R. C. Bryfogle, eds. *Urban Problems: A Canadian Reader.* Toronto, 1971.
—— . "From Villages to Cities". In J. M. S. Careless and R. C. Brown, eds. *The Canadians, 1867-1967.* Toronto: Macmillan, 1967.
Pinfold, T. "The Role of Land in the Urban Economy". *Canadian Issues*, vol. 1, no. 1 (Spring 1975): 29-54.
Plunkett, T. J. *Understanding Urban Development in Canada.* Toronto: Canadian Foundation for Economic Education, 1977.
Powell, A., ed. *The City: Attacking Modern Myths.* Toronto: McClelland and Stewart, 1972.

Rashleigh, E. T. "Observations on Canadian Cities". In R. M. Irving, ed. *Readings in Canadian Geography.* Toronto, 1966.
Richardson, B. *The Future of Canadian Cities.* Toronto: New Press, 1972.
Robinson, I. M. *New Industrial Towns on Canada's Resource Frontier.* Chicago: University of Chicago Press, 1962.
Rose, Albert. "The Challenge of Metropolitan Growth". *Community Planning Review*, vol. 4, no. 4 (1954): 97-103.

Saarinen, E. *The City: Its Growth, Its Decay, Its Future.* Cambridge, Mass.: The MIT Press, 1943.
Schnore, L. F., and G. B. Petersen. "Urban and Metropolitan Development in the United States and Canada". *Annals of the American Academy of Political and Social Sciences*, no. 316 (March 1958): 60-68.
Science Council of Canada. *Cities for Tomorrow: Some Applications of Science and Technology to Urban Development.* Ottawa: Queen's Printer, 1971.
Simmons, J. W., and R. Simmons. *Urban Canada.* 2nd ed. Toronto: Copp Clark, 1974.
Simmons, J. W. *Canada as an Urban System: A Conceptual Frame-*

work. Toronto: Centre for Urban and Community Studies, University of Toronto, 1974.

――― . *Canada: Choices in a National Urban Strategy*. Toronto: Centre for Urban and Community Studies, University of Toronto, 1975.

Sjoberg, Gideon. *The Pre-Industrial City—Past and Present*. New York: The Free Press, 1960.

Slater, D. W. "The Political Economy of Urban Changes in Canada". *Queen's Quarterly*, vol. 67, no. 4 (Winter 1961): 586-604.

――― . "Decentralization of Urban Peoples and Manufacturing Activity in Canada". *Canadian Journal of Economics and Political Science*, vol. 27, no. 1 (February 1961): 72-84.

Stelter, Gilbert A. "The Urban Frontier in Canadian History". In A. R. McCormack and I. MacPherson, eds. *Cities in the West*. Ottawa, 1975.

――― , ed. "The Canadian City in the Nineteenth Century". *Urban History Review*, no. 1-75 (June 1975): 2-54.

――― , and Alan F. J. Artibise, eds. *The Canadian City: Essays in Urban History*. Toronto: Macmillan of Canada, 1979.

Stone, L. O. *Urban Development in Canada*. Ottawa: Dominion Bureau of Statistics, 1967.

――― . "Recent Trends in Urbanization and Metropolitan Growth". Canada Year Book (1969): 156-65.

Tremblay, M. A., and W. J. Anderson, eds. *Rural Canada in Transition: A Multidimensional Study of the Impact of Technology and Urbanization on Traditional Society*. Ottawa: Agricultural Economics Research Council of Canada, 1966.

Vance, James E. *This Scene of Man: The Role and Structure of the City in the Geography of Western Civilization*. New York: Harper and Row, 1977.

Whitaker, J. R. "Regional Contrasts in the Growth of Canadian Cities". *Scottish Geographical Magazine*, vol. 53 (November 1937): 373-79.

Wolforth, J., and R. Leigh. *Urban Prospects*. Toronto: McClelland and Stewart, 1971.

Walker, Harry W. "Canadian 'New Towns'". *Community Planning Review*, vol. 4, no. 4 (1954): 80-87.

Weaver, J. C. *Shaping the Canadian City: Essays on Urban Politics and Policy, 1890 – 1920*. Monographs on Canadian Urban Government, vol. 1. Toronto: Institute of Public Administration of Canada, 1977.

Yeates, M. *Main Street: Windsor to Quebec City.* Toronto: Macmillan, 1975.

Yeomans, W. C. "The Pressures of Urbanization". *Community Planning Review*, vol. 20, no. 4 (Winter 1970-71): 4-9.

B. GOVERNMENT AND POLITICS

Aitchison, J. H. "The Municipal Corporations Act of 1849". *Canadian Historical Review*, vol. 30 (1949): 107-22.

Anderson, G. "A Comparative Study of Local Government Development in Canada". MA thesis, University of Saskatchewan, 1974.

Anderson, J. D. "Nonpartisan Civic Politics in Canada and the United States". MA thesis, University of Alberta, 1971.

Axworthy, L. "The Politics of Urban Innovation". In A. M. Linden, ed. *Living in the Seventies.* Toronto 1970.

Bettison, D. G. *The Politics of Canadian Urban Development.* Edmonton: University of Alberta Press, 1975.

Blake, D. E. "Role Perceptions of Local Decision-Makers". MA thesis, University of Alberta, 1967.

Blumenfeld, H. "The Role of the Federal Government in Urban Affairs". *Journal of Liberal Thought*, vol. 2 (Spring 1966): 35-44.

Bourinot, J. G. *Local Government in Canada: An Historical Study.* Baltimore: John Hopkins University, 1887 [Reprinted 1973 by Johnson Reprint Corporation, New York].

Brittain, H. L. *Local Government in Canada.* Toronto: Ryerson, 1951.

Callard, K. "The Present System of Local Government in Canada: Some Problems of Status, Area, Population, and Resources". *Canadian Journal of Economics and Political Science*, vol. 17, no. 2 (May 1951): 204-17.

Clark, R. M. "Some Aspects of the Development of the Personal Income Tax in the Provinces and Municipalities of Canada up to 1930". PHD thesis, Harvard University, 1946.

Crawford, K. G. *Canadian Municipal Government.* Toronto: University of Toronto Press, 1954.

Curtis, C. A., and Carl H. Chatters. "War-Time Problems of Local Government". *Canadian Journal of Economics and Political Science*, vol. 9, no. 3 (August 1943): 394-407.

——— . "Municipal Finance and Provincial-Federal Relations". *Cana-*

dian Journal of Economics and Political Science, vol. 17, no. 3 (August 1951): 297-306.

———— . "Canadian Municipal Finance". *Canadian Tax Journal*, vol. I, no. 6 (1953): 532-39.

———— . "The Changing Form of Municipal Government". *Canadian Tax Journal*, vol. 6, no. 5 (1958): 339-45.

Draper, J. A., ed. *Citizen Participation: Canada, A Book of Readings*. Toronto: New Press, 1971.

Duncan, Lewis. "The Political Basis of Municipal Democracy". *Canadian Journal of Economics and Political Science*, vol. 8, no. 3 (August 1942): 427-32.

Feldman, L. D., and D. Goldrick, eds. *Politics and Government of Urban Canada*. 3rd rev. ed. Toronto: Methuen, 1976.

Frankel, S. J., and R. C. Pratt. *Municipal Labour Relations in Canada: A Study of Some Problems Arising from Collective Bargaining between Municipalities and Municipal Trade Unions*. Montreal: McGill University, 1954.

Fyfe, S. "Governing Urban Communities". *Queen's Quarterly*, vol. 67, no. 4 (Winter 1961): 605-16.

Gibbons, K. M., and D. C. Rowat, eds. *Political Corruption in Canada: Cases, Causes, and Cures*. Toronto: McClelland and Stewart, 1976.

Goldenberg, H. Carl. *Municipal Finance in Canada: A Study Prepared for the Royal Commission on Dominion Provincial Relations*. Ottawa: King's Printer, 1939.

———— . "Municipal Finance and Taxation: Problems and Prospects". *Canadian Tax Journal*, vol. 4, no. 3 (1956): 158-65.

Graham, J. F. "Fiscal Equity Principle in Provincial-Municipal Relation". *Canadian Public Administration*, vol. 3, no. 1 (March 1960): 24-30.

Hahn, H. "Ethos and Social Class: Referenda in Canadian Cities". *Polity*, vol. 2, no. 3 (Spring 1970): 294-315.

Hall, G. E. "Municipal Government's 100th Anniversary". *Municipal World*, vol. 59 (December 1949): 369-74.

Hardy, E. "Provincial-Municipal Financial Relations". *Canadian Public Administration*, vol. 3, no. 1 (March 1960): 14-23.

Hickey, P. "The Changing Structure of Municipal Government in

Canada". *Canadian Chartered Accountant*, vol. 89 (September 1966): 182-86.

Higgins, D. J. H. *Urban Canada: Its Government and Politics*. Toronto: Macmillan, 1977.

Hochstein, A. P. "The Wage Determination Process in Selected Municipal Governments". MA thesis, McGill University, 1969.

Institute of Local Government, Queen's University. *Single Enterprise Communities in Canada*. Ottawa: Central Mortgage and Housing, 1953.

Johnson, I. C. "Provincial and Municipal Debt in Canada, 1946-66". MA thesis, University of Western Ontario, 1971.

Joyce, J. G. "Municipal Political Parties in Canada". MA thesis, University of Western Ontario, 1969.

Joyce, J. G., and H. A. Hossé. *Civic Parties in Canada*. Ottawa: Canadian Federation of Mayors and Municipalities, 1970.

Kaplan, H. *The Regional City: Politics and Planning in Metropolitan Areas*. Toronto: CBC, 1965.

Leo, Christopher. *The Politics of Urban Development; Canadian Urban Expressway Disputes*. Monographs on Canadian Urban Government, vol. 3. Toronto: Institute of Public Administration, 1978.

Lightbody, James. "The Rise of Party Politics in Canadian Local Elections". *Journal of Canadian Studies*, vol. VI, no. 1 (February 1971): 39-44.

Lighthall, W. D. "The Elimination of Political Parties in Canadian Cities". *National Municipal Review*, vol. 6, no. 2 (March 1917): 207-09.

Lithwick, N. H. "Urban Policy-Making: Shortcomings in Political Technology". *Canadian Public Administration*, vol. XV, no. 4 (1972): 571-84.

——— . "Towards a New Urban Politics". *Community Planning Review*, vol. 22, no. 3 (1972): 3-8.

Long, J. A., and B. Slemko. "The Recruitment of Local Decision-Makers in Five Canadian Cities". *Canadian Journal of Political Science*, vol. 7, no. 3 (September 1974): 550-59.

Lorimer, James. "Expertise *Versus* Participation: Who Will Govern Canada's Cities in the Seventies?" In A. M. Linden, ed. *Living in the Seventies*. Toronto, 1970.

——— . *The Real World of City Politics*. Toronto: James, Lewis and Samuel, 1970.

_____ . *A Citizen's Guide to City Politics*. Toronto: James, Lewis and Samuel, 1972.

McIver, J. M. "A Survey of the City Manager Plan in Canada". *Canadian Public Administration*, vol. 3, no. 3 (September 1960): 216-32.

Manning, H. E. *Assessment and Rating: Municipal Taxation in Canada*. Toronto: Cartwright, 1951.

Marshall, A. H. *Financial Administration in Local Government*. Toronto: Thomas Nelson, 1960.

Masson, J., and J. D. Anderson. eds. *Emerging Party Politics in Urban Canada*. Toronto: McClelland and Stewart, 1972.

Mooney, G. S. "The Canadian Federation of Mayors and Municipalities". *Canadian Public Administration*, vol. 3, no. 1 (March 1960): 84-92.

_____ . *The Municipality's Role in the National Economy: A Selection of Papers Prepared for the Silver Jubilee of the Canadian Federation of Mayors and Municipalities*. Montreal: CFMM, 1962.

Morse, C. "Municipal Institutions in England and Canada". *Canada Law Journal*, vol. 41 (1905): 505-21.

Munro, W. B. "Boards of Control and Commission Government in Canadian Cities". *Papers and Proceedings*, Canadian Political Science Association. Ottawa, 1913.

_____ . *American Influences on Canadian Government*. Toronto: Macmillan, 1929.

Newcomer, M., and R. G. Hitchison. "Taxation of Land Values in Canada". *Journal of Political Economy*, vol. 40 (June 1932): 366-78.

Owens, H. T. *Land Value Taxation in Canadian Local Government*. Westmount, Quebec: Henry George Foundation of Canada, Inc., 1953.

Perry, Harvey. "Municipal Finance Needs and Federal Fiscal Policy". *Canadian Tax Journal*, vol. 7, no. 4 (1959): 308-17.

Plunkett, T. J. *Municipal Organization in Canada*. Montreal: Canadian Federation of Mayors and Municipalities, 1955.

_____ . "Metropolitan Government in Canada". *University of Toronto Law Journal*, vol. 14, no. 1 (1961): 29-51.

_____ . *Urban Canada and Its Government: A Study of Municipal Organization*. Toronto: Macmillan, 1968.

_____ , et al. *Urban Population Growth and Municipal Organization*. Kingston: Institute of Local Government, Queen's University, 1973.

———— . "Structural Reform of Local Government in Canada". *Public Administration Review*, vol. 33, no. 1 (January – February 1973): 40-51.

———— and G. M. Betts. *The Management of Canadian Urban Government: A Basic Text for a Course in Urban Management.* Kingston: Institute of Local Government, Queen's University, 1978.

Powell, C. W. "Provincial-Municipal Financing". *Canadian Public Administration*, vol. 6, no. 1 (March 1963): 84-91.

Raney, E. F. "Municipal Taxation in Canada: A Reconstruction". PHD thesis, University of Toronto, 1912.

Robson, W. A. "Metropolitan Government: Problems and Solutions". *Canadian Public Administration*, vol. 9, no. 1 (March 1966): 45-54.

Rowat, D. C. "Do We Need the Manager Plan?" *Canadian Public Administration*, vol. 3, no. 1 (March 1960): 42-50.

———— . *The Canadian Municipal System: Essays in the Improvement of Local Government.* Toronto: McClelland and Stewart, 1969.

———— . "The Role of Canada's Urban Municipalities in Governmental Decision-Making". *Studies in Comparative Local Government*, vol. 8, no. 1 (1974): 43-49.

———— . "The Problem of Federal-Urban Relations in Canada". *Quarterly of Canadian Studies*, vol. 3, no. 4 (1975): 214-24.

———— . *Your Local Government: A Sketch of the Municipal System in Canada.* 2nd ed. Toronto: Macmillan, 1975.

Rutherford, P. "Tomorrow's Metropolis: The Urban Reform Movement in Canada, 1880-1920". In G. A. Stelter and A. F. J. Artibise, eds. *The Canadian City: Essays in Urban History.* Toronto: Macmillan, 1979.

———— , ed. *Saving the Canadian City: The First Phase, 1880-1920. An Anthology of Early Articles on Urban Reform.* Toronto: University of Toronto Press, 1974.

Scanlon, T. J. "Board of Control: Its Merits and Defects". *Canadian Public Administration*, vol. 3, no. 4 (September 1960): 331-36.

Silver, Sheldon. "The Feasibility of a Municipal Income Tax in Canada". *Canadian Tax Journal*, vol. 16, no. 5 (1968): 398-406.

Tindal, C. R. *Structural Changes in Local Government: Government for Urban Regions.* Monographs on Canadian Urban Government, vol. 2. Toronto: Institute of Public Administration of Canada, 1977.

Vineberg, S. *Provincial and Local Taxation in Canada*. London: P. S. King and Son, 1912.

Weaver, J. C. "Elitism and the Corporate Ideal: Businessmen and Boosters in Canadian Civic Reform, 1890-1920". In A. R. McCormack and I. MacPherson, eds. *Cities in the West*. Ottawa, 1975.

_____ . "Approaches to the History of Urban Reform". *Urban History Review*, No. 2-76 (October 1976): 3-11.

_____ . "Tomorrow's Metropolis Revisited: A Critical Assessment of Urban Reform in Canada, 1890-1920". In G. A. Stelter and A. F. J. Artibise, eds. *The Canadian City: Essays in Urban History*. Toronto: Macmillan, 1979.

Whalen, H. "Ideology, Democracy, and the Foundations of Local Government". *Canadian Journal of Economics and Political Science*, vol. 26, no. 3 (August 1960): 377-95.

Wickett, S. M. "City Government in Canada". *Canadian Magazine*, vol. 18, no. 1 (November 1901): 53-65.

_____ , ed. *Municipal Government in Canada*. Toronto: University of Toronto Studies, History and Economics, 1907.

Wickwar, W. H. *The Political Theory of Local Government*. Columbia, S. C.: University of South Carolina Press, 1970.

Wrenshall, C. M. *Municipal Administration and Accounting*. Toronto: Pitman, 1937.

Young, D. A. "Canadian Local Government Development: Some Aspects of the Commissioner and City Manager Forms of Government". *Canadian Public Administration*, vol. 9, no. 1 (March 1966): 55-68.

C. PLANNING AND ARCHITECTURE

Adams, Thomas. *Town Planning and Land Development*. Ottawa: Commission of Conservation, 1918.

_____ . *Outline of Town and City Planning*. New York: Russell Sage, 1935.

Adamson, A. "Form and the 20th Century Canadian City". *Queen's Quarterly*, vol. 69 (Spring 1962): 49-68.

Armstrong, Alan H. "Federal Aids to Urban Repair and Replacement". *Community Planning Review*, vol. 4, no. 2 (1954): 49-63.

_____ . "Thomas Adams and the Commission of Conservation". *Plan Canada*, vol. 1, no. 1 (1959): 14-32.

Ashworth, W. *The Genesis of Modern British Town Planning*. London: Routledge and Kegan Paul, 1954.

Aubin, Henry. *City for Sale; International Finance and Canadian Development*. Toronto: James Lorimer and Company, 1977.

Bacon, E. N. *Design of Cities: An Account of the Development of Urban Form, From Ancient Athens to Modern Brasilia*. New York: Penguin Books, 1976.

Baker, J. "Private and Government Planning". In *Housing and Community Planning*. McGill University Monograph Series. Montreal, 1944.

Baldwin, M. "Exhibition as a Medium for the Study and Teaching of History: Town Planning in Early Days in Canada". Canadian Historical Association, *Annual Report* (1941): 55-64.

Benevolo, L. *The Origins of Modern Town Planning*. London: Routledge and Kegan Paul, 1967.

Blair, D. E. "Traffic, Transportation and Terminal Facilities". In *Housing and Community Planning*. McGill University Monograph Series. Montreal, 1944.

Bland, John. "The Growth of Physical Planning". In *Housing and Community Planning*. McGill University Monograph Series. Montreal, 1944.

———. "Regional Planning". In *Housing and Community Planning*. McGill University Monograph Series. Montreal, 1944.

Blumenfeld, H. "Transportation in the Modern Metropolis". *Queen's Quarterly*, vol. 67, no. 4 (Winter 1961): 640-53.

Bourne, L. S. "Trends in Urban Redevelopment: The Implications for Urban Form". *Appraisal Journal*, vol. 37 (1970): 24-36.

———, ed. *Internal Structure of the City: Readings on Space and Environment*. Toronto: Oxford University Press, 1971.

———, and J. W. Simmons, eds. *The Form of Cities in Central Canada: Selected Papers*. Toronto: University of Toronto Press, 1973.

Bryant, R. W. G. *Land: Private Property/Public Control*. Montreal: Harvest House, 1972.

Buckley, K. A. H. "Urban Building and Real Estate Fluctuations in Canada". *Canadian Journal of Economics and Political Science*, vol. 18, no. 1 (February 1952): 41-62.

Capling, A. J. "Ornamental Aspects of Cities". MArch. thesis, McGill University, 1967.

Carver, H. M. S. "Planning in Canada". *Habitat*, vol. 3 (Autumn 1960): 2-5.

——— . *Compassionate Landscape.* Toronto: University of Toronto Press, 1975.

Cherry, G. E. *The Evolution of British Town Planning.* London: Leonard Hill Books, 1974.

Clark, Douglas. "Urban Renewal and Municipal Taxation". *Canadian Tax Journal*, vol. 10, no. 6 (1962): 387-94; vol. 11, no. 1 (1963): 76-82.

Clark, R. "The Crisis in Canadian City Planning". *City Magazine*, vol. 1, no. 8 (January – February 1976): 17-25.

Collier, R. W. *Contemporary Cathedrals: Large Scale Developments in Canadian Cities.* Montreal: Harvest House, 1975.

Cousineau, A. "Planning Public Services". In *Housing and Community Planning.* McGill University Monograph Series. Montreal, 1944.

Crerar, A. D. "Land for Our Future—The High Cost of Sprawl". *Community Planning Review*, vol. 9, no. 2 (June 1959): 44-48.

Cross, K. J. "Urban Redevelopment in Canada". PHD thesis, Cornell University, 1958.

Dant, Noel. "People, Planning, Politics, Publicity and the Press". *Community Planning Review*, vol. 12, no. 2 (1962): 3-12.

Dawson, Carl A. "City Planning and Our North American Social Heritage". In *Housing and Community Planning.* McGill University Monograph Series. Montreal, 1944.

Deacon, P. A. "Community Planning in Canada". *Canadian Forum*, vol. 31 (November 1951): 175-76.

Denhey, M. "Conserving Neighborhoods and Landmarks: The Canadian Problem". *Urban Forum*, vol. 2, no. 1 (Spring 1976): 27-35.

Detwyler, T. R. *Urbanization and Environment: The Physical Geography of the City.* Belmont, California: Duxbury Press, 1972.

Dickinson, R. E. *City Planning and Regionalism.* London: Kegan, Paul, 1947.

Erickson, A. "Architecture, Urban Development and Industrialization". *Canadian Architect*, vol. 20 (January 1975): 35-38.

——— . *The Architecture of ArthurErickson.* Montreal: Tundra Books, 1975.

Faludi, E. G., and A. Adamson, "Plans for Eight Communities: Regina, Hamilton, Windsor, Peterborough, Stratford, Kenora, Terrace Bay, and Etobicoke". *Journal of the Royal Architectural Institute of Canada.* vol. 23, no. 11 (November 1946): 276-93.

Firestone, O. J. "Measurement of Housing Needs, Supply and Post-

War Requirements". In *Housing and Community Planning*. McGill University Monograph Series. Montreal, 1944.

French, R. de L. "Community Street Systems". In *Housing and Community Planning*. McGill University Monograph Series. Montreal, 1944.

Fulton, D. *Design for Small Communities*. Toronto: Macmillan, 1975.

Gerecke, K. "Toward a New Model of Urban Planning". PHD thesis, University of British Columbia, 1974.

——— . "The History of Canadian City Planning". *City Magazine*, vol. 2, nos. 3 and 4 (Summer 1976): 12-23.

Gertler, L. O. "Regional Planning and Development". *Resources for Tomorrow: Conference Background Papers*, vol. I. Ottawa, 1961.

——— , ed. *Planning the Canadian Environment*. Montreal: Harvest House, 1968.

——— . *Regional Planning in Canada: A Planner's Testament*. Montreal: Harvest House, 1972.

Gowans, Alan. *Building Canada: An Architectural History of Canadian Life*. Toronto: Oxford University Press, 1966.

——— . "Towards a Meaningfully Built Environment". *Canadian Issues*, vol. 1, no. 1 (Spring 1975): 55-84.

Grimble, L. G. "Gaits: A Proposed Public Transit System". *Community Planning Review*, vol. 18, no. 3 (Fall 1968): 4-9.

Gutstein, D. "Arthur Erickson: The Corporate Artist-Architect". *City Magazine*, vol. 1, no. 1 (October 1974): 6-15.

Higgins, B. H. "Financial Planning at the Community Level". In *Housing and Community Planning*. McGill University Monograph Series. Montreal, 1944.

Horsbrugh, P. "Pride of Place". *Queen's Quarterly*, vol. 67, no. 4 (Winter 1961): 617-29.

Hugo-Brunt, M. *The History of City Planning: A Survey*. Montreal: Harvest House, 1972.

Jackson, J. T. "The House as a Visual Indicator of Social Status Change, 1861-1915". MA thesis, University of Western Ontario, 1973.

James, F. C. "The Economic Background of Housing and Community Planning in Post-War Canada". In *Housing and Community Planning*. McGill University Monograph Series. Montreal, 1944.

Jones, M. V. "Urban Focus and Regional Planning". *Canadian Public Administration*, vol. 9, no. 2 (June 1966): 177-80.

Kellough, W. R., *et al.* "Anatomy of the Housing Shortage". *Community Planning Review*, vol. 19, no. 1 (Spring 1969): 18-26.

Kruegar, R. R. "Community Planning and Local Government". *Community Planning Review*, vol. 18, no. 4 (Winter 1968): 16-22.

Kuwabara, B., and B. Sampson. "Diamond and Myers: The Form of Reform". *City Magazine*, vol. 1, nos. 5 and 6 (September 1975): 29-47.

Lamb, A. S. "Planning for Health and Recreation". In *Housing and Community Planning*. McGill University Monograph Series. Montreal, 1944.

Leo, Christopher. *The Politics of Urban Development: Canadian Urban Expressway Disputes*. Monographs on Canadian Urban Government, vol. 3. Toronto: Institute of Public Administration in Canada, 1977.

Levin, Earl. "Land Planning and Land Costs". *Community Planning Review*. vol. 9, no. 2 (June 1959): 54-64.

Lorimer, James. *The Developers*. Toronto: James Lorimer and Company, 1978.

Lovendan, P. "Problèmes fondamentales de l'urbanisme". *Revue de l'Université Laval*, vol. 4 (juin 1950): 950-59.

MacRossie, W. "Land Policy". In *Housing and Community Planning*. McGill University Monograph Series. Montreal, 1944.

Marsh, Leonard. "Government Planning in Canada". In *Housing and Community Planning*. McGill University Monograph Series. Montreal, 1944.

McCann, L. D. "The Changing Internal Structure of Resource Towns". *Plan Canada*, vol. 18 (1978): 46-59.

Meyerson, M., and E. C. Banfield. *Politics, Planning and the Public Interest*. Toronto: Macmillan, 1955.

Michelson, William. *Man and His Urban Environment*. Don Mills: Addison-Wesley, 1970.

Milner, J. B. "Town and Regional Planning in Transition". *Canadian Public Administration*, vol. 3, no. 1 (March 1960): 59-75.

Nobbs, P. E. *Report on Town Planning Legislation in the Provinces of Canada*. Montreal: Department of City Planning, 1946.

Nordland, R. V. "Settlement Planning in the Arctic". MCP thesis, University of Manitoba, 1972.

Oberlander, H. Peter. "Critique: Canada's New Towns". *Progressive Architecture*, vol. 9 (August 1956): 113-19.

———. "Community Planning and Housing: Stepchildren of Canadian Federalism". *Queen's Quarterly*, vol. 67, no. 4 (Winter 1960-61): 663-72.

———. "Urban Planning and Federalism". *Proceedings of the 1964 Annual Conference of the American Institute of Planners*. Newark, N.J., 1964.

Parent, Honoré. "City Planning and the Law". In *Housing and Community Planning*. McGill University Monograph Series. Montreal, 1944.

Pressman, N. E. P. "Urbanism—Toward a More Humanized Environment". *Plan Canada*, vol. 11, no. 1 (December 1970): 13-22.

———. *Planning New Communities in Canada*. Ottawa: Ministry of State for Urban Affairs, 1975.

———. "Hans Blumenfeld: Humanist and Urban Planner". *Plan Canada*, vol. 16, no. 1 (March 1976): 25-36.

Renfrew, Stewart. "Commission of Conservation". *Douglas Library Notes*, vol. 19, no. 3-4 (Spring 1971): 17-26.

Reps, J. W. *The Making of Urban America: A History of City Planning in the United States*. Princeton: Princeton University Press, 1965.

Richardson, D. "Canadian Architecture in the Victorian Era: The Spirit of the Place". *Canadian Collector*, no. 10 (1975): 20-29.

Richardson, Nigel H. "Let's Stop Building Tomorrow's Slums". *Community Planning Review*, vol. 9, no. 2 (June 1959): 32-41.

Ritchie, T. *Canada Builds, 1867-1967*. Toronto: University of Toronto Press, 1967.

Rowat, D. C. "Planning and Metropolitan Government". *Canadian Public Administration*, vol. I, no. 1 (March 1958): 14-21.

Rowland, K. *The Shape of Towns*. London: Ginn and Co., 1966.

Saywell, John T. *Housing Canadians: Essays on the History of Residential Construction in Canada*. Economic Council of Canada. Discussion Paper No. 24. Ottawa, 1975.

Schneider, Kenneth R. "The Destruction of Urban Space". *Community Planning Review*, vol. 21, no. 1 (Spring 1971): 11-16, 31-36.

Scott, M. *American City Planning Since 1890*. Berkeley: University of California Press, 1970.

Simmons, James W. "The Location of Land for Public Use in Urban Areas". *Canadian Geographer*, vol. 14, no. 1 (Spring 1970): 45-56.

Sise, Hazen. "The Townscape Revealed". *Canadian Geographical Journal*, vol. 73, no. 4 (October 1966): 128-37.

Spreiregen, P. D. *Urban Design: The Architecture of Towns and Cities*. New York : McGraw-Hill, 1965.

Spurr, P. *Land and Urban Development: A Preliminary Study*. Toronto: J. Lorimer, 1976.

——. "Five Land Banks [Kingston, Peterborough, Hamilton, Saskatoon, Red Deer]". *City Magazine*, vol. 2, no. 1 (March – April 1976): 10-21.

Slater, David W. "Planning In Smaller Communities". *Community Planning Review*, vol. 11, no. 3 (1961): 6-17.

Smith, C. Ray, and David R. Witty. "Conservation, Resources and Environment, An Exposition and Critical Evaluation of the Commission of Conservation, Canada". *Plan Canada*, vol. 11, no. 1 (1970): 55-71; and vol. 11, no. 3 (1972): 199-216.

Stelter, Gilbert A. and Alan F. J. Artibise, "Canadian Resource Towns in Historical Perspective". *Plan Canada*, vol. 18 (1978): 7-16.

Tanimura, H. "Urban Development Models as Planning Tools". MCP thesis, University of Manitoba, 1966.

Tardif, J. P. E. "An Ecological Interpretation of City Planning". MCP thesis, University of Manitoba, 1969.

Van Nus, W. "The Plan-Makers and the City: Architects, Engineers, Surveyors, and Urban Planning in Canada, 1890-1939". PHD thesis, University of Toronto, 1975.

——. "The Fate of City Beautiful Thought in Canada, 1893-1930". In Gilbert A. Stelter and Alan F. J. Artibise, eds. *The Canadian City: Essays in Urban History*. Toronto: Macmillan, 1979.

Vinton, Warren J. "The Planning of Public Housing". In *Housing and Community Planning*. McGill University Monograph Series. Montreal, 1944.

Walker, H. W. "Canadian 'New Towns'". *Community Planning Review*, vol. 4 (1954): 80-87.

Webster, Donald H. *Urban Planning and Municipal Public Policy*. New York: Harper and Brothers, 1958.

D. BIBLIOGRAPHICAL AND METHODOLOGICAL

Anderson, B. L. *Special Libraries and Information Centres in Canada: A Directory*. Ottawa: Canadian Library Association, 1970.

Armstrong, F. H. "Urban History in Canada". *Urban History Group Newsletter*, no. 28 (December 1969): 1-10.

Association of Canadian Archivists. *Directory of Canadian Records and Manuscript Repositories*. Ottawa: Association of Canadian Archivists, 1977.

Bourne, L. S., and C. M. Biernacki. *Urban Housing Markets, Housing Supply and the Spatial Structure of Residential Change: A Working Bibliography*. Toronto: Centre for Urban and Community Studies, University of Toronto, 1977.

Bowsfield, H. "Writing Local History". *Alberta Historical Review*, vol. 17, no. 3 (Summer 1964): 10-19.

Brown, R. A., and W. G. Tyrell. *How To Use Local History*. Washington: National Council for Social Studies, 1961.

Bryfogle, R. C. *Urban Problems: A Bibliography of Non-Print and Audio-Visual Material for a Secondary Geography Course*. Monticello, Illinois: Council of Planning Librarians, Exchange Bibliography No. 259, 1972.

——— , compiler. *City in Print: An Urban Studies Bibliography*. Agincourt, Ont.: GLC Publishers, 1975. [Supplements are available, bringing material up-to-date].

Canadian Council on Urban and Regional Research. *Urban and Regional References, 1945-1969*. Ottawa, 1970. [Supplements published annually].

Careless, J. M. S. "Somewhat Narrow Horizons". Canadian Historical Association, *Annual Report* (1968): 1-10.

——— . "Nationalism, Pluralism and Canadian History". *Culture*, vol. 30 (March 1969): 19-26.

——— . "Localism or Parochialism in Canadian History". *B.C. Perspectives*, no. 2 (October 1972): 4-14.

Carter, Harold. *The Study of Urban Geography*. London: Edward Arnold, 1972.

Chamberlain, S. B., and Crowley, D. F. *Decision-Making and Change in Urban Residential Space: Selected and Annotated References*. Toronto: Centre for Urban and Community Studies, University of Toronto, 1969.

Cook, G. L. "Some Uses of Local and Regional History as an Introduction to the Study of History". *B. C. Perspectives*, no. 2 (October 1972): 15-24.

Cooper, Ian, and J. D. Hulchanski, eds. *Canadian Town Planning,*

1900-1930: An Historical Bibliography. 3 vols. Toronto: Centre for Urban and Community Studies, University of Toronto, 1978.

Dahl, E. H., ed. "Resources for the Study of Urban History in the Public Archives of Canada". *Urban History Review*, No. 2-72 (June 1972): 3-13.

Davey, P. "Quantitative Methods in the Study of Local History". *The History and Social Science Teacher*, vol. 10, no. 2 (Winter 1974): 9-16.

Dempsey, Hugh A. *How To Prepare a Local History*. Calgary: Glenbow-Alberta Institute, 1969.

Dickinson, R. E. *City and Region: A Geographical Interpretation*. New York: Humanities Press, 1964.

Dill, John, and Pamela Macri. *Current References Relating to Housing and Land Issues in Canada*. Monticello, Illinois: Council of Planning Librarians, Exchange Bibliography no. 842, 1975.

Douch, R. *Local History and the Teacher*. London: Routledge and Kegan Paul, 1967.

Dyos, H. J., ed. *The Study of Urban History*. London: Edward Arnold, 1968.

Finan, W. M. *Urban Reference Service and Its Implementation at the Local Level*. Ottawa: Canadian Council on Urban and Regional Research, 1975.

Finberg, H. R. P. *The Local Historian and His Theme*. Leicester: University of Leicester Press, 1952.

Freer, K. M. *Vancouver: A Bibliography*. Vancouver Public Library, 1962.

Gibbs, J. P., ed. *Urban Research Methods*. Toronto: Van Nostrand, 1961.

Goldfield, D. R. "Living History: The Physical City as Artifact and Teaching Tool". *The History Teacher*, vol. 8, no. 4 (August 1975): 535-56.

Graff, Harvey J. "Counting on the Past: Quantification in History". *Acadiensis*, vol. 6, no. 1 (Autumn 1976): 115-28.

Hall, P. "The Future of Cities and the Future of Urban Research". In W. R. Derrick Sewell and H. D. Foster, eds. *The Geographer and Society*. Victoria, 1970.

Hamilton, W. B. "Structuring a Program in Local History." *The History and Social Science Teacher*, vol. 10, no. 2 (Winter 1974): 3-8.

Handlin, O., and J. Burchard, eds. *The Historian and the City*. Cambridge, Mass.: Harvard University Press, 1963.

Harvey, D. C. "The Importance of Local History in the Writing of General History". *Canadian Historical Review*, vol. 13, no. 3 (September 1932): 244-51.

Hauser, P. M. *Handbook for Social Research in Urban Areas*. Paris: UNESCO, 19649

——— , and L. F. Schnore, eds. *The Study of Urbanization*. New York: John Wiley and Sons, 1965.

Hayward, R. J. "Sources for Urban Historical Research: Insurance Plans and Land-Use Atlases". *Urban History Review,* No. 1-73 (May 1973): 2-10.

Hulchanski, J. D. *Citizen Participation in Planning: A Comprehensive Bibliography*. Toronto: Department of Urban and Regional Planning, University of Toronto, 1974.

——— . *Thomas Adams: A Biographical and Bibliographical Guide*. Toronto: University of Toronto, Department of Urban and Regional Planning, 1978.

Johnson, J. H. *Urban Geography: An Introductory Analysis*. Toronto: Pergamon Press, 1967.

Knight, D. B., and Clark, J. "Some Reflections on a Conference on the Historical Urbanization of North America". *Urban History Review*, No. 1-73 (May 1973): 10-14.

Knight, R. *Work Camps and Company Towns in Canada and the U.S.: An Annotated Bibliography*. Vancouver: New Star Books, 1975.

Lambert, R., and L. Lavallee. *Bibliography on Canadian Land Market Mechanisms and Land Information Systems*. Ottawa: Ministry of State for Urban Affairs, 1976.

——— . *A Canadian Bibliography of Urban and Regional Information System Activity*. Ottawa: Ministry of State for Urban Affairs, 1976.

Lemon, J. T. "Study of the Urban Past: Approaches by Geographers". Canadian Historical Association, *Historical Papers* (1973): 179-90.

Lubove, R. "The Urbanization Process: An Approach to Historical Research". *Journal of the American Institute of Planners*, vol. 33, no. 1 (January 1967): 33-58.

McCann, L. D. "The Local Historian and the Urban Past." Archival Association of Atlantic Canada, *Newsletter*, vol. 4, no. 2 (1976): 21-23.

Marsh, L. *Communities in Canada: Selected Sources*. Toronto: Mc-Clelland and Stewart, 1970.

Marshall, J. U. "Geography's Contribution to the Historical Study of Urban Canada". *Urban History Review*, No. 1-73 (May 1973): 15-23.

Murphy, R. "Historical and Comparative Urban Studies". *Journal of Geography*, vol. 65 (1966): 212-19.

National Capital Commission. *History and Heritage Bibliography of The National Capital Region*. Ottawa, 1976.

Pressman, N. E. P. "The Built Environment: A Planning Approach to the Study of Urban Settlement". *Contact: Bulletin of Environmental Studies*, vol. 6 (1974): 6-13.

Preston, R. A. "Is Local History Really History?" *Saskatchewan History*, vol. 10, no. 3 (Autumn 1957): 97-103.

Schnore, L. F., ed. *Social Science and the City: A Survey of Urban Research*. New York: F. A. Praeger, 1968.

Simmons, James W. "Urban Geography in Canada". *Canadian Geographer*, vol. 11, no. 4 (1967): 341-56.

Sizler, V. J. *Housing Rehabilitation and Neighbourhood Change: Britain, Canada, and the U.S.A.: An Annotated Bibliography*. Toronto: Centre for Urban and Community Studies, University of Toronto, 1975.

Sloane, D. L., J. M. Rosender, and M. J. Hernandez, eds. *Winnipeg: A Centennial Bibliography*. Winnipeg: Manitoba Library Association, 1974.

Smith, P. J. "Geography and Urban Planning: Links and Departures". *Canadian Geographer*, vol. 19, no. 4 (Winter 1975): 267-78.

Stelter, Gilbert A. *Canadian Urban History: A Selected Bibliography*. Sudbury: Laurentian University Press, 1972.

———. "The Use of Selected Quantifiable Sources in Canadian Urban History". *Urban History Review*, No. 1-72 (February 1972): 15-18.

———. "Current Research in Canadian Urban History". *Urban History Review*, No. 3-75 (February 1976): 27-36.

———. "A Sense of Time and Place: The Historian's Approach to Canada's Urban Past". In Gilbert A. Stelter and Alan F. J. Artibise, eds. *The Canadian City: Essays in Urban History*. Toronto: Macmillan, 1979.

———. "Urban History in North America: Canada". *Urban History Yearbook*. University of Leicester, England, 1977.

———, and Alan F. J. Artibise. "Urban History Comes of Age: A

Survey of Current Research". *City Magazine*, vol. 3, no. 3 (September – October 1977): 22-36.

_____ , and John Rowan. *Community Development in Northeastern Ontario: A Selected Bibliography*. Sudbury: Laurentian University Press, 1972.

Sutcliffe, A. R. *The History of Modern Town Planning: A Bibliographic Guide*. Birmingham: Centre for Urban and Regional Studies, University of Birmingham, 1977.

Symonds, H., ed. *The Teacher and the City*. Toronto: Methuen, 1971.

Thompson, W. R. *A Preface to Urban Economics*. Baltimore: Johns Hopkins Press, 1965.

Thrupp, S. L. "Pedigree and Prospects of Local History". *British Columbia Historical Quarterly*, vol. 4 (October 1960): 253-65.

Van Nus, Walter. "Sources for the History of Urban Planning in Canada, 1890-1939". *Urban History Review*, No. 1-76 (June 1976): 6-9.

Weaver, J. C. "Living in and Building up the Canadian City: A Review of Studies on the Urban Past". *Plan Canada*, vol. 15 (September 1975): 111-17.

Wellman, B., *et al. Community – Network – Communication: An Annotated Bibliography*. 2nd rev. ed. Toronto: Centre for Urban and Community Studies, University of Toronto, 1974.

Wickett, S. M. "Bibliography of Canadian Municipal Government". In S. M. Wickett, ed. *Municipal Government in Canada*. Toronto, 1907: 121-30, 193, 365.

Winchester, I., and P. Davey. "Record of the Past – A Way to Study Canadian History". *Orbit*, vol. 7, no. 1 (February 1976): 3-7.

Notes on Editors

ALAN F. J. ARTIBISE is an Associate Professor of History at the University of Victoria. He is the author of *Winnipeg: A Social History of Urban Growth, 1874 – 1914* (Montreal, 1975); *Winnipeg: An Illustrated History* (Toronto, 1977) and several other books and articles on Winnipeg. He is the editor of the *Urban History Review* and the general editor of the *History of Canadian Cities Series*, a joint project of the National Museum of Man and James Lorimer and Company. Professor Artibise is currently working on a comparative history of prairie cities, 1870 – 1950.

GILBERT A. STELTER, an Associate Professor of History at the University of Guelph, co-ordinated the Guelph Urban History Conference where most of the papers in this volume were first presented. He co-edited (with Alan F. J. Artibise) *The Canadian City: Essays in Urban History* (Toronto, 1977), and a special issue of *Plan Canada* on the history of Canadian resource towns. He has published numerous articles on Canadian urban historiography and on frontier towns. Professor Stelter is currently writing a general history of Canadian urban development prior to 1850.

Notes on Contributors

JAMES D. ANDERSON is a PH D candidate in the Department of Political Science at the University of Alberta. He is co-editor of *Emerging Party Politics in Urban Canada* (Toronto, 1972).

TERRY COPP is an Associate Professor in the History Department at Wilfrid Laurier University. He has also taught history at Loyola College, McGill University, and Sir George Williams University. He is now writing a sequel to his *The Anatomy of Poverty: The Condition of the Working Class in Montreal, 1897 – 1929* (Toronto, 1974).

MAX FORAN is a PH D candidate in the History Department of the University of Calgary. He is the author of *Calgary: An Illustrated History* (Toronto, 1978).

THOMAS I. GUNTON is a doctoral candidate in the School of Community and Regional Planning, University of British Columbia.

PETER W. MOORE completed his MA at the University of Canterbury, New Zealand, and is currently a PH D candidate in the Geography Department at the University of Toronto.

J. E. REA is a Professor of History at the University of Manitoba. He has published several articles on Winnipeg politics and recently completed a study for the Committee of Review, City of Winnipeg Act, entitled *Parties and Power: An Analysis of Winnipeg City Council, 1919 – 1975* (Winnipeg, 1977).

OIVA SAARINEN is an Assistant Professor of Geography at Laurentian University. He has published several articles on urban and regional development in Northeastern Ontario and edited the *Proceedings of the Conference on Regional Development in Northeastern Ontario* (Sudbury, 1976).

JAMES W. SIMMONS is a Professor of Geography at the University of Toronto and is also associated with the Centre for Urban and Community Studies. He has written numerous articles on a variety of Canadian urban topics and co-authored the book *Urban Canada* (Toronto, 1974). His current research interest is the study of growth within the urban system. A book on this subject is forthcoming, as is a book of readings on the national urban system.

Notes

P. J. SMITH is a Professor of Geography at the University of Alberta. He has written many articles on planning, and has been involved with planning in Alberta since 1956, first on the staff of the Calgary Planning Department and later as a teacher of planning at the University of Alberta.

SHIRLEY SPRAGGE is a PH D candidate in history at Queen's University.

WALTER VAN NUS is an Assistant Professor of History at Concordia University. His article in this volume is part of an extensive study of urban planning in Canada up to the Second World War.

JOHN C. WEAVER is an Associate Professor of History at McMaster University. He has published several articles on Canadian urban reform, and is currently writing a history of Hamilton for the *History of Canadian Cities Series*.

THE CARLETON LIBRARY